D1155012

Commercial Banking

Second Edition

EDWARD W. REED, PH.D.

RICHARD V. COTTER, PH.D.
University of Nevada

EDWARD K. GILL, PH.D.
Idaho First National Bank

RICHARD K. SMITH, J.D., PH.D.
University of Montana

Prentice-Hall, Inc., Englewood Cliffs, New Jersey 07632

Library of Congress Cataloging in Publication Data

Main entry under title:

Commercial banking.

Includes bibliographies and index.
  1. Banks and banking—United States. I. Reed,
Edward Wilson,
HG2491.C64   1979   332.1'2'0973   79-18376
ISBN 0-13-152785-1

© 1980 by Prentice-Hall, Inc.
Englewood Cliffs, New Jersey

Editorial production and interior design
by M. L. McAbee
Cover design by Allyson Everngam
Manufacturing buyer: Anthony Caruso

10 9 8 7 6 5 4 3 2

Printed in the United States of America

PRENTICE-HALL INTERNATIONAL, INC., *London*
PRENTICE-HALL OF AUSTRALIA, PTY. LTD., *Sydney*
PRENTICE-HALL OF CANADA, LTD., *Toronto*
PRENTICE-HALL OF INDIA PRIVATE LIMITED, *New Delhi*
PRENTICE-HALL OF JAPAN, INC., *Tokyo*
PRENTICE-HALL OF SOUTHEAST ASIA (PTE.) LTD., *Singapore*
WHITEHALL BOOKS LIMITED, *Wellington, New Zealand*

Contents

Preface

Although the First Edition of *Commercial Banking* was published only a few years ago, significant changes have necessitated a Second Edition. These changes have occurred in many areas—new legislation, regulations, financial markets, deposits, lending, and taxation, to mention the major ones. Commercial banks still remain the heart of our financial system, holding the deposits of millions of persons, governments, and business units. They make funds available through their lending and investing activities to borrowers—individuals, business firms, and governments. In so doing they facilitate both the flow of goods and services from producers to consumers and the financial activities of governments. They provide a large portion of our medium of exchange and are the media through which monetary policy is effected. These activities demonstrate that the commercial banking system of the nation is important to the functioning of our economy.

The ability of our commercial banking system to perform its tasks efficiently and in harmony with our needs and economic goals depends in large measure on efficient management. As in any other type of organization—business, government, charitable, or even household—commercial banks must be managed efficiently. There is too much at stake to do otherwise. They must be managed prudently, safely, and profitably if we are to have a strong, growing, adaptable banking system capable of meeting the demands of society. This book reviews the management aspects of commercial banks. It has been written with the objective of providing professionals and students alike with a description and an analysis of the operations of our commercial banks. It is an investigation of the techniques and principles followed by commercial banks in the performance of their many functions. Although its major concern is with management, and the individual bank occupies the spotlight, the book does not lose sight of the social and monetary importance of the system.

From an organizational standpoint, the text covers structure, organization and management, deposits, cash and liquidity management, lending, investing, trust services, international banking, capital structure, and profitability. Because of the quasi-public nature of commercial banking, we consider each of these topics in relation to banking laws and administrative rulings by bank regulatory bodies. Moreover, the pertinent recommendations made by various commissions in recent years, including the Report of the President's Commission on Financial Structure and Regulation, are evaluated.

We are indebted to several people, both practitioners and academicians. A number of bankers have given helpful suggestions and have read portions of the manuscript. Teachers of commercial banking and related subjects have made suggestions regarding arrangement, presentation, and coverage of material. These people are too numerous to mention, but to all of them we owe a debt of gratitude. This does not mean, however, that they or anyone else who was helpful are responsible for any errors or omissions; these must be assumed by the authors.

1

Commercial Banking: An Overview

Commercial banking is one of our oldest industries. The first bank was organized in 1782 before the adoption of our federal Constitution, and many of the banks that were organized in the 1800s are still in operation. Commercial banks are the most important type of financial institution in the nation in terms of aggregate assets. The growth of their assets and liabilities is presented in Figures 1–1 and 1–2. Total assets exceed one trillion dollars. In terms of employment, banking is one of our largest industries, with over one million employees.

Functions of Commercial Banks

The business of banking is very broad and far-reaching; with the introduction of the one-bank holding company and the possibility of relaxation of some of the restrictions imposed on banking, the number and variety of services provided by commercial banks and their affiliates have expanded. Recent innovations in banking include the introduction of credit cards, accounting services for business firms, factoring, leasing, participating in the Eurodollar market, and lock box banking. Moreover, many banks are employing management science techniques to improve the numerous financial services provided. The importance of commercial banks can best be illustrated by a brief explanation of their major functions.

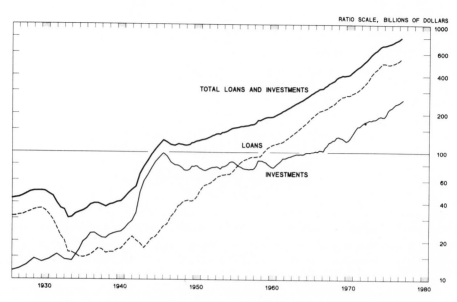

Fig.1-1   Principal assets of commercial banks. (Source: Board of Governors of the Federal Reserve System, *Historical Chart Book, 1977.*)

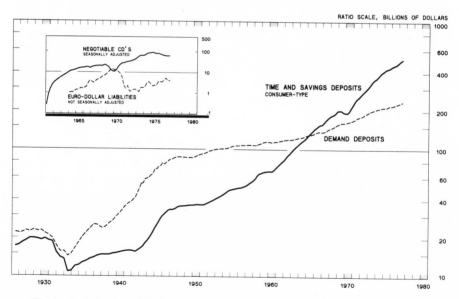

Fig.1-2   Principal liabilities of commercial banks. (Source: Board of Governors of the Federal Reserve System, *Historical Chart Book, 1977.*)

Creating Money

One of the major functions of commercial banks and a distinguishing feature that separates them from other financial institutions is the ability to create and to destroy money.[1] This is accomplished by the lending and investing activities of commercial banks in cooperation with the Federal Reserve System. The power of the commercial banking system to create money is of great economic significance. It results in the elastic credit system that is necessary for economic progress at a relatively steady rate of growth. If bank credit were not available, the expansion of our productive facilities and operations would be in many cases impossible and in other instances delayed until funds could be accumulated from profits or obtained from other outside sources. Moreover, productive units would be forced to maintain larger working balances to meet the fluctuating requirements for funds. Such a practice would be uneconomic since large sums would have to be held idle for some periods, while during the seasonal peaks of business activity such sums might be insufficient.

Our economy needs an adequate but not excessive money supply. If the money supply increases at a more rapid rate than does the production of goods and services, inflation is the result, with all of its ill effects on the various economic processes. Conversely, if the money supply lags behind production, the economy may suffer from deflation with equally undesirable effects. The objective of Federal Reserve policy is to provide a money supply commensurate with the national objectives of stable prices, sound economic growth, and a high level of employment. Commercial banks play a very important role in the implementation of these policies. They serve as a conduit through which the money supply is increased or decreased in an effort to attain these worthy objectives.

Payments Mechanism

Providing for a payments mechanism or the transfer of funds is one of the important functions performed by commercial banks, and it is increasing in importance as greater reliance is placed on the use of checks and credit cards. The increasing efficiency with which funds are managed is indicated by the gradual decline in money holdings relative to the gross national product over the years, despite an increase in the number of financial transactions. In recent years the only kind of money that has increased relative to national income is coin, primarily because of the growth of metering and vending machines. Demand deposits are assuming a larger portion of the

[1]The definition of money as used here is the widely accepted definition which includes not only coins and currency but also demand deposits, and is commonly designated as M_1 by economists.

3

transaction load, and they are being used more efficiently. This is a result of improved technology, the desire of business firms and individuals to use their funds more efficiently, and the ability of depositors to synchronize their receipts and expenditures.

Most of the checks in the nation are cleared through the commercial banking system. Checks drawn on and deposited in the same bank merely transfer funds from one account to another. If only two banks are involved in the same town, there is a direct exchange of checks. When several banks are involved within the same city, a clearinghouse arrangement is usually employed. The process becomes a bit more complicated, time-consuming, and expensive when checks are cleared between banks located in different parts of the country. Such clearings are often handled through the correspondent banking system. Banks located on the West Coast, for example, might send checks drawn on East Coast banks to banks in New York City, which would in turn route the checks to the banks in their area on which the checks were drawn. Checks may also be cleared through regional banks of the Federal Reserve System in a manner similar to clearings through the correspondent banking system. Less than half of the checks are cleared through the Federal Reserve System, and the dollar amount is even less.

Banks have employed computers and other sophisticated equipment to speed the clearing process, reduce costs, and improve accuracy. In recent years considerable thought and research have been given to what has become known as *checkless banking* or the *checkless society;* that is, the use of some form of electronic transfer of funds that would eliminate the bank check and most of the work attendant to it. Experiments have already been made with a system that would involve placing a card similar to a bank credit card into a terminal at a retail store. This would activate computers in banks throughout the nation and thus transfer funds from the purchaser's account to the seller's account. A forerunner of this system is the use of automated teller machines now installed by many banks, whereby a bank credit card can be used to withdraw cash from a depositor's account, make deposits and loan payments, and transfer funds between a depositor's savings and checking accounts. A fuller discussion on the transfer of funds is found in Chapter 6.

Pooling of Savings

Commercial banks perform a very important service to all sectors of the economy by providing facilities for the pooling of savings and making them available for economically and socially desirable purposes. The saver is rewarded by the payment of interest on his savings, which are safe and in a highly liquid form. These pooled funds are made available to businessmen who may use them for the expansion of their productive capacity and to consumers for such items as housing and consumer goods. Our society enjoys a high degree of affluence that enables us to save a substantial portion of our income. A large part of these savings flows into the savings departments of commercial banks.

Extension of Credit

The primary function of commercial banks is the extension of credit to worthy borrowers. From the beginning of time, organizers of banks have been motivated by the opportunities presented by the lending function, and charters have been granted by governments primarily because there was a need for credit in a particular community. In making credit available, commercial banks are rendering a great social service; through their actions production is increased, capital investments are expanded, and a higher standard of living is realized.

Bank lending is very important to the economy, for it makes possible the financing of the agricultural, commercial, and industrial activities of the nation. It makes possible what economists have called indirect or roundabout production, as compared to direct production where consumable goods are secured by the direct application of labor to land or natural wealth. Bank loans also make possible production for inventory. The food industry provides us with an excellent example: all of the food that is harvested and processed cannot be consumed immediately. Loans to canners enable them to purchase, process, can, and store the food which may at a later time be sold to retailers and ultimately to consumers. During this interval of time—from producer to canner, to wholesaler, to retailer, and finally to consumer—bank loans have made possible the economic handling of the food crop.

The farmer, because of the availability of bank loans, is able to purchase seed, feed, fertilizer, and the many other items necessary for raising and harvesting the agricultural commodities that feed our expanding population. Bank loans to manufacturers make possible the purchase of raw materials and machinery and the employment of labor which in time produce goods demanded by industry, government, and consumers. Retailers and wholesalers are able to stock their shelves and move goods for people to consume because of the funds made available in the form of loans by commercial banks. Goods can be transported from producers to the ultimate consumers because of the financial assistance of banks to transportation enterprises. In addition to financing the agricultural, commercial, and industrial activities of the nation, commercial banks facilitate consumption by making consumer loans. Funds may be extended to consumers by banks for the purchase of such items as houses, automobiles, and appliances.

Although the investment activities of commercial banks are usually considered separately from lending, the economic effects and social results are the same. Because government receipts are not always equal to expenditures, temporary borrowing from commercial banks is not uncommon; therefore, the provision of bank credit provides for the smooth operation of government. In general, capital improvements made by governments are not financed out of operating revenue but out of a bond issue. Thus, when banks purchase municipal securities, they are providing funds for such capital improvements as the building of schools and hospitals and the purchasing of new fire trucks. Because of these expenditures our standard of living is improved. When securities issued by the federal government are purchased, these funds are used for a multitude of purposes, such as the construction of highways and dams, and for national defense.

Facilities for the Financing of Foreign Trade

Although foreign trade is basically the same as domestic trade, some differences necessitate that international banking services be provided by commercial banks. These differences arise because of the existence of national monetary systems, unfamiliarity with the financial ability of buyers and sellers in foreign countries, and, in some cases, language barriers. A person who orders wine from France, a car from Germany, shoes from Italy, or a subscription to the *Economist* from England may discover that foreign sellers are not willing to take American dollars in payment. Therefore, arrangements must be made to pay in the currency of the foreign country, for example, in francs, marks, lira, or pounds. To do this, the purchaser can go to a commercial bank and quickly and efficiently arrange for the amount of foreign exchange needed. The bank may have foreign currency of these countries on hand but, if not, can arrange for it quickly through another bank. The purchaser may encounter a situation where the foreign seller is not willing to place the goods on a ship and wait for payment to arrive in the next mail. In fact, the purchaser might not want this type of loose arrangement but would prefer something more binding and businesslike. The transaction might be handled more satisfactorily through the issuance of a commercial letter of credit, which is a written statement on the part of a bank to an individual or firm guaranteeing that the bank will accept and pay a draft, up to a specified sum, if presented to the bank in accordance with the terms of the letter of credit. When a commercial letter of credit is issued, both seller and purchaser are protected; the type and condition of the goods are specified, and the credit of the bank has been substituted for that of the purchaser whose financial standing is not known to the seller. Much of our international trade is financed on this basis.

Many Americans who travel abroad demand the foreign banking services of a commercial bank. Although travelers might want to convert a few dollars into a foreign currency, they would probably purchase travelers letters of credit or traveler's checks. The financing of foreign trade and travel by commercial banks contributes to a freer flow of trade between nations and at lower prices than if these services did not exist. As foreign trade has increased throughout the world, so have the foreign banking services of commercial banks.

Trust Services

Increased incomes have made possible the accumulation of wealth which in turn has contributed to the growth of the trust services of commercial banks. Individuals who have accumulated an estate, even of moderate size, have an interest in providing for the distribution of the assets before death. Many of these individuals have made wills and have asked trust departments to act as executor. Moreover, many of these wills have provided for the creation of personal trusts under which trust departments have the responsibility of investing and caring for the funds and distributing the proceeds as established by the trust agreement.

Trust departments provide many services for corporations. One such service is the administration of pension and profit-sharing plans which have grown rapidly in recent years. In addition to this important function, trust departments serve as trustees in connection with bond issues and as transfer agents and registrars for corporations. They may also administer sinking funds and perform other activities associated with the issuance and redemption of stocks and bonds.

Safekeeping of Valuables

The safekeeping of valuables is one of the oldest services provided by commercial banks. They have vaults that are difficult to enter even by the best of burglars and have established a record of proper custody. The protection of valuables falls into two areas or departments of a bank: safe deposit boxes and safekeeping. Safe deposit boxes are made available to customers on a rental basis. Under such an arrangement the customer has control of his valuables at all times. The bank merely provides the vault, the box, and the other facilities necessary for a proper safe deposit box operation. Finally, and most importantly, the bank controls access to the vault; that is, the bank guarantees that the customer who has rented the box or his authorized representative is the only one permitted access. The procedure consists of proper identification, double locks, and very careful supervision by cautious attendants. A safe deposit box provides a place for securities, deeds, insurance policies, and personal items that may be of value only to the owner. There is no way of estimating the value of all the articles in bank safe deposit boxes. How would a person place a value on the contents of another's safety deposit box: a love letter, a Purple Heart, a Congressional Medal of Honor, a wedding ring, a bit of lace, a rare coin, or a lock of hair? Items of this nature are sometimes found in safe deposit boxes when they are opened with the approval of legal authorities upon the death of a customer.

Safekeeping differs from safe deposit box services in that the bank has custody of the valuables and acts as an agent for the customer. Although the services as well as the items accepted vary considerably, safekeeping is concerned primarily with caring for securities such as stocks and bonds. This department, for example, would be concerned with the holding of securities that have been pledged as collateral for a loan. Securities that are held in trust by the trust department of a bank would also be cared for in safekeeping. Relatively small banks that do not have facilities for the safe-keeping of securities might use those of a larger bank. It is common practice for corporations, both financial and nonfinancial, that own securities to keep them with a bank. Sometimes a holder of securities will ask a bank not only to hold his securities in safekeeping while he is away from his home for a prolonged period but also to clip and cash bond coupons and receive dividends and credit them to his account.

A Brief Look at Assets, Liabilities, and Income

Many of the functions of commercial banking can be illustrated by reviewing the major assets and liabilities of all insured commercial banks of the nation presented in Table 1–1; in fact, much of the subject matter of the following chapters can be highlighted by examining these items. Of the *assets* shown in this table, the entry "Cash and due from banks," which accounted for about 13 percent of total assets as of December 31, 1977, includes a variety of items such as currency and coin kept in banks' vaults for customers who need cash for the usual small transactions. Because of the protective measures that must be observed, banks keep the amount of coin and currency to a minimum and rely when possible on the various Federal Reserve banks as a source of supply. Large banks in some areas of the country serve as warehouses for smaller banks. "Cash items in the process of collection" is the largest item under "Cash and due from banks" and consists primarily of checks drawn on other banks that have been presented to the bank by depositors or other banks for payment. Through a clearing process provided by the correspondent banking system and the Federal Reserve System, these checks are routed to the drawee banks and the paying bank is finally reimbursed. Banks usually refer to this important category of bank assets as *float*. Steps are being taken to reduce the amount of float in the

Table 1–1
Assets and Liabilities of All Insured Banks
December 31, 1977

	Amount (in millions)	Percent of Total
ASSETS		
Cash and due from banks	$ 160,353	14.1
Cash items in process of collection	66,448	5.8
Currency and cash	13,999	1.2
Balances with banks		
Domestic	45,155	4.0
Foreign	5,410	0.5
Reserves with Federal Reserve Bank	29,340	2.6
Securities	258,408	22.7
Investment securities	250,393	22.0
U.S. Treasury	95,961	8.4
Obligations of U.S. Government agencies	35,812	3.2
Obligations of States and local governments	112,900	9.9
Other securities	5,719	0.5
Corporate stock	1,612	0.1
Trading account securities	6,404	0.6
Federal funds sold and securities purchased under agreements to resell	49,875	4.4
Loans, net	591,313	52.0
Plus: Reserve for loan losses	6,692	0.6
Unearned income on loans	14,701	1.3
Loans, gross	612,706	53.9
Commercial and industrial	197,092	17.3
Real Estate	178,607	15.7
Consumer	141,252	12.4
All others	95,756	8.4
Direct lease financing	5,810	0.5
Bank premises and other real estate	21,435	1.9
Customer liability on acceptances	11,492	1.0
All other assets	39,001	3.4
Total	$1,137,687	100.0
LIABILITIES		
Business and personal deposits	775,304	68.2
Government deposits	84.607	7.4
Domestic interbank deposits	49,297	4.3
Foreign government and bank deposits	19,962	1.8
Total deposits	929,169	81.7
Demand	378,723	33.3
Savings	220,090	19.4
Time	303,356	26.7
Federal funds purchased and securities sold under agreements to repurchase	82,946	7.3
Acceptances outstanding	12,084	1.1
All other liabilities	28,461	2.5
Subordinated notes and debentures	5,739	0.5
Equity capital	79,288	7.0
Total	$1,137,687	100.0

Source: FDIC, *Annual Report*, 1977.
Note: Figures will not necessarily add to totals because of rounding.

commercial banking system. As the electronic transfer of funds becomes more common, this sizable figure will be reduced substantially.

Banks that are members of the Federal Reserve System are required to carry reserves equal to a certain percent of their time and demand deposits. These reserves must be in the form of cash in the vault or deposits in a Federal Reserve bank. Banks that are not members of the Federal Reserve System may carry their reserves with other commercial banks commonly referred to as correspondent banks. Even member banks may carry accounts with other banks for reasons that will be discussed in the following chapter. Banks that provide international banking services carry accounts with foreign banks just as domestic banks carry deposits with larger city correspondent banks and for the same reasons.

Approximately 25 percent of all bank assets are invested in securities. "Investment securities" are those securities that banks purchase for income and liquidity. U.S. Treasury securities represent the direct debt of the United States and are considered by banks and regulatory authorities as prime investments. Agency securities are those issued by the various agencies of the federal government such as the Federal Home Loan Bank, the Bank for Cooperatives, the Federal Land Bank, etc. State and local issues account for nearly half of the investment securities of commercial banks. As the name implies, these securities are issues of state and local governments such as schools, counties, cities, etc. Banks are attracted to these securities because they normally provide a higher after-tax yield than do U.S. Government securities. Two of the following chapters are devoted to the investment activities of commercial banks. "Other securities" include those issued by the International Development Bank, the World Bank, etc. Banks frequently underwrite general obligation securities of state and local governments, make a market in such issues, and sell them to customers, including other banks; hence, the term "Trading account securities." The item "Corporate stock" includes the amount of stock held in the Federal Reserve banks by member banks and other stocks that banks have acquired through foreclosure.

"Federal funds sold and securities purchased under agreements to resell" arise from the sale of excess reserves of member banks held in the Federal Reserve System. These represent funds purchased by banks that are short of required reserves and have decided to buy funds in the federal funds market rather than sell securities or call loans to correct their reserve position. One method of selling (lending) federal funds is to purchase securities under a repurchase agreement from a bank that needs funds. Under such agreements the borrower of the funds (seller of the securities) agrees to repurchase the securities at a specified price on a specified date. Management of the liquidity position of a commercial bank is important, as is the management of the investment portfolio, both of which are discussed in later chapters.

"Loans" account for the largest percentage of bank assets. There are many types of loans as the student will realize after reading the chapters on lending. Here they have been classified into only four categories. From the total amount of commercial and industrial loans, it is fairly obvious why we refer to banks as commercial banks. Lending to business has been the major lending activity from the beginning of banking. Real estate and consumer lending have increased over the years, however. In Table 1–1, the "Reserve for loan losses" shows the amount set aside to cover potential losses. "Unearned income on loans" arises when the amount of the loan recorded on the books of the bank includes the interest on the loan as well as the amount advanced to the borrower. As interest is earned and loan payments received, appropriate amounts are transferred from unearned income to current income. "Direct lease financing" includes the outstanding balances of all types of leases and is discussed in Chapter 13.

"Bank premises and other real estate" includes the depreciated value of bank buildings, furniture, fixtures, and various pieces of equipment necessary for the bank's operation. Some banks lease part of their equipment, such as computers, and some lease their building or buildings. This is especially true of banks in the bigger cities that are housed in very large buildings, the cost of which may exceed the capital account that serves as a limit on the amount of assets that can be invested in real estate. Unless special permission is granted, a bank can invest in bank premises only an amount equal to its capital stock. Also included in this item is real estate owned other than bank premises, such as parking lots.

Many banks provide their customers with international banking services. The item "Customer liability on acceptances" includes claims of the bank on its customers for drafts and bills of exchange that have been issued in their favor and accepted by the bank. This item will be discussed in greater detail in the chapter on international banking. "Other assets" include a multitude of items that do not fit into the above categories, such as income accrued but not collected, and prepaid expenses.

By far the largest *liability* of commercial banks is deposits. In the table deposits are listed according to ownership and by type. The great proportion of bank deposits is owned by individuals and business firms. The item "Domestic interbank deposits" includes those deposits carried by banks primarily for the purpose of clearing checks. Governments, too, must have deposits in order to carry on their activities. Foreign governments that have business relations with entities in the United States may carry accounts with U.S. banks, and foreign banks also maintain deposits in U.S. banks if they are in the business of providing international services to their customers.

"Demand deposits," as the name implies, are deposits that are withdrawable on demand. Some identify these deposits as checking deposits, meaning that they are normally withdrawn by the use of a bank check. "Savings deposits" are the most common consumer type of savings account and are frequently called passbook savings. These deposits can normally be withdrawn anytime, but technically a waiting period could be imposed since banking rules and regulations provide for this treatment. "Time deposits" may take several forms and are for stated periods of time. Time deposits may be held by individuals, corporations, partnerships, or governments and are usually in larger denominations than savings deposits. Time deposits are also known as certificates of deposits or, simply, CDs. They are normally evidenced by a certificate rather than a passbook. The deposits in foreign branches and international subsidiaries are both demand and time deposits, but the breakdowns are not indicated in Table 1–1.

"Federal funds purchased and securities sold under agreements to repurchase" is the opposite of the item "Federal funds sold and securities purchased under agreements to resell" under assets. The reason for funds purchased being larger than funds sold is that these transactions occur not only with domestic commercial banks but also with brokers and dealers in securities as well. "Acceptances outstanding" is the offsetting entry to "Customer liability on acceptances" under assets. "All other liabilities" includes a variety of items such as expenses accrued and unpaid, minority interest in consolidated subsidiaries, and deferred income taxes. The item "Subordinated notes and debentures" includes for the most part liabilities of relatively large banks. "Equity capital" in Table 1–1 represents the sum of preferred and common stock outstanding, surplus, undivided profits, reserve for contingencies, and other capital reserves.

The income and expense items of insured commercial banks operating throughout 1977 are shown in Table 1–2. Many of these items can be related to asset and liability items in Table 1–1. From a brief examination of Table 1–2 it can be seen that banks receive most of their income from "interest and fees on loans;" in fact, nearly two-thirds of the operating income of all banks derives from this source. Investment income is the second largest source of income for commercial banks. Income from both U.S. Treasury and state and local securities is a significant part of this total. Another source is "income from fiduciary activities," that is, from trust departments which will be discussed further in detail in the chapter on trust services. "Service charges on deposit accounts" are an important source of income, as are numerous other service charges, commissions, and fees. Although the various service charges are not as important as income from loans and securities, they have increased significantly over the years and they will probably become a more important source of income in the future.

The major expenses of commercial banks consist of "salaries and em-

Table 1-2

Income of Insured Commercial Banks Operating throughout 1977

	Total (in millions)	As a Percent of Operating Income
OPERATING INCOME		
Interest and fees on loans	$58,991	65.3
Interest on balances with banks	4,888	5.4
Income on federal funds sold and securities purchased under agreements to resell	2,476	2.7
Interest on U.S. Treasury securities	6,395	7.1
Interest on obligations of U.S. Government agencies and corporations	2,469	2.7
Interest on States and local securities	5,365	5.9
Interest on other securities	859	1.0
Dividends on stock	110	0.1
Income from direct lease financing	699	0.8
Income from fiduciary activities	1,980	2.2
Service charges on deposit accounts	1,807	2.0
Other service charges, commissions, and fees	2,409	2.7
Other income	1,910	2.1
Total	$90,358	100.0
OPERATING EXPENSES		
Salaries and employee benefits	16,346	18.1
Interest on time certificates of deposit of $100,000 or more issued by domestic offices	6,763	7.5
Interest on deposits in foreign offices	10,216	11.3
Interest on other deposits	21,833	24.2
Expense of federal funds purchased and securities sold under agreements to repurchase	4,543	5.0
Interest on other borrowed money	818	0.9
Interest on subordinated notes and debentures	392	0.4
Net occupancy expense	3,603	4.0
Furniture and equipment expense	1,931	2.1
Provision for possible loan losses	3,301	3.7
Other expenses	9,599	10.6
Total	$78,792	87.2
Income before income taxes and securities gains or losses	11,566	
Applicable income taxes	2,832	
Income before securities gains or losses	8,734	
Securities gains or losses, gross	142	
Applicable income taxes	43	
Securities gains or losses, net	98	
Income before extraordinary items	8,833	
Extraordinary items, gross	55	
Applicable income taxes	8	
Extraordinary items, net	47	
Net income	$ 8,879	

Source: FDIC, *Annual Report*, 1977.
Note: Total may not necessarily add to totals because of rounding.

ployee benefits," and "interest on deposits." Table 1–2 shows that interest expenses accounted for more than one-half of total operating expenses. This amount has increased dramatically in recent years due, in large part, to rising interest rates; with increased competition for deposits, it may continue to rise in the future. Although salaries and employee benefits as a percent of total operating income have declined in recent years, the total amount has increased significantly. Since 1970, this item of expense has doubled. Banks expend a sizable amount for federal funds. Some banks do not enter the federal funds market but borrow directly from the Federal Reserve banks and/or correspondent banks. This latter procedure is accounted for by the item "Interest on other borrowed money." "Interest on subordinated notes and debentures" is the payment of interest on these debt instruments; and "Net occupancy" and "Furniture and equipment" expenses are associated with the ownership of real estate and personal property including maintenance, depreciation, rental expenses, and outlays for lease payments.

Like all other business firms, banks are profit-oriented institutions. In 1977 the gross income of insured banks amounted to nearly $11.6 billion, and after income taxes and various adjustments net income approximated $8.9 billion. Although profitability varies from bank to bank, in the aggregate the return on equity was approximately 11.7 percent.

Competitive Environment

Commercial banks operate in a competitive environment, and competition is increasing. Banks compete with each other as well as with thrift institutions—savings and loan associations, mutual savings banks, and credit unions—and also with other participants in the money and capital markets. In recent years national and state banks have also been facing a substantial increase in competition from foreign banks operating in this country. Savings and loan associations, mutual savings banks, and credit unions have been broadening their services and competing with commercial banks on an ever-widening front. In lending to business borrowers, commercial banks must compete with other suppliers of funds in the money and capital markets, and in seeking funds, commercial banks must compete with government as well as with other corporate issuers of commercial paper and long-term securities. Commercial banks, therefore, are subject to competition in their endeavor to attract funds as well as in the area of lending and investing those funds.

Traditionally, banks and thrift institutions have been viewed as separate "lines of commerce"; in fact, the Supreme Court, in a landmark decision that will be discussed in Chapter 3, decreed that commercial banking was a relevant line of commerce. This was a very narrow interpretation and not realistic since banks compete with other financial institutions in a very broad market. Regulatory and technological changes are contributing to greater similarity between banks and thrift institutions and, hence, to an increase in competition. In many cases thrift institutions are offering third party payment accounts, which are similar to the demand deposit accounts of commercial banks. These third party transfers are called negotiable orders of withdrawal, commonly referred to as NOW accounts. The NOWs are drafts that depositors can write against interest-bearing saving accounts. Although few have done so, credit unions can issue share drafts which are similar to NOW accounts. Some states are permitting state chartered savings and loan associations to issue non-interest bearing accounts, commonly referred to as NINOWs, which are comparable to demand deposits at commercial banks.

Technological changes involving the electronic transfer of funds have been researched and pioneered by the major commercial banks and have been made available to thrift institutions via various laws and court decisions. The effect of this development is to make banks and thrift institutions more competitive. Increased competition between banks and thrift institutions is occurring not only in the area of deposits but in assets as well. Commercial banks are diversifying their assets toward higher percentages of mortgages and consumer loans, whereas thrifts are changing their asset composition and clamoring for greater freedom. Legislative bodies are becoming more attentive to their demands. Thrift institutions contend that when market rates of interest exceed the legal ceiling that they can pay on savings deposits, *disintermediation* occurs; that is, funds are withdrawn from the thrifts and transferred to higher-yielding investment instruments such as commercial paper and Treasury Bills. Moreover, thrifts suffer from financing long-term assets (mortgages) with short-term funds (savings). Since only a small fraction of a thrift's mortgage portfolio is replaced each year, the average return on assets may not rise as fast as short-term rates; consequently, a squeeze on earnings develops. One solution of this problem is to diversify the loan portfolio and/or shorten its maturity. This is now done by some thrift institutions in those states that already permit loan diversification, and it is being requested in others. Thrifts have recently been authorized to provide credit card services, and many large thrift institutions have begun to issue these.

Evidence of increased competition between banks and thrift institutions is presented in Figure 1–3. Note that the share of deposits held by commercial banks declined from 69 percent in 1960 to 62 percent in 1978. The most rapid growth was experienced by credit unions during this period, followed by savings and loan associations. Mutual savings banks had a slower growth rate than did commercial banks. Although commercial banks have been

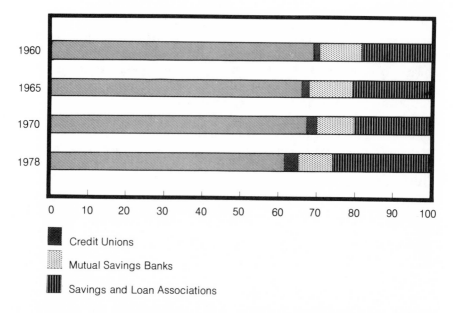

Credit Unions

Mutual Savings Banks

Savings and Loan Associations

Fig.1–3   Percent of deposits held by commercial banks and thrift institutions, selected years (Source: Board of Governors of the Federal Reserve System, *Federal Reserve Bulletins.*)

aggressive lenders, they have encountered stiff competition from thrift institutions, sales finance companies, mortgage companies, insurance companies, leasing companies, pension funds, and the commercial paper market. As a result of this strong competition, the share of total public and private debt held by commercial banks has declined over the years. In 1960, for example, loans and investments of commercial banks accounted for nearly 27 percent of the total public and private debt of the nation, but by 1978 this percentage had dropped to 25. Despite the decline in the banks' share of deposits, loans, and investments over the years, commercial banks remain the single most important financial institution in the nation.

SELECTED REFERENCES

CANDILIS, WRAY O.   *The Future of Commercial Banking,* New York, Praeger Publishers, 1975.

BAUGHN, WILLIAM H., and CHARLES E. WALKER, editors, *The Bankers' Handbook,* Homewood, Illinois, Dow Jones-Irwin, 1978.

MCKINNEY, GEORGE W., JR. and WILLIAM J. BROWN, *Management of Commercial Bank Funds,* Washington, The American Institute of Banking, the American Bankers Association, 1974.

2

Structure of the Banking System

The structure of banking is determined by two basic forces—economic and legal. As in any market the demand for the final product influences the number of sellers. The demand for banking services also affects bank size. In addition, government regulations have a great impact on bank structure. These regulations may be classified as those that restrict the formation of new banks and those that affect structure through the impact on bank organization.

Early History of Banking

Many factors have influenced our banking structure, among them war, economic crisis, constitutional authority, and fiscal leadership. During the Colonial period very little money circulated in the American colonies. Money brought from Europe by the settlers soon flowed back because of an unfavorable balance of trade. At the beginning of the American Revolution there was less than $12 million in coin in circulation—a little less than $5 per person. Barter was common, and commodities such as corn in Massachusetts and tobacco in Virginia were legal tender. In 1690 Massachusetts printed "bills of credit" to finance King William's war, a practice that was adopted by some of the other colonies. These bills of credit became the first paper money introduced in the British Empire. A few "land banks," which issued bank notes secured by real estate, were established. The creation of these banks, as well as the issuance of bills of credit, raised the ire of the British Parliament, which insisted on "sound" money throughout the Empire.

In 1782 the Continental Congress granted a charter to The Bank of North America. Doubts concerning the authority of the Continental Congress to grant a charter to a financial institution led the bank to seek a charter from the state of Pennsylvania and later from New York, Massachusetts, and Delaware. In 1784 the Bank of New York and the Bank of Massachusetts were organized. All of these banks are still in operation, although under different names. A significant development was the 20-year chartering of the Bank of the United States by Congress in 1791. Alexander Hamilton, our first Secretary of the Treasury, promoted the creation of the bank, a proposal that started an important and lasting controversy as to the proper roles of the federal government and the states. Supporters of the bank pointed out the need for such an institution and held that Article 1, Section 8 of the Constitution, which states that "Congress shall have the power . . . To coin money and regulate the Value thereof, and of foreign Coin . . .", was an implied power sufficient to justify the creation of a bank. Although the bank performed many functions, probably the most important was to regulate the money supply and thus protect the economy from inflation. Since the bank served as the depository for the federal government, it could present bank notes for payment in gold and silver to the bank in issue. In the performance of this function the bank served as a central bank and regulated the amounts of money in circulation—a role not welcomed by those who favored an expanding money supply. The first Bank of the United States grew and prospered and at the time of its expiration in 1811 operated nationwide, with branches in the major port cities. When the bank passed from the scene, the number of state banks increased rapidly, as did the amount of their bank notes. Unfortunately, the value of their notes declined even more rapidly. This situation plus the economic impact of the War of 1812 set the stage for the return of a national bank. In 1816 the Second Bank of the United States was chartered. Although it performed the same basic function as the first bank, it lacked sound management and became embroiled in politics; consequently, in 1832 President Jackson vetoed a bill that would have extended its life beyond its original twenty years. In his criticism Jackson referred to "the 'moneyed aristocracy'" and described the bank as an 'odious monopoly' operating 'to make the rich richer and the potent more powerful'."[1] Opposition to the bank was so great that the state of Maryland imposed a tax on a branch of the bank to force it out of business. The Supreme Court held such a tax unconstitutional in the celebrated case

[1]Paul B. Trescott, *Financing American Enterprise: The Story of Commercial Banking*, New York, Harper & Row, Publishers, 1963, pp. 27–28.

of *McCulloch v. Maryland* and paved the way for an increasing role of the federal government in the area of money and banking.

Following the demise of the second Bank of the United States, there was a substantial increase in the number of state banks. In too many instances, unsound banking practices prevailed, including excessive issue of bank notes and little or no provision for note redemption. Commenting on the shortcomings of our monetary system, Senator John Sherman stated that "In 1862 there were fifteen hundred banks, the notes of 253 of which had not been counterfeited. The variety of imitations was 1,861; of alterations, 3,039; of spurious notes, 1,685."[2]

The very unsatisfactory condition of the currency together with the needs associated with the financing of the Civil War led to the passage of the National Bank Act of 1863. This Act created the Office of the Comptroller of the Currency whose responsibility it was to charter and regulate national banks. In an effort to create a uniform currency and to help finance the war, banks were encouraged to purchase government bonds, which could then be used as the basis for the issuance of national bank notes. Further, a tax of 10 percent was imposed on all state bank notes in the hope that this would render such issues unprofitable and drive the state banks out of existence. Although their notes disappeared, the state banks did not, since by then note circulation was not essential to banking. Deposit banking had come of age; consequently, state banks remained in existence, which assured a dual banking system.

Although relatively unimportant in number and in assets held, a few private banks—those that have neither a federal nor a state charter—have continued to exist. Most private banks have operated informally, often in conjunction with the operation of a general store. The National Bank Act and the tax levied on bank notes forced many private banks into the national banking system and restricted the activities of those that remained. At the present time there are only 14 private banks in the nation,[3] and the formation of others is not possible since all states now require newly organized banks to have a charter.

Dual Banking

A unique feature of the dual banking system is that both the states and the federal government have rights regarding the chartering, supervision, and examination of commercial banks. Several features of the system are responsible for its uniqueness. Although banking is recognized as a very

[2]Ibid, p. 47.
[3]*The Wall Street Journal,* May 9, 1977, p. 1.

important industry nationally and one that affects interstate commerce, it is subject to state regulation. With the exception of a few industries, such as oil production and insurance, business activity involving interstate commerce is usually subject to federal regulation. Since both state and federal bank regulatory agencies are concerned with chartering, regulation and supervision, and examination of bank management, the dual system results in a competitive rather than cooperative federalism which is found in so many areas of government such as welfare and education. Another unusual feature is that banks may select the jurisdiction that will regulate and supervise them, a practice not found elsewhere in government regulation. Some delegation of policy decisions exists in the dual banking system, the most important of which is branch banking. Here the states have supreme authority in that they determine whether banks—state or federally chartered—can engage in branch banking. Despite these unique features a considerable amount of cooperation exists between state and national banking authorities. This cooperation is found in several areas, including examinations and financial reporting.

The efficiency of the dual banking system has been debated for years. Some observers hold that it has created *competition in laxity* between national and state governments, that is, as one regulatory agency lowers its standards to maintain its membership or to attract additional banks the other is forced to follow, since it is possible for banks to switch charters from one regulatory agency to the other. Some, however, look upon the dual banking system as desirable, believing that it reduces the possibility of overburdensome control. This point of view is expressed in a publication of the American Bankers Association which states that "the historical value of dual banking lies in its ability to provide an escape valve from arbitrary or discriminatory chartering and regulatory policies at either the state or federal level."[4] This statement raises a question that is fundamental to our political system, namely, are many facets of our society overregulated? This statement also implies that equity and justice may not always be forthcoming from one regulatory agency and that some degree of competition in government is desirable.

An argument for the support of dual banking is that the states should have the ability to decide which type of banking structure is best suited to their needs. Although the strength of the dual banking system is dwindling, it still plays an important role in our banking structure. The major stronghold now possessed by the states is in the area of branch banking. Here the states are supreme.

The major reason for the continuation of the dual banking system is that the small rural bank has more political power than the large city bank. Small

---

[4]William J. Brown, *The Dual Banking System in the United States* (New York, The American Bankers Association, 1968), p. 59. Excerpt with permission.

rural banks exist in a marketplace that is often less competitive than that found in most large cities. Rural and small town banks favor the status quo, and in many states they have been able to achieve that objective.

The dual banking system has served as a check and balance system that has probably deterred unduly restrictive legislative and regulatory action by both levels of government. One reason for not favoring the exclusive regulation and supervision by the federal government stems from its performance record in other areas of regulation, including the railroads and motor carriers.

Organization of Banking

Banks may be classified into unit, branch, and group. Many nations are characterized by only one type. American banking is noted for all types, although unit banking is the most common historically. Since branch, holding company, and group banking are forms of expansion, these will be analyzed in the following chapter.

Unit Banking

Unit banking exists when banking services are provided by a single-office institution. Today approximately a third of American banking offices are unit banks. Despite an increase in other types of banking over a period of years, some sections of the country still favor unit banking. The presence of unit banking in our banking system is a result of tradition, law, vested interests, and the ability of this type of organization to meet the demands of banking customers. Because of inadequate transportation and communication facilities when the country was young, the most practical banking organization was unit banking. The first and second Banks of the United States provided for branches, but few branch systems existed on the state level. When communities were more homogeneous and smaller than they are at present, and small business and farming were more dominant, unit banking worked well. However, with the economic interdependence of large geographical areas, the importance of transportation and communication, the growth of big business firms, a more mobile population, and increasing emphasis placed on location and convenience, unit banking is giving way to branch banking in many parts of the country.

Branch Banking

Branch banking exists when a single banking firm conducts operations at two or more places. The branches are controlled from one location, referred to as the head office. The branch offices may be located in the same city, county, state, and, if permitted, across state and even national lines. The head office and all the branches are controlled by the same board of directors and are owned by the same stockholders. The affairs of the branches are directed by their managers in accordance with the regulations and policies of the head office. Although some banking services are basic, the extent and variety performed at the branch level vary. Such activities as the management of the reserve position and of the investment account are performed at the head office.

Presently there are different degrees of branching throughout the country (see Figure 2–1). Some states like Texas and Illinois prohibit branch banking entirely while others like California and North Carolina permit statewide branching. Other states limit branching to areas such as the town, city, or county in which the head office is located; sometimes banks are

Fig. 2–1 States permitting unit, limited, and statewide branching. (Source: FDIC)

permitted to branch within their home county and in continguous counties. At the present time 20 states permit statewide branching, 15 permit unit banking only, and 15 permit limited branching. At the end of 1977 nearly 69 percent of the banking offices throughout the nation were branches. Bank of America leads all banks in the nation in the number of branches and at the end of 1978 had more than 1,000 domestic and over 100 foreign branches. To be sure, this number of branches is quite impressive, but it is considerably less than the nearly 6,000 domestic and foreign branches of Barclays Bank of England.

Number of Commercial Banks and Commercial Banking Offices

The number of banks and branches has fluctuated greatly (see Figure 2–2). The number of banks has declined and the number of branches increased. The shift of population from rural areas to urban centers has reduced the need for many rural banks. Improved transportation now makes

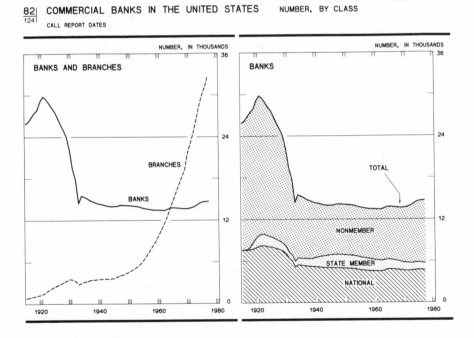

Fig. 2–2 Number of banks and branches and classification of banks. (Source: Board of Governors of the Federal Reserve System, *Historical Chart Book,* 1977.)

it possible for most people to do their banking miles away from their homes, which would have been practically impossible in the 1920s. The productivity and efficiency of banking offices, resulting from their ability to handle an increased volume of business, have also reduced the need for banks. This increased productivity has stemmed from improved physical layouts, increased automation of operations, drive-in teller windows, the use of bank-by-mail facilities, specialization on the part of bank personnel, and improved organization and management. The introduction of electronic data processing machines is an example of an innovation that has greatly increased the efficiency of banks.

While the number of banks has remained relatively stable since 1940, the number of branches has increased greatly, especially in the 1960s when the number more than doubled. The most important factor responsible for the growth of branch banking has probably been a change in attitude toward branch banking, which has been reflected in the liberalization of state banking laws. Other factors include the growth of suburbs, the increased congestion of city traffic, and the movement of industry out of the central cities. Banks have followed the population and the demand for banking services. From information available on the granting of new charters and the establishment of branches, it appears that regulatory agencies regard new branches with greater favor than new unit banks.

The consolidation of banks through purchase has been responsible for a great part of this branch banking growth. The financial return on funds invested in a new unit bank has been lower than alternative investments, therefore, there have been few unit banks organized in the past thirty years. Since it takes time for a newly organized bank to operate at a profit, investors have been reluctant to invest their funds in new banks. Established banks are in a better position to expand their banking services into a new community. Some communities are too small to support a full-service unit bank, but a branch bank can provide the necessary services since it can be operated at less cost than a unit bank.

The slight increase in the number of banks in recent years has all occurred in state banks (see Figure 2–2). Although state banks account for 68 percent of the banks of the nation, they hold only 43 percent of the bank assets. National banks have held the majority of bank assets since the mid-1930s.

Banks are frequently classified as member and nonmember banks to identify their relationship with the Federal Reserve System, which is optional for state banks but mandatory for national banks. The most significant development in bank classification in recent years has been an increase in the number of nonmember banks. Although many factors influence a bank's decision to be a member of the Federal Reserve System, the major one involves reserve requirements. Every member bank is required by law to maintain a reserve based on the amount of deposits held. A member bank is required to maintain reserves in the form of cash in the vault and deposits in the Federal Reserve bank in the district in which it is located. Such reserves are nonearning assets. Although nonmember banks must also maintain reserves, except in Illinois, the requirement varies from state to state in accordance with state law. In many instances a portion of the reserve of nonmember banks may be in the form of earning assets such as time deposits at other banks or certain short term U.S. government securities. Moreover, a part of a cash requirement of nonmember banks is usually carried in other banks, and in some state uncollected funds serve as reserves.

Since one objective of bank management is to maximize earning assets and income, an earning asset that can serve as a legal reserve is very attractive. Because the reserves of member banks must be in the form of nonearning assets, more and more newly formed state banks have elected not to become members of the Federal Reserve System, and an increasing number of member banks have withdrawn from the system. At mid-1978, only 10 percent of the state banks of the nation were members of the Federal Reserve System. This trend has not gone unnoticed by banking authorities and students of banking. The development has given rise to the recommendation that all banks be required to be members of the Federal Reserve System, a regulation that would result in greater equity and would allow the Federal Reserve System to carry out monetary policy more effectively. In the past twenty-five years, the percent of total bank assets held by member banks has declined from 86 to 71.

Another classification of banks not presented in Figure 2–2 is insured banks. As the term implies, insured banks are those whose deposits are insured by the Federal Deposit Insurance Corporation (see Table 2–1). Practically all banks in this nation are insured banks. In fact, 98 percent of the banks were insured by the FDIC as of mid-1978, and these held approximately 99.5 percent of the bank assets of the nation.

Size of Commercial Banks

One of the surprising features of our banking system is the great variation in the size of banks and the number of relatively small banks (see Table 2–1). Nearly 65 percent of the banks in 1977 held deposits of $25 million or less while only 1.7 percent of the banks held deposits in excess of $500 million. Banks with deposits of $25 million and less held only 11 percent of the bank assets of the nation, whereas the banks of $500 million and more held 54 percent. This great disparity in size is not characteristic of the banking system of any other nation. The major reason for the great difference in the

Table 2–1

Insured Commercial Banks in the United States (states and other areas)
Grouped According to Assets, December 31, 1977

Assets (in millions)	*Num-ber*	*Per-cent*	*Cumula-tive Per-centage*	*Assets (in millions)*	*Per-cent*	*Cumu-lative*
Less than $5.0	1,197	8.3		$ 4,217	0.4	
$5.0 to $9.9	2,593	18.0	26.3	19,258	1.7	2.1
$10.0 to $24.9	4,911	34.1	60.4	81,025	7.2	9.3
$25.0 to $49.9	2,980	20.7	81.1	103,275	9.1	18.4
$50.0 to $99.9	1,485	10.3	91.4	102,909	9.1	27.5
$100.0 to $299.9	824	5.7	97.1	132,354	11.7	39.2
$300.0 to $499.9	157	1.1	98.2	60,466	5.3	44.5
$500.0 to $999.9	124	0.9	99.1	85,370	7.5	52.0
$1,000.0 to $4,900.0	120	0.8	99.9	229,082	20.2	72.2
$5,000.0 or more	21	0.1	100.0	315,470	27.8	100.0
Total	14,412	100.0		$1,133,427	100.0	

Source: FDIC, *Annual Report*, 1977.
Note: Figures will not necessarily add to totals because of rounding.

size of banks in the United States is the type of banking system. Unit banking contributes to a multitude of small banks while branching results in fewer banks and as many, if not more, banking offices.

Unit banking, the small independent banks, is still well entrenched in many areas, although slowly giving way in the United States. As previously mentioned, tradition, law, vested interest, and special customer demands are responsible for their continuation. An additional factor, our individualistic attitude, probably should not be overlooked. Local communities desire the development of their own area. The feeling persists that a board of directors composed of local residents knows best the problems and needs of the area and will be more concerned with its economic development. This attitude has been ably expressed by a well-known writer on banking when he stated that,

> Small-town America is inordinately proud of its little banks and jealous of so-called invasions of local autonomy. Merge a small bank into a larger, more efficient institution or open a branch of a city bank in a rural area, and local hackles rise. This ingrained parochialism has combined with the outsize power of local small-bank lobbies to preserve the nation's crazy-quilt and obsolete branching and merger laws.[5]

This attitude is still prevalent, but it is slowly changing as shown by the increase in the number of branches and by the branching issue that is so frequently discussed in state legislatures.

[5]Sanford Rose, "Are Those 11,400 Banks Really Necessary?" *Fortune*, November 1970, p. 113.

Incorporation of Commercial Banks

As outlined earlier, those who wish to engage in commercial banking must either secure a charter or license from the appropriate state agency or request and receive a federal charter from the Comptroller of the Currency. Certain rules and regulations must be complied with regarding board of directors, capitalization, quality of management, location, etc., at either governmental level. For many years, it was not necessary in many states to receive government sanction to engage in banking. Those banks without a government charter were referred to as private banks. The major reason for requiring incorporation was to provide for closer, more efficient control of banking activities to assure higher safety and liquidity standards. For a time the issuance of bank charters was a prerogative of the legislative body on the state as well as the federal level. Under such an arrangement "politics" crept in, abuses were prevalent, and in many instances qualified persons were prohibited from entering the banking business.

Any group may now apply for permission to engage in commercial banking activities, but an application does not necessarily mean a charter will be granted. The granting of bank charters has taken on the public utility concept; that is, banks are "natural monopolies," and charters are granted only if banking services are needed and banks can operate profitably and in a safe manner.

Correspondent Banking

Correspondent banking is an arrangement that exists between banks throughout the country based on the practice of smaller banks carrying deposits with larger banks in exchange for the performance of various services. This arrangement originated in colonial times and developed because of the need for redemption centers for banknotes. Later, as deposits became more acceptable and popular, the major service performed was the clearing of checks. As the banking system further developed, additional services were performed. This cooperative mechanism contributes to more efficient services, greater fluidity of funds, and higher banking standards. Two basic reasons support the existence of correspondent banking: banks find it impossible in many instances to provide certain services that they consider important; or, if these services are provided, the banks find them quite expensive. This is another way of saying that banks can purchase certain services more economically than they can produce them, primarily as a result of the economies of scale in the production of banking services. Although all banks derive benefits from correspondent banking, small banks probably derive the greater benefit.

Banks that receive checks drawn on other banks must arrange for presentation either to the bank on which they are drawn or to some location where the drawee bank maintains an account. Sometimes it is desirable for the receiving bank to keep an account with the paying bank, especially if the volume of checks is quite sizable. Although the Federal Reserve System provides a check clearing service for member banks, many rely instead on the correspondent banking system for this service since the process is faster, in many instances. Only about 45 percent of the checks in the nation are cleared through the Federal Reserve facilities. For many years a bank had to be a member of the Federal Reserve System to use its clearing facilities, but in recent years this requirement has been relaxed, in part, to encourage membership. Nonmember banks are permitted to use the clearing facilities of the Federal Reserve Regional Check Processing Centers. If a nonmember bank wants to clear beyond the center, however, it must rely on the correspondent banking system.

In addition to clearing checks, correspondent banking provides some useful asset management services. Small banks encounter two basic limitations in this area. The staff of a small bank often has insufficient expertise, and the relatively small units—loans, investments, deposits, and the like—in which small banks are forced to deal tend to be expensive. It is not uncommon for them to be confronted with a loan request by a valued customer in excess of their legal limit. Such a loan in excess of the small bank's limit can be carried by a correspondent bank, however. The correspondent bank may also share a portion of its loan portfolio with its country cousin if the latter needs an increased loan portfolio and the larger bank is just about "loaned up." In addition, the correspondent bank may serve as an investment counselor and purchase, sell, and hold securities for the small bank.

The correspondent bank is also a source of information and help on various phases of bank operation and may dispatch one of its technicians to the smaller bank to aid in the installation of new machines and equipment or in the introduction of an improved method of operation. The correspondent bank with a foreign department may make its services available to a smaller bank which is called upon to perform such services only occasionally. The larger bank with an extensive credit department may share some of its information if asked to do so.

A very valuable service performed by correspondent banks is lending to banks to enable them to increase their reserves. This service is especially important to those banks that are not members of the Federal Reserve System. Correspondent banks that are located in the large money market centers of the country also assemble and make federal funds available to their smaller correspondents during tight money periods. During periods when small banks have excess reserves the larger correspondent banks stand ready to purchase their federal funds. Since small banks sometimes find the demand for federal funds greater on the national level than locally and the rate on these funds is relatively high, their sale becomes an important source of revenue.

Correspondent banking relations are both regional and national. Smaller banks usually carry an account with larger banks that are located at the center of the area's economic activity and are able to provide the services desired. These correspondent banks in turn carry deposits with banks in larger cities. Banks may also carry accounts with major banks beyond the immediate area if the latter are in a position to provide some special banking services. For example, banks in New York have enjoyed correspondent bank relations with many banks throughout the nation, in part because of their location in the heart of the export and import center of the nation. The correspondent banking system is not limited to banks within the U.S., but includes foreign banks as well. Many U.S. banks that do not have branches abroad carry accounts with foreign banks in order to provide foreign trade services for their customers. Foreign banks carry deposits with American banks for the same reason. At the end of 1977 interbank deposits of all insured commercial banks amounted to approximately $50 billion (see Table 1–1).

For many years, payment for services of correspondent banks has often been in the form of a deposit, which can be invested in earning assets. Since it is difficult sometimes to measure the actual value of correspondent bank services, these deposits may be larger than necessary to cover all costs and provide a reasonable profit. Although deposits are still employed as a means of payment, a shift has occurred toward the use of a specific service charge that actually covers the cost of providing a correspondent bank service. The reasons for this change are the desire to control costs, greater reliance on computerization of certain functions which has resulted in more accurate measurements of services performed, and improved cost accounting. Although actual payment may not be made for the various services, the cost is expressed in the amount of deposit balances at a stipulated earnings rate that would cover the costs. For example, if the services performed by a correspondent bank were valued at $400,000 and an earnings rate of 8 percent were agreed upon, a deposit of $5 million would be required.

When the Federal Reserve System was introduced, it was thought that correspondent banking would decline in importance or fail completely because the legal reserves of member banks were required to be maintained at the Federal Reserve banks. However, correspondent banking continues since it provides a number of useful services in our banking system.

Supervision of Commercial Banking

Commercial banking is one of the most closely regulated businesses. Few businesses are examined as often and as meticulously by supervisory and regulatory authorities to determine whether they are operating in accordance with the various laws and administrative rulings. This close regulation and supervision reflect their quasi-public nature. Commercial banks hold deposits of millions of people, which may be requested on demand; they can withhold or make credit available to individuals and businesses, and they are closely involved with the nation's money supply. Because of these factors, banks are vested with a public interest and are regulated to assure that these very basic functions are adequately performed.

Nearly every phase of banking activity is regulated by federal and state banking laws. The numerous regulations can be categorized as follows:

1 Restrictions on the right of entry into the banking business
2 Restrictions on expansion via branching and merging
3 Curbs on the competition for earning assets by prohibiting and restricting both the volume and composition of assets
4 Limits on a bank's ability to compete for funds by prohibiting the payment of interest on demand deposits and the imposition of ceilings on the amount of interest that can be paid on time and savings deposits
5 Reserve requirements on demand and time deposits
6 Requirements regarding bank capital

From the standpoint of regulation, banks can be divided into four groups: national banks, state member banks, nonmember banks that are members of the Federal Deposit Insurance Corporation (FDIC), and noninsured nonmember banks. National banks are under the control of the Comptroller of the Currency, a part of the Treasury Department, and are subject to all federal banking laws and regulations, including those imposed by the Federal Reserve System and the FDIC. State member banks are subject to the laws and regulations of the state in which they are chartered and operate, and to applicable federal laws since they are members of the Federal Reserve System and the FDIC. Nonmember insured banks are subject to state regulations plus the rules and regulations of the FDIC, and noninsured government nonmember banks are subject to state banking laws only. On the state level, the government officer responsible for the supervision and regulation of banks is known by such titles as state bank commissioner, commissioner of banks, and superintendent of banks.

The functions of banking supervisors such as the Comptroller of the

Currency and Superintendent of Banks (or whatever title may be used on the state level) are:

1. Passing on applications for charters for new banks, applications for branch permits, proposed mergers and consolidations, and proposed changes in banks' capital structures
2. Liquidation of closed banks
3. Issuance of regulations, ruling, and instructions to supplement or clarify legislation
4. Periodic detailed examinations of the condition, operations, and policies of individual banks
5. Taking corrective action
6. Counsel and advice to bankers
7. Compilation of reports and statistical data

Although these functions vary in some details between the federal and state governments, the general objective is the same: to establish and maintain a sound banking system.

The most important and effective tool of bank supervision and control is the bank examination. An examination is conducted by regulatory officials usually twice a year and may require anywhere from a few days to several weeks, depending on the size of the bank. The agencies that perform examinations are individual state regulatory agencies, the FDIC, the Federal Reserve System, and the Comptroller of the Currency. The objectives and methods employed by these agencies are similar. As stated by the Comptroller of the Currency, the objectives are:

". . . (1) to provide an objective evaluation of a bank's soundness; (2) to permit the OCC to appraise the quality of management and directors; and (3) to identify those areas where corrective action is required to strengthen the bank, to improve the quality of its performance, and to enable it to comply with applicable laws, rulings and regulations. The evaluation of the prudency of practices, adherence to laws and regulations, adequacy of liquidity and capital, quality of assets and earnings, nature of operations, and adequacy of internal control and internal audit are among the procedures utilized to accomplish these objectives."[6]

Although a bank examination involves all aspects of bank operations, the most significant is the appraisal of assets, especially loans and securities. The reason for this emphasis is to ascertain the soundness and liquidity of

[6]Comptroller of the Currency, *Comptroller's Handbook for National Bank Examiners,* Section 1.1.

a bank. Assets that do not meet acceptable standards are placed in specific categories and must be treated different from assets in general. Those, for example, that involve a loss must be charged off—that is, charged to a reserve account specifically created for that purpose—or deducted from the capital account. Sometimes only a portion of a questionable asset is charged off. Other questionable assets may be designated as below standard and requiring careful supervision.

The supervision and regulation of banks appear to be complicated because of overlapping state and federal laws and the many agencies with authority. Cooperation among the various regulatory agencies has reduced some of this overlapping, however, particularly in the field of examinations, a uniform classification of securities, and the exchange of information regarding chartering and branching. The complexity and duplication of bank regulations, nevertheless, have not gone unnoticed by banking authorities, congressional committees, and students of banking.

Governor J. L. Robertson, a member of the Board of Governors of the Federal Reserve System, has proposed that "the bank supervisory powers now exercised by the Comptroller of the Currency and the Federal Reserve and all powers and functions now vested in the Federal Deposit Insurance Corporation would be transferred to a new independent agency, consisting of five members, who would be appointed by the President on a nonpartisan basis for staggered ten-year terms."

According to Governor Robertson, our present arrangement "represents an unnecessary and undesirable fragmentation of responsibility that invites confusion and opportunities for the regulated industry to play off one administrative body against the other."[7]

Governor Henry Wallich, Board of Governors of the Federal Reserve System, in discussing the regulation of commercial banks, pointed out that:

> Public regulation of business has a long history of coddling regulated industries to death. The pattern of excessive solicitude began with the ICC and the railroads. Today the Federal Reserve, together with the other bank regulators and Congress, is doing the same to banking. The Fed keeps banks from paying competitive rates on deposits. Old limitations, such as the restrictions on branching, become increasingly anachronistic in today's world of instant communication. The House of Representatives has passed a measure that would keep the banks from going after new types of business. And the Federal Reserve has been flirting with legislation to "improve," i.e., probably toughen, the regulatory setup. If the banks cannot break out of this pattern, they are in danger of going the way of the railroads.

[7]J. L. Robertson, "Federal Regulation of Banking: A Plea for Unification." Reprinted, with permission, from 31 *Law & Contemp. Prob.* 687(1966).

... In other countries, banks have been allowed to take advantage of their technological freedom to engage in a wide variety of financial activities. By spreading out, functionally and geographically, they have been able to compensate for the constant erosion of their traditional base. In the U.S., the constraints that the laws of nature do not impose upon the business have been imposed by the laws of man. Banking, with its three federal and fifty state supervisory authorities, and bodies of law to match, is the most overregulated industry in the country.

Why, in an economy freer than most, is banking singled out for this excess of governmental solicitude? The U.S. has some of the best banks in the world, but it surely has the worst banking system of any major nation. This is not the fault of the banker. It is the fault of the legislator. To be sure, the legislator has tried to deal with real problems. The frequent miscarriage of his more or less well meant efforts was not always foreseeable. But this is precisely the usual fate of well-intentioned regulation."[8]

A presidential commission commonly referred to as the Hunt Commission stated that,

... greater flexibility and operational freedom in the financial structure will improve the allocation of resources to the nation's economic and social needs. Within the limits necessary for soundness and safety, the Commission seeks to remove unworkable regulatory restraints as well as provide additional powers and flexibility to the various types of financial institutions.

Very generally, the recommendations authorize depository institutions to engage in a wider range of financial services. At the same time, the recommendations require that after a transitional period, all institutions competing in the same markets do so on an equal basis. It is essential, for example, that all institutions offering third party payment services have the same reserve requirements, tax treatment, interest rate regulations, and supervisory burdens. The critical need for competition on equal terms causes the Commission to emphasize the interdependence of the recommendations and warn against the potential harm of taking piece-meal legislative action. When financial institutions compete on equal terms, with respect to reserves, taxes, rate regulations, and supervision, there should be no need for *ad hoc* protective policies in future periods of economic stress.

The recommendations are interrelated and the Commission urges that they be considered as a package, even though some of the proposed changes, if enacted separately, would improve the financial system. The Commission believes that piece-meal adoption of the recommendation raises the danger of creating new and greater imbalances.[9]

[8]Henry C. Wallich, Professor of Economics, Yale University, "Banks Need More Freedom to Compete," *Fortune,* March 1970, p. 114. This article was written prior to Professor Wallich's appointment to the Board of Governors of the Federal Reserve System.

[9]*The Report of the President's Commission on Financial Structure and Regulation,* Washington, D.C., December 1971, pp. 8–9.

The commission went ahead and made 89 recommendations, most of which applied to commercial banks. These regulations will be discussed in the chapters that follow.

A look at the history of banking shows that regulations are a product of financial crises instead of constructive planning. Examples are those arising out of the Civil War years, the period from 1907–1914, and between 1927 and 1935. Although some changes have been made, for the most part the structure of regulation is very much the same as was established in the 1930s when the safety of the depositor was uppermost in the minds of legislators. Changes in banking rules and regulations come slowly; however, because of the many technological developments that now appear on the horizon, changes may be more rapid in the future. Legislators should remember the words of the commission:

> Well-functioning financial intermediaries should be able to develop and use technological opportunities without significant strain on the system. It is widely believed that the financial sector has entered a period of rapid change. Technology is expected to influence the operating methods and structure of financial institutions in important but as yet uncertain ways. In the next few decades, technology may well have a more pervasive impact on financial structure than inflation has had in recent decades. The Commission is concerned with achieving a regulatory framework that allows adequate freedom for financial firms to adjust to new technological possibilities, encourages new types of financial firms to emerge, and at the same time assures that the resulting benefits will flow to the public.
>
> . . . Modifications in the structure and regulation of the financial system are urgently needed.[10]

Specifically, the commission made several recommendations in the area of regulation and supervision. The most significant was probably the creation of an Administrator of State Banks. This agency would consolidate the examining and supervisory functions of the FDIC and the Board of Governors of the Federal Reserve System. The insurance of deposits would be transferred to a Federal Deposit Guarantee Administration, which would not only administer the present insurance fund of commercial banks but also the funds for savings and loan associations and for credit unions. The Comptroller's Office would be retitled the Office of the National Bank Administrator and would be an independent agency separate from the Treasury Department. This office would continue to charter, examine, and supervise national banks. It would also provide the same regulatory and supervisory functions for mutual savings banks when provision is made for their federal chartering, which was recommended by the commission. The com-

[10]Ibid., pp. 14–15.

mission also recommended that the Board of Governors of the Federal Reserve System limit its activities primarily to monetary responsibilities. It did, however, recommend that the Board continue to supervise bank holding companies and certain international activities. Many observers have held that the Board of Governors should be concerned exclusively with monetary matters and leave the examining and regulatory activities to other agencies. This would contribute to greater efficiency and uniform standards. In the opinion of these observers, it is unfortunate that the commission did not recommend a clean break in this particular area.

A more recent study, known as the FINE Report, came up with some far-reaching recommendations regarding the total financial structure of the nation.[11] Many of the recommendations applicable to commercial banking are similar to those made by the Hunt Commission. The FINE Report recommends a further concentration of regulatory agencies. The Federal Reserve System would be stripped of its regulatory and supervisory powers and left with only one major function; namely, the formulation and administration of monetary policy. A super agency known as the Federal Depository Institutions Commission would be concerned with all federal regulations of all financial institutions that are now regulated by agencies of the federal government. Such agencies as the Comptroller of the Currency, the FDIC, and the Federal Credit Union Administration would be abolished, and their functions assigned to this commission. The Federal Home Loan Bank System would receive a new charter giving it authority to administer the Federal Home Loan Corporation and a program of housing finance utilizing all depository institutions as sources of mortgage funds for low- and moderate-income housing. The super agency would have jurisdiction over all depository institutions operating under federal charters or insured by a federal agency. Only those institutions that are state chartered and whose liabilities are not insured by a federal agency would be free of federal regulation. Since 98 percent of all U.S. banks are insured by the FDIC, the banking industry, for all practical purposes, would be subject to federal regulation. State Banking Commissions would cease to exist in those states that have no uninsured banks.

The regulation of commercial banks is based on some generally accepted objectives: First, the government should control the supply of the nation's medium of exchange. Second, since banks hold a large portion of the business and personal assets of the country, the safety of banks should be given high priority. Third, the government should prohibit anti-competitive mar-

[11]U.S. Congress. House. Subcommittee on Financial Institutions Supervision, Regulation and Insurance of the Committee on Banking, Currency and Housing. *Financial Institutions and the Nation's Economy (FINE) "Discussion Principles":* Hearings, vols. I–III. 94th Cong., 1st sess., December 1975, January 1976.

ket practices. Finally, the government should take steps to insure that fair and equitable treatment is extended to those seeking credit.

In order to attain these objectives, the breadth of coverage and the intensity of bank regulation have increased considerably in recent years. Increased regulation raises a very basic question: In what areas can government regulation attain an objective more efficiently than can increased reliance on a free market? We have been searching for an answer to this question over the years, not only in banking, but in other areas as well.

Foreign Banks in the United States

In addition to the domestic banks operating in the United States, at year end 1978 there were 123 foreign banks operating 305 banking facilities, holding total assets of approximately $130 billion—about 8.4 percent of the total commercial bank assets in the nation. Approximately 42 percent of these assets were controlled by banks from common market member countries and 24 percent by banking offices of Japan.

Since 1972 the number of foreign banks in this country has increased substantially and their assets increased at four times the rate of the three hundred largest banks in the U.S. These foreign banks are concentrated in about a dozen states; about 90 percent of their assets are located in California, Illinois, and New York. These banks provide a wide range of services, including what we normally regard as commercial banking, investment banking, venture capital financing, and real estate development.

A foreign branch is a banking office of a foreign owned bank that performs the usual banking services such as accepting deposits, making loans, and financing international trade. A subsidiary is not a branch but a separate entity, and may be owned in whole or in part by a foreign bank or a bank holding company. It, too, may perform a wide range of banking services. An agency differs from a foreign branch and a subsidiary in the breadth of services performed. Although an agency may finance international trade and make loans, it does not have legal permission to accept deposits. The funds an agency employs in the performance of its functions are derived from the home country. A foreign affiliate is not owned by a foreign bank, but the foreign bank and its affiliate may have common ownership in that the stock of both may be owned by a holding company. A foreign affiliate may perform broad or limited banking services, depending on the permission granted by the state in which it operates.

For many years the entry of foreign banks was controlled exclusively by the states since no federal legislation had been enacted governing entry. Foreign banks were touched by federal law only if they became members of the Federal Reserve System or controlled a subsidiary bank, in which case the Bank Holding Company Act applied. The lack of a national policy regarding foreign banks gave them a competitive advantage over domestic banks which in recent years became a matter of concern in the domestic banking community. Foreign banks were permitted to branch across state lines, a privilege denied domestic banks by the McFadden Act of 1927. They were also permitted to operate security affiliates to underwrite and sell stocks in the U.S., an activity that was denied domestic banks by the Glass-Steagall Act of 1935. Finally, foreign banks have not been subject to Federal Reserve requirements imposed by the Federal Reserve System since they were not required to join.

Because of the unequal impact of the various banking rules and regulations, foreign banks have been in a position to enter choice markets. This is evidenced by the fact that half of the foreign banks operated in two or more states and approximately one-fourth of their assets were found outside their home state. Although foreign banks, like branches of U.S. banks abroad, are interested primarily in financing foreign trade, some have engaged in domestic banking, aggressively seeking deposits of U.S. businesses and residents and making loans domestically. Since foreign banks were not subject to the same reserve requirements as domestic banks, their lending costs were lower, which made them strong competitors for loans.

The rapid growth in the number of foreign banks and foreign bank assets culminated in the International Banking Act of 1978, which was designed to remove some of the competitive inequities that existed. A foreign bank must now select one state as its "home state" of operation and can establish a new branch or agency outside the home state only with that state's express permission. Although the new branch or agency located outside the home state may conduct full banking services in accordance with state law, the new branches may accept deposits only from non-residents or from activities related to international trade financing. The new legislation provides that all banks shall be subject to reserve requirements imposed by the Federal Reserve System if the parent bank has world-wide assets of $1 billion or more. Although foreign banks operating in the U.S. are not required to be members of the Federal Reserve System, they may enjoy the services of the central bank on terms comparable with member banks.

The above legislation is a step toward the removal of inequities. Foreign banks still have important advantages over domestic banks, however, because of a "grandfathering" provision; that is, the exemption of existing out-of-state branches, agencies, and subsidiary banks. Moreover, state chartered subsidiary banks of foreign banks are exempt from this new legislation. The existing operations of security affiliates of foreign banks are also "grandfathered," but new entries are prohibited. Although a national policy for the regulation of foreign banks has been developed for the first time, it falls short of equal treatment of foreign and domestic banks. This is probably not the end of close scrutiny and legislation in this area.

Questions

1. If you had been a member of the British Parliament during the Colonial period, what would have been your attitude toward the organization of banks in America? Would you have favored restrictions? What kind? Why?

2. Do you think a dual banking system is desirable or undesirable? Why or why not?

3. Discuss how the taxation of state bank notes by the federal government contributed to the organization of national banks.

4. How do you account for the difference in the size of banks in the U.S.?

5. If you were to recommend the type of banking the nation should have, what would you suggest—unit or branch banking? Why? Would you suggest greater or less restrictions on entry? Why?

6. Why did correspondent relationships develop between banks? How would you evaluate the performance of the correspondent banking system? Would it be advisable to permit this system to perform many of the services that are now a responsibility of the Federal Reserve System such as clearance of checks, transfer of funds, safekeeping, providing the nation with coin and currency, etc.?

7. Why have governments chartered and regulated commercial banking? What are the objectives of bank supervision?

8. A multitude of recommendations has been made regarding the structure of commercial banking and how and by whom banks should be regulated. What would you recommend in these two areas?

9. Frequently we hear and read about the concentration of business firms in various industries. Compare the degree of concentration in banking with other industries. From a societal standpoint, is there any reason for concern? Why?

10. From the standpoint of a free competitive market, how would you evaluate the International Banking Act of 1978? Explain.

SELECTED REFERENCES

BOARD OF GOVERNORS OF THE FEDERAL RESERVE SYSTEM, *Banking Studies,* Washington, D.C. August 1941.

COMMISSION ON FINANCIAL STRUCTURE AND REGULATION, *The Report of the President's Commission on Financial Structure and Regulation,* Washington, D.C., December 1971.

FINE-Financial Institutions and the Nation's Economy-Compendium of Papers Prepared for the FINE Study, Books 1 and 2. Committee on Banking, Currency and Housing, U.S. House of Representatives, 94th Cong., 2d sess., June 1976.

FISHER, GERALD C., *American Banking Structure,* New York, Columbia University Press, 1968.

TRESCOTT, PAUL B., *Financing American Enterprise: The Story of Commercial Banking,* New York, Harper & Row Publishers, 1963.

"Symposium of the FINE Study," *Journal of Money, Credit and Banking,* Vol. IX No. 4, November 1977, pp. 605–661.

REPORT OF THE COMMISSION ON MONEY AND CREDIT. *Money and Credit: Their Influence on Jobs, Prices, and Growth,* Englewood Cliffs, N.J., Prentice-Hall, 1961.

U.S. CONGRESS, Subcommittee on Financial Institutions Supervision, Regulation, and Insurance, of the House Committee on Banking, Currency, and Housing. *Financial Institutions and the Nation's Economy (FINE) "Discussion Principles": Hearings,* vols. I-III. 94th Cong., 1st sess., December 1975–January 1976.

3

Expansion of
Commercial Banking

Economic forces, constantly at work, contribute to changes in the commercial banking structure. On a system-wide basis, expansion is largely a product of how rapidly the policymakers at the national level allow the money supply to expand. The major components of both the narrowly defined money supply, commonly termed M1, and the broadly defined money supply, called M2, constitute most of the liabilities of commercial banks. M1 is composed of currency in the hands of the public and demand deposits at commercial banks. M2 is composed of M1 plus savings deposits, time deposits open account, and certificates of deposit other than negotiable certificates of deposit over $100,000. If decisions in Washington, D.C., result in rapid growth of M1 and M2, a concomitant expansion of the banking system occurs. The extent of the expansion that results at an individual bank depends on its own local economy, its competitive environment, and its objectives.

There are many other determinants of an individual bank's ability to expand. Economic activity quickens in some areas of the country and declines in others. Population increases and shifts. New business firms come into being, some pass from the scene, and others change location. Traffic patterns are altered, and business firms—including banks—that were once accessible may encounter difficulties in keeping or attracting customers. To increase earning assets and improve profitability, banks may change their organizational form. The avenues of expansion or structural change that are open to banks are merging, branching, and the formation of holding companies.

Mergers of Commercial Banks

The two types of business combinations that are available to business firms in general are also available to banks, namely, mergers and consolidations. A merger occurs when one bank ceases to exist and its assets are combined with those of another. A consolidation results when two or more banks combine to form a new one and the participating banks lose their individual identities. Most combinations in banking are mergers. Although the term merger has a technical meaning, it is used here, as it is in most discussions of the concentration of banking, to mean any form of combination whereby two or more operating banks are joined under a single management.

Reasons for Merging

Several factors motivate banks to merge. Cutting the costs of operation and increasing volume in order to increase profits are the two most important reasons. Population shifts to suburban areas stimulate expansion as banks make an effort to increase deposits and loans and thus increase earnings. Another reason for expanding is to diversify banking operations. Some banks engaged in wholesale banking—catering to large depositors and borrowers—branch out into consumer and other forms of lending.

The size of loan requests has grown, and since the size of loans to any one borrower is limited by the size of a bank's capital and surplus, banks have combined to increase loan limits. In this manner, old customers can be held and new ones attracted. The prestige associated with "bigness" has probably contributed to the desire to expand also. In states that permit branch banking, the purchase of a bank may be less expensive than setting up a new office, with its construction and promotional costs and personnel recruitment problems. The absorption of another bank may eliminate some competition also.

Banks that have agreed to be absorbed by larger banks have done so for a variety of reasons. Some have agreed because of difficulties in raising needed capital, and others to avoid failure. One very important reason has been the problem of management. Many small banks, realizing that competent management is not available to replace present personnel who may be nearing retirement age, decide to merge, consolidate, or sell to a larger bank. An attractive offer also motivates small banks to sell out to larger banks. The stock for small banks usually has a limited market and often sells at a price below book value. In addition, some small banks have conservative management, and as a result growth is stifled and earnings impaired. If stockholders exchange their stock for shares in the purchasing bank, often more diversified and progressive, they may enjoy a broader market for their stock, and receive larger dividends. Competition from other banks and financial institutions has also encouraged some smaller banks to unite with others.

Although mergers occur every year, a very large number, approximately 1,600, took place during the 1950s. Most of the banks involved were relatively small institutions which became branches of the acquiring bank, but mergers did occur between billion-dollar banks, some of the largest in the nation. This increase in mergers caused some legislators to become concerned about the concentration of banking.

For many years the task of making rules governing bank mergers was assigned to the various banking agencies, but no specific standards were established for exercising this authority. It was assumed that since banks were closely regulated, banking agencies would approve only those mergers that were desirable from the standpoint of banking competition and the needs and convenience of the public.

Because of the impact of bank mergers on banking competition, the Bank Merger Act of 1960 was enacted. This made all bank mergers involving insured banks subject to one of the three federal agencies. Mergers that would result in national banks were placed under the Comptroller of the Currency. Mergers involving banks that were to be state member banks were under the jurisdiction of the Board of Governors of the Federal Reserve System. If a bank were to be a state nonmember, insured bank, authority to merge was vested with the FDIC. The act departed from previous legislation on bank mergers by listing criteria to be used in the evaluation of merger applications, but it did not assign relative weights to the individual factors. The factors to be considered were:

1 The financial history and condition of each bank involved
2 The adequacy of each bank's capital structure
3 The merged bank's earnings prospects
4 The general character of its management
5 The convenience and needs of the community to be served
6 Whether the merged bank's corporate powers are consistent with the purposes of the Federal Deposit Insurance Corporation Act
7 How the merger will affect competition

In addition to these requirements, each agency was required in the interest of uniform standards to request a report from the other two agencies and from the Attorney General on the competitive factors involved. The agency concerned, however, was not bound by these reports. Although there was nothing in the act that required or authorized the Attorney General to make an antitrust attack if evidence indicated this should be the proper procedure, he was certainly not barred from doing so.

Merging and the Courts

It soon became evident that the Bank Merger Act of 1960 was not only unclear but also confusing. The wording of the act was very general, allowing great flexibility. No time limit was set for the reports the various agencies were to file with the banking agency supervising a merger. No weight was given to the various criteria set forth. The role of the Attorney General was not specific. It was not long, however, before bank mergers were to play a central role in our banking history. In a series of Supreme Court decisions[1] it was held that banking is subject to the provisions of the Sherman Act of 1890 and the Clayton Act of 1914, the cornerstones of federal antitrust legislation. In the Philadelphia case, the first and probably the most celebrated case involving a bank merger, the court ruled that banking was a line of commerce and even though a merger was approved by the federal banking agencies, it could be challenged under the antitrust laws. The court held that the proposed merger of two large Philadelphia banks which would have resulted in a single bank controlling 36 percent of the deposits in a four-county area was sufficiently anticompetitive to be in violation of the Clayton Act. Thus banks were declared subject to the same antitrust rules as other business firms.

The Bank Merger Act of 1966, an amendment to the Act of 1960, was enacted primarily to reconcile the differences between the courts and the banking agencies. The courts stressed competitive factors, while banking agencies placed greater emphasis on the convenience and needs of the public. It was a compromise between two views; that the antitrust laws should be rigorously applied to bank mergers and that banking agencies should have exclusive control of bank mergers. In this compromise the 1966 act assigned greater weight to the competitive factors than did the 1960 act. It provided, for example, that,

> The responsible agency shall not approve . . . any proposed merger transaction which would result in a monopoly, or would be in furtherance of any

[1]*United States* v. *Philadelphia National Bank,* et al., 210 F. Supp. 348 (1962); 83 S Ct. 1715 (1963). *United States* v. *First National Bank and Trust Company of Lexington,* et al., 208 F. Supp. 457 (1962); 84 S Ct. 1033 (1964).

combination or conspiracy to monopolize or attempt to monopolize the business of banking in any part of the United States . . .[2]

Not many bank merger cases have come before the U.S. Supreme Court since the passage of the Bank Merger Act of 1966, but a sufficient number have to indicate the Court's reasoning on this subject. In the first two cases[3] the Court's decisions relied heavily upon concentration ratios as an indication of bank competition. In the first case the merging banks accounted for only 14 percent of the commercial bank deposits in a market in which the five largest commercial banks controlled 71 percent, yet the merger was denied. In the other case the market share of the proposed merging banks would have been 32 percent while the five largest banks in the area accounted for 66 percent of the deposits. In both cases the district courts did not see this amount of concentration to be in violation of the antitrust laws. Two major procedural questions were answered in these early cases. The Court asserted that the Department of Justice need only challenge a bank merger on the grounds of a violation of the antitrust laws. The Court was not required to prove a violation of the Bank Merger Act of 1966, and an opinion of a banking agency was not binding on the courts. The Court also ruled that the burden of proof that the convenience and needs consideration outweighed the anticompetitive effects rested with the defendant banks.

The first case involving relatively large branch banks was the Crocker-Anglo Citizens Bank case in 1967.[4] This case involved the fifth and seventh largest banks in California, where branch banking is widespread. The Court approved the merger on the grounds that the new bank would be in a stronger position to compete with the largest bank in the state. Before the merger, one bank operated in northern California and the other in the southern part of the state with some overlapping in only one county. After the merger Crocker-Citizens was the fourth largest bank in the state.

A very interesting case, because of the competitive weakness of one of the banks involved, was the Third National Bank case in 1968.[5] The Third National Bank of Nashville, the second largest bank in Davidson County, wanted to merge with the fourth largest bank in the area, which held only 4.83 percent of the deposits in the county, a percentage that had been declining since 1960. If the merger had been allowed, the new combination

[2]Bank Merger Act of 1966, 80 Stat. 7; Public Law 356, 89th Cong., 2d sess., 1966.

[3]*United States* v. *Provident National Bank,* et al., 262 F. Supp. 297 (1966); 87 S. Ct. 1088 (1967). *United States* v. *First City National Bank of Houston,* et al., Supp. 397 (1966); S. Ct. 1088 (1967).

[4]*United States* v. *Crocker-Anglo National Bank,* et al., 263 F. Supp. 125 (1966); 277 F. Supp. 133 (1967).

[5]*United States* v. *Third National Bank of Nashville,* et al., 260 F. Supp. 869 (1966); 88 S. Ct. 882 (1968).

would have held nearly 40 percent of the deposits of the commercial banks in the county. Prior to the merger the three largest banks controlled 93 percent of the deposits. The lower court had approved the merger on the grounds that the bank being acquired held a relatively small amount of deposits in the area and that it was not a vigorous competitor because of the lack of aggressive management. In other words the merger would not have resulted in weakened bank competition in the area. For several years banking agencies had approved mergers when one of the banks was in a similar situation. They had also approved mergers when the acquired bank was in a floundering or failing condition. Although the acquired bank in the Third National Bank case was not failing, the district court had termed it a *stagnant* or foundering bank. Despite this description the Supreme Court denied the merger, pointing out that the defendant did not show that the gains expected from the merger could not have been attained through other means.

The Court has not been reluctant to reject proposed mergers of relatively small banks. This was evident in the *Phillipsburg National Bank* case which involved two banks, each with deposits of less than $30 million, which when merged would control only 23 percent of the total deposits of a two-city area, while the remaining two banks controlled 56 percent. In deciding upon the relevant geographic area the Supreme Court considered the two-city area of Phillipsburg, New Jersey, and Easton, Pennsylvania, separated by the Delaware River.[6]

A sufficient number of merger cases have come before the courts after the enactment of the 1966 legislation to establish a pattern that will probably be followed for some time. The convenience and needs of the public test so long relied upon by banking agencies is a less powerful force than the competitive factor in bank mergers. Moreover, the courts are not bound by the opinions of the banking agencies in their analysis of mergers. For many years regulatory authorities would approve a merger if one of the banks was on the verge of failing. This is no longer true unless it is the only realistic solution.

Is Banking a Line of Commerce?

One of the most debatable topics in bank merger discussions is the determination of the relevant market. In the Philadelphia case the Court took a narrow view of the relevant market and in so doing precluded any evaluation of the competition that arose from other financial institutions or financial markets. The defendants held that banking consisted of two main functions: the securing of deposits and the granting of loans, both of which could be further subdivided into areas or markets. The banks, in their defense, fur-

[6]*United States* v. *Phillipsburg National Bank and Trust Company,* et al., 306 F. Supp. 645 (1969); 90 S. Ct. 2035 (1970).

ther pointed out that each type of deposit or loan attracted different customers, some located in different geographical areas. The banks also held that varying degrees of competition existed in each of these markets. For example, in the competition for funds, banks compete with savings and loans associations, mutual savings banks, and, during tight money periods, even with Treasury securities for time deposits. In the large certificate of deposit market, banks compete locally as well as nationally for funds. Banks also compete with other institutions for all types of loans.

The concepts of *markets* and *industries* have fundamentally changed over the years. The Court's concept of industry and market as it applies to a segment of the banking industry is quite archaic and applicable to a great extent only to small banks, which provide a limited number of services. To say, as the Court has, that banking is a single line of commerce implies that an analysis of local market conditions is not necessary in merger considerations. This seems to have been the Court's position in the Philadelphia case when it said that "so also we must be alert to the danger of subverting congressional intent by permitting too broad an economic investigation."[7]

Until recently commercial banks were the sole producers of demand deposits. This unique function undoubtedly influenced the Court in its conclusion that banking is, in its entirety, a line of commerce. The Court was not on firm ground, however, when it stated that demand deposit accounts were costless to the banks. It is true that banks do not pay interest on demand deposits because they have been prohibited from doing so by law since 1933, but they are certainly not costless. Banks can no longer exclusively provide demand deposit service. Since 1976 negotiable orders of withdrawal (NOW) accounts[8] have been authorized for mutual savings banks, savings and loan associations, and commercial banks in all the New England states. In addition, mutual savings banks in the New England and five other states now offer demand deposit accounts. In 1977 it was reported that "all but 15 of the nation's 470 mutual savings banks have either NOW accounts, traditional checking accounts, or a combination of the two."[9] Legislation has been proposed to extend authorization for NOW accounts to all states. Credit unions in 46 states now issue demand deposits called "share draft accounts."[10]

A logical conclusion is that banking includes several distinct lines of commerce, each of which faces competition from nonbanking enterprises. This is not true of each individual bank, however. For example, the large

---

[7] *United States* v. *Philadelphia National Bank.*

[8] NOW accounts are discussed in chapter 6.

[9] Jean M. Lovati, "The Growing Similarity Among Financial Institutions," Federal Reserve Bank of St. Louis *Review,* October 1977, pp. 7–8.

[10] *Ibid.,* p. 8.

banks of New York City compete for business loans and time deposits nationally and even worldwide, unlike the small rural banks located throughout the nation. The small bank may not seek large certificates of deposit and does not provide the numerous services that are made available to customers of New York banks. Thus, if the concept of the line of commerce is applicable to commercial banking, it should be recognized that banking involves a cluster of products, and that nonbanking competition should be included in the courts' evaluation of bank mergers.

Competition in Banking

Economists hold that competition refers to rivalry among firms in a given market. Theory tells us that the strength of this rivalry depends upon the number and size of the buyers and sellers in a given market. In fact, pure competition could be defined as a situation in which we have so many buyers and sellers that one can enter or leave the market without having an appreciable effect upon it.

The many advantages to competition can be summarized by saying that an industry that is highly competitive is efficient—the smaller the number of sellers or the greater the concentration of business firms, the lower the quality of services and the higher the price for goods and services. Based upon this reasoning it would seem that in highly concentrated banking markets interest on loans would be higher than in areas where there was less concentration, lower rates of interest would be paid on various classes of time deposits, the ratio of time to total deposits would be lower, and earnings would be higher. Moreover, less emphasis would be placed on direct lending, especially in small amounts, than on the purchase of securities. These hypotheses are not fully supported by the research on competition in banking: the results have been inconclusive, and complete agreement on many issues has not been reached. Research on bank competition has been hampered by the unavailability of data and, more importantly, by the inability to hold other things equal when measuring the effects of specific factors in different market situations.

Some studies on the relationship of banking markets to loan rates show that the larger the number of banks, the lower the rates of interest, and others have found just the opposite. One study concluded that "no easily identifiable relationship exists between concentration ratios and the level of interest rate charged by commercial banks on business loans."[11]

With the growth of branch banking there has been great interest in its effect on market conditions. Most research on this subject indicates that

---

[11]Theodore G. Fleching, *Banking Market Structure & Performance in Metropolitan Areas* (Washington, D.C., Board of Governors of the Federal Reserve System, 1965).

when banks acquire additional branches through merger, consumers of banking services are benefited. Several studies show that interest rates paid on savings accounts were higher after a merger and several loan rates were lower, including residental real estate and automobile loans.[12] The maturities of these loans were also more liberal than before the merger. The results of research that relates performance to size are not as convincing as we would like. The reason is largely conceptual in that concluding what banks produce is difficult. Banks of different size and location cater to different clienteles and produce different services. It is difficult to measure these services and, in many instances, comparison is impossible. Studies have shown, however, that large banks paid higher interest rates on savings than did small banks and also charged lower rates on loans. Large banks had a higher ratio of time to total deposits, were more aggressive in their lending, and had a higher ratio of loans to deposits. Several factors are responsible for some of these developments. Loans made by large banks to large business firms entail less credit risk and require less administration than many small loans made by small banks. Moreover, large banks, in general, have a greater share of their time deposits in large certificates of deposit, which require less administrative costs and on which relatively higher rates are paid. Large banks tend to be more aggressive and innovative in new bank services and in the employment of a larger amount of their assets in loans and investments. A brief but penetrating discussion of competition in banking concludes with the following:

> If the findings are taken at their face value—which, as has repeatedly been indicated, is very hazardous—they would seem to suggest the desirability of a public policy toward banking structure that discouraged concentration, encouraged new entry, liberalized branching and permitted banks to grow to large size.[13]

Bank size is an important factor in efficiency and the capacity to provide a wide range of banking services to the public. This was recognized by Governor Mitchell of the Board of Governors of the Federal Reserve System when he said,

> A competitive banking system must be based on the *capacity* to compete. For many types of services this capacity requires large size. It also requires considerable talent. An arena of sufficient scope must be provided for the exercise of that talent and for its development. The alternative is some sort of shelter-

[12]Larry R. Mote, "The Perennial Issue: Branch Banking," *Business Conditions,* Federal Reserve Bank of Chicago, February 1974. This publication contains an excellent bibliography on branch banking.

[13]"Competition in Banking: What is Known? What is the Evidence?" *Business Conditions,* Federal Reserve Bank of Chicago, February 1967.

ing—the kind exemplified by statutory home office protection and regulatory prescription of over-banking. If we believe that competition will provide higher quality and lower prices for banking services, then we cannot assume that the requisite competitive talent will be attracted by a dead-end future.[14]

Although much of the early research on bank markets concluded or implied that economies of scale were not substantial in banking, greater value has recently been assigned to bank size. One researcher takes the position that because of uncertainties the stochastic nature of banking activities and economies of scale of a special kind exist. Professor Baltensperger points out, for example, that,

> Exploitation of economies of scale due to uncertainty is in some sense "raison d'etre" for banks. Banks are financial intermediaries consolidating risk by having as assets the debt of a large number of different people independent in their solvency, and having as liabilities deposits of a large number of independently acting depositors. This permits them to hold relatively small amounts of liquid reserves against their liabilities and the associated risk of cash-drains, and relatively small amounts of capital account against their assets and the corresponding risk of capital losses and bankruptcy. It is surprising, therefore, that the existing literature on economies of scale in banking either does not mention uncertainty at all as a possible source of these economies, or treats it only as of secondary importance.[15]

To promote a competitive structure the Justice Department introduced in 1968 what has become known as the *doctrine of potential competition*. This doctrine was developed from a set of merger guidelines set forth by the Department of Justice and stated that mergers would be challenged between firms if the parties to the mergers controlled certain percentages of the market. Some degrees of concentration that would trigger a challenge were as follows:

1 Any firm with approximately 25% or more of the market;

2 One of the two largest firms in a market in which the shares of the two largest firms amount to approximately 50% or more;

3 One of the four largest firms in a market in which the shares of the eight largest firms amount to approximately 75% or more, provided the merging firm's share of the market amounts to approximately 10% or more; or

4 One of the eight largest firms in a market in which the shares of these firms amount to approximately 75% or more, provided either (A) the

[14]Governor George W. Mitchell, "The Changing Structure of Banking" (Speech delivered to the Graduate School of Banking at the University of Wisconsin, Madison, August 16, 1972).

[15]Ernst Baltensperger, "Economies of Scale, Firm Size, and Concentration in Banking," *Journal of Money, Credit, and Banking*, Vol. 4 (August 1972), p. 467. Copyright © 1972 by The Ohio State University Press.

merging firm's share of the market is not insubstantial and there are no more than one or two likely entrants into the market, or (B) the merging firm is a rapidly growing firm.[16]

The legal doctrine of potential competition is a recent development. The concept implies that although the acquisition of one bank by another may not result in a noncompetitive situation immediately, it might do so at some time in the future. In considering potential competition there are several hypothetical questions that must be answered. One is: What would be the acquiring bank's alternate moves in the event entry by acquisition were denied; that is, would the acquiring bank be likely to enter the market by establishing a branch and thus add to competition? Would the acquiring bank be so strong and aggressive that potential competition would be lessened? Finally, would the acquisition leave so few competitors that competition would eventually be stifled? These questions are difficult to answer, of course. Since short-run developments cannot be seen clearly sometimes and the view is dimmer further down the road, it is not surprising that this doctrine has not been supported by the courts.

There have been periods when the American banking system was weak and many failures occurred, such as after the demise of the Second Bank of the United States in the 1830s and the decades of the 1920s and 1930s. Thus, factors other than efficiency warrant consideration, most importantly, financial soundness. In a competitive environment the inefficient firms are forced out of the market because they are not in a position to charge high enough prices to cover their costs. Under monopolistic conditions, firms with high costs are afforded a certain degree of immunity from the rigors of competition. For a number of years the banking system has tried to stay between these two extremes, since this position appeared more compatible with financial soundness. In recent years emphasis has been placed on moving the industry toward greater competition. The problem faced by regulatory agencies and the courts is not maintaining perfect competition but supporting a market condition that is as competitive as possible, yet recognizing the advantages of economies of scale and financial soundness. To provide such an environment is a difficult task, but one of great importance.

Establishing Branches

Banks that are permitted to engage in branch banking on either a statewide or limited basis expand their plant capacity by establishing new branches or by absorbing smaller independent unit banks. Banks engaged

[16]U.S. Department of Justice, "Merger Guidelines," Policy Release, May 30, 1968.

in branch banking are, in general, guided in their expansion decisions by the same factors as are the organizers of a new unit bank: the potential growth of the area and an analysis of present banking facilities. They may take a long-run view of their actions because of their pool of capital. For example, a bank might take the view that it can afford to operate a particular branch at a loss for three years, whereas organizers of a unit bank might decide that if the location would not be completely self-supporting at the end of two years it would not be a good investment. This difference has probably been recognized by supervisory and regulatory agencies and has also contributed to the expansion of branch banking.

A significant piece of legislation that restricted national banks from branching was the McFadden Act of 1927, which allowed national banks to establish branches only in their home office city, if branches were permitted by state law. The act encouraged many states to enact legislation against branching, and such laws were upheld by the courts. This antibranching attitude, which was quite strong in the 1920s, softened somewhat in the early 1930s during the collapse of the banking system. Shortly thereafter many states revised their branching laws to permit statewide or limited branching. In the Banking Act of 1933, national banks were placed on a par with state banks; that is, if state banks were permitted to branch statewide, so were national banks. The legislation regarding branching is quite interesting in that the federal government, which has the authority to charter national banks and permit branching by these institutions, turned over to the states the responsibility of deciding whether branching will be permitted.

Despite a growing interest in branching, state legislatures have been slow to revise their branching laws, with few notable exceptions such as New Jersey and New York. Moreover, no movement has been organized to promote branch banking on the federal level. The Congress has been satisfied, it seems, to permit the states to determine the kind of multi-office banking structure each desires. This reluctance to change our banking structure, primarily established in the 1930s, has continued despite many significant changes in our economy and social patterns. The 1971 Commission on Financial Institutions seemed to accept this position but did indicate that branching was a desirable development when it said that, "The public should benefit from the option granted financial institutions to branch statewide."[17] Statewide branching would rule out *home office protection* statutes in many states that prohibit banks from establishing new branches in communities already served by other banks. Obviously, this type of legislation is designed to limit the entry of banks in the area and is certainly anticompetitive.

---

[17] *The Report of the President's Commission on Financial Structure and Regulation* (Washington, D.C.: Government Printing Office, 1971), pp. 61–62.

A very important issue in the area of bank structure is the question of branching across state lines. Obviously some bank markets straddle state lines and will continue to do so as metropolitan areas continue to grow. The Commission on Money and Credit, which made a study of financial institutions in the early 1960s, recommended that banks be permitted to establish branches within trading areas. An Advisory Committee on Branching appointed by the Comptroller of the Currency made a similar recommendation in 1962, and Governor Mitchell referred to state lines as they applied to branching as "Berlin walls" and said that, "there is no economic or institutional reason for not negotiating interstate compacts to enrich the banking alternatives for citizens who live in metropolitan areas."[18] In March 1972 the New York Superintendent of Banks introduced in the New York legislature a bill that would permit out-of-state bank holding companies to acquire New York banks provided the state in which the banking company was located would grant reciprocal privilege to New York bank holding companies.[19] The President's commission on financial institutions skirted this issue very cleverly and placed this responsibility on the states.

> Although this Commission rejects proposals to permit interstate branching or metropolitan area banking by federal legislation, it urges states to be progressive in changing their laws. Failure to act could encourage the use of inferior organizational and technological means for extending markets.[20]

Actually, the federal government has unlimited alternatives regarding branching, one of which is to permit national banks to branch within relevant economic areas, regardless of state law and whether such areas cut across state lines. Should this come about, states would be placed in a position of having to adopt similar laws; if they did not, state banks that they charter would be at a competitive disadvantage. The most far-reaching change that the federal government could adopt would be to permit nationwide banking for national banks. Both of these proposals are revolutionary in terms of our past history of banking structure. Perhaps in the future they may not be considered so extreme. At the moment, the first proposal is probably the most realistic and sound. It would permit improved banking service in a marketing area and provide a structure that could be regulated without an undue burden.

Several arguments have been set forth against branch banking. One of the oldest is that it is monopolistic and will tend to develop a *money trust*. A second argument is that a branch bank will become impersonal in its activi-

---

[18]*American Bankers,* October 28, 1968.

[19]Ibid.

[20]*The Report of the President's Commission on Financial Structure and Regulation,* p. 62.

ties and the needs of the small communities and small borrowers will be neglected, as a result. However, no convincing evidence exists that such has happened. Among the arguments advanced in favor of branch banking, the most important is that it leads to better bank management. Because of greater resources and better training facilities, branch banking probably does have an advantage in the development of better management. More skilled people can be employed, and there are greater opportunities for specialization. Another argument is that a greater diversification of assets can take place, allowing a greater diversification of risks. Advocates of branch banking contend that geographical mobility of funds to meet emergencies and seasonal needs and larger amounts of deposits and capital than unit banks usually have are definite advantages. Communities may need funds in excess of the deposits of a unit bank, and the lending limit of branch banks may be greater than that of unit banks. With branch banking, these demands can be met, and larger loans can be made to one borrower. Advocates of branch banking often state that a branch office can be organized more quickly and economically than a new bank in a rapidly developing area, and that there can be more diversified banking services. It is true that branching has made banking facilities available in areas where unit banks would have difficulty surviving. Moreover, branch banking has demonstrated economies of scale that have benefited the banking public.

The basic reason for opposing branch banking is that small banks fear they will be placed at a competitive disadvantage and ultimately be forced from the market. Although there is some truth in this assumption, the fear, in many cases, is more imaginary than real. The New York State Banking Department has conducted some valuable research in this area which shows that,

1 Small banks did not serve the public as well as large banks did with respect to prices, lending terms, and credit availability. Although the deposit growth of small banks . . . continued to increase, the rate of growth was reduced by the entry of large banks.
2 The profitability of most small banks was not adversely affected by the entry of large banks into a community.
3 Broadening of branching powers does not necessarily create insurmountable difficulties for local institutions, large or small.[21]

It is interesting to note that primarily because of these studies the New York legislature enacted legislation that permits statewide as opposed to regional branching.

[21]Ernest Kohn, "Branching and Competition" (Statement before the 16th Annual Trustees' Day, Group V Savings Banks, January 23, 1970).

Chain Banking

Another form of bank organization is chain banking, which is usually defined as the control of two or more commercial banks by the same individual or group of individuals. Control may be accomplished through stock ownership, common directors, or any other manner permitted by law. Each bank that is a member of the chain maintains its own identity and has a separate board of directors. Although this type of organization has been around for years, comprehensive information about its size and operation is fragmentary, primarily because it is not regulated as are multibank and one-bank holding companies; hence, there are no published reports on chain organizations. There have been, however, some special studies on chain banking over the years that are quite helpful to students of banking.[22]

Chain banking was introduced in this country near the end of the 19th Century, and most of the early development was found in the northwestern and southern agricultural states. Chain banking has expanded in states that prohibit branching and multibank holding companies. Banks that are members of a chain are relatively small, and the chain operates in a relatively small area. This has not kept some chains from moving across state lines, however. Usually chain organizations are built around a key bank that is considerably larger than the others in the organization. A recent study of chain banking in the 7th Federal Reserve District,[23] a stronghold of this type of banking, showed that there were 86 chains, 70 of which were located in the states of Illinois and Iowa, both of which prohibit branch banking. These chains controlled 322 banks which held around $14 billion in deposits, or 11 percent of the total deposits in the District. Although information regarding the performance of chains is not known, it appears that a philosophy of management, common goals and objectives could be introduced via the board of directors. Moreover, banks within the chain organization that have personnel with special management techniques and expertise could share this with other members and thus increase the overall efficiency of the organization. Despite these possible advantages, one study in the late 1960s that examined the profitability of chain and non-chain banks revealed that chain banks were less profitable.

[22]C. E. Cagle, "Branch Chain and Group Banking," *Banking Studies*, Board of Governors of the Federal Reserve System, August 1941; Jerome C. Darnell, "Profitability Comparisons Between Chain and Non-Chain Banks," *The Bankers Magazine*, Spring 1968; Joseph T. Keating, "Chain Banking in the District," *Economic Perspectives*, Federal Reserve Bank of Chicago, September/October 1977.

[23]Includes the states of Illinois, Iowa. Wisconsin, Indiana, and Michigan.

Bank Holding Companies

One of the significant developments in banking in recent years has been the growth of bank holding companies which own or control directly or indirectly one or more banks. The banks owned by a holding company may be unit banks or banks with branches. Such banks retain their own board of directors, responsible to the stockholders and regulatory authorities for the proper operation of their banks. The two general types of bank holding companies are the multibank and the one-bank holding company.

Multibank Holding Companies

A multibank holding company is defined by law as one that controls two or more banks. Multibank holding companies have existed since the turn of the century and have developed primarily in states that limit or prohibit branch banking. In essence, the same reasons that contributed to the growth of branch banking also contributed to the growth of group banking. Although group banking has become a significant force on the American banking scene, it has not developed without opposition. The critics have pointed out that group banking tends to lessen competition, is not sufficiently concerned with the needs of local communities, and is a subterfuge employed to evade state banking laws. Federal regulation was introduced in 1933, but it proved relatively ineffective. Consequently, additional legislation was enacted in 1956.

The Bank Holding Company Act of 1956 defines a holding company as one that controls two or more banks by the ownership of 25 percent of the voting shares, or controls in any manner the election of a majority of the directors of two or more banks. The law prohibits new acquisitions outside the state of the holding company's principal place of business, unless the company is authorized to make the acquisition by the state in which it is desired. Since no states have such legislation, the act precludes the expansion of interstate group banking and insulates those groups already established from competition from other similar groups. An important provision of the 1956 act, with certain exceptions, prohibits bank holding companies from owning voting shares in nonbanking corporations and from acquiring such interests in the future. Furthermore, they were given the choice of relinquishing all their banking interests with the exception of a single bank, or relinquishing their nonbanking interests.

The Board of Governors of the Federal Reserve System is charged with the responsibility of administering the Bank Holding Company Act and in so doing supervises the formation and expansion of bank holding companies. Organizers of a holding company are required to have board approval before a holding company is formed, before a company can acquire over five percent of the voting stock of any bank, and before bank holding companies can merge. The act sets forth the five factors that the board is required to consider before granting approval of these actions. They are:

1 The financial history and condition of the company or companies and the banks concerned
2 Their prospects
3 The character of their management
4 The convenience, needs, and welfare of the communities and areas concerned
5 Whether the effect of the acquisition, merger, or consolidation would be to expand the bank holding company system involved beyond limits consistent with adequate and sound banking, the public interest, and preservation of competition in the field of banking[24]

In 1966 an amendment to the act clarified the last factor with the following language:

1 Any acquisition . . . which would result in a monopoly, or which would be in furtherance of any combination or conspiracy to monopolize or attempt to monopolize the business of banking in any part of the United States.
2 Any other proposed acquisition . . . whose effect in any section of the country may be substantially to lessen competition, or tend to create a monopoly, or which in any manner would be in restraint of trade, unless it finds that the anti-competitive effects of the proposed transaction are clearly outweighed in the public interest by the probable effect of the transaction in meeting the convenience and needs of the community to be served.[25]

The Bank Merger Act of 1966 discussed earlier in this chapter included the same provision.

In 1970 several legislative developments contributed to the growth of multibank holding companies. The Bank Holding Company Act of 1956 was amended in a manner that erased for all practical purposes the regulatory distinction between corporations holding one bank and those holding two or more banks. Furthermore, some states liberalized their legislation as it applied to multibank holding companies.

Since bank holding companies range greatly in size, it is difficult to discuss a typical group system. Many bank holding companies control banks

---

[24]Public Law 89-356, Sec. 1, 80 Stat. 7; 12 U.S. Code 1828.

[25]Bank Holding Company Act of 1956 as amended by Act of July 1, 1966 Sec. 8(b), 80 Stat. 239; an Act of Dec. 31, 1970 Sec. 103, 84 Stat.

with aggregate total assets of less than $100 million, and many have resources in excess of $1 billion. Some bank holding companies operate in a local area only, some statewide, and some across state lines. Citicorp of New York (principal asset Citibank) is the largest multibank holding company in the nation and held banks with deposits of some $61 billion at the end of 1978. The largest multibank holding company as far as area covered is Western Bancorporation of Los Angeles. At the end of 1978, Western Bancorporation controlled 22 banks located in 11 states with 797 domestic offices that held $21 billion in deposits. At year-end 1977, 306 multibank holding companies throughout the nation controlled 2,301 banks with a total of $300 billion in deposits. (See Table 3–1)

The success of group banking stems in large part from the services provided by bank holding company offices to their subsidiary banks. Such services include auditing, investment counseling, the purchasing of supplies, data processing equipment, insurance, research on operating methods and procedures, advertising, tax guidance, personnel recruitment and transfer between banks, and advisory services for building and remodeling. These services, and possibly many others, permit a certain degree of personnel specialization and free local bank personnel to carry on other banking services.

Several studies have been made on the effects of holding company acquisitions on the performance of acquired banks. A recent study involving the examination of 82 banks that were acquired by holding companies between 1966 and 1969 revealed that the impact was not very great. This study showed:

> . . . that the major effect of holding company acquisitions is to alter the portfolio composition of acquired banks. These banks tend to switch out of U.S. Government securities and into State and local government securities and loans, particularly instalment loans. These portfolio changes suggest that holding company acquisitions result in acquired banks making more credit available in their localities. Holding company acquisitions, however, do not result in significant changes in the capital, prices, expenses, or profitability of acquired banks. Therefore, the fact that a bank is acquired by a holding company does not appear to have a broad impact on that bank's performance.[26]

Group banking does not have the advantages of mobility of funds, larger lending limits to one borrower, and availability of funds in excess of local deposits to the same extent that branch banking does. Neither does group

---

[26]Samuel H. Talley, *The Effect of Holding Company Acquisitions on Bank Performances,* Staff Economic Studies, Washington, D.C.: Board of Governors of the Federal Reserve System, 1971.

Table 3–1
Banking Offices, Assets, and Deposits in Holding Company Groups,
December, 1977

Holding Company Groups	*Offices*			*Amounts (in billions)*	
	Banks	*Branches*	*Total*	*Assets*	*Deposits*
Total	1,913	3,903	20,340	24,243	$795.1	$624.3
Multibank	306	2,301	10,562	12,863	409.1	324.6
One-bank	1,607	1,602	9,778	11,380	385.8	299.7
All insured commercial banks		14,412	33,088	47,506	1,137.4	929.2

Source: Board of Governors of the Federal Reserve System, *Annual Statistical Digest, 1973–77* and Federal Deposit Insurance Corporation, *Annual Report, 1977.*

banking offer the same economy of operations nor the same specialized management to the extent offered by branch banking. The history of bank holding companies indicates that their opening of new banks is not as common as is their acquiring control of already established and successful banks. In group banking less flexibility exists in management, so vital in financial institutions, than in branch banking. This is evidenced by the fact that holding company banking is not nearly so prevalent in those states where branch banking is permitted.

One-Bank Holding Companies

An important development in banking has been the formation of one-bank holding companies, which offer certain economic advantages as do branch banking and the multibank holding company-type of organization. Faced with rising costs, bank management relied on several avenues to maintain profit margins in the 1960s. One of these was an increase in earning assets evidenced by a substantial rise in the loan-deposit ratio. This method cannot be used indefinitely since there is a point beyond which the loan–deposit ratio cannot be increased.

Another method of increasing bank earnings is to place bank funds into high earning assets commensurate with prudent banking practices. This was done by bank management and took many forms, one of which was investing increasing amounts in municipal securities providing tax-free income. An excellent way of increasing profits is increasing loan rates. This was also done, especially in the late 1960s, as interest rates soared due to the great demand for credit, and to monetary and fiscal policies. Of course, this method cannot be relied upon forever as a means of solving the pressure on profits. Although keeping expenses down is a worthwhile objective of any

business enterprise, banks found this difficult to accomplish with rising inflation, especially in the late 1960s. The two largest expense items of commercial banks are salaries and wages and interest paid on time deposits, both of which have increased rapidly in recent years. The final avenue available to any business firm that desires to increase its profits is to increase its output, that is, produce more goods and/or services and hope that increased sales will result in additional income. Banks that formed one-bank holding companies were following this approach to the problem of profit maximization. In a sense they attempted to form a supermarket of financial services.

Banks were encouraged to broaden their financial services by a changing attitude and administrative rulings on the part of the Comptroller's Office, the regulatory agency that supervises national banks. In the early 1960s a new Comptroller of the Currency adopted policies permitting banks to perform financial services that were "closely related to banking" if in so doing they did not impair their solvency and liquidity. This attitude was well received by most bankers as evidenced by the large number of banks that exchanged their state charters for national charters. The Federal Reserve System and several state regulatory agencies soon began to relax some of their restrictions. Although banks welcomed this change in attitude, the less restrictive environment was not as free as some had hoped, since many newly adopted services were challenged by politicians and various competitors on the grounds that banks were exceeding their authority. In many instances the courts agreed. This was especially true in the areas of travel and messenger services, service bureaus, and mutual funds. It was fairly obvious, therefore, that if banks were to broaden their services, a different organizational arrangement would be needed; hence the formation of the one-bank holding company.

The one-bank holding company involves the formation of a corporation with broad business powers. Stock in a bank is exchanged for stock in a newly formed corporation, and the bank thus becomes a wholly owned subsidiary. A bank might also be acquired by a tender offer. The holding company can then purchase stock in approved corporations that engage in activities from which banks are either barred or seriously restricted, or organize new corporations to perform certain desired services. Firms that are owned and operated by a holding company may engage in such activities as factoring, data processing, and leasing companies. Although some of these activities could be performed by a bank, because of a multiplicity of regulations these services are provided with greater flexibility by subsidiaries of a holding company. An example of regulations that restrict a bank in providing a particular service, in contrast to the holding company, is mortgage financing. If funds are needed for this service in addition to those

derived from the deposit function, a bank could raise funds in the open market by the issuance of debt claims. These claims would have to be subordinated to the claims of depositors, however, which in all likelihood would result in higher interest costs to the bank and in turn to the borrower. However, a mortgage firm owned by a holding company could issue debt claims that would not be subordinated, leading to lower rates for borrowers, assuming competitive conditions.

As far as services performed are concerned, one-bank holding companies in most instances are congeneric rather than conglomerate; that is, the subsidiaries of the holding companies provide services that are similar rather than unrelated. Bank personnel are knowledgeable in the area of finance, and although lending, leasing, or factoring are not the same, they are certainly similar. Customer demand has also contributed to banks broadening their services. If banks do not maintain their competitive position, customers will turn to other institutions for financial services. This is one reason banks entered the credit card field. Other financial congeneric businesses such as national sales finance companies have demonstrated a wide array of financial services that have proved to be appealing to customers.

In 1970 amendments to the Holding Company Act of 1956 reaffirmed the principle of separation of banking and commerce that was embodied in the 1956 legislation. The definition of a bank holding company was extended to bring in all companies (corporations, partnerships, business trusts, and associations) that directly or indirectly own 25 percent of the stock or exercise a controlling influence over the management or policies of one or more banks as interpreted by the Board of Governors of the Federal Reserve System.[27] The Federal Reserve System is authorized to review all nonbanking subsidiaries of the bank holding companies regardless of the date they were acquired and to determine whether any of them are logically and closely related to banking.

One-bank holding companies are permitted to own or retain shares of companies whose activities the Board of Governors of the Federal Reserve System determines

> to be so closely related to banking or managing or controlling banks as to be a proper incident thereto. In determining whether a particular activity is a proper incident to banking or managing or controlling banks, the Board shall consider whether its performance by an affiliate of a holding company can reasonably be expected to produce benefits to the public, such as greater convenience, increased competition, or gains in efficiency, that outweigh pos-

[27]Bank Holding Company Act of 1956 as amended by Act of July 1, 1966 Sec. 7(c), 80 Stat. 238.

sible adverse effects, such as undue concentration of resources, decreased or unfair competition, conflicts of interest, or unsound banking practices.

In accordance with this directive the board has approved several activities. Some of the most important (with some limitations) are:

1 Making loans for its own account or for the account of others including, for example, operating mortgage, finance, credit card, or factoring companies

2 Operating a Morris Plan Bank or an industrial loan company

3 Servicing loans and mortgages

4 Acting as fiduciary

5 Investment and financial advisory services

6 Leasing personal and real property where the initial lease provides for payment of rentals that will reimburse the lessor for the full purchase price of the property including cost of financing

7 Acting as insurance agent or broker, principally in connection with extention of credit by the holding company or any of its subsidiaries and also as insurer for the holding company and its subsidiaries

8 Providing bookkeeping or data processing services for (a) the holding company and its subsidiaries, (b) others, provided that the value of services performed by the company for such persons is not a principal portion of the total value of all such services performed

9 Making equity investments in community rehabilitation and development corporations engaged in providing housing and employment opportunities for low and moderate income persons

10 Providing courier services

11 Providing management consulting advice to nonaffiliated banks

12 Trading and arbitraging gold and silver bullion

13 Issuing money orders and general purpose variable denominated payment instruments

14 Issuing traveler's checks

One-bank holding companies may engage in any of these financial activities via the purchase of existing businesses or by de novo. Starting an activity is looked upon with greater favor by regulatory authorities, however, than is the purchase of a going concern. If a one-bank holding company acquires more than five percent of a going concern engaged in permissible nonbanking activities, it must first obtain the approval of the Board of Governors of the Federal Reserve System. The law requires that the Board analyze the competitive effects of the proposal as well as a number of other public interest considerations, such as the efficiencies that would be forthcoming from such ownership and management, convenience to the public, conflict of interest, and undue concentration. A relatively sensitive area in an acquisition is the competitive aspect; if a proposed acquisition would reduce existing competition or thwart future competition, the Board would be reluctant to extend approval.

As more experience is gained from the operation of bank holding companies under the amended Holding Company Act, other activities may be added. There are some activities in addition to those listed above in which bank holding companies may participate. They may own shares in companies whose activities are closely related to the primary function of banking. These are functions that could be carried on by banks including holding properties for the use of a holding company's subsidiary, conducting a safe deposit business, or liquidating assets acquired from the holding company or its banks.

Congress was concerned that unfair competition might arise from the expansion of bank holding companies into related areas and therefore added what has become known as the anti-tie-in provision. This provision prohibits any bank (whether or not it is a holding company subsidiary) from requiring a customer purchasing one of its services to obtain another service from the bank, its holding company, or affiliates. A bank is also prohibited from requiring a customer to refrain from doing business with competitors of the bank or its holding company affiliates unless reasonably imposed to assure soundness in a credit transaction. This provision bars banks from packaging their services or tieing one of their services to the activities of their affiliates. The only exceptions to this rule are transactions exclusively involving the traditional banking services of loans, discounts, deposits, and trusts. One-bank holding companies have entered many areas of financial activity, the most important of which are mortgage banking, consumer financing, factoring, and leasing. Despite the rapid entry into many areas and the successful operation of those endeavors, the assets of nonbanking affiliates account for less than 5 percent of the consolidated assets of bank holding companies.

The spread of one-bank holding companies has been phenomenal. Since mid-1968, when large banks discovered this type of organization was highly desirable, to year-end 1977 more than 1,900 banks organized one-bank holding companies. (Table 3-1) Increased demand for financial services and the restrictions that surrounded commercial banking for many years were responsible for this spread.

Questions

1. How do you account for the trend in the assets and liabilities of the bank or banks in your community?
2. What is meant by the term "convenience and need of the community" that is so often employed in bank merger cases?
3. Do you consider commercial banking to be a "line of commerce"? Explain.
4. Bank regulatory authorities and the courts have been concerned with the degree and level of competition in banking. Has this concern been desirable?
5. There are several methods of bank expansion—branching, merging, holding companies, etc. Which do you consider to be the most desirable and why?
6. Why the rise of multibank and one-bank holding companies? Do you consider these developments to be desirable? Explain.
7. Chain banking has never been regulated. Do you see any reason why it should be?

SELECTED REFERENCES

Association of Registered Bank Holding Companies, *The Bank Holding Company, Its History and Significance in Modern America*, Washington, D.C., The Association, 1973.

BENSTON, G. J. "Economies of Scale of Financial Institutions," *Journal of Money, Credit and Banking*, May 1972.

Board of Governors of the Federal Reserve System, *Operating Policies of Bank Holding Companies*, Staff Studies, 1971.

Board of Governors of the Federal Reserve System, *Recent Changes in Banking Structure in the United States*, Washington, D.C., U.S. Government Printing Office, 1970.

CARTER H. GOLEMBE AND ASSOCIATES, *The Future of Registered Bank Holding Companies: Operation, Regulation, and Potential in a Changing Financial Environment*, Washington, D.C., Association of Registered Bank Holding Companies, 1971.

Federal Reserve Bank of Chicago, *Proceedings of the Conference on Banking Structure and Competition*, 1972, 1975, 1976, and 1977.

SCHWEITZER, STUART A., "Economies of Scale and Holding Company Affiliation in Banking," *Southern Economic Journal*, XXVIX, October 1972.

4

Management
and Internal Organization
of Commercial Banks

Commercial banking, with its great reliance on public confidence and influence on the nation's economic life, needs high quality management and organizational structure. With them, banks can attain maximum operating efficiency and profitability. Commercial banks are quasi-public financial institutions and must abide by many regulations, so their organizational structure differs in some respects from that of other business firms.

The Board of Directors

Stockholders, depositors, and regulatory authorities look to directors for policy decisions and management ability that will result in the safety of funds and profitable operations. A board of directors is not directly concerned with the day-to-day operations of its banks since it delegates authority to various officers, but the directors are ultimately responsible for the success of the bank's operation.

Requirements of Bank Directors

Federal law requires that a national bank board consist of from five to twenty-five directors. State banks that are Federal Reserve System members must conform to this provision. National bank directors are elected by the stockholders for one-year terms. State laws generally have similar provisions. A majority of national bank directors must be citizens of the United States and each must directly own shares of the capital stock in the bank he directs, the aggregate par value of which shall not be less than $1,000.[1]

The federal government has followed a policy of prohibiting interlocking directorates. This policy has been seen as necessary to prevent the creation of a *money trust,* the concentration of capital and credit in the hands of relatively few men. Apparently, this fear does not extend to interlocking directorates between banks and large businesses, since there are no national laws prohibiting such relationships. Indeed, many boards, especially in large banks, are made up of presidents and chairmen of relatively large private corporations with which the banks have business connections. In recent years, however, regulatory authorities have not looked with favor on a bank board member serving on the board of directors of a competing financial institution such as a savings and loan association. The reason for this concern stems from the possibility of a conflict of interest.

Responsibilities of Bank Directors

Bank directors have considerable authority in the performance of their duties. Although the objectives of a bank may be formulated by the officers of a bank and members of the board of directors, in the final analysis the approval of the objectives is the responsibility of the board. The board has the authority to appoint and discharge officers and employees, and may require bonds of various officers or employees. It may name, appoint, and define the duties of as many committees from its membership as it desires. The board may determine the type of reports it wants from the officers of the bank.

The directors also have the power to amend the by-laws, in any legal way, as long as such amendments do not materially affect the stockholders' interest. If a change affecting their interest is thought desirable, their approval must be secured at a stockholders' meeting. The board has the authority to declare a dividend or transfer funds from the undivided profits account to surplus. In the final analysis, the board has the authority to determine the amount that will be invested in loans, bonds, and other assets.

Functions of the Board of Directors

In meeting their responsibilities to the depositors, stockholders, and supervisory agencies, the members of the board of directors perform many functions, which vary considerably among banks. Some boards of directors are

---

[1]If the capital stock of the bank is $25,000 or less, however, the amount of stock required is only $500.

more active than others, depending upon the occupations of the members, the time they have to devote to the affairs of the bank, their interest in the bank's progress, and their investment in the bank. In general, however, the directors of banks would be concerned with some or all seven of the following activities.

Determination of Bank Objectives and Formulation of Bank Policies.   Probably the most important functions of the board of directors of a commercial bank are the establishment of its objectives and the determination of its policies. Establishing objectives is the first task, since these are basic to the determination of the bank's policies and affect the organizational structure and influence the employment of personnel. This contributes to the molding of the bank's personality.

The development of policies is necessary in planning a course of action. Policies may appear in the minutes of the board or standing committees or in the manual of organization. Smaller banks have little written policy, but larger banks find this is almost a necessity. Policies may be established by the board of directors, by committees, or by the officers and employees in any department of the bank. Unit banks can formulate policy more easily than can branch banks because of the proximity of personnel and their smaller trade territory. Since branch banking organizations may cover larger geographical areas, their board of directors should not disregard the policy contribution made by a branch manager. A branch bank organization may have a different policy on a particular matter for each area of its operation. Areas differ in economic growth, activities, needs, and people's attitudes.

Policies should be flexible, and the board should review them periodically with the idea of making improvements. Economic conditions, among other factors, may make change necessary. Although many matters in bank management require the establishment of policy, it should not become a straitjacket for management. A few policies that need periodic reviewing are those on charge-offs, loans, investments, and insurance. These, and others, will be discussed at length later.

Selection of Bank Management.   Employment of good management is an important function of the board of directors. Usually it is difficult to find skilled bankers on the board of directors, except for those members who are also officers of the bank. Nonofficer members may have good business judgment and be capable of determining the policies of the bank, but they are not trained bankers with knowledge of the actual operations of a bank. They often are busy people, operating their own businesses, who can spare only a few hours each week to the supervision of the bank's activities. Bank operations are complex and require trained personnel with a knowledge of investments, credits, operations, people, and machines; therefore, the selection of capable personnel demands careful consideration. The board selects personnel with the policies it has set in mind, since the officers of the bank will be responsible for carrying out those policies.

Creation of Committees. In addition to selecting the officers, the board of directors creates certain standing committees and elects the members. The use of committees in banking has developed for several reasons. It has been found that nonofficer directors, who are local businessmen, have a knowledge of the community and various business endeavors. The committee form of organization has been encouraged, and in some instances required, by the supervisory authorities. Since banking primarily involves the employment of depositors' funds in earning assets, a belief has developed that group decision will result in fewer bad loans and investments.

The use of committees has also developed because of their value in coordinating the various departments of the bank and serving as a medium of communication. Therefore, it is customary to set up various standing committees which may meet weekly, or more often, to handle certain matters. Special committees may be created to handle something of an exceptional nature, for example, remodeling the banking quarters or building a new building.

In general there are four principal standing committees of the board of directors. These committees and their duties are:

1 Executive Committee. The executive committee is primarily an administrative committee handling matters that would ordinarily be taken up by the board but require attention between the regular meetings. This committee may make various studies which will be reported to the board as a whole at a future meeting.

2 Discount Committee. The discount committee is one of the busiest and most important committees of the board of directors. This committee may pass on all loans or loans above a certain amount, lines of credit, interest rates on loans, and the amount to be placed in the various classes of loans, such as real estate, personal, and commercial.

3 Trust Committee. The trust committee is concerned with the investment of funds and other matters incident to the various trust accounts.

4 Examination Committee. The examination committee examines the bank at unstated intervals. In a sense its work is comparable to a supervisory agency examination. The examination of the bank can be done by either the members of the examining committee or an outside agency employed by the committee.

The activities of committees vary considerably among banks. In some banks, especially small ones, committees are quite active in actual management, whereas in larger banks they are concerned primarily with matters of policy. In some small banks, for example, the loan or discount committee approves most of the loans made by the bank. In larger banks this function is usually reserved for a committee made up of the loan officers of the bank, who are skilled in lending and who have greater knowledge of the request than do members of the board of directors.

Supervision of Loans and Investments. Supervision of loans and investments by the board does not mean it actually directs these two important functions. It does mean that the board is responsible for seeing that lending and investing are carried out in accordance with sound principles, banking laws, and the regulations imposed by regulatory and supervisory authorities. Supervision of loans and investments involves a periodic review of portfolios to determine whether the bank has been following its established loan and investment policies. It also involves changing established policies to better meet the bank's objective in view of changes that may have occurred in loan demand, interest rates, and liquidity needs.

Counseling. A very important function of a board of directors is to counsel—to give advice to the officers of the bank which will aid them in making decisions. Their business and professional experiences give them a knowledge of the community and its people somewhat different from that of the officers of the bank, which is certainly of value in counseling with the officers. Since the directors are in contact with many people, they may be able to evaluate the actions of the bank better than people within the bank. They may also be able to predict the degree of public acceptance of some proposed change in bank policy. Bank management relies heavily on the counsel of business and professional members of the board. If a retailer is on the board, his advice in his field would be invaluable to the officers of the bank. Naturally, the same could be said about contractors, doctors, lawyers, manufacturers, and any other business or professional people who might be members.

Business Development. Well-respected leaders in the community can certainly influence many depositors and borrowers to patronize the bank of which they are directors. A bank that has an outstanding retailer, manufacturer, doctor, lawyer, et cetera, on the board, who is active in his or her respective field, locally and nationally, and is a member of various civic committees is certainly in a better position to attract new business than one with directors of lesser stature.

Review of Bank Operations. Even though bank directors are usually busy people primarily concerned with their own businesses and professions, they must maintain general supervision of the affairs of the bank. To a great extent, this is accomplished by periodic review of bank operations, usually at a monthly meeting at which various reports prepared by the executive officers are reviewed. Oral reports or visual presentations may be employed, followed by questions and a discussion of the bank's progress. In larger banks, the review must be quick because of the volume of business. Therefore, it is necessary that the reports be concise, yet adequate to give the board a picture of the month's operation.

Liabilities of Directors

Bank directors cannot take their positions lightly. Both statutory law and common law impose penalties on directors for mismanagement of the bank's affairs. It is impractical to mention all the laws and situations that give rise to such responsibilities, but a few, applicable to national banks, will be presented to illustrate the importance of the directors' liabilities.

Criminal Liabilities.   Violation of criminal laws carries a fine of $5,000, or imprisonment of not more than five years, or both. Some of the violations that apply to directors, as well as to officers, agents, and employees of the bank are:

1   False entries, false reports, and the like

2   False certification of checks

3   Theft, embezzlement, or misapplication of funds

4   False representation as to Federal Deposit Insurance coverage

5   Loans to bank examiners

6   Loans of trust funds to directors

7   Receiving fees for procuring loans

8   Making political contributions[2]

In addition to being exposed to criminal liabilities, bank directors may become liable for losses sustained by the bank as a result of some breach of statutory requirements in which they have participated, assented to, or caused because they have not exercised the due care required under common law. Issues of this kind involve both liability for statutory violations and common-law liability for negligence.

The statutory liability of directors is based upon the provisions of the National Bank and Federal Reserve Acts. Paragraph 34 of the National Bank Act states the liability as follows:

[2]U.S., Treasury Department, Office of the Comptroller of the Currency, *Duties and Liabilities of Directors of National Banks* (Washington, D.C.: Government Printing Office, October 1969).

If the directors of any national banking association shall knowingly violate, or knowingly permit any of the officers, agents, or servants of the association to violate any of the provisions of this title (Title LXII of the U.S.R.S., consisting of the National Bank Act and related laws), all the rights, privileges, and franchises of the association shall be thereby forfeited. Such violation shall, however, be determined and adjudged by a proper circuit, district, or Territorial Court of the United States, in a suit brought for that purpose by the Comptroller of the Currency, in his own name, before the association shall be declared dissolved. And in cases of such violation, every director who participated in or assented to the same shall be held liable in his personal and individual capacity for all damages which the association, its shareholders, or any other person, shall have sustained in consequence of such violation.[3]

The courts have held that directors are personally liable for the violation of national banking statutes. Directors may become civilly liable if they knowingly authorize or acquiesce in the making of false reports to any person who is injured by relying on such published reports. In *Chesbrough* v. *Williams,* for example, the directors were held liable for falsifying the capital account of the bank, which induced the plaintiff to purchase stock in the bank.[4] In *Yates* v. *Jones National Bank* the Court said that "An action for deceit may be maintained against the directors of a bank by depositors induced to become such by false representations in statements of the bank's condition made by such director."[5] Directors may incur personal liability for damages sustained by the bank as a result of paying dividends contrary to law.[6]

Directors are also personally liable for losses resulting from their failure to investigate a matter that is within their power to investigate, "if bank directors deliberately refrain from investigating a matter which it is their duty to investigate, or having knowledge of facts which put them on notice of irregular or criminal acts, they deliberately refrain from utilizing available accounting methods and from employing independent auditors to determine the full extent of the loss to the bank, any resulting violation of the statute may be regarded as 'in effect intentional' or as having been committed 'knowingly.' "[7]

Thus bank directors have a duty at common law to exercise ordinary care and prudence in administering the affairs of their bank. They "cannot, in justice to those who deal with the bank, shut their eyes to what is going on

[3]12 U.S.C., sec. 93.
[4]*Chesbrough* v. *Williams,* 244 U.S. 72 (1916).
[5]*Yates* v. *Jones National Bank,* 206 U.S. 158 (1906).
[6]*United States* v. *Britton,* 108 U.S. 199 (1883); *Dudley* v. *Hawkins,* 239 Fed. 386 (1917).
[7]*F.D.I.C., Receiver of the Commercial National Bank of Bradford, Pa.* v. *Mason,* (C.C.A. 3d 1940) 115F (2d) 548.

around them. It is their duty to use ordinary diligence in ascertaining the condition of its business, and to exercise reasonable control and supervision of its officers."[8] Directors are also personally liable for losses resulting from *ultra vires*—acts that are beyond the power conferred upon the bank.[9] The court has been very strict in interpreting the section of federal law that prohibits national banks from making loans in excess of ten percent of the bank's capital and surplus, with certain exceptions. "Where the directors assent to the making of loans in excess of the maximum permissible amount, they may be held liable for any losses sustained, regardless of their motives, or the financial standing of the borrowers at the time the loans were made, or the value of any security taken; and any such liability will not be limited to the portion of the loans in excess of the prescribed limit but may include the whole amount plus interest and less recovery on the loans."[10] Furthermore, liability cannot be avoided by resorting to a loan to two or more persons who are closely affiliated in a business. This same general restriction also applies to investments of commercial banks.

Common-Law Liability for Negligence. Directors are subject to common-law liability for negligence. As pointed out in *Gamble* v. *Brown,* the "National Bank Act does not relieve directors from common-law duty to be honest and diligent, and the degree of care required in such respect is that which ordinarily prudent men would exercise under similar circumstances."[11]

Analysis of Directors' Liabilities. The criminal and common-law liabilities of bank directors are severe, but they are not as harsh as they may appear at first sight. They may be eliminated or lessened in several ways. The directors can protect themselves against these liabilities by becoming thoroughly acquainted with banking law, the regulations of supervisory authorities, and the bank's operations; by the employment of honest officers and employees, as far as this is possible; by insurance; and by internal controls. Because of the quasi-public nature of banking, dishonesty cannot be tolerated. Not only does it result in losses to depositors and stockholders, but it also erodes public confidence in the banking system. Therefore, officers and employees, as well as directors, must have a high concept and a fair code of business ethics and must respect the various banking laws and regulations imposed by the supervisory and regulatory authorities.

Directors may insure themselves and the bank against many of the statutory and common-law liabilities, and against various risks that may arise from the nature of the bank's operations. The Insurance and Protective

---

[8]*Martin* v. *Webb,* 110 U.S. 7 (1883).

[9]*Cockrill* v. *Abeles,* 86 Fed. 505 (1898).

[10]*Corsicana National Bank* v. *Johnson,* 251 U.S. 68 (1919).

[11]*Gamble* v. *Brown,* 29F. (2d) 366, (1928).

Committee of the American Bankers Association has done much to improve and standardize insurance coverage for banks. This committee has from time to time published suggested amounts of minimum and maximum coverage for banks of various deposit size. Many risks are now included in one bond, commonly referred to as a blanket bond for banks. These policies cover losses from such criminal acts as embezzlement, burglary, robbery, theft, larceny, and forgery, and provide for indemnity for loss of money and securities. Insurance that covers many of the risks associated with safe-deposit operations can be purchased. There are policies to cover losses arising from errors and omissions in mortgages or other legal documents and from fraudulent, counterfeit, fictitious, raised, invalid, or nonexistent accounts receivable. Banks may also purchase insurance that will protect them against court costs and attorney's fees.

Directors may reduce their liability, as well as that of the bank, by the adoption of a system of audit or internal controls. This method is so important that most chartering agencies require that banks have an examination committee, and, in addition, require the board of directors to examine the bank a minimum number of times each year. This examination may be done by the directors themselves, or they may hire an outside accounting firm to perform the audit. The ideal situation is for the bank to have a full-time auditor reporting directly to the board, as many large and medium-size banks do. The auditor's function is primarily to improve accounting methods and systems in such a manner that they will reflect the complete record of the transactions of the bank accurately and economically, and leave little, if any, room for dishonesty to be hidden.

The liabilities of bank directors are large, to be sure, but they are not of such magnitude as to prohibit the participation of capable, interested, and honest individuals in bank management, as the history of banking in this country has proved. Many ways of reducing and eliminating these liabilities exist, but none has been designed that will substitute for the basic ingredient of business and personal relations—honesty.

Administrative Officers

In a bank, especially a large one, several officers are responsible for the management function. The most important are the chairman of the board, president, executive vice president, vice presidents, assistant vice presidents, cashier, and comptroller. In some banks the title of senior vice president, denoting a rank above that of vice president, is quite often used. In addition to these management officers, an auditor is found in larger banks.

The position of chairman of the board carries with it a great deal of dignity and respect in banking circles. The chairman is usually the chief executive officer of the bank, keeps the board of directors informed on the progress of the bank, and implements the policies established. This officer is also concerned with planning, public relations, and broad banking policies. The president is the administrative head of the bank and is responsible for administering the business affairs of the bank. It is through the president, primarily, that the personality of the bank emanates. A president may not be concerned with the bank's actual operations but would concentrate instead on building good will for the bank through personal, business, and social contacts. However, many bank presidents take part in all activities of the bank, such as interviewing customers, granting loans, and making credit investigations. Most presidents probably fall somewhere between these two extremes, as far as the nature of their activity is concerned. Officers with the title of executive vice president, senior vice president, or vice president are usually placed in charge of a major department, or in charge of a branch if the bank is engaged in branch banking.

The office of the cashier is nearly as old as banking itself. Each national bank and some state banks are required by law to have a cashier. For a long time, the cashier was a person with many years of experience who had worked up the ladder from a messenger, bookkeeper, teller, or perhaps all three. His customary and traditional duties, especially in small banks, include all those incident to the internal operations of the bank and may involve personnel, records, acting as secretary to the board, insurance, and safekeeping of cash and securities. His traditional control over the money of the bank is reflected in the term *cashier's check*. The cashier is usually responsible for all reports to the regulatory agencies, such as the call report which sets forth the assets and liabilities of the bank as of a certain date and the earnings and dividend reports.

The comptroller of a bank is its chief accounting and statistical officer. Few small banks have a comptroller, but one is often found in the larger banks. Only in recent years have the duties of the comptroller become as important as those of the other major functional officers. It is the comptroller's responsibility to gather and interpret data of value to the bank management so that wise decisions may be made regarding policy and operations. In addition to such cost-accounting work, the comptroller checks on the actual operations of the bank. For example, s/he determines whether the note teller can skip one step of the operation and save the bank a few dollars and still maintain efficiency and accuracy of operation. The comptroller is concerned with new improvements, new machines, and new methods.

Most large banks and many small ones operate on a budget, and it is the comptroller's responsibility to draw up a tentative budget and supply the budget committee with information so that a realistic final budget can be adopted. This official is also responsible for supplying a large portion of the information included in the officers' monthly report to the board of directors.

The auditor is responsible for verifying the accounts resulting from the bank's daily operations and operating methods. The auditor's major duty is to examine the bank continually to ascertain whether the business is being conducted in accordance with acceptable accounting procedures, policies established by the board of directors, and rules imposed by regulatory authorities. The objective of this work is to safeguard the assets of the bank against manipulation, misappropriation, and waste. Through examinations of the bank's procedures the auditor is able to detect discrepancies. The auditor should be, and in many banks is, a direct representative of the board. The auditor reports, usually monthly, to the board, along with an account of any discrepancies found or any suggestions for improvement that are deemed advisable. All large banks have an auditor as, in recent years, do some smaller banks.

In branch banking the chief administrative officer of a branch is usually the manager, or sometimes a vice president. This position is similar to that of bank president, and the responsibilities vary with the size of the branch and the amount of business conducted, which may be more significant than those of many small bank presidents in the country. A branch manager's immediate supervisor is the branch administrator from whom flows authority, instructions, regulations, and policies that emanate from the head office. If branches are of sufficient size, they may have one or more assistant managers, who are comparable to vice presidents in smaller unit banks.

Examples of Bank Organization

Banks in general are highly departmentalized. Departmentalization in banking, as in other business organizations, results from the inability of one person to perform all the tasks connected with one group of activities. It is an outgrowth of a need to assemble the specialized knowledge that develops from an increasing volume and from the complexities of bank operations and the varied services rendered to customers. Departmentalization enables improved and expanded services to customers, develops more efficient officers and employees, and reduces the costs of operation.

The degree of departmentalization varies with the size and work of the bank. The absence of one or another department does not mean that a particular function is not performed in a bank. Some banks without a consumer loan department make consumer loans; similarly, all banks purchase securities, but many do not have a bond department, and all banks have public relations even though some may not have a public relations department. Only in banks where the volume of business is sufficient to have several people concerned with a particular function do we usually find departmentalization.

The organization of banks for management purposes also varies because of differences in size, personalities and capabilities of officers and employees, the importance of the different functions performed and services offered, and the workload of the bank. The number of employees also varies from one bank to another, ranging from as few as three or four people to thousands.

Banks utilize both the line and staff functions in their organization. Functions that are directly involved in accomplishing the objectives of the bank are line functions and include activities such as lending, investing, trust services, international banking, and the acceptance and processing of deposits. Staff functions involve assistance and advice to those in the line and include accounting, personnel, education, marketing, control, methods, and building planning and maintenance. In small banks, line and staff functions are mixed, with some officers and employees performing both types. As banks become larger, line and staff functions are more clearly separated.

For efficient management in those banks that engage in branch banking some form of regional organization is necessary, since some branch banks may have a hundred or more branches. In branch banking we usually find the banking market, which may be statewide, divided into geographical areas with a vice-president and regional manager in charge of each area. This officer would have a staff of technicians to help in the supervision of the branches in the region. The size and composition of the regional staff depend on the number of branches, the degree of decentralization approved by top management, the type of banking in the area, and the capabilities of the branch managers. A regional organization includes one or more loan supervisors. If there are several loan supervisors, they probably specialize in the areas of commercial, real estate, agricultural, and consumer loans. The staff would certainly have an operations and personnel officer, a marketing officer, and probably others. The functions performed and the number of officers and employees in a branch depend on its size and the type of clientele. The banking functions that are always present are lending and operations. If trust services and international banking are demanded, they too are provided. If the demand for these services is insufficient to warrant skilled personnel, the services would still be provided by other branch personnel, with some assistance and close supervision from the head office. Although the handling of deposits is an important function in any bank or branch, it has become less of a chore for branches since the actual preparation and posting of statements have been computerized and performed at regional centers or at the head office. This development has made possible greater accuracy at less cost, plus the release of personnel for more customer-oriented services.

Historically and traditionally banks have been organized around two basic concepts—a strong executive and heavy reliance upon committees as decision-making bodies. A strong executive, or what has been referred to by some as *rule at the top*, is probably an outgrowth of the fact that many banks started out as family enterprises. In the history of banking such names as Medici and the House of Rothschild are well known in Europe. In America the names of Robert Morris, Mellon, and Giannini are well known in banking circles. Many small banks in rural areas are still dominated by single families. Since the family had a great interest in the success of the bank, one of its members served as the chief executive officer and made most of the major decisions. The use of committees had its roots in the 1930s when banking was searching for sound financial decisions in the midst of bank failures. Much was at stake then since the risks were very great. Committees, it was hoped, would come to sounder and more reliable decisions than would a single individual because of the basic philosophy that "two heads are better than one."

Organization charts are often helpful in explaining the structure of a firm. In Figure 4–1 a hypothetical organization chart for a relatively small unit bank is presented. Note that we have six departments—loans, investments, operations, trust, marketing, and auditing. In our example the investment department may not be very large or perform much work, while the trust department may have several officers and employees and enjoy a great deal of activity. The loan department is very important and is usually the largest in the bank. In our example there are four areas of lending—commercial, consumer, real estate, and agricultural. The credit department is included under the officer in charge of loans, as is the note-collector function. Although the investment department is important in a bank, it is normally not as large as some of the others. The reasons, of course, are that the investment department deals in relatively large units and operates in an organized and impersonal market rather than in a negotiated market, as does the loan department.

Several phases of bank operations are listed under the vice-president and cashier. It would appear from the chart that the duties are numerous and that some are unrelated. To be sure, this is true; but the department would contain several officers skilled in these various areas. Many of these functions are "housekeeping" in nature and are not directly customer oriented, but they are important nevertheless. Note that the marketing department is also concerned with a wide range of activities, including advertising, market research, and business development. Business development can be quite broad and interesting. It normally includes an officer's call program, that is, visiting with customers and potential customers to increase the bank's busi-

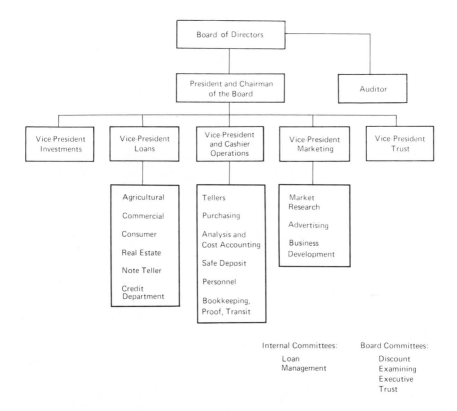

Fig. 4–1 Hypothetical organization of a unit bank

ness. It might also include contacts with national accounts and correspondent banks. Since Chapter 18 is devoted to trust services, the trust function and its organization will not be discussed here.

It may be noted that some bank services are not included in the organization chart. This does not mean necessarily that these functions are not performed. One example is international finance, which would probably be managed by the loan department in cooperation with one of the bank's city correspondents. The same may be true of issuing a bank credit card. In Figure 4–1 note that the auditor reports to the board of directors, which is the normal practice. Each of the functions in this chart is headed by a vice-president. In small banks this would normally be the title used, but we might find the title of senior vice-president or executive vice-president. Strict uniformity does not exist in the use of titles in commercial banking; however, the larger the bank, the wider the range of titles.

In the chart the various committees are classified as board and internal. Board committees are the usual ones created by the board of directors and are dominated by the board as far as membership is concerned. Board committees would contain some bank officers who are also members of the board of directors, since their presence is necessary because of their familiarity with the subjects with which the committee is concerned. This is not necessarily true of the examining committee, which in many instances does not include any administrative officer, in the interests of objectivity. The president is usually a member of all committees, except the examination committee. In general, this is a desirable situation in a bank of this size since the president must carry out all policies and decisions of the board of directors; membership on these committees provides him with first-hand knowledge of the decisions and thinking of the board members on the various issues.

Although internal committees are similar to the board committees, the membership does not normally include outside board members. This is due to the frequency of the meetings and the fact that they deal with day-to-day operational problems that are of no immediate concern to the board of directors. If they were, the matters would be referred to the board of directors. The management committee is made up of the top bank officers and is concerned with the coordination of all activities necessary for attainment of the bank's objectives. The loan committee is concerned with loan applications that are in excess of the lending officers' limits or that deviate in some manner from established bank policy.

The great increase in banking business has resulted in a decrease in the use of committees, since it would be physically impossible for board committees to handle the many problems that arise. In larger banks the discount or loan committee could not approve all loans, because of the time involved and the waiting that would be required of borrowers. Some borrowers might resent a period of waiting and might interpret the delay to mean that the bank considered them questionable risks.

The use of a loan committee also tends to curb the loan officer's talents. He cannot become a versatile and competent loan officer if all the decisions regarding loans must be made by a committee. For people to develop professionally, they must assume responsibility. This is true not only of lending but of all phases of commercial bank operations. Committees that are extremely active in management do not encourage decision making on the part of individual officers, and many functions in banking require skills that might not be possessed by committees.

In addition to the decline of committees in banking, an identifiable trend has developed toward restructuring the role of the chief executive. Since there is more to manage in a large organization, the delegation of authority to lower levels of management has increased. The extent to which this is accomplished successfully depends on the effectiveness of the bank's planning, control, and information systems. Accompanying this delegation of authority has been a more formal designation of the executive's responsibilites among those concerned with management at the top echelon. This can be seen in Figure 4–2, an organization chart for a relatively large branch banking system.

As bank functions have increased, top management has been organized into groups, with several functions placed under one individual. There is a simple explanation of this development. With the increase in banking functions it is impossible, from the standpoint of the span-of-control principle, for the chief executive to administer all of them. Consequently, different functions that are similar in nature are grouped together. The asset management group shown in Figure 4-2 is an example. For many years the loan and investment functions were separate and, to a certain degree, competed for funds. Obviously, these two functions should complement one another since the size of the investment and loan portfolios varies, depending on the stage of the business cycle. For example, in periods of expansion, loans would increase while the investment portfolio would decrease; in periods of low demand the opposite would occur. Because of this, it is logical that one person could more effectively manage the overall function, keeping in harmony with the bank's objectives.

Note that a public service group has been created to handle community and government relations, a function that for years was considered an exclusive province of the chief executive. Profit planning is also a division under staff services, and this, too, was once jealously guarded by the chief executive officer. This does not mean that the officer is unfamiliar with these areas or unconcerned with their performance. This has developed because of the increase in management duties and because the functions are of such importance that a full-time person is necessary for their performance.

A final development in recent years has been the improvement and expansion of staff capability to support a bank's line management. This trend is illustrated in the organization chart in Figure 4-2, with the cluster of functions under the staff services group. Included here are administrative services, personnel, profit planning, the comptroller function, and the data processing. A lending officer cannot have at his fingertips all the data that would be of value to him in performing his function. He increasingly relies on such staff services as the credit department. The computer has made it possible to assemble information of great value to a lending officer. He is not, however, required to write his own program or operate the computer. Skilled technicians provide these services. Strong staff capabilities are not limited to the lending function but are found in all areas of the bank, including investments, trust services, and marketing.

The asset management group is concerned with the two most important

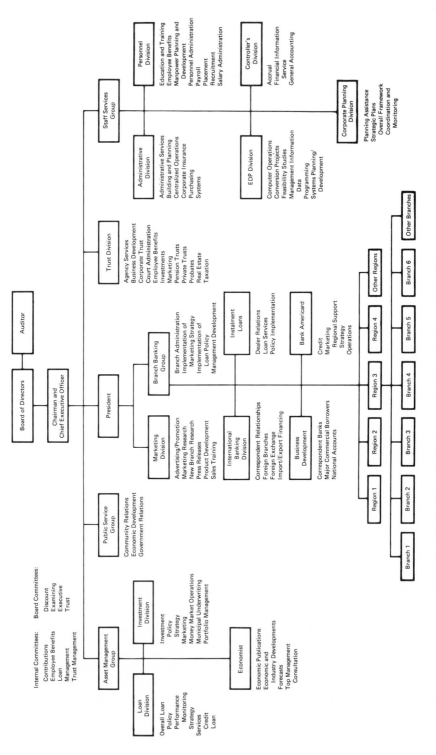

Fig. 4-2 Hypothetical organization of a branch banking system

Internal Committees:
Contributions
Employee Benefits
Loan
Management
Trust Management

Board Committees:
Discount
Examining
Executive
Trust

Board of Directors

Auditor

Chairman and Chief Executive Officer

President

Asset Management Group

Loan Division
Overall Loan Policy
Performance Monitoring
Strategy
Credit Services
Loan

Investment Division
Investment Policy
Strategy
Marketing
Money Market Operations
Municipal Underwriting
Portfolio Management

Economist
Economic Publications
Economic and Industry Developments
Forecasts
Top Management Consultation

Public Service Group
Community Relations
Economic Development
Government Relations

Marketing Division
Advertising/Promotion
Marketing Research
New Branch Research
Press Releases
Product Development
Sales Training

Branch Banking Group
Branch Administration
Implementation of Marketing Strategy
Implementation of Loan Policy
Management Development

International Banking Division
Correspondent Relationships
Foreign Branches
Foreign Exchange
Import/Export Financing

Instalment Loans
Dealer Relations
Loan Services
Policy Implementation

Business Development
Correspondent Banks
Major Commercial Borrowers
National Accounts

Bank Americard
Credit
Marketing
Regional Support
Strategy
Operations

Trust Division
Agency Services
Business Development
Corporate Trust
Court Administration
Employee Benefits
Investments
Marketing
Pension Trusts
Private Trusts
Probates
Real Estate
Taxation

Staff Services Group

Administrative Division
Administrative Services
Building and Planning
Centralized Operations
Corporate Insurance
Purchasing
Systems

Personnel Division
Education and Training
Employee Benefits
Manpower Planning and Development
Personnel Administration
Payroll
Placement
Recruitment
Salary Administration

EDP Division
Computer Operations
Conversion Projects
Feasibility Studies
Management Information
Data Programming
Systems Planning/Development

Controller's Division
Accrual
Financial Information Service
General Accounting

Corporate Planning Division
Planning Assistance
Strategic Plans
Overall Framework
Coordination and Monitoring

Region 1
Region 2
Region 3
Region 4
Other Regions

Branch 1
Branch 2
Branch 3
Branch 4
Branch 5
Branch 6
Other Branches

classes of assets of the bank: investments and loans. The investment of bank funds is an operating function while the loan division is a staff function concerned with overall loan policy and the quality of loans. The bank economist is a part of the asset management group since his expertise is of value in the allocation of bank resources. A large bank is responsible to the community, and these functions are listed under the public service group in Figure 4-2.

The president heads the branch banking group, the most important operating area of the bank, and the marketing division. The latter is included here since marketing is concerned with new services, new branches, advertising, and promotion, all of which contribute to the successful operation of the various branches. The branch banking group provides some staff services necessary for the efficient operation and administration of the branches. Instalment loans and business development would probably be staff functions, but international banking and credit card would probably be operating units as well. Under the branch banking group are the various regions; under each region are the various branches.

Banks with branches differ in organization from unit banks even though the functions performed are basically the same. The major differences in organizational structure are found in the control of the various branches and in the functions performed by the senior officers at the head office. Branch banks are organized along line and staff lines, as are unit banks, although they probably place greater emphasis upon staff functions. The nature of branch banking necessitates the presence of a branch administrator, through whom lines of control usually pass to the several branches of the organization.

The local branch bank organization is similar to that of a unit bank and performs those functions warranted by the amount of banking services required in the community. If the branch is located in a large community, it would probably be departmentalized similarly to the hypothetical unit bank. If it is located in a small community where the amount of business done is relatively small, it would not be departmentalized, but might take a form of organization similar to that of the small unit bank. One special advantage a small branch can offer is the service and advice of skilled personnel available to it from the head office.

Some functions of a small branch are performed at the central location, however. One of these is the investment function, which can be performed more efficiently and economically at the head office. Such concentration permits greater specialization. The correspondent banking function is also performed by personnel at the head office. Most of the personnel function is also centered in the head office where personnel needs are known for all branches, and where greater opportunities for a supervised and planned training program exist. The branch managers interview and hire local personnel at the non-officer level, however. No mention has been made of titles in our hypothetical organization in Figure 4-2, but in a bank of this size the heads of the various groups would probably be executive vice-presidents or at least senior vice-presidents. It is not necessarily true that as we drop down the organization the titles follow accordingly. It is entirely possible that a branch manager would carry the title of vice-president. After all, some branch banks are larger than unit banks.

Branch managers are responsible to their regional administrator. The officers located at the head office perform a staff function, and their advice usually flows through the regular chain of command to the various branches. Branch managers have a certain amount of authority; but if a problem should arise that requires anything in excess of this predetermined authority, the head office is contacted for advice and counsel.

Lending is an example of this limited authority. A branch manager is usually given a certain lending limit. When requests in excess of this limit are received, he is required to contact his supervisor, who may have the authority to approve the request. If not, the request moves to the central office where an investigation is made by skilled people with adequate facilities at hand to determine the credit worthiness of the applicant. A decision is then reached. The argument that branch banking has more capable management than have unit banks is illustrated by this example. The skilled people at the top in every phase of banking stand ready to lend assistance to all branches at a moment's notice.

Branch managers must be skilled in two separate areas. They must possess expertise in the field of banking—lending, operations, marketing bank services, and the like; they must be managers. Branch managers are responsible for assembling the resources—human and material—at hand to attain the goals and objectives of the bank. They must be able to motivate people to accomplish their assigned tasks. In a very real sense, they weld together a team that has common goals and objectives. In addition to these important functions, the public expects a branch manager to be a financial advisor as well as a leader in the community. He is expected to serve on the local hospital board, help raise funds for the Community Chest or United Fund, attend P.T.A. meetings, and participate in chamber of commerce activities. Branch managers wear many different hats.

As already noted, small banks are not usually departmentalized, so it is not uncommon to find officers and employees performing a variety of tasks incident to the bank's operations. All officers, including the president, may be concerned with making loans of all types—business, agricultural, and consumer. However, certain officers may specialize by performing designated duties such as handling bank investments, trust services when performed, personnel, public relations, business development, and the preparation of reports required by the regulatory and supervisory agencies.

Moreover, one officer, usually the cashier, may be delegated the task of supervising such internal operations of the bank as the bookkeeping, purchasing, and deposit functions. Employees in small banks perform a variety of jobs—acting as bookkeeper, paying and receiving tellers, and note teller. It is doubtful, under these conditions, that a person can become a specialist in a particular field, and that the bank's services can be as efficient as those of a more specialized bank. It is also doubtful that internal control and security attain the standards found in larger departmentalized banks. In some very small banks the president is not an active officer, and the bank is headed, in fact, by the cashier or a vice-president.

Even though a small bank may not be departmentalized, certain services are still provided. For example, if some foreign operations service were demanded by a customer, this small bank could probably perform the service by working with one of its city correspondents. A number of other demands for services could be performed in the same manner. This is one of the advantages of the present correspondent banking relationship that exists in the banking system. A small bank may not have a credit department, but this does not mean that credit analysis or the retention of credit information is not performed. Each lending officer is probably required to maintain records on the loans s/he supervises. Too often in small banks, this information is carried in the head rather than in a written and orderly form, however. Small banks may not have an auditing department or an auditor, but the function may be performed by the officers at irregular and slack periods during the year and an examination performed annually by a private accounting firm under the supervision of the board of directors.

Planning

Planning is the activity through which a business firm charts its future course of action. The end result of planning is to develop a strategy for utilizing the resources of a business within its projected environment so as to attain its overall objectives. Many banks realize the importance of this function and have planning departments staffed with technical personnel. Others do it intermittently.

Planning is important because of the competitive environment within which banks operate and their desire to improve efficiency that will, it is hoped, result in increased growth which in turn will result in an increase in the return on equity. Planning is an exercise; in fact, the process may be as useful as the plan itself in that it requires management to look ahead, recognize problems, and search for solutions to them.

A schematic diagram of commercial bank planning is shown in Figure 4–3. Although the five elements are usually studied, researched, discussed,

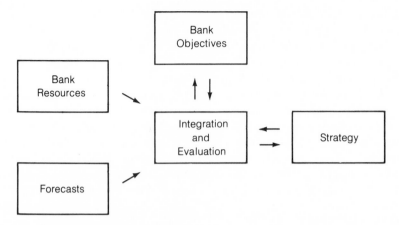

Fig. 4–3   Planning arrangement in a commercial bank

and formulated simultaneously, the key step in the process is to arrive at the bank objectives. This involves a substantial amount of subjective evaluation and covers many areas. Objectives may change over time, but once formulated, they are looked upon as a firm and binding contract. Bank objectives are usually stated in short, concise terms and limited to ten to twelve items. A few items from a list of one bank's objectives follow.[12]

1   Our business is the sale of financial services in Oregon and in selected regional, national and international markets. We will extend our business into areas which provide sound expansion opportunities meeting predetermined profit criteria.

2   We will strive for stability in earnings growth, acquire investments of high quality, and pursue sound and innovative tactics. Through strategic planning and strong management, we will aggressively expand income sources while remaining in control of costs.

3   Our primary marketing objective is to increase our share of market through superior service and appropriate products consistent with corporate strategic plans.

4   Management will provide continuity of policies and direction. Changes will be implemented quickly and in a manner that considers both individual and corporate needs.

5   Our objective is to promote people within the organization. However, expansion into new fields and the need for specialized talent may require hiring people from other sources.

[12]U. S. Bancorp, *Annual Report,* 1977.

6 We are sensitive to social and economic concerns and recognize our responsibilities as a corporate citizen. We support and participate in activities to improve social and economic conditions.

Once a bank's objectives are formulated, the next step is to arrive at a strategy to accomplish these goals and objectives. While objectives represent a subjective choice as to quality, direction, and pace of the enterprise, strategy is the plan by which a bank can best realize the established objectives. It is a quantification of ideas. While an objective of a bank may be to increase its market share, a strategy would deal with how this could be implemented. It might take the form of providing the public with a new higher yielding certificate or paying a higher rate of interest on certain certificates of deposit. The initiation of a *call program,* that is, bank personnel making personal calls on all the business firms in the community in an effort to secure commercial and industrial loans, is a strategy. The introduction of a bank credit card or "pay by telephone" are examples of strategies designed to increase the customer base of a bank.

In moving from objectives to strategy, factors that must be considered are the bank's resources and what the environment might be in the future. A bank's resources include such items as size of its assets, physical facilities, image, financial resources, and personnel. All of these would influence the kind of strategy that a bank would adopt. It would be pointless for a bank to attempt to make oil loans if it has no personnel experienced in this type of lending. A bank with assets of $25 million or less would encounter some difficulty in attracting national firms that have lines of credit in the amount of $100 to $150 million from five to ten banks and are entitled to the prime rate. Banks operate in an economic environment; consequently, an economic forecast for the next three to five years would certainly be helpful in adopting a plan. Aggressiveness in lending is influenced by the phase of the business cycle within which the bank is operating. The level and direction of interest rates also influence the investment strategy of a commercial bank. Forecasting is not limited to economic matters alone but includes political and cultural developments as well. Local and national legislation influences banking, and population movements influence both the need for bank services and the sources of funds.

As the arrows indicate in Figure 4–3, bank objectives influence integration and evaluation; in turn, integration and evaluation influence objectives and strategy. Although there is no magical period for which a bank should plan, a five-year plan seems to be quite common. Because of many changes, it is doubtful that a plan introduced today would still be valid five years hence, but this does not lessen the value of the planning process. If major changes occur that affect the adopted plan, it should be changed. Planning is a continuous process, not a "once every five years" exercise. In a very real sense, planning is necessary because of our inability to forecast with reliability.

The planning process in banks may be administered by a management committee, a task force, or the creation of a separate department that is concerned with planning continuously. A staff department approach to planning is found in larger banks of the nation. Although formal planning occurs more frequently in large banks than in small ones, some planning, consciously or unconsciously, is done in all banks, just as most individuals have personal budgets even though they may not be in written form.

Questions

1. The management of banks is regulated closely by laws and regulatory authorities. Would management be improved if there was less regulation? Why?

2. Considering the many liabilities of bank directors, would you like to serve on a bank board? Would you rather be a director of a non-financial corporation such as a manufacturing firm? Why?

3. From your knowledge of management, how would you evaluate the organization charts presented for hypothetical unit and branch banks? What suggestions would you make for improvement?

4. Do you think that there is too much reliance on committees in banking? Why?

5. Of all the responsibilities of the board of directors, which would you consider to be the most important and why?

6. Do you agree that the most important function of management is planning? Why?

7. If the management of a bank came up with the idea that it should earn 12 percent on its net worth, would that be an objective or a part of its strategy? Why?

SELECTED REFERENCES

BAUGHN, WILLIAM H., and CHARLES E. WALKER, eds. *The Bankers Handbook*, Rev. Ed., Homewood, IL, Dow Jones-Irwin Inc., 1978.

The Comptroller of the Currency, *Duties and Liabilities of Directors of National Banks,* Washington, D.C. June 1972.

DAVIS, SAVILLE R., "Planning in the 1970s," *The Creative Interface,* Washington, D. C., American University Press, 1970.

FISHER, DAVID I., *Commercial Banking in 1975 and 1980,* Philadelphia, Robert Morris Associates, 1970.

JOHNSON, RICHARD B., ed., New Perspectives for Bank Directors, (Southwestern Graduate School of Banking, Series; 4) Dallas, Southern Methodist University Press, 1977.

PORTER, L. W., E. E. LAWLER III, and J. R. HACKMAN, *Behavior in Organizations,* New York, McGraw-Hill, 1975.

RUBIN, HARVEY W., "A Banker's Guide to Directors' and Officers' Liability," *The Bankers Magazine,* May–June, 1978.

WARREN, E. KIRBY, *Long Range Planning: The Executives Viewpoint,* Englewood Cliffs, N.J., Prentice-Hall, Inc., 1966.

WEBBER, ROSS A., *Management,* Homewood, Ill, Irwin, 1975.

5

Asset Management

Asset management is the term used to describe the allocation of funds among investment alternatives. Applied to commercial banking, the term refers to the distribution of funds among cash, security investments, loans, and other assets. Specialized areas of asset management include securities portfolio and loan management relating to the composition of securities and outstanding loans. A discussion of these specialized areas is included in later chapters. In this chapter we will be concerned with the broader aspects of the problem—that is, the conversion of deposits and capital funds into cash and earning assets.

The obvious solution to the funds-allocation problem is to purchase those assets (make loans and investments) that promise the highest rate of return for the level of risk that a bank's management is prepared to assume. The management of funds in commercial banking is complicated by several factors, however. First, as banks are the most regulated of all business enterprises, funds must be managed within the legal and regulatory framework established by statutory and supervisory authorities. Second, the relationship between a bank and its loan and deposit customers is one of trust as well as accommodation. Finally, the stockholders of a commercial bank, like other investors, require a rate of return commensurate with the risk of the investment and competitive with the return available on similar investments.

The effects of legal and regulatory provisions on commercial bank asset management may be classified as those that specify how a part of a bank's assets must be invested and those that limit the use of funds in certain types of assets. An example of the first type of restriction is the provision that banks must hold a percentage of their deposits in cash or its equivalent. The second is illustrated by the prohibition on investing funds in common stocks of industrial corporations.

The greatest portion of commercial bank liabilities is payable on demand, or with only short notice. Demand deposits are, of course, payable at the request of the depositor, and while prior notice of withdrawal may be required on time and savings deposits, banks generally regard savings deposits as payable on demand. Therefore, the first requirement of prudent bank management is to assure the bank's ability to meet the claims of depositors. The second requirement is to make available sufficient funds to satisfy the legitimate credit needs of the bank's customers and surrounding community. The provision of such credit is the principal profit-making activity of a commercial bank. Failure to accommodate reasonable and legitimate loan requests from customers will result in immediate loss of business and, ultimately, the possible failure of the bank as a viable business organization.

Commercial banks are privately owned business firms that seek satisfactory profits subject to the constraints of liquidity and safety. At the same time, the role of banks as suppliers of most of the nation's money supply requires members of the industry to assume important public responsibilities. The public must never have reason to question the solvency, liquidity, or integrity of the banking system; and depositors must be able to maintain full confidence in the individual banking firm. The objectives of a bank's depositors and those of its stockholders are incompatible to some extent. This incompatibility is reflected in the unavoidable conflict between necessary liquidity and desired profitability which is present in virtually every financial transaction of a commercial bank.

This conflict between liquidity and profitability may be regarded as the central problem in the management of bank funds. Bank managers feel pressure from stockholders for greater profits, which may be earned by investing in longer-term securities, extending credit to borrowers with marginal credit worthiness, and reducing idle cash balances. On the other hand, the managers are acutely aware that these actions greatly reduce liquidity, which may be needed to meet deposit withdrawals and the credit demands of long-standing customers.

The risk of investing in loans and securities is defined sometimes as the dispersion of possible returns. An investment in a very short-term U.S. Government security, for example, would be expected to have a virtually certain return. An investment in a low-grade corporate bond due in 20 years, on the other hand, would be subject to both credit risk and money-rate risk, and the return to be realized may vary from the loss of the entire investment to the full return promised if held to maturity. This wider dispersion of possible returns usually requires a promise of a higher interest rate in order to induce an investor to take the risk that the returns may be lower

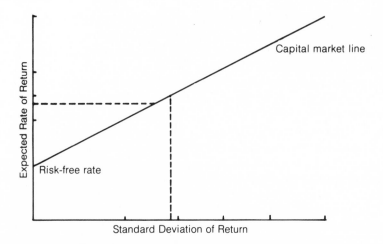

Fig. 5-1   Tradeoff between risk and return.

than promised. The tradeoff between risk and rate of return is illustrated in Figure 5-1 where the risk (dispersion of possible returns) is indicated by the standard deviation of the expected rate of return on an investment. As the risk increases, due to increased credit risk or increased time to maturity, the expected rate of return also increases. The capital market line expresses the tradeoff between risk and the rate of return required by the market. Thus a bank that takes on investments or loans which promise a higher rate of return also takes on more risk.

There is an interdependence between the management of assets and the management of liabilities, to be discussed in Chapter 6. Liquidity may be provided by holding cash and other liquid assets and also may be provided by an ability to attract additional deposits or to borrow from other sources. In addition, the high volatility of deposits and need for early repayment of debt require larger holdings of liquid assets. Furthermore, there is a relationship between the cost of deposits and borrowed funds and the returns available from various categories of assets. A careful analysis of the marginal costs of funds relative to the marginal revenues available from loans and investments can enhance the profitability of a bank while staying within the constraints of liquidity.

Commercial Bank Assets

Commercial bank assets may be divided into four basic categories: cash assets, security investments, loans, and fixed assets. The problem of asset management centers primarily on the allocation of funds among and within the first three categories; management is normally not involved on a day-to-day basis with the investment of funds in buildings and equipment. When such expenditures are planned, however, provision must be made to have sufficient cash available at the appropriate time.

Table 5-1 shows some of the complexity of the problem, presenting the asset structure of a typical billion dollar commercial bank in the United States. A considerable difference exists between the asset structure of banks

Table 5–1
Hypothetical National Bank Structure of Assets

	Amount in Thousands of Dollars	Percent of Total Assets[a]
Cash Assets		
Currency and coin	$ 13,300	1.33
Reserves with Federal Reserve Bank	41,100	4.11
Balances with domestic banks	18,800	1.88
Cash items in process of collection	69,400	6.94
Total Cash Assets	$ 142,600	14.26
Securities		
U.S. Treasury bills	$ 15,000	1.50
U.S. notes and bonds maturing 1 year	15,300	1.53
U.S. notes and bonds maturing 1–5 years	40,400	4.04
U.S. notes and bonds maturing after 5 years	6,800	0.68
Federal agency certificates of participation	5,000	0.50
Obligations of states and subdivisions	94,500	9.45
Other securities	24,800	2.48
Total securities	$ 201,800	20.18
Loans		
Federal funds sold and repurchase agreements	46,200	4.62
Commercial and industrial loans	195,500	19.55
Agricultural loans	9,900	0.99
Loans for purchasing or carrying securities	15,100	1.51
Loans to nonbank financial institutions	34,600	3.46
Real estate loans	142,800	14.28
Loans to commercial banks	10,800	1.08
Consumer installment loans	91,600	9.16
All other loans	40,700	4.07
Less Loan reserve and unearned income	(17,000)	(1.70)
Total loans	$ 570,200	57.02
Other assets		
Investments in subsidiaries not consolidated	3,100	0.31
Bank premises and other assets	82,300	8.23
Total other assets	85,400	8.54
Total assets	1,000,000	100.00

[a]Percentages of total assets are approximately the same as those for large commercial banks outside New York City reporting weekly. See *Federal Reserve Bulletin*, January 1978, p. A22

and that of nonfinancial business firms. Most commercial bank assets are financial claims. Banks have relatively large cash balances and relatively small investments in land and buildings. In contrast, a typical manufacturing firm requires relatively small cash balances and has relatively large investments in inventories and fixed assets. The financial claims of a manufacturing firm are, for the most part, limited to accounts receivable and temporary investments of surplus cash.

The differences between the composition of a bank's assets and those of an industrial firm result from differences in the nature of their liabilities and the character of the profit-making activities in which the firms engage. An industrial firm derives most of its profits from the sale of goods that are manufactured from raw materials. Merchandising requires maintenance of a substantial finished goods inventory and manufacturing requires maintenance of a raw materials inventory as well as the use of expensive equipment housed in a modern plant. In contrast, bank profits are derived mostly from lending and investing and result in the bank holding notes, bonds, and other financial instruments evidencing the amounts to be repaid in the future.

Cash Assets

Commercial banks are required by the regulatory authorities to maintain a portion of their assets in cash or demand balances with other banks. In addition. working balances are required to make change, meet withdrawal requests, accommodate requests for loans, and provide the various operating expenses including salaries, wages, supplies, and services. The category "cash assets" includes balances at the Federal Reserve banks and at other commercial banks, currency and coin, and cash items in the process of collection.

Legal Reserves of Member Banks

All commercial banks that are members of the Federal Reserve System are required to hold, as a collected balance at a Federal Reserve bank or in vault cash, a stipulated percentage of their net demand deposits and time and savings deposits. Net demand deposits are gross demand deposits minus cash items in the process of collection and demand balances due from domestic banks. The amount of reserves required to be held varies with the classification of banks and the size and classification of the deposits. The legal reserve requirements of member banks are determined by the Board of Governors of the Federal Reserve System within limits established by

Congress.[1] Within these broad limits, the Board of Governors has broad authority to vary reserve requirements for all or just one classification of banks. It can change the designation of cities for reserve purposes. It may permit banks located in reserve cities to maintain only the reserves required of banks located in country districts for their outlying branches. The greatest power that the board has over legal reserves is to suspend for 30 days any and all requirements in extreme emergencies.

The amount of average daily legal reserves a member bank is required to have during any week depends on its average daily net deposits of each kind during the second preceding week. For this purpose, the week (often referred to as the *settlement week*) is a period of seven days ending on Wednesday. The required reserve percentages for member banks are covered by Regulation D of the Board of Governors of the Federal Reserve System, and are modified by the Board from time to time. Current requirements are published regularly in the *Federal Reserve Bulletin*. Excess reserves or deficiencies may be carried over for one settlement week as long as the amount does not exceed two percent of the required reserves.

Legal Reserves of Nonmember Banks

In many states the required reserve percentages for nonmember banks are lower than the Federal Reserve requirements for member banks. At the extreme, the state of Illinois requires no reserves for nonmember banks. Even more important than differences in the amount of reserves required are the differences in the kinds of assets that qualify as legal reserves. In 18 states, cash items in the process of collection are counted as reserves; in 28 states nonmember banks can meet all or some proportion of their required reserves with earning assets. The earning assets that qualify always include U.S. Government securities (limited, in some cases, to short-term) and, in some states, one or more of the following: Federal agency securities, debt securities of the state, certificates of deposit, and Federal funds sold. The proportion of total reserve requirements that can be satisfied with interest-bearing securities varies considerably from state to state.[2]

[1]The legal limits are as follows:

	Minimum	*Maximum*
Net demand deposits, reserve city banks	10%	22%
Net demand deposits, other banks	7%	14%
Time deposits	3%	10%

[2]Alton Gilbert and Jean M. Lovati, "Bank Reserve Requirements and Their Enforcement: A Comparison Across States," Federal Reserve Bank of St. Louis, *Review*, March 1978, pp. 22–31.

Vault Cash

As the term implies, vault cash is the amount of coin and currency carried by banks in their vaults. Even though the amount is considered part of legal reserves, bank management attempts to keep it as low as possible for security reasons. Moreover, the cost of protection and insuring cash against loss is relatively high, and cash balances earn no interest.

The amount of cash needed by individual banks varies widely. In some areas of the nation transactions are settled in cash to a greater extent than in others where greater reliance is placed upon the use of checks. Most banks experience seasonal demands for cash. Vault cash must be increased temporarily for anticipated events such as the crop harvesting season when cash is needed for the payment of labor, and the Christmas season when merchants and customers are accumulating larger than usual cash balances. Bank location is also an important factor influencing the size of cash balances. Banks situated relatively far from a Federal Reserve bank or branch or their correspondent banks are forced to carry more cash than banks located closer to a cash supply. When a depositor requests currency or coin, it is neither good manners nor proper protocol to reply that it will arrive by courier later in the day. Country banks generally carry a larger amount of cash in relation to deposits than do city banks, partially because of their location.

Correspondent Bank Balances

The efficient collection of checks by commercial banks and the provision of services not available from the Federal Reserve banks have contributed to the continuation and growth of correspondent banking in America. Normally correspondent banks are compensated for the services they provide by investing for profit a portion of the correspondent bank account. The size of this account will vary roughly with the amount of services performed. However, the amount carried in a correspondent balance may not truly reflect the extent of the services rendered by the correspondent bank since many banks carry accounts that are seldom used. Often such accounts are maintained because of the friendship of bank executives, and much time and energy are devoted to generating and maintaining this type of account. The rising cost of providing banking services is forcing many banks to place correspondent relationships on a cost-benefit basis. This involves the pricing of individual services used by correspondent banks and asking these banks to maintain a balance sufficient to provide earnings equal to the full cost of the services provided.

Security Investments

Commercial banks purchase securities for liquidity purposes, to augment income, and to serve as collateral for deposit liabilities to federal, state, and local governments. The largest proportion of security investments is in government obligations—either federal, state, or local. Investments in short-term U.S. government securities generally provide limited income but are highly liquid with no credit risk and little market-rate risk. Longer-term obligations normally offer greater income over extended periods of time. Often they are held until maturity or near-maturity. Municipal securities are attractive bank investments because the interest (usually lower than for U.S. government or corporate securities) is exempt from federal income taxes and, in many cases, from state income taxes. In addition to providing attractive income when compared to the after-tax earnings on other securities, the purchase of municipal securities sometimes is viewed as a way to support the activities of local governments—in effect, to be a good citizen by providing a market for the securities of state and local political subdivisions.

Banks also hold relatively small amounts of other securities, including those held primarily to provide liquidity, such as bankers' acceptances, open market commercial paper, brokers' loans, and Commodity Credit Corporation certificates of interest. To augment income, investments are made in the obligations of some government agencies and, on a limited basis, in high-grade corporate bonds. A complete discussion of bank security investments will be found in Chapters 16 and 17.

Bank Loans

The principal profit-making activity of commercial banks is making loans to its customers. In the allocation of funds to the loan portfolio, the primary objective of the bank management is to earn income while serving the credit needs of its community. The degree of liquidity a particular loan commitment may have is of secondary importance. For example, few loans may be liquidated by sale to other institutions or individuals because of the lack of a secondary market in this type of financial claim. An exception has been the development of a secondary market for residential mortgage loans.

The bank management must decide, too, upon the distribution of funds *within* the loan portfolio; that is, funds must be assigned to instalment loans, commercial loans, real estate loans, and others. This assignment is made on the basis of the relative profitability of and demand for various classes of loans, subject to constraints required by prudence and imposed by regulation. Detailed consideration will be given to loan policy and various classes of loans in Chapters 10 through 15.

Management of Assets

The allocation of bank funds to various asset classifications is constrained by regulations and law, by the need to maintain a high degree of liquidity, and by the need to earn sufficient income. Three different approaches to asset management have been espoused in attempts to resolve the liquidity-profitability dilemma. Each differs in its emphasis on the form of the management process and in the degree to which quantitative analysis is employed in evaluating the alternatives available. No one approach can be considered a panacea for bank management because problems and deficiencies are associated with each. Some elements of each approach probably should be considered for applicability to the particular problems of an individual commercial bank. The first approach, called the *pool-of-funds* approach, is the simplest to administer. It has served many bankers well, particularly during periods when funds were plentiful. The second, the *asset allocation* or *conversion of funds* approach, was developed to meet some of the deficiencies of the pool-of-funds approach. The third approach involves the application of management-science techniques and, usually, computer-aided analysis.

Whatever approach or combination of approaches is chosen as a model for allocating funds to various types of assets, a banker recognizes the tradeoff between risk and return among the various categories of assets and among various loans and investments within the categories. Profitability goals can be realized more easily with careful analysis of the marginal cost of funds as compared with marginal revenues available from earning assets.

The Pool-of-Funds Approach

The funds available to the portfolio manager of a commercial bank are derived from a number of sources, including demand deposits, savings deposits, time deposits, and capital funds. The basic idea underlying the use of the pool-of-funds approach is that all funds should be pooled together. Funds then should be allocated from the pool to whatever asset investment (loans, government securities, cash, and so forth) is appropriate. The source from which funds were derived to make a particular investment is immaterial to the pool-of-funds model as long as the investment will contribute to meeting the objectives of the bank. This idea is illustrated schematically in Figure 5–2.

This approach requires the bank management to identify their liquidity and profitability requirements. Then funds are allocated to the asset categories that best satisfy those requirements. Allocation is undertaken according to several priorities, which are established to assist operating management

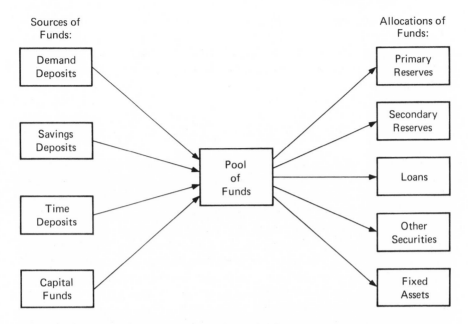

Fig. 5-2   The pool-of-funds model for asset management.

in solving the dilemma between liquidity and profitability. These priorities have to do with the proportion of each available dollar to be placed in primary reserves, secondary reserves, loans, and security investments for income. Investments in land, buildings, and other fixed assets usually are considered separately.

Primary Reserves

The first priority in the allocation scheme is to establish the proportion of funds that will be allocated to primary reserves. This category of assets is a functional category that does not appear on the statement of position of a commercial bank. Nevertheless, it is an important concept to a commercial banker and relates to those assets that can be used immediately to meet withdrawal requests and satisfy loan applicants. It is the primary source of liquidity for a commercial bank. In most instances, primary reserves are grouped under the heading "Cash and Due from Banks." Assets held as primary reserves include collected balances at the Federal Reserve banks, correspondent balances (deposits) at other commercial banks, vault cash, and cash items in the process of collection.

Note that the primary reserves include both legal reserves against deposit liabilities and the working balances that a bank's management judges to be sufficient. A common approach to establishing the proportion of funds to be allocated to the primary reserves is to use the average ratio of cash assets to deposits or total assets for all banks of similar size. Banks whose asset structure is illustrated in Table 5–1 might have established a rule that about 14 percent of new sources of funds should be set aside in the form of cash to meet the primary reserve priority.

Secondary Reserves

The second priority in the funds-allocation process is providing for noncash liquid assets that contribute to the earning power of the bank. These reserves of a commercial bank consist of highly liquid earning assets that can be converted into cash with little delay and little risk of loss. The major function of these secondary reserves is to replenish and supplement the primary reserve. Like *primary reserve,* the *secondary reserve* refers to an economic concept rather than an accounting one, so it does not appear in the statement of condition. The assets that make up this reserve are found in the securities investment portfolio usually and in the loan accounts in some instances.

The size of the secondary reserve is determined indirectly by those factors that influence the variability of deposits and loans. A bank that experiences great variation in deposits and a highly erratic credit demand would need a larger secondary reserve than a bank with stable loans and deposits.

As with the primary reserve, a proportion of total funds usually is established for the secondary reserve. While the national average may not meet the needs of the individual bank, this percentage might be considered a starting point. The ratio of cash and U.S. government securities to total deposits for all commercial banks sometimes is used as an approximation of the liquidity of the banking system. An individual bank's management may decide to set the proportion of funds to be allocated to the secondary reserve as equal to the ratio of U.S. government securities due in five years or less to total assets. The hypothetical bank of Table 5–1, then, might allocate about 7 percent of available new funds to the secondary reserve.

Loan Portfolio

The third priority in the use of bank funds under the pool-of-funds approach is the allocation of funds to the loan portfolio. After a bank has taken care of its primary and secondary reserve needs, it is free to make loans to its customers. This is the major profit-making activity of a bank. Loans represent the most important part of total bank assets, and income from loans is the greatest contributor to bank profits. Most risks inherent in banking activities are carried in the loan portfolio.

Investment for Income

The final priority is the allocation of funds to the investment portfolio. Funds remaining after the legitimate credit needs of customers have been met may be placed in relatively long-term, high-quality securities. The functions of the investment portfolio are to provide income to the bank and additions to secondary reserves as the long-term securities approach maturity.

The pool-of-funds approach to commercial bank asset management provides broad rules for a bank to follow in allocating funds to various asset categories. The approach emphasizes priorities that are stated in rather general terms. The method does not provide an explicit means for determining the proportion of funds that should be invested in each asset classification, nor does it provide a solution to the dilemma between liquidity and profitability in asset management. These problems are left to the judgment and intuition of a bank's management.

The Asset-Allocation Approach

It has been contended that the pool-of-funds approach to bank asset management places too much emphasis on liquidity and fails to distinguish among the different liquidity requirements of demand deposits, savings deposits, time deposits, and capital funds. Many bankers think that this deficiency caused an increasing amount of erosion to the profitability of commercial banks during the 1950s and 1960s. During those years time and savings deposits that required less liquidity grew more rapidly than did demand deposits. The asset-allocation approach, also known as the conversion-of-funds approach, was developed to meet this deficiency.

Banks within a Bank

The asset-allocation model recognizes that the amount of liquidity needed by a bank is related to the sources from which its funds are obtained. This idea is described schematically in Figure 5–3. The model attempts to distinguish different sources of funds according to legal reserve requirements and the velocity, or turnover, of the sources. Demand deposits have a higher legal reserve requirement, for example, than do savings and time deposits and typically have a higher velocity, or turnover rate, than do the other types of deposits. Therefore, a greater proportion of each demand deposit dollar should be allocated to the primary and secondary reserves and a smaller proportion to investments such as residential morgage loans or long-term municipal bonds. The model establishes several liquidity–profitability centers within a bank for allocating funds obtained from different sources.

Sources of Funds from
Liquidity — Profitability Center:

Uses of Funds as Allocated
by Liquidity — Profitability Center:

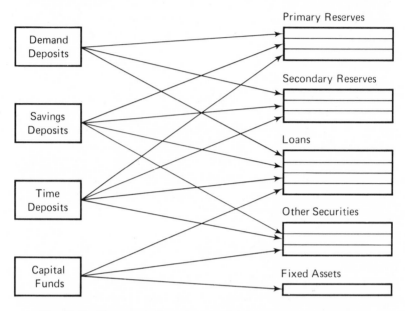

Fig. 5–3 The asset-allocation model for asset management.

These centers sometimes have been called banks within a bank because the allocation of funds from each center is made independently from the allocation of funds from other centers. Thus there may exist a demand-deposit bank, a savings-deposit bank, a time-deposit bank, and a capital-funds bank within a given commercial banking organization.

Once the liquidity-profitability centers have been identified and established, management must formulate a policy regarding the allocation of funds generated within each center. Demand deposits require the highest percentage of legal reserves and have the greatest velocity, perhaps turning over as often as 30 to 50 times per year. The demand-deposit center, then, would allocate a high proportion of the funds generated in this center to primary reserves—say one percent more than the required reserve percentage—then the bulk of uncommitted funds would go to secondary reserves for investment in short-term government securities. Relatively small amounts would be committed to loans—mostly in the form of short-term commercial loans. In Figure 5–3 no allocation is made from the demand-deposit center to other securities or to fixed assets. The savings-deposit and time-deposit centers would require relatively less liquidity and so would allocate larger amounts to loans and investments. Capital funds require little liquidity and would be used to finance land and buildings, with the balance committed to long-term loans and less liquid security investments in order to enhance income.

The principal advantage claimed for this asset-allocation approach is that it reduces liquid assets and allocates additional funds to the loan and investment accounts thus tending to increase profitability. Advocates of this approach maintain that the improvement in profitability is obtained by eliminating excess liquidity carried against time and savings deposits and capital funds.

This model also has limitations impairing its effectiveness. While the velocity of different kinds of deposit liabilities is used as a basis for defining different liquidity-profitability centers, little relationship may exist between the velocity of a particular group of deposit accounts and the variability of the total amount of deposits within that group. A bank's demand deposits, for example, may turn over as many as 40 times per year. With some customers writing checks while others make simultaneous deposits, the sum of individual balances (or the total deposit liability of the bank) may vary by as little as 10 percent over the course of a year. As long as a bank operates it will have a minimum deposit liability. From a practical standpoint, some funds derived from demand deposits in the aggregate may never be withdrawn and could be invested in long-term high-yielding investments prudently.

Another limitation of the model is that it assumes sources of funds are independent of the use to which the bank puts them. This is not a realistic assumption. Practicing bankers seek to attract business deposits, for example, because business firms tend to borrow from the same bank where they maintain their checking account. An acceptance of new deposits, therefore, implies an obligation on the part of the bank to fulfill some of the credit requirements of the new depositors. Accordingly, a portion of the new deposits should be allocated to new loans for the same depositor group.

Other limitations apply both to the pool-of-funds model and the asset-allocation model. Both models emphasize the liquidity of legal reserve requirements and the possible withdrawal of deposits, while giving relatively less consideration to the requirement for a bank to satisfy its customers' loan requests. It is well known that both deposits and loans tend to rise along with rising business activity. Aside from legal reserve requirements, little additional liquidity is needed to take care of withdrawal requests when this occurs, particularly if the bank's economist is able to forecast accurately when business activity and deposits are likely to taper off. In this circumstance liquidity is needed primarily to satisfy loan demand, which is likely to be rising more rapidly than deposits.

It should be noted also that there are seasonal variations for individual banks in which loan demand may be up when deposits are at a low level. Also, because of monetary policy actions, loan demand in periods of rising activity outstrips deposit growth and, for all banks, deposit growth is more rapid in recessionary periods because of monetary policy actions, with modest growth in boom periods of high loan demand.

Both of the asset management models described have another shortcoming. They emphasize *average* liquidity requirements rather than *marginal* requirements. While the average ratio of cash and government securities to total deposits may be appropriate for judging the adequacy of liquidity in the banking system, it does not tell the management of an individual commercial bank how much cash it must have on hand to meet withdrawal requests and loan applications during the coming week. Only an analysis of the bank's individual customer accounts and knowledge of local business and financial activity can help in estimating immediate requirements.

The pool-of-funds and asset-allocation models are somewhat simplistic in nature. Rather than providing a complete set of guidelines as a basis for decision making, each model should be considered a general framework within which management might formulate policies for handling the asset-management problem. Within either framework, a competent management team should be able to recognize the complex interrelationships and use the degree of sophistication in analysis and decision-making appropriate to the particular bank's individual situation.

The Management-Science Approach

The management-science or operations-research approach to asset management uses sophisticated models and advanced mathematical techniques to analyze the complex interrelationships among various components of the balance sheet and income statement. This approach can provide powerful aids to management in the decision-making process. The solution of management problems with the aid of operations-research techniques was an outgrowth of attempts by the military to solve complex logistical problems during World War II. They have since been widely used in industry as aids in production scheduling, blending of raw materials, transportation and distribution, inventory control, development of advertising strategies, job assignment, capital budgeting, and funds allocation.

The asset-management approaches described in previous sections utilize simple management-science techniques as aids in the decision making process. Both approaches use simple models to analyze relationships among the various asset classifications and the different categories of liabilities. The models are used then to prescribe how a bank's management should allocate whatever funds are available for investment to provide adequate profitability while operating within the liquidity constraints imposed by management (from within), or by regulatory authorities (from without).

More sophisticated techniques involve a scientific approach to management's problem solving that utilizes advanced mathematical techniques and computer-based technology for examining the interaction of elements in complex models. The examination and manipulation of such models may be of great assistance to commercial bank management in realizing increased profitability from bank operations.

The scientific method for the solution of problems involved in bank asset management requires a statement of objectives, identification of the relationships among various elements of the problem, identification of variable elements that are, and are not, under the control of management, an estimate of the way noncontrolled variables may behave, and identification of constraints imposed on the behavior of management (either from within or without). The method attempts to provide answers to three questions: What is the problem? What are the alternatives? Which alternative is best?

Linear programming is one technique used by management scientists for solving business problems. This technique will be described as an illustration of the management-science approach to decision making in commercial bank asset management. It combines the asset management problem with the liability management problem and can incorporate both profitability and liquidity constraints.

Other techniques of management science could be used profitably by commercial bank managers in this and other management activities. Some of these techniques will be described in subsequent chapters.

The Linear-Programming Model

A linear program is a mathematical model that expresses the relationships among various decision elements in a standard mathematical form. The model uses one of several standardized computational methods, such as the simplex algorithm, for determining the optimal combination of elements that are subject to the control of the decision maker. The mathematical and computational aspects of the model and its use are rather intricate, but it is not essential that a user master these aspects. Outside of a classroom, no one calculates a linear program manually. Standard computer codes have been devised to make the use of such complex models feasible. However, it is important for management to recognize the types of decision problems that are capable of solution by linear-programming models, to be familiar with the banking and economic implications of the model's assumptions, to be able to assist the mathematician or operations-research specialist in analyzing the problem, and to be able to interpret and evaluate the results of the analysis.

Every linear-program model has certain characteristics. It is assumed that the objective is to be most successfully reached by means of the variables under the control of the decision maker. Alternative courses of action with regard to the use of such variables must exist. The courses of action are limited by one or more constraints on the ability of the decision maker to control the decision variables. The linear program is a deterministic model that leads to a single optimum solution,[3] therefore, the exact nature of the constraints must be known or able to be approximated. The objective function must be continuous; that is, the coefficients of the decision variables must be able to assume any value. The objective must be stated—sometimes by approximation—in linear form; that is, each decision variable must make a proportional contribution to the value of the objective function and in the equations describing the constraints.

The Objective Function

The linear-program model requires an explicit statement of an objective to be optimized. Optimization, for example, may consist of maximization of profits or minimization of costs. In the asset management problem the objective is to maximize profits realized from investments in various categories of assets that may be purchased. In a simplified situation, for example, a bank's management may wish to undertake the combination of investments that would contribute most to profits. The decision variables, or alternatives available might be short-term government securities yielding 4 percent, long-term government securities yielding 5 percent, high-grade commercial loans with an average yield of 6 percent, term loans to business firms with an average yield of 7 percent, automobile instalment paper yielding 8 percent, and/or other consumer instalment loans yielding 12 percent. These yields are on a net basis, after deduction of the bank's expenses of servicing the various types of assets.[4] If we let the variable x represent the amounts to be invested in the different categories of assets, the profits (P) to be derived from these investments can be described as follows:

$$P = .04x_1 + .05x_2 + .06x_3 + .07x_4 + .08x_5 + .12x_6$$

[3]Each time the program is run there is a single solution. Management probably would run the program a number of times, in practice, to test the effect of changing some of the constraints or estimated relationships.

[4]Space limitations have required many simplifications in this discussion of linear programming. One such simplification in this example is the built-in assumption that the costs of administering the various classes of assets are directly proportional to the amounts invested in those assets. Obviously, it does not cost ten times as much to manage $100 million of U.S. government bonds as it does to manage $10 million.

The objective of solving the linear program would be to maximize the value of P. If a banker is free to take on any risks, is not concerned with liquidity, and is not subject to any legal restrictions on investments, the solution of the equation, of course, is trivial. The answer would be to invest all of the available funds in consumer instalment loans (x_6) for a yield of 12 percent. This is unrealistic since banks have other customers to be cared for, and regulations and prudent banking would not permit such specialization.

Formulation of Constraints

The investments of commercial banks are limited by constraints imposed by law and the regulatory authorities, some of which are necessary because of the economic environment, and others desired by management to conform to good banking practices. Some constraints are more difficult than others to formulate in mathematical terms. Some constitute absolute limitations and others are a matter for the judgment of management. The amount of cash and deposits with the Federal Reserve bank, for example, must be at least equal to the minimum reserve requirements for a member bank. This amount can be easily formulated as the sum of the percentages of the various categories of deposits. The maximum amount that could be invested in high-grade term loans, on the other hand, would be limited to the volume of loan applications the bank might receive. This volume, even for the near future, is subject to some uncertainty. Management must do some forecasting and estimate the expected demand.

The constraint on high-grade term loans can be formulated mathematically when management has estimated the maximum demand for such loans. Suppose that maximum demand for such loans at a net yield of 7 percent (x_4, as shown in the illustration of the objective function) is estimated at $5 million. Then the maximum value of x_4 in the objective function would be $5 million. Stated mathematically, this is shown as $x_4 \leq 5,000,000$. While some constraint formulations are more complex, the principle of formulation is the same.

Examples of other constraints that might be incorporated in a linear program for bank asset management would include those relating to risk, liquidity, and legal restrictions. The inclusion of a limitation on the total volume of risk assets according to the value of capital funds, or perhaps a version of the capital adequacy formula (described in Chapter 7) might be desirable in order to limit the risk of loss to amounts that would be considered reasonable percentages of the capital funds available to absorb the losses. To assure sufficient liquidity, short-term government securities might be related to total deposits with a minimum percentage specified. This type of limitation should be considered by management based on likely withdrawal requests, the range of expected demands for loans in subsequent periods, and the way that investors and depositors are likely to view the liquidity position of the bank. The linear-program model is flexible enough to incorporate whatever restrictions are desired by management or required by regulatory authorities.

A multi-period model also would incorporate restrictions that provide linkages from one period to the next. An example of this type of constraint is to limit the amount of funds available in one period to amounts derived from loan repayments, securities matured or liquidated, new deposits received, and net profits in the immediately preceding period. A multi-period formulation of the model also would permit the solution to reflect management's beliefs about what will happen to demand for various types of loans, the way that interest rates are likely to change, and even expected changes in regulatory restrictions such as reserve ratios. For example, if interest rates are expected to fall, it is good business practice to invest more funds for a longer term, provided the subsequent periods will have sufficient liquidity. Such expectations can and should be incorporated to maximize profitability over time.

The Linear-Programming Solution

The linear-programming solution would indicate the appropriate amounts to be invested in each asset category for maximum profitability, given the set of assumptions that were included in the formulation of the model. It is likely that the program will need to be run several times with different sets of assumptions in order to test the sensitivity of the results to changes in the assumptions. For example, if interest rates two periods hence are subject to some uncertainty, it would be helpful to try a range of possible rates in different iterations to see what the effect would be on optimal allocation of funds to different asset categories in the current period.

The solution would also identify the opportunity costs associated with the constraints that were included in the model. Either relaxing the requirements for liquidity or actively seeking additional funds through the issue of capital notes might substantially increase the profits of a bank. The linear-program solution, for example, may include *shadow prices* for each constraint that limits the value of the objective function in this type of problem: that is, limit the amount of profit. A shadow price is the amount by which the objective function would increase if the constraint were relaxed by one additional unit.

Suppose that the solution of the problem given above, including additional constraints specified by management, showed that maximum profitability would be achieved by investing the maximum amount possible ($5 million) in high-grade term loans. The amount of profit could likely be increased, therefore, if loan demand were greater. If the shadow price on this constraint were shown to be 0.03 over an additional range of 1,000,000, this would be interpreted as meaning each dollar of additional loan demand up to $1 million more would contribute an additional three cents to profits. In other words, the shadow price that management could afford to pay for additional promotion to generate greater loan demand would be up to three cents per dollar of additional loans or say, $3,000 to generate an additional $100,000 in loans.

Consideration of shadow prices generated by a program is a useful kind of sensitivity analysis for management to utilize in reaching policy decisions. New business development activities may take on added importance in the light of shadow price analysis like that shown above. It would not be unreasonable for management to allocate additional funds for such activities if experience shows that new loan business can be generated at a cost less than the shadow price. Or suppose the linear-program solution shows a funds constraint (limiting the amount of funds available for investment) to have a shadow price of .095 per dollar of additional funds. Management might well consider a policy of expanding capital by issuing capital notes with a net interest cost not exceeding 9.5 percent. Management must rely on experience to judge whether the cost of additional promotion activities or of issuing additional capital notes can be justified.[5]

Implementation

The management-science approach to bank asset management offers distinct advantages to those banks that have staff members or consultants with the mathematical sophistication to employ the techniques. The bank management should consider these techniques a way to improve the decision-making process and not a way to replace its own judgment and expertise. The use of a comprehensive linear-programming model may help a bank's management to recognize the implications of some of their decisions. It may be used to test the sensitivity of those decisions to changes in the economic environment or to errors in forecasting. It certainly will be helpful in utilizing the processing speed of the computer to summarize the complex interactions among the large number of variables with which management must deal when allocating funds to different investments.

In the final analysis, however, the management must accept the responsibility for the formulation of the model and for the decisions based on information derived from the model. The formulation of the model perhaps offers one of the principal advantages to management in that it requires a careful formulation of objectives and an explicit statement of the various

[5]See Chapter 6 for a discussion of liability management and Chapter 7 for a discussion of capital notes.

constraints under which it operates. Moreover, management is forced to examine the loan and investment portfolio to determine the characteristics of the various types of investment, the likely return from each, and the costs associated with each. This information is extremely valuable, no matter which approach is utilized for the asset-management process.

The principal disadvantage of the use of management-science techniques applies primarily to small banks. The use of these techniques requires the availability of bank personnel or consultants who have technical competence in this type of analysis, as well as adequate computer facilities to permit the use of large-scale models. Both are relatively high in cost in relation to the possible benefits for a small organization. More and more banks (and other business organizations) will be utilizing computers on a regular basis, either with their own facility or through leased time-share services. And more bankers will have received at least minimal education in management-science techniques. These factors will tend to reduce the marginal cost to small banks of using these techniques.

The problem of whether to use or not use computer techniques is the same as with allocating funds to various loans and securities. If the expected benefits exceed the marginal costs and the risks are not inappropriate, then sophisticated techniques should be implemented.

Liquidity of Assets

Commercial banks, like virtually all economic units, need liquidity; this is the quality of an asset that makes it easily convertible into cash with little or no risk of loss. Assets might be arrayed along a continuum from most to least liquid. Cash is the most liquid asset, and the ease with which other assets can be converted (through sale or collection) provides the standard of liquidity. U.S. Treasury bills provide perhaps the most liquidity of any security because they can be sold readily in an active market without substantial loss. Among the least liquid of assets are bank premises. A bank's loans are in a sense, though, the least liquid of its assets. Buildings usually can be sold, even though the transaction may be subject to some delay and substantial discount. For many types of loans there is no resale market, and the only way they can be converted to cash is to collect them at maturity. Regular amortization of the principal through monthly payments can provide considerable liquidity to a loan portfolio, but it would be difficult to liquidate the entire portfolio.

A bank is considered to be liquid when it has sufficient cash and other liquid assets, together with the ability to raise funds quickly from other sources, to enable it to meet its payment obligations and financial commitments in a timely manner. In addition there should be a sufficient liquidity buffer to meet almost any financial emergency.

How much liquidity to hold and in what forms to hold it are a constant concern of bank management. As we have discussed, banks are required to comply with legal reserve requirements. In addition, banks need liquidity to meet seasonal and unexpected loan demands and deposit fluctuations. The majority of these transactions can be anticipated in advance and met from expected cash inflows from deposits, loan repayments, or earnings. Cash reserves also are needed to take advantage of unexpected profit opportunities, or for what might be termed aggressive purposes. When a business firm that the bank has been working to secure as a customer finally presents a loan application, or a particularly desirable investment develops, the bank must have funds available to seize these opportunities. During periods of expanding economic activity, banks are frequently presented with attractive loan situations that cannot be met because the bank is "loaned-up."

It may be advisable for banks to maintain a certain amount of liquidity to meet unforeseen contingencies or emergencies. Despite management's planning efforts, unexpected deposit outflows often develop. The occurrence of a prolonged labor strike, the closing of a locally important industry, or the relocation of a military installation are situations that can adversely affect bank deposits in a community. Thus, a liquid reserve to protect the integrity of the bank against such contingencies is highly desirable.

Liquidity may be regarded as either a *stock* or *flow* concept. To measure liquidity from a stock viewpoint, one must appraise holdings of assets that may be turned into cash. To determine the adequacy of liquidity within this framework, one has to compare holdings of liquid assets with expected liquidity needs. This is a rather narrow concept of liquidity since it fails to take into consideration that liquidity may be obtained through the credit markets and revenue flows. When viewing liquidity from a flow approach, one considers not only the ability to convert liquid assets but also the ability of the economic unit to borrow and to generate cash from operations.

Liquidity Measurement

A standard for liquidity is difficult to determine, since future demands are not known. To obtain a realistic appraisal of a bank's liquidity position would require an accurate forecast of cash needs and the expected level of liquid assets and cash receipts over a given time period. In other words, a meaningful measure of liquidity would incorporate the flow concept in the calculation. However, the most widely used liquidity measures are gauged from the stock concept. One of these measures is the ratio of loans to deposits. When the ratio rises to a relatively high level, bankers become less inclined to lend and to invest. Moreover, they become more selective and, as standards are increased and credit is more strictly allocated, interest rates tend to rise. Although a high loan-to-deposit ratio has never been quantified, it is a force that influences lending and investment decisions. The loan-to-deposit ratio that bank management has been willing to live with has increased over the years for all banks but has been higher for the larger banks of the nation. This higher ratio can be explained primarily by the ability and willingness of large banks to solve their liquidity problems by liability management, or borrowing in the market, rather than relying solely on asset adjustments.

The use of the loan-to-deposit ratio as a measure of liquidity is based on the premise that loans are the most nonliquid of bank earning assets. Therefore, as the portion of deposits invested in loans rises, liquidity declines. The loan-to-deposit ratio as a measure of liquidity has some limitations in that it tells us nothing about the maturity or quality of the loan portfolio. Appraising the liquidity of the loan portfolio requires knowledge of the average length of maturity of loans, of whether the loans are amortized or single payment, and of the credit record of the borrowers. The ratio gives no indication of liquidity needs. A bank with a loan-to-deposit ratio of 70 percent, for example, may be relatively more liquid than one with a 50 percent ratio if the deposits of the former bank are stable while those of the latter are subject to wide variations. Finally, the loan-to-deposit ratio does not provide information concerning the nature of bank assets outside the loan portfolio. One bank might have 20 percent of its deposits invested in cash and short-term government securities while another bank might have the same percentage in bank buildings and real estate, but both banks could have the same loan-to-deposit ratio. Obviously, the banks would not have the same level of liquidity. Despite these shortcomings, the loan-to-deposit ratio does have some value in that as it rises it serves as a caution signal and stimulates bank management to make an evaluation of its overall expansion program. It is not intended to be a perfect measure of liquidity but a rough indicator.

Other liquidity measures that reflect the stock concept relate liquid assets to total deposits or to total assets. The ratio of cash assets to total deposits, for example, is superior in some ways to the loan-to-deposit ratio because this relates liquid assets directly to deposit levels rather than indirectly by considering loans, the least liquid assets, to deposits. A serious deficiency of this ratio lies in the fact that a substantial portion of cash assets are not really available to meet the liquidity needs of the bank. That portion of cash assets that is required to meet legal reserve requirements is, of course, not available to satisfy loan demand and only the legal reserve percentage is available to meet deposit withdrawal requests. Another deficiency of this ratio is its failure to include other liquid assets such as Treasury bills and short-term liquid securities. It gives no consideration to a bank's ability to raise funds from other sources.

Determining Liquidity Needs

Liquidity is one of the many problems with which bank management struggles constantly, and a foolproof formula for determining a bank's liquidity needs has not yet been developed. The amount of liquidity needed by an individual bank depends on the amount of variation that occurs in deposits and the demand for loans.

There are many movements in the economy—irregular, seasonal, cyclical, and secular. It is difficult to predict the occurrence or the severity of irregular movements since they do not follow established patterns. They do, however, affect the level of deposits and the demand for loans. Examples of irregular movements are a labor strike, the effects of some natural catastrophe such as an earthquake or a flood, a war scare, or some unusual economic or political development.

Seasonal movements, directly related to the changing seasons, differ from irregular movements by repeating themselves every year. The precise seasonal pattern may change with the passage of time. A bank located in an agricultural area might enjoy a high level of deposits in the fall after crops are harvested and experience a high loan demand in the spring. The demand for construction loans normally is higher in the summer months than in the winter. Weather is the most important factor responsible for seasonal patterns, but social custom has an influence—for example, retail sales normally rise in December because of the Christmas season.

Cyclical movements are more difficult to predict than seasonal movements. During the contraction period of a business cycle, loan demand declines and bank deposits may shrink. In recent years, however, the monetary policy of the Federal Reserve System has tended to offset the contraction of deposits in the banking system during an economic slump. During the prosperity phase, loan demand increases and so do deposits, but not always at the same rate. In some periods of prosperity, *disintermediation* of deposits occurs, presenting serious liquidity problems for many commercial banks.

Disintermediation occurs during a "tight money" period when monetary policy is geared to slow economic expansion by limiting the availability of excess reserves to the banking system and pushing interest rates up. For example, when interest rates on commercial paper rise above those available on time certificates of deposit, funds invested in CDs tend to shift into commercial paper. This shift from commercial banks and other financial intermediaries to money market instruments is called disintermediation.

The process of disintermediation has a somewhat different effect on an individual commercial bank than it has on the banking system as a whole. If a holder of a CD decides to take the proceeds at maturity and invest them in commercial paper, the issuer of the commercial paper will probably use the proceeds to reduce his bank loans. Thus, for the banking system as a whole there is a decrease in time deposits and a decrease in loans. This actually gives rise, at least temporarily, to an increase in excess reserves for the system. If the funds are used to finance expansion, they likely would be shifted to demand deposits, which require a higher percentage of reserves, and there would be a temporary decrease in the amount of excess reserves for the banking system. The net effect on the system would depend upon the activities of the Federal Reserve Board in implementing monetary policy. For the bank whose CD was "cashed" it represents a loss of reserves to other banks and a decrease in liquidity.

Secular movements or trends persist over a long period relative to the duration of the business cycle. Secular movements may encompass several business cycles and are a product of both short- and long-run influences such as changes in consumption, savings, investment, population, labor force, and technological developments.

The amount of variation in deposits may be considerable. An illustration of deposit variation and fluctuation in loan demand is presented in Figure 5–4. This chart shows the deposit and loan movements in large New York

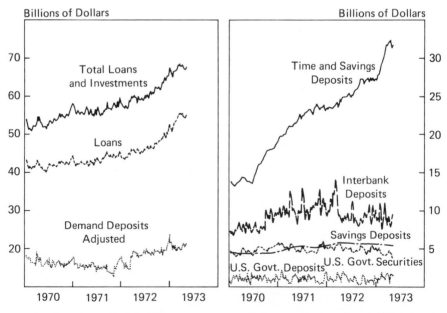

Fig. 5–4   Loans, investments, and deposits—large commercial banks in New York City. (Source: Board of Governors of the Federal Reserve System, *Federal Reserve Monthly Chartbook,* May 1973)

City banks during a period extending from recession to prosperity. Note that both deposits and loans followed a seasonal pattern. Loans declined in February and again in May but picked up during the last quarter of each year, and showed a definite increase in December. Both loan and demand deposits on an adjusted basis showed sharp increases in 1972 and early 1973, reflecting the strong economic recovery from the 1969–70 recession. Savings deposits in New York City banks were very stable compared with deposits of the U.S. government and interbank deposits. The rapid rise in total time and savings deposits was due primarily to the sharp increase in CDs issued to meet the strong demand. It can also be observed from this chart that other banks needed funds in 1972 and 1973 and drew down their interbank deposits. It is evident that the many movements in the economy create forces that influence the level of bank deposits. These forces make planning for liquidity purposes highly important.

In calculating requirements for a particular time period, a bank may determine the expected changes in deposits and loans from a given base period. Three things cause the changes in liquidity or excess reserves: the gain or loss in funds due to the increase or decrease in deposits; the gain or loss in funds due to the decrease or increase in loans and/or investments; and the increase or decrease in required legal reserves due to the increase or decrease in deposits. The calculation of the liquidity needs of a hypothetical commercial bank is illustrated in Table 5–2. Liquidity needs may be estimated for any time period desired by management. In the illustration, excess funds are expected to flow into the bank during the first quarter of the year, but funds will have to be obtained to meet heavy liquidity needs for the remainder of the year. These needs are reflected mainly in the anticipated growth of loan demands rather than in deposit outflows. Note that the increases in deposits toward the end of the year require additional legal reserves, thus offsetting the funds released from reserves earlier in the year.

If deposit changes and the demands for loans and investments could be forecast accurately, the problem of determining liquidity would be greatly simplified. Despite the difficulty, banks must attempt to predict loan and deposit levels. The forecasts of large banks are developed primarily by two basic methods. One way is to analyze the credit needs and expected deposit level of each principal customer. Forecasts constructed by this approach are usually prepared by loan officers, with each officer preparing forecasts for his accounts. Responsibility for coordinating and assembling these forecasts may rest with the economics department, comptroller's department, cashier's division, or a special group of officers assigned to planning. The other method of estimating loan and deposit volume involves a forecast of sources and uses of investment funds for the entire economy. Estimates are made of the public and private sectors of the economy, generally employing eco-

Table 5-2
Calculation of Liquidity Needs for a Hypothetical Commercial Bank (in thousands of dollars)

	Deposits	Change from Prior Month	Change in Required Reserves (10%)	Loans	Change from Prior Month	Liquidity Needs (–) Surplus (+)	Cumulative Needs (–) Surplus (+)
December	$10,900	–	–	$7,000	–	–	–
January	10,800	–100	–10	6,500	–500	+410	+400
February	10,750	–50	–5	6,490	–10	–35	+375
March	10,440	–310	–31	6,400	–90	–189	+186
April	9,900	–540	–54	6,440	+40	–526	–340
May	9,840	–60	–6	6,460	+20	–74	–414
June	9,810	–30	–3	6,500	+40	–67	–481
July	9,720	–90	–9	6,530	+30	–111	–592
August	9,790	+70	+7	6,720	+190	–127	–719
September	9,840	+50	+5	6,800	+80	–35	–754
October	9,980	+140	+14	7,200	+400	–274	–1,028
November	10,500	+520	+52	7,680	+480	–12	–1,040
December	10,940	+440	+44	8,040	+360	+36	–1,004

nometric forecasting techniques. The private sector's estimated needs for funds are balanced against estimated supplies. Total bank loan volume then can be determined as the balancing item in the sources and uses of funds statement, and the individual bank can estimate its share of the total market. This method is used primarily by large banks, since small banks usually do not have the trained personnel to engage in such sophisticated forecasting. In predicting deposit and loan levels, such banks rely heavily on past experience. Charts and tables showing monthly averages for several years or during the course of a business cycle are frequently used to give management an indication of expected loan and deposit fluctuations.

In forecasting bank liquidity needs, whether for a large or small bank, both local and national considerations must be taken into account. At the local level, the type, source, and stability of deposits are primary factors to consider. It is generally assumed that savings deposits are more stable than time deposits and time deposits fluctuate less than demand deposits. This is probably true for individual accounts but not necessarily true for the aggregate deposits of an individual bank. A demand deposit structure consisting of the deposits of many small- and medium-sized accounts generally is more stable than one made up of the accounts of a few business firms or large individual depositors, because the fluctuations of only a few business accounts are more likely to be correlated with each other.

Seasonal fluctuations in deposits and loans result largely from a lack of economic diversification in a bank's market area. Local economies that are heavily dependent on one or on a few industries that produce related commodities are not uncommon. Seasonal fluctuations are reflected in deposits and loans and must be recognized in planning liquidity reserves.

Although the majority of banks are primarily "small business firms" and operate in a local economy, they are influenced by factors that arise beyond their trade territory. For example, the effects of monetary and fiscal policies tend to be felt first in money-market centers, but sooner or later all banks are affected. No bank, no matter how small or remote, can escape the effects of restrictive monetary policy; consequently, the management of an individual bank must keep abreast of national developments. Monetary policy is likely to be restrictive during a period of economic expansion as demand for goods and services expands more rapidly than does productive capacity. To slow down the rate of expansion of the economy, Federal Reserve officials may act to restrict the growth rate of the money supply. When this occurs, the banking system, and thus individual banks within the system, will have limited excess reserves with which to make additional loans. Liquidity can be critical for a bank at such times. Loan demand is likely to be growing more rapidly than deposits. Interest rates may rise to unusually high levels. If a bank has sufficient liquidity to meet its loan demand, it can capitalize on the high interest rates available and thereby increase its profitability. If liquidity is low, a bank may have to turn down profitable loans or sell less liquid securities at a loss in order to accommodate its loan customers.

Theories of Bank Liquidity Management

Theories of liquidity management have existed since the early days of commercial banking. At present four separate theories can be identified: commercial loan, shiftability, anticipated income, and liability management. The first three theories are concerned with the management of assets and are discussed in this section. Liquidity through liability management will be discussed in Chapter 6.

The Commercial-Loan Theory

The commercial-loan theory was the outgrowth of English banking practices during the eighteenth century. Proponents of this theory maintain that a commercial bank's liquidity is assured as long as its assets are held in short-term loans that would be liquidated in the normal course of business; that is, banks should finance the movement of goods through the successive stages of production to consumption. Such loans today would be termed inventory or working-capital loans. Throughout much of our history it was considered inappropriate for banks to make loans for the purchase of securities, real estate, or consumer goods, or to make long-term agricultural loans.

The commercial-loan theory was the predominant banking theory in the United States from colonial times through the 1930s. For example, the rules of the Bank of New York in 1784 provided that discounts

> . . . will be due on Thursday in every week, and bills and notes bought for discount must be left at the bank on Wednesday morning, under a sealed cover, directed to William Seton, Cashier. The rate of discount is at present fixed at six percent *per annum;* but no discount will be made for longer than thirty days, nor will any note or bill be discounted to pay for a former one.[6]

The philosophy of this theory was embodied in early banking legislation, and its dominance is reflected in current Federal Reserve rules covering the rediscounting of notes for member banks. Commercial or agricultural paper that is eligible for discounting is required to be secured by staple agricul-

[6]Bray Hammond, *Banks and Politics in America from the Revolution to the Civil War,* p. 74. Copyright © 1957 by Princeton University Press; Princeton Paperback, 1967. Reprinted by permission of Princeton University Press.

tural products or other goods, wares, or merchandise—further, it must have a maturity at the time of discount of not more than 90 days, except that agricultural paper may have a maturity at the time of discount of 9 months or less.

While the commercial-loan theory was widely expounded by economists, regulatory authorities, and banks, it was followed rather loosely in practice. The theory's principal limitation was that it failed to take into account the credit needs of the nation's expanding economy. Rigid adherence to the theory prohibited banks from financing expansion of plant and equipment, home purchases, livestock acquisition, and land purchases. The failure of banks to meet these types of credit needs was an important factor in the development of competing financial institutions such as mutual savings banks, savings and loan associations, consumer finance companies, and credit unions.

This theory also failed to take into account the relative stability of bank deposits. Bank deposits *may* be withdrawn on demand, but all depositors are unlikely to remove their funds at the same time. This stability of deposits enables a bank to extend funds for a reasonably long period without becoming nonliquid. Further, the theory assumed that all loans would be liquidated in the normal course of business. During periods when economic activity is high, business firms have no difficulty meeting their obligations. However, in periods of economic depression or during money panics, the movement of goods from cash to inventory to sales to accounts receivable to cash is interrupted, and business finds it difficult, if not impossible, to liquidate bank credit.

The theory's final limitation is that the short-term self-liquidating commercial loan provides liquidity during normal economic circumstances, but may not do so during periods of economic recession when liquidity is most needed. During such times, inventories and accounts receivable tend to have lower turnover rates, and many business firms have difficulty paying their loans when due. Whereas individual banks might maintain liquidity by investing in self-liquidating loans, the banking system as a whole could be short of liquidity during hard times.

The Shiftability Theory

The shiftability theory is based on the proposition that a bank's liquidity is maintained if it holds assets that could be shifted or sold to other lenders or investors for cash. If loans are not repaid, the collateral from secured loans (marketable securities, for example) could be sold in the market for cash; if funds are needed, loans could be shifted to the central bank. Thus the individual commercial bank should be able to meet its liquidity needs, provided it always has assets to sell; similarly, the banking system would be liquid, provided that the central bank stands ready to purchase the assets offered for discount.

Highly marketable securities have long been considered an excellent source of liquidity. Such securities can easily be converted to cash and frequently are referred to as secondary reserves. To insure convertibility without delay and appreciable loss, assets of the secondary reserve must meet three requirements: high quality, short maturity, and marketability. They must be free of credit and money rate risk and be saleable in the market on short notice.

No definite rule exists regarding the maturity of assets held as liquid reserves, but a general one is, the shorter the maturity the better. A more realistic position is that they should be of such length that the effects of the money rate risk encountered in buying them would be relatively insignificant. Many bankers now think in terms of a maturity of one year or less before high-grade marketable securities are included in the secondary reserve. This rule of thumb could change, however, depending on money rates. If rates were stable or declining, longer maturities would be acceptable; if rates were subject to considerable fluctuations or rising, shorter maturities would be a necessity.

The requirements of quality and marketability may be met by a number of different types of securities. Treasury bills are the most common security held for the secondary reserve. In addition, banks hold other securities issued by the federal government and its agencies. Government bonds are eligible if the maturity date is close, since the money-rate risk becomes less as maturity shortens. Short-term securities of such agencies as the Farmer's Home Administration, Export-Import Bank, Federal Intermediate Credit Bank, Federal Home Loan Bank, and the Bank for Cooperatives are suitable also.

Some high-grade short-term securities from the private sector are eligible for the secondary reserve, too. Included in this category are bankers' acceptances and open-market commercial paper. A bankers' acceptance is a draft that has been accepted by a bank for payment at a later date, usually 180 days or less. The use of this instrument arises primarily from the financing of international trade, although it may arise from financing the movement and storage of goods in domestic trade. Bankers' acceptances are traded in a fairly active market, and are eligible for discount at the Federal Reserve banks.

Open-market commercial paper is often purchased by commercial banks for their secondary reserve portfolios. Such paper consists of promissory notes issued by corporations for relatively short periods, usually not exceeding four to six months. To borrow in this market, a corporation must have a very high credit rating. Notes usually are issued in large denominations that are payable to the issuer and endorsed without qualification. In this manner they become *bearer instruments* and pass freely from hand to hand without further endorsetment. Commercial paper often is held by a bank until maturity, although dealers may repurchase it under prior agreement. Commercial paper may be rediscounted at a Federal Reserve bank, provided it is within 90 days of maturity and is otherwise eligible for discount.

Although the shiftability theory has some validity, adherence to its provisions did not prevent hundreds of banks from encountering liquidity problems in the 1920s and 1930s. Some banks placed great reliance for liquidity on *call loans* collateralized by securities on the grounds that they could be called within a 24-hour period. Unfortunately, when the market price of securities fell, banks found that these loans could only be liquidated at a loss. Since the loans were not eligible for discounting at the Federal Reserve banks, no additional reserves were made available by the central bank. As previously mentioned, Federal Reserve rules of eligibility were based primarily on the commercial-loan theory, and as long as banks held short-term self-liquidating commercial loans, they could be assured of receiving credit at the Federal Reserve. However, the growth of American business required banks to extend longer-term credit and for purposes not recognized by the eligibility rules. Despite the unfortunate experience of the 30s the shiftability theory, has attracted many adherents. In recent years the emphasis has been on holding highly marketable U.S. government securities to meet liquidity needs.

The Anticipated-Income Theory

The anticipated-income theory of commercial banking holds that a bank's liquidity can be planned if scheduled loan payments are based on the future income of the borrower. This theory does not deny the applicability of the commercial loan and shiftability theories. It emphasizes instead the desirability of relating loan repayment to income rather than relying heavily on collateral. Also, it holds that a bank's liquidity can be influenced by the maturity pattern of the loan and investment portfolios. Short-term business loans would have more liquidity than would term loans, and consumer instalment loans would have more liquidity than would those secured by residential real estate.

The theory recognizes the development and rapid growth of certain types of loans that now constitute a major portion of the portfolios of commercial banks: business term loans, consumer instalment loans, and residential real estate loans. These have one thing in common that adds to their liquidity, namely, the fact that they can be amortized. A portfolio having many loans with regular monthly or quarterly payments of principal and interest has liquidity because of the regular cash flow month in and month out that can be anticipated. When liquidity is needed, the cash can be used. Otherwise it may be reinvested for future liquidity.

The anticipated-income theory has encouraged many commercial bankers to adopt a *ladder effect* in the investment portfolio; this means a staggering of maturities so that redemptions will occur on a regular and predictable basis. The securities portfolio thus takes on the cash flow characteristics of a loan portfolio with regular amortization of principal and interest.

The Liability-Management Theory

Advocates of the liability-management theory of liquidity maintain that banks can meet liquidity requirements by bidding in the market for additional funds. This approach originally found its strongest advocates in the large money-market banks but soon spread throughout the nation. It has its roots in the rejuvenation of the federal funds market in the 1950s, and the later development of the negotiable time certificate of deposit as a major money-market instrument. Banks also rely for liquidity on borrowing at the Federal Reserve banks, in the Eurodollar market, or from a parent bank holding company. Liability management for liquidity will be discussed in more detail in the next chapter.

Management of Liquidity Position

Those in charge of managing a bank's liquidity position probably are not conscious of following any one liquidity theory. From a practical viewpoint, all theories are employed to some degree, with some bankers emphasizing one and some another.

It is possible to distinguish two distinct policies followed by banks in managing their reserve position. At one extreme is the policy of close supervision of reserves to assure that no nonearning funds, or virtually no funds, are held in excess of the requirement. At the other extreme is the policy of maintaining reserves sufficiently large at all times to meet the reserve requirement when deposits are at their peak. The majority of banks probably fall within these extremes. All large banks find it profitable to manage their money position closely, and small banks are becoming more aware of the contribution that cash management can make to overall profitability.

The first task in planning for the liquidity needs of a bank is to manage the money position, that is, to comply with the legal reserve requirements and have a sufficient amount of coin and currency on hand to meet customer demands. The holding of cash balances is affected constantly during banking hours as numerous transactions cause a flow of payments into and out of the bank. This task is as important as it is difficult. Cash yields no income; consequently, the objective of bank management is to hold it to a minimum.

In the management of the money position, many computations and reports are required by regulatory authorities. Nonmember banks must report their reserve data to their respective regulatory agencies at the state level, and member banks to the Federal Reserve banks. Member banks are required to compute reserves weekly, beginning Thursday, on the basis of average deposit balances. In computing legal reserves, demand deposits are adjusted so that cash items in the process of collection and demand balances due from other banks are subtracted from total demand deposits. Time deposits require no adjustment. To aid the manager of the money position, the Federal Reserve bank informs him of the average reserves the bank must carry during the coming week. This information is based on the second previous week's experience. Since day-to-day cash flow estimates cannot be absolutely accurate, an excess or deficiency in reserve requirements averaging up to 2 percent of the required reserve may be carried forward to the next reserve week. Although this leeway may make the task of managing the reserve account less difficult, it still is not an easy one, especially when a bank is attempting to keep the reserve at a minimum. This is the reason banks frequently miss their target and are forced to borrow to correct their reserve position. Unless additional reserves are needed for a relatively long period, banks often prefer to make adjustments through the federal funds market or by borrowing from the Federal Reserve, even though the cost may be greater. This is due partly to the cost involved in frequent trading of securities and the reluctance of management to disturb the maturity structure of the portfolio.

An example of how a large bank might meet its liquidity requirements is presented in Table 5–3. Sources and uses of funds are shown for four time periods. These periods may be for a day, a week, a month, or even longer. The funds in our example are needed for increasing security holdings, meeting loan demands, and caring for a decline in deposits, (listed as a minus entry under "sources of funds"). Note that demand deposits declined in the first and fourth periods, and CDs declined in every period but the second. Other time deposits were relatively stable, with the exception of the second period when there was definite disintermediation.

Our hypothetical bank used several liquidity-management techniques sometime during the four periods. It borrowed from the Federal Reserve bank in two periods, then substantially entered the Eurodollar market in the third and fourth periods. It was in the federal funds market every period. Some securities matured during the first period and some were sold from the secondary reserve in the first and fourth periods. A final method used was the sale of securities to a nonbank investor under agreement to repur-

Table 5-3

Example of Liquidity Management by a Hypothetical Commercial Bank
(in thousands of dollars)

	Periods			
	1	*2*	*3*	*4*
Uses of Funds				
U.S. government securities	—	1,000	600	300
Other securities	1,000	400	1,600	1,300
Loans	1,500	2,600	3,500	2,700
Total	2,500	4,000	5,700	4,300
Sources of Funds				
Demand deposits	−700	1,300	1,000	−1,200
Certificates of deposit	−2,500	200	−1,400	−500
Other time deposits	1,100	700	1,600	1,200
Borrowing from F.R. bank	500	1,100	—	—
Federal funds purchased	2,100	700	1,500	1,700
Eurodollars purchased	—	—	2,000	2,100
Maturity of securities	1,000	—	—	—
Sale of securities	1,000	—	—	1,000
Sale and repurchase of securities	—	—	1,000	—
Total	2,500	4,000	5,700	4,300

chase for a stated length of time and at a predetermined price or yield. This might have been a large corporate customer with excess funds to invest, a government securities dealer, or a local public body with excess funds derived from a bond issue or tax collections. Although our example is unrealistic in that all these methods would not be used by a bank in a relatively short time and no consideration was given to costs, it does give us an idea of how they might be used in liquidity management. This illustration has concentrated on management of liquidity as it relates to the loan and investment portfolio and to the deposits and other liabilities of a commercial bank. In addition, the manager of the liquidity position must consider funds provided from operations as well as from dividends and capital investments. It is appropriate to prepare a complete cash budget, including all expected cash receipts and an estimate of all cash payments that will be required.

Questions

1. How does the asset structure of a commercial bank differ from that of a manufacturing corporation? What are the reasons for the differences?

2. How would you define and quantify the risk associated with investments in loans and securities? What is an appropriate tradeoff between risk and profitability for a commercial bank?

3. Describe the principal differences between the nature of legal reserves for member banks and those of nonmember banks. All other things being equal except legal reserve requirements, which classification of bank would be more profitable?

4. From which category of earning assets do banks derive most of their profits? Where does that category rank with regard to liquidity? Why?

5. Describe the pool-of-funds approach to bank asset management. What problems do you see in its use?

6. Differentiate between primary and secondary reserves.

7. What are the strengths and weaknesses of the asset–allocation model for asset management?

8. For the linear programming example given in the text, formulate the constraint to reflect the requirements for legal reserves of member banks. Add two variables to the Model: x_7 to represent vault cash and deposits with the Fed and x_8 to represent demand deposits. Assume that the bank has no time deposits. Formulate another constraint to limit the total investment in x_1 through x_7 to the total deposit funds available.

9. How does the rather strict definition of bank asset liquidity given in the text differ from a somewhat looser definition that might be used, say, by the New York Stock Exchange?

10. How would you determine the degree of liquidity of a particular commercial bank from its statement of condition? What factors might be overlooked with a ratio analysis?

11. What aspects of federal monetary policy are likely to affect bank liquidity late in a period of economic expansion? How would liquidity likely be affected?

12. How would liquidity requirements be likely to differ for a bank located in a city dependent on summer tourists as compared with a bank located in a city with diversified manufacturing for an economic base?

13. Compare and contrast the commercial-loan theory of liquidity management with the shiftability theory.

14. Using the anticipated-income theory of liquidity management, show how liquidity is dependent upon regular amortization of loans.

15. Obtain the annual report of a local bank. From its statement of condition for the last two years, prepare a statement of sources and uses of funds. Comment on apparent changes in the liquidity position of the bank.

SELECTED REFERENCES

COHEN, KALMAN J. and STEN THORE, "Programming Bank Portfolios Under Uncertainty," *Journal of Bank Research,* Spring 1970, pp. 42–61.

COOK, TIMOTHY Q. ed., *Instruments of the Money Market,* Federal Reserve Bank of Richmond, 1977.

CRAMER, ROBERT H., and JAMES A. SEIFERT, "Measuring the Impact of Maturity on Expected Return and Risk," *Journal of Bank Research*, Autumn 1976, pp. 229–235.

CROSSE, HOWARD and GEORGE A. HEMPEL, *Management Policies for Commercial Banks,* Englewood Cliffs, N.J., Prentice-Hall, Inc., 1973.

FORTSON, JAMES C. and ROBERT R. DINCE, "An Application of Goal Programming to Management of a Country Bank," *Journal of Bank Research*, Winter 1977, pp. 311–319.

GOLDBERG, LAWRENCE G. and JOHN T. ROSE, "Do State Reserve Requirements Matter?" *Journal of Bank Research*, Spring 1977, pp. 31–39.

GUP, BENTON E. "Risk Management of Commercial Bank Portfolios," *Journal of Contemporary Business*, University of Washington, Summer, 1977, pp. 15–29.

HEMPEL, GEORGE H., and JESS B. YAWITZ, *Financial Management of Financial Institutions,* Englewood Cliffs, N.J., Prentice-Hall, Inc., 1977, Ch. 5, pp. 82–123.

JOHNSON, HARRY L., "Deposits, Reserves, and Bank Earnings," *The Bankers Magazine,* Spring 1968.

ROUSSAKIS, EMMANUEL N., *Managing Commercial Bank Funds.* New York, Praeger Publishers, 1977. Chs. 2 and 3, pp. 50–94.

SEALY, CALVIN W. JR., "Commercial Bank Portfolio Management with Multiple Objectives," *Journal of Commercial Bank Lending,* February 1977, pp. 39–48.

WOODWORTH, G. WALTER "Theories of Cyclical Liquidity Management of Commercial Banks," *National Banking Review,* June 1967.

6

Liability Management

Commercial banks utilize a high degree of financial leverage with borrowed funds supplying about 93 percent of total assets. The use of relatively low-cost borrowed funds, including deposits, enables slim profit margins to be magnified to provide a reasonable return to the shareholders. Deposits are the chief source of borrowed funds, accounting for about 86 percent of all commercial bank liabilities. Other sources of funds include federal funds purchased from other banks, securities sold under agreements to repurchase, bankers' acceptances outstanding, Eurodollar borrowings, and capital notes.

In a broad sense, liability management consists of the activities involved in obtaining funds from depositors and other creditors and determining the appropriate mix of funds for a particular bank. In a narrower sense, liability management has come to be known as the activities involved in supplementing liquidity needs by actively seeking borrowed funds when needed. The ability to sell certificates of deposit and to borrow Eurodollars or federal funds enables a bank to rely less on low-earning secondary reserve assets for liquidity, which may enhance the earning power of a bank. These activities are not without risk. Liability management requires consideration of the extra risk as well as the difference between the cost of obtaining funds and the return that can be earned when the funds are invested in loans or securities. Thus the relationship between asset management and liability management is a critical determinant of a bank's profitability.

Commercial banks are in the business of borrowing money (mostly from depositors) and lending or investing it at higher rates. This is the business of a financial intermediary, acting as a go-between for those who have funds to save and those who need funds. The activities of lending money to those of high credit standing and investing in high quality securities result in relatively low profit margins when compared with those of nonfinancial corporations (See Chapter 8). This necessitates using a high degree of financial leverage to magnify the profits for shareholders. In the United States capital stock and retained earnings provide only about 7 percent of total bank funds. Commercial bank deposits and short-term borrowings are discussed in this chapter, together with their relationship to asset management. The management of capital funds, including long-term debt, is reserved for Chapter 7.

Many kinds of depositors—individuals, business firms, non profit organizations, governments, and political subdivisions—are willing to carry deposits with commercial banks for a variety of reasons. Banks provide safety —more safety than a mattress or a cooky jar. Practically all banks are insured by the Federal Deposit Insurance Corporation, an agency of the federal government, which provides $40,000 in insurance for each account. Demand deposits serve as a medium of exchange, and deposits carried in the form of savings or time deposits provide a return. Many depositors place a value on liquidity, or the availability of funds, and this is provided by commercial bank deposits, especially when they are in the form of demand deposits.

Demand Deposits

From the standpoint of withdrawal, deposits may be classified as demand and time. Demand deposits may be withdrawn by the depositor or transferred to someone else at any time, without previous notice to the bank. They are maintained by depositors who need a liquid balance, and account for about 38 percent of total bank deposits. Demand deposits withdrawn by checks account for about 74 percent of our money supply (M_1 currency and demand deposits), and it is commonly estimated that 90 percent of our exchange transactions are effected by the use of checks.

The reason for the popularity of checks is obvious. They are an economical and safe method of transferring a sizeable amount of money, from the standpoint of transportation costs and the possibility of loss from robbery. When checks are used, the transfer is made through the clearing of checks by banks without either party, the payer or payee, giving the matter much thought. The drawer of the check worries little, even about forgery, since the bank is at fault in the event a forged check is paid. Check money also has another advantage in that cancelled checks returned to the depositor

Table 6–1
Gross Demand Deposits of Individuals, Partnerships, and Corporations,
All Insured Commercial Banks (September 1978)

Holder	Billions of Dollars	Percent Distribution
Financial business	25.1	9.3
Nonfinancial business	142.5	52.0
Consumer	95.0	34.1
Foreign	2.5	0.9
Other IPC	13.1	4.7
Total	278.8	100.0

Source: Board of Governors of the Federal Reserve System, *Federal Reserve Bulletin*, November 1978, p. A25.

serve as receipts for payments made. Even though the depositor may lose or destroy his cancelled checks, he can in most cases be furnished with a copy. A majority of banks microfilm all checks paid and keep the film for an indefinite period. Gross demand deposits of individuals, partnerships, and corporations as of September 1978 are presented in Table 6–1. Slightly more than half of these deposits were held by nonfinancial business and a third by consumers.

Time Deposits

Time deposits, as the term implies, are deposited with banks for a certain period of time. For a deposit to have time status, which permits banks to pay interest to depositors and carry a smaller reserve than is permitted in most instances on demand deposits, it must be left with the bank for a definite period of time and/or notice of withdrawal must be a part of the contract that exists between the holder and the bank. Notice of withdrawal, usually 30 days, is normally waived, especially on savings accounts. Time deposits cannot be withdrawn by check but must be converted into currency or demand deposits. Automatic transfer services (described below) make possible the transfer of funds from savings accounts to checking accounts in order to cover an overdraft or to maintain a minimum balance in a checking account.

Savings Deposits

Time deposits may take several forms. The most common type is a savings deposit, which is referred to as a *regular* or *passbook* savings account. This type of account is evidenced by a passbook containing the rules governing the account. The passbook contains all transactions relative to the account and must usually be presented to the teller when the owner makes a deposit or withdrawal. One of the objectives of a savings account is the promotion of thrift. Regular savings deposits are most widely held by individuals and nonprofit institutions. Other corporate or institutional accounts are limited to a maximum of $150,000. Savings deposits, the largest component of time deposits, account for about 40 percent of total time deposits.

Certificates of Deposit

Another form of time deposit is the time certificate of deposit, evidenced by a formal negotiable or nonnegotiable receipt issued for funds left with the bank for a specified period of time. These deposits are payable only on surrender of the properly endorsed receipt. They are carried on the general ledger of the bank under the heading of "time certificates of deposit" rather than on the individual ledger under the name of the person to whom the certificate was issued, as regular savings accounts are carried. These deposits are usually referred to as *CDs*. Certificates of deposit may be purchased any time, and the funds start bearing interest on the date of purchase.

A wide variety of types of CDs is common among commercial banks. Maturities may range from 30 days to more than eight years. Minimum balances may range from $500 to $100,000. Rates of interest may vary according to size of deposit and maturity date. Most types are non-negotiable and thus can be converted to cash only by redeeming them at the issuing bank. Funds may be withdrawn prior to maturity only by incurring a penalty for early withdrawal. The penalty consists of forfeiting three months' interest and a reduction of interest for the balance of time held to the rate for passbook savings accounts.

Special types of CDs have been developed to meet the competition for deposit funds. For example, *negotiable certificates of deposit* in large denominations are issued by many large banks. Security dealers make a secondary market for these certificates, and thus banks are able to attract funds from large investors that otherwise might place their funds in Treasury bills or other money market instruments. These negotiable CDs are generally sold to corporations, pension funds, and government bodies in $100,000 to $1 million denominations. They are generally short-term instruments with maturities of one year or less. On average, three-month certificates yield returns 30 to 40 basis points above the bond yield equivalent on three-month Treasury bills. The CDs are negotiable instruments, being issued in bearer form, and may be traded in secondary markets before maturity. At the end of 1978 outstanding negotiable CDs issued by large commercial banks approximated $100 billion, compared to about $1 billion outstanding in 1961. The acceptance of this money market instrument by corporations has been phenomenal.

Banks also seek to attract smaller investors with short-term *money market certificates.* First offered in 1978, these are non-negotiable CDs with minimum balances of $10,000 and maturities of six months. Banks may pay rates as high as the average yield (calculated on a discount basis) of the most recent auction of six-month Treasury bills. Particularly when money-market rates are higher than those available on other types of CDs, this instrument can be directly competitive with Treasury bills even to the smaller investor.

A form of deposit known as a *savings certificate* is similar to a certificate of deposit in that it is issued for a definite period, usually three years. Since savings certificates are long coming to maturity, they usually bear a relatively high rate of interest. They were designed to attract the intermediate investor who would like to have a higher rate of interest than is paid on a regular savings account but who is not interested in a bond of five to ten years' maturity.

Banks also have some minor time deposit plans, including Christmas club, vacation, tax, and other so-called savings clubs. These are offered to encourage savers to deposit in the savings department a stated sum each week that will within a stated period be a large enough amount to enable the depositor to pay his Christmas or vacation bills. Banks find these savings programs desirable because they increase deposits and stimulate thrift on the part of the savers. Many people possibly would not save if banking programs of this type were not provided.

Distribution of Time and Savings Deposits

Table 6–2 presents the distribution of time and savings deposits by type and ownership. Note that "other time deposits" (primarily certificates of deposit and savings certificates) accounted for nearly half of total time deposits on

Table 6–2
Distribution of Time and Savings Deposits of Insured Commercial Banks
March 31, 1978 (amounts in billions)

	Amount	*Percent*
Total individual, partnerships, and corporations	$486.6	86.1
Savings	219.4	38.8
Other time and savings deposits	267.2	47.3
Banks and governments	78.7	13.9
United States government	0.9	0.2
States and subdivisions	61.0	10.8
Banks in the United States	6.8	1.2
Banks in foreign countries	1.4	0.2
Foreign governments, central banks	8.5	1.5
Total	$565.2	100.0

Source: *Federal Reserve Bulletin*, November 1978. Figures may not add to totals because of rounding.

March 31, 1978. This latter form of deposit has become popular because of relatively high rates that have been paid in recent years and the liquidity such an investment provides. Savings deposits, owned for the most part by individuals, make up another large category. Individuals save at commercial banks for many reasons, principally convenience and safety. Savers may also have a checking account, a safe-deposit box, a personal loan, or make use of the facilities of the trust department of a commercial bank. They feel secure that their deposits are insured by the Federal Deposit Insurance Corporation. Further, many savers, especially small ones, are interested in the stability of the dollar value of their savings in commercial banks rather than investing in securities such as stocks and bonds whose current market value may vary with the market rate of interest and be influenced by other factors.

The Level of Bank Deposits

A distinction must be made between the deposits of the commercial banking system and the deposits of individual banks. This distinction is necessary because individual banks cannot control the level of deposits of the nation although they are able to influence to a limited extent the amount of deposits they hold.

Level of Deposits of the Commercial Banking System

Students who have completed a course in basic economics were introduced to deposit expansion and contraction and the influence of the Federal Reserve System and Treasury Department monetary powers on the level of deposits in the commercial banking system. Since we are concerned here with the operation of individual banks rather than with the commercial banking system, this subject will not be discussed in detail. However, this does not mean that it is unimportant.

In the commercial banking system the level of deposits depends primarily on the amount of credit extended by banks in the form of loans and investments. If banks did not engage in lending and investing, they would have deposits equal only to the amount of currency left with them by depositors. They would be completely liquid, for the most part, and their earnings would reflect income only from their charges for performing various services. Banks are profit-seeking enterprises, however, and attempt to loan and invest prudently as much as possible of the funds they receive from shareholders and depositors to increase operating earnings. Individual banks are normally in a position to lend or invest amounts equal to the amount of their excess funds, or what are commonly referred to as *excess reserves*.

The term excess funds or reserves as used here includes the amount of funds that are in excess of legal reserve requirements and whatever additional funds are considered necessary for liquidity purposes by commercial bankers to support the liabilities. For example, if deposits of a commercial bank are $100,000 and the reserves (including legal and liquidity reserves) necessary to back up the deposits are $25,000, the bank would be in a position to lend its excess funds of $75,000. If this were done and the $75,000 withdrawn from the lending bank and deposited in another, this second bank could in turn follow the same procedure (assuming the same reserve requirements) and lend or invest 75 percent of the newly acquired deposit, or $56,250 . As these deposits were withdrawn by check and deposited in other banks, these banks in turn could do the same and the process could be repeated numerous times.

Deposit expansion of the banking system can be done only with the cooperation of all banks and a willingness on the part of monetary and fiscal authorities to permit such expansion by making additional reserves available. Individual banks may lure deposits away from other banks, but the total in the banking system will remain the same. Excess reserve creation is an exclusive function of the Federal Reserve System. Reserves can be increased or decreased, and hence so can deposits, by the use of open market operations, varying reserve requirements, and supervision of the discount or borrowing function. The Federal Reserve System is continually employing these basic monetary powers to attain broad economic goals such as the promotion of economic growth, a high level of employment, and stable prices. In the attainment of these goals, the central bank influences the level of deposits of the banking system since, in a very real sense, banks serve as the conduit through which monetary policy is transmitted to the economy.

Level of Deposits of Individual Banks

Although individual banks do not have absolute control over the level of their deposits, they are in a position to influence the amount they hold. Since deposits are so important to their profitable operation, banks compete aggressively for them. Bankers burn the midnight oil thinking of ways to increase them, and advertising agencies are employed to make a bank's services more appealing to prospective customers. Progressive banks undertake sophisticated market research to identify factors that are important to their particular situation. While the monetary and fiscal policies of government are major factors that determine the level of deposits in the banking system, economic and personal factors are important to individual banks.

Physical Features and Personnel. In general, people like to do business with a firm that has attractive quarters and is staffed by personable employees. Many banks have recognized these qualities and have made improvements in these areas. The hard marble benches and nondescript terrazo floors have been replaced by comfortable chairs and divans and carpets more in keeping with the draped windows and beautiful walls. Bank personnel are encouraged to be friendly and efficient in the performance of their tasks.

Services Offered by Banks. Banks that offer better and more diversified services usually have an advantage over those whose services are limited. Shortage of downtown parking places those banks with ample parking facilities in an advantageous position. The same may be said for those that have drive-in-teller windows, bank-by-mail, automated payment systems, and improved, time-saving deposit services.

Some customers are attracted to banks that have specialized loan departments, a convenient safe-deposit box department, an accurate bookkeeping department, or a trust department that has an outstanding reputation. Business firms may select a bank because of its after-hour depository service, its foreign department, and its correspondent bank relations, especially if the firm has need of loans in excess of the bank's lending limit or has business dealings in cities throughout the nation and abroad. Farmers may be attracted to a bank that has an outstanding farm representative trained in agriculture and willing to advise farmers who have production, marketing, or financial problems.

Fundamental Policies and Strength of a Bank. Bank policies regarding loans, investments, and other matters provide an important yardstick by which outsiders can judge the competence and capacity of the management. A bank that has gone through a "money crunch" or other economic crises either nationally or locally has the advantage of experience, and this is important to many depositors. A well-disciplined and stable organization indicates to the public that banking transactions will be handled correctly and soundly. Confidence in banks lessens the possibility of "runs." This trust is a reflection of the depositors' faith in the bank management. The presence of outstanding persons of the community on the board of directors, capable officers and employees of the bank, a record of fair dealing, sound investment and loan portfolios, and a strong capital structure are reflections of good bank management.

The loan policies of one bank may be more appealing to people than those of another. A bank may enjoy increased deposits because of the instalment loan, credit card, personal line of credit, real estate, or commercial loan departments. Interest rates on loans are also important to those who borrow. Some instances probably occur where one bank would permit a person to borrow on an open basis but another would insist upon security. If such is the case, borrowers would probably favor the former and carry their deposit there. Some banks specialize in certain types of loans, and people are often drawn to them because of their expertise or specialty. Banks that have a reputation of caring for their borrowing customers who need credit often are selected over those that are reluctant to lend to steady customers in periods of economic stress.

Level of Economic Activity. Deposits grow more rapidly during the prosperity phase of the business cycle than in periods of recession and depression. During periods of prosperity, business firms build up the level of deposits to support a higher level of sales and economic activity. Local communities and areas compete with each other. In recent years, economic activity in the country has undergone several shifts. The Southwest, Southeast, and West have grown more rapidly in personal income and populations than other areas of the nation. A change in demand for certain products of a community leads to price increases and thus to increased deposits. An increase in crude oil prices means an increase in deposits in those banks located in the oil-producing areas. Banks in a section of the country producing lumber or wood products gain in deposits from an increase in the prices of forest products. This fact, of course, applies to all commodities produced, whether cotton or cars. Conversely, a decline in the price of locally produced commodities results in a decline in bank deposits.

Location. Because of the shift in population and the increase in traffic, location has become a force influencing the ability of banks to attract deposits. Research has shown that while business borrowers may be inclined to travel great distances to consummate a loan, consumers are less inclined to do so. The individual who needs an instalment loan for the purchase of a car or a television is not inclined to fight the traffic when there is an alternative. Nonborrowing customers are even more influenced by location when selecting a bank. To the average household depositor, banks are very much alike. Virtually all banks provide depositors with monthly statements and insure their deposits. Obviously, differences exist between banks, but when there is great similarity, accessibility becomes more important to bank customers.

Commercial banks realize that location is important and that those with excellent locations are in a better position to attract depositors. This is the major reason many banks favor branch banking. Most banks with branches have departments that are responsible for studying population movements and deposit and loan potential throughout their trade territory in order to select the most profitable location for new branches. A prestigious address long-valued in the city center loses some of its glitter as the population moves to the suburbs. In unit banking states, those in the financial district are forced to remain there, but new banks are being organized in outlying areas with several objectives in mind, one of which is to attract deposits.

Momentum of an Early Start. A Bank does not differ much from any other business that enjoys a dominant position in an industry because of the momentum of an early start. Although it is not always true, an old established bank sometimes has an advantage over the newer banks. This is especially true in localities where there has not been a rapid increase in business activity and deposits. In these areas, son and daughter have a tendency to conduct their banking business where father and mother carried their account. They have been influenced by the various favors that were extended to the parents when they were just getting started. The same thing applies to local business firms. Junior executives are trained to patronize the old established bank that extended the first loans to the struggling business. Once such ties are established they are difficult to break.

Growth of Deposits

In general, the growth of bank deposits has been upward, with the exception of the recession in the early 1920s and the depression of the 1930s. The upward trend, however, has not been uniform. Growth was relatively slow during the 1950s, as compared to the 1960s and 1970s. Monetary and fiscal policies were more restrictive in the earlier period, and such government policies are very important to the direction and level of bank deposits. The past two decades were also characterized by a relatively rapid expansion in the gross national product, which contributed to rising personal and business incomes. In the 1960s and 1970s regulations were liberalized regarding maximum interest rates that could be paid on time and savings deposits.

The Shift in Deposit Mix

Time deposits have increased more rapidly than have demand deposits, thus altering the composition of commercial bank deposits. In 1950 demand deposits accounted for 74 percent of total deposits and time deposits 26 percent, while in 1978 these percentages were 38 and 62 percent, respectively (see Table 6–3). Rising interest rates and the liberalization of the ceilings applicable to time deposits account for this development.

As interest rates rose during the 1960s bank depositors became more interest-conscious and turned to time deposits as a means of increasing income; consequently, time deposits increased at a more rapid rate than did demand deposits. Corporate treasurers began to manage their demand balances more efficiently and invest their excess funds in short-term financial assets. These assets included commercial paper, U.S. government trea-

Table 6–3
Relative Importance of Commercial Bank Demand and Time Deposits

	Total	Demand	Time
1950	100	74	26
1955	100	72	28
1960	100	65	35
1965	100	52	48
1970	100	48	52
1975	100	41	59
1976	100	40	60
1977	100	41	59
1978	100	38	62

Source: Board of Governors of the Federal Reserve System, *Federal Reserve Bulletins.*

sury bills, bank CDs, and, in some instances, Eurodollar balances abroad. Business concerns with several locations throughout the nation employed lock boxes to collect funds more quickly and consolidate them in central locations. Compensating balances, or minimum amounts of funds required to be maintained in checking accounts under many loan agreements, were more closely scrutinized in an effort to reduce the amount of idle funds. Increasingly, individuals have followed the lead of corporate treasurers in an attempt to hold down their demand balances. Deposits have been shifted from checking accounts to savings accounts to obtain higher interest income from deposits. Individuals have also expanded their credit facilities to help synchronize money receipts and payments and, in so doing, reduce their demand balances. Many consumers use a bank card to pay for goods and services and, at the end of the month or billing cycle, write one check to cover the month's outlays. Under such an arrangement funds can be invested in a savings account or in some other earning asset. The widespread use of hospital and medical insurance, unemployment insurance, and the like also reduce the need to maintain higher checking balances to meet emergencies. Hence the precautionary motive for holding cash balances has been reduced. Such developments have contributed to a slow growth in demand deposits of commercial banks.

Competition for Deposits

Banks have encountered strong competition for savings and time deposits in recent years. While commercial banks are in competition with all forms of investment alternatives, the strongest competition is from thrift institutions—savings and loan associations, mutual savings banks, and credit unions. These groups offer services comparable to savings accounts and a wide array of savings certificates. Figure 6–1 presents the growth of savings accounts in commercial banks and the major thrift institutions since 1955.

Billions of Dollars

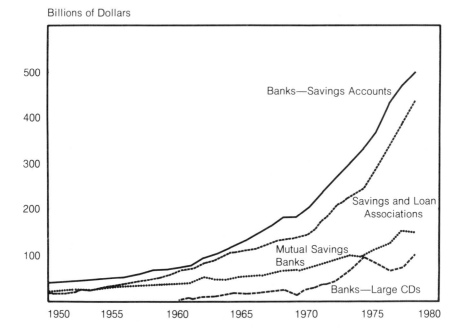

Fig. 6-1 Growth in Time and Savings Deposits at Commercial Banks, Savings and Loan Associations, and Mutual Savings Banks. (Source: Board of Governors of the Federal Reserve System, *Flow of Funds Accounts 1945–1971; Federal Reserve Bulletins.*)

Savings and loan associations have experienced a higher growth rate in savings than have commercial banks except for the decade of the 1960s. Since 1970, savings and loan growth has averaged nearly 15 percent per year compared to a little more than 12 percent annually for commercial bank savings. Although the rate of growth at mutual savings banks has accelerated since the early 1960s, it has lagged behind the growth of deposits at both commercial banks and savings and loan associations. Credit unions are not as large as banks and the other thrift institutions, but they have proved to be strong competitors. For example, in 1950 credit union deposits were less than one billion dollars but by 1960 they had increased to nearly $5 billion and by 1978 exceeded $52 billion.

Although many factors have contributed to the strong competition for savings and time deposits, the major one has been the rate paid on savings accounts. For many years banks did not actively seek time deposits as intensely as did savings and loan associations and credit unions. For example, the average rate paid on savings accounts by all insured commercial banks in 1950, was only 0.9 percent compared to a rate of 2.5 percent for savings and loan associations. This was a spread of 1.6 percent. Over the years, however, banks became much more competitive, and the spread narrowed considerably so that by 1965 it had dwindled to 0.54; by 1973 banks were paying 0.15 percent more on savings and time deposits than did savings and loan associations.[1]

For many years the banking industry had a monopoly on demand deposits, that is, they were the only financial institutions that were permitted to enter into an agreement with customers to make deposits available on demand. Although most demand deposits are presently held by commercial banks, the acceptance of deposits on demand is no longer their exclusive privilege. Since 1976 savings and loan associations, mutual savings banks, and commercial banks in the New England states have been authorized to have a new type of account known as a negotiable order of withdrawal—commonly referred to as a *NOW account*—which in effect allows the depositor to initiate a withdrawal form that can be negotiated in the same manner as a regular bank check. It also permits the payment of interest on such an account, which is for all practical purposes a demand deposit.

Additional competition for deposits has arisen from authorization in several states for mutual savings banks to offer demand deposits and from authorization of credit unions in most states to offer a new type of service called *share draft accounts.* The share draft account is similar to a NOW account, and enables credit union shareholders to write drafts on their interest-bearing savings accounts. In 1976 it was reported that "all but 15 of the nation's 470 mutual savings banks have either NOW accounts, traditional checking accounts, or a combination of the two. . . . Share drafts are now available at more than 940 credit unions in 46 states."[2]

Automatic transfer services (ATS), first authorized and introduced in 1978, placed commercial banks on a similar footing with savings institutions offering NOW accounts and other third-party payment services. ATS permits automatic transfers of funds from the savings accounts of individual customers to their checking accounts in order to cover overdrafts or to maintain a minimum balance in a checking account. ATS accounts permit customers to earn interest on funds that otherwise might be carried in checking accounts. Most such plans involve service charges (monthly maintenance fees and transactions costs) that offset part or all of the interest earnings unless

[1]United States League of Savings Associations, *'74 Savings & Loan Fact Book,* Chicago, 1974, p. 17.

[2]Jean M. Lovati, "The Growing Similarity Among Financial Institutions," Federal Reserve Bank of St. Louis *Review,* October 1977, pp. 7–8.

relatively large minimum balances (ranging from $300 to $5,000) are maintained in the savings account.[3]

Recent developments to increase competition for deposits by expanding the ability of thrift institutions to offer third-party payment services follow, in part, recommendations that were made by the Hunt Commission in 1971. The commission's recommendations included provision for third-party payment services for mutual savings banks, savings and loan associations, and credit unions, as well as permitting thrift institutions to offer a wider variety of time and savings deposits and certificates.[4] At the same time, they recommended that thrift institutions be put on an equal basis with regard to "taxation, ceilings on interest rates for time deposits, reserve requirements, and regulatory supervision."[5] Several factors contributed to the commission's recommendations. It pointed out, for example, that greater flexibility was needed to improve the allocation of resources to meet the nation's economic and social needs. It was also concerned with the future of thrift institutions when it said that,

> Without changes in their operations, there is serious question about the ability of deposit thrift institutions to survive. The power of the rate ceilings to isolate deposit markets from the rest of the short-term money market has eroded with continued reliance on this regulation. In time, they will probably have little effectiveness. Thus the major deterrent to losses of income and liquidity and the possible failure of thrift institutions during past periods of rising interest rates will not provide the same protection in the future.[6]

From our past experience with presidential commissions, we know that their recommendations are implemented slowly, sometimes reluctantly, and in some instances never. It is too early to predict the fate of the Hunt Commission recommendations, but some forces are at work that will contribute to the adoption of some of them. The concept of equality in competition is certainly a force contributing to the adoption of some of the recommendations, as is the idea that monetary policy might be improved if all thrift institutions are required to maintain the same or similar reserve

---

[3]Although ATS was outlawed by the U.S. Court of Appeals in 1979, banks were permitted to maintain such accounts until January 1, 1980. Since the Court implied that the authorization of such accounts was a responsibility of the Congress rather than a bank regulatory body, we may see renewed interest in these or similar accounts in the future.

[4]*The Report of the President's Commission on Financial Structure and Regulation.* (Washington, D.C.: Government Printing Office, 1971). pp. 33, 55.

[5]Ibid., p. 40.

[6]Ibid., p. 37.

requirements. The need for additional revenues and the opposition to so-called tax loopholes are forces that will contribute to equality of taxation. The concept of convenience and needs of the customer may also be forces contributing to the broadening of the powers of all financial institutions.

Regulation of Interest Paid on Deposits

Banking is subject to many regulations, and those that are most debilitating involve deposits. Banks are prohibited from paying interest on demand deposits, and the amount that can be paid on time and savings deposits is closely regulated. Of all the regulations applicable to commercial banks, none have been more far-reaching and disruptive to financial markets than those on deposits. The regulations applicable to deposits penalize savers, lead to nonprice competition, misallocate resources, distort the impact of monetary policy, and contribute to disruption of the international monetary system.

Demand Deposits

The Banking Act of 1933 prohibited payment of interest on demand deposits. A commonly held view at that time was that the holding of high risk assets had been encouraged by high interest rates paid on deposits, and that these assets of an inferior quality had been a major factor in bank losses and failures during the great depression. Thus the prohibition of interest payment on deposits would protect banks from interest-rate competition. A second reason advanced for such a prohibition was the fear that large city banks would outbid smaller rural banks for funds; consequently, credit for small local borrowers would be in short supply. Some advocates of interest-rate prohibition went even further in their arguments and pointed out that bank costs would be reduced, and thus the cost of credit would be less. The congressional attitude towards the prohibition of interest on demand deposits and the limitations placed on time and savings deposits was influenced greatly by the adoption of legislation providing for the insurance of bank deposits.

Although these arguments may have appeared plausible at the time, evidence does not support such conclusions. Several researchers have pointed out that high deposit rates will not necessarily induce banks to invest in more risky assets and thus endanger bank solvency. In fact, it has been discovered that an inverse relationship existed between deposit rates and failures of country banks in the 1920s and the 1930s.[7] It is also doubtful that higher interest rates by large city banks resulted in the attraction of

[7]George Benston, "Interest Payments on Demand Deposits and Bank Investment Behavior," *Journal of Political Economy*, October 1964.

interbank deposits from rural areas and thus contributed to speculation in the call loan market, and to less credit in rural areas. The Heller Committee of 1963 pointed out that with the advent of margin requirements, high reserve requirements, and other restrictions this was not a serious problem.[8] If we were to assume that the relationship of loans to assets was an indication of credit availability, it would appear that rural banks have had the ability to lend over the years. If we were to define small banks as those with $10 million and less in deposits, we would find that their loans, as a percent of total assets, have been below the average for all banks. For example, in 1960 loans as a percent of total assets in banks with deposits of $10 million and less were only 41 percent, compared to 46 percent for all banks. It was not until 1976 that this percentage approximated the all-bank average. Finally, the small number of bank failures and losses since the adoption of the insurance of deposits indicates that this fear was unwarranted.

The arguments advanced by supporters of the prohibition of interest payments on demand deposits failed to take into account some very basic economic facts. In order to make loans a bank must have loanable funds, and interest rates are an effective way of attracting deposits. Because of this simple fact and the inability to pay interest on demand deposits, banks have engaged in nonprice competition as a means of attracting deposits. This nonprice competition has taken many forms, one of which is lower loan rates for borrowers who carry large deposit balances. It also manifests itself in reduced service charges for those who carry rather large balances. A few banks have even eliminated service charges as a means of attracting deposits. Some banks have introduced premiums for new accounts, and others have aided corporate customers in the investment of corporate funds in such money market instruments as commercial paper, bankers' acceptances, and other short-term instruments. In effect, these arrangements provide for the receiving of interest on assets, serving the same purpose that demand deposits did a few years ago. In a very real sense, the negotiable certificate of deposit falls into this category, as does the practice of encouraging automatic transfer services from savings accounts to demand deposits and the payment of interest on savings accounts from day of deposit to day of withdrawal. The reason banks engage in such practices is simply a choice of the lesser of two evils. If they did not make such services available, depositors motivated by a desire to earn more on their assets would invest directly or move their deposits elsewhere. Money and capital markets are quite competitive and impersonal, and banks as well as other financial institutions compete for deposits.

[8] *Report of the Committee on Financial Institutions to the President of the United States* (Washington D.C.: Government Printing Office, 1963).

The prohibition of the payment of interest on demand deposits has caused many depositors, especially business firms, to spend considerable time and effort to conserve the use of demand deposits; consequently, cash holdings of corporations have declined considerably in recent years. Excess funds have been invested in such earning assets as short-term securities and CDs. The economical use of demand deposits is reflected in the *income velocity of money*.[9] The annual turnover rate has increased steadily in recent years from a ratio of approximately 2.5 in 1950 to 5.7 in 1977. This is another way of saying that the money supply, of which demand deposits are a major part, has been made to operate more efficiently.

The economic effects of the prohibition of interest payments on demand deposits were fully recognized by the Hunt Commission when it stated that, "The interest rate prohibition, therefore, causes resources to be misallocated." The commission did not recommend removal of the ban, however, but did say that "the prohibition should be reviewed in the future." It is obvious that the Hunt Commission recognized that the prohibition of interest payment on demand deposits is uneconomic, but that this prohibition had already created so many dislocations in our economy that an abrupt change would be very upsetting.[10]

Savings and Time Deposits

Although banks are permitted to pay interest on time and savings deposits, the amount is closely regulated by the Federal Reserve System and the Federal Deposit Insurance Corporation. Federal Reserve regulations are implemented through the Board's Regulation Q, "Interest on Deposits." The reason offered for regulating the amount of interest paid on time and savings deposits is the same as that given for the prohibition of the payment of interest on demand deposits, that is, discouraging the commercial banking system from investing in high risk assets.

From 1937 until the early 1950s, the ceilings on interest rates established by Regulation Q were well above market interest rates, and thus, for all practical purposes, were not effective. During this period banks were not very competitive with one another or with other financial institutions. The commercial banking system was in an excess reserve position, and interest rates were at historically low levels. By the mid-1950s the situation had changed. Banks were hard pressed for loanable funds, and the effects of

[9]The income velocity of money is defined as the ratio of Gross National Product to the Money Supply (M1). M1 includes demand deposits at commercial banks other than domestic interbank and U.S. Government, less cash items in process of collection and Federal Reserve float; foreign demand balances at Federal Reserve banks; and currency outside the Treasury, Federal Reserve banks, and vaults of commercial banks.

[10]*The Report of the President's Commission on Financial Structure and Regulation*, p. 27–28.

Regulation Q were felt for the first time. Under Regulation Q banks could not exeed 2.5 percent on savings accounts, which was below the rate being paid by many savings and loan associations, mutual savings banks, and credit unions—none of which came under a similar regulation. After some discussion, Regulation Q was revised upward in July 1957 to permit banks to compete more effectively for time and savings deposits. Since then, maximum rates have been changed a number of times. Maximum rate ceilings on CDs in denominations of $100,000 or more were suspended in 1973. Maximum rates on other time and savings deposits, except for money market certificates of less than $100,000, ranged from 5 to 8 percent in early 1979, depending on time to maturity and, in some cases, on size of minimum balance. Current rates are published monthly in the *Federal Reserve Bulletin*.

Although savers may be motivated by other factors, the rate of interest paid is of major consequence. Evidence of the importance of rate was the growth in savings deposits after the change in the ceiling on time and savings deposits in 1957. From 1945 to 1956, time and savings deposits had increased at a compounded annual rate of approximately 5 percent, but in 1957 the rate jumped to 13.8 percent. At the end of 1956 commercial bank time and savings deposits were approximately $52.6 billion, which constituted about 25 percent of total bank deposits, but by the end of 1964 these deposits had tripled in amount and at the end of 1977 had increased to $551 billion and accounted for 63 percent of total bank deposits. During the 1950s, time and savings deposits increased at a 7.1 percent compounded annual rate while savings and loan associations had a rate of 16 percent and mutual savings banks 6.1 percent. During the 1970–77 period these growth rates changed considerably; for commercial banks the rate was 12.4 percent, savings and loan associations 14.9 percent, and mutual savings banks 9.2 percent.

Despite the fact that the liberalization of Regulation Q has resulted in an increase in time and savings deposits, it has had a perverse effect on the flow of funds and the money market in general. During tight money periods it has contributed to disintermediation, that is, caused funds to leave the commercial banking system. In 1959, for example, when interest rates increased substantially, bank savings deposits increased by only 2.7 percent, compared to an increase of 13.8 percent in share accounts of savings and loan associations. In 1969, another year of rapidly rising interest rates, savings deposits increased by only 1.7 percent in commercial banks while share accounts in savings and loan associations rose by 3 percent. During the same year large CDs in commercial banks declined from $23.5 billion to $10.9 billion. A large part of these funds that left the commercial banking system was invested in commercial paper and other short-term assets, and some was transferred abroad to the Eurodollar market. Thus the inability of commercial banks to compete for funds because of the ceiling imposed by Regulation Q caused the Eurodollar market to increase in size. To meet commitments to borrowers, American bankers were forced to enter the Eurodollar market and borrow funds at very high rates. For a time in 1974 the rate on a Eurodollar loan of three months maturity exceeded 13 percent.

This inability to compete for time deposits was partly alleviated when maximum rates were suspended in mid 1973 on time deposits of $100,000 or more. In 1978 the introduction of six-month money market certificates with interest rates competitive with Treasury bills took additional pressure off the banking system. The last half of 1978 showed an increase in net time deposits at an annual rate approaching 10 percent.[11] This increase was during a period when money market rates were rising and generally were above the maximum rates available on other certificates of deposit. Thus, the harmful effects of disintermediation were avoided at least to some degree.

Several committees and responsible individuals have recommended removing Regulation Q or placing it on a standby basis. Both the Commission on Money and Credit and the Heller Committee recommended this. Alfred Hayes, president of the Federal Reserve Bank of New York, agreed with a former chairman of the Board of Governors of the Federal Reserve System, Mr. Martin, when he said that, "the time is close when it would be well for the System to start moving away from the imposition of interest rate ceilings on deposits and related liabilities."[12] The Hunt Commission made several recommendations regarding maximum rates of interest, two of which were quite significant:

1　the power to stipulate deposit rate maximums be abolished for time and savings deposits, certificates of deposit and share accounts of $100,000 or more.

2　the power to stipulate deposit rate maximums on time and savings deposits, certificates of deposit and share accounts of less than $100,-000 at commercial banks, mutual savings banks, savings and loan associations, and credit unions be given to the Board of Governors of the Federal Reserve System for use on a standby basis, to be exercised only when serious disintermediation is threatened.[13]

[11]Net time deposits are defined as savings deposits, time deposits open account, plus time certificates of deposit other than negotiable time certificates of deposit issued in denominations of $100,000 or more by large weekly reporting commercial banks. Federal Reserve Bank of St. Louis, *U.S. Financial Data,* Week ending January 3, 1979, p.8.

[12]Alfred Hayes, "Recent Developments in Banking Structure and Monetary Policy," *Monthly Review,* June 1970, p. 122.

[13]*The Report of the President's Commission on Financial Structure and Regulation,* p. 23.

Despite the desirability of removing Regulation Q, the removal will probably be slow and reluctant. It is difficult for legislative bodies with the power to adopt regulations and those who administer such regulations to give them up. The removal of the ceiling on large CDs in 1973 may, however, pave the way to future relaxation and possible elimination of interest rate regulations.

Clearing and Collection of Checks

The widespread use of checks in our economy makes their clearing and collection no small task. This is done quickly and efficiently by commercial banks, however, through their own devices and in cooperation with other banks and with the Federal Reserve System. Funds are transferred from one account to another in the same bank by debiting one account and crediting another. When checks are drawn on one bank and deposited in another within a community, the banks merely exchange daily claims on each other. If a difference exists, it is ordinarily paid by a check drawn on the bank's account carried at a Federal Reserve bank or in one of its correspondent banks. In communities and cities with several banks, all or at least most, would be members of a clearinghouse which would have as its major function the clearing of checks.

When checks are drawn on banks several miles from the depositing bank, they may be cleared through the correspondent banking system or through the Federal Reserve System. Member banks carry a portion of their reserves with the Federal Reserve bank of their district, and a bank receiving a check drawn on another bank in the same district would receive credit to its account and the latter's account would be debited a like amount. Checks may be cleared between Federal Reserve districts by the use of the interdistrict Settlement Fund in Washington, D.C. Each Federal Reserve bank maintains a balance in the fund, and daily computations are made based on reports received from each Federal Reserve bank of checks received during the day involving collections in each of the other Federal Reserve bank districts.

The method employed to clear checks depends on which will be the quickest and most efficient. Banks are interested in clearing checks as soon as possible, since a prolonged collection period results in a loss of earnings for the bank and, in some instances, an inconvenience to depositors. The use of electronic data-processing equipment by commercial banks has facilitated the clearing of billions of checks. The inception of coded check and deposit information has also resulted in expediting the time involved in check clearings. However, the volume of checks processed each year has grown significantly, and some experts estimate that it could reach 36 billion by 1980.[14]

The Board of Governors of the Federal Reserve System recognized this problem, and on June 17, 1971, issued a policy statement calling for basic changes in the money transfer system of the nation. These changes were labeled as essentially transitional steps towards replacing the use of checks with the electronic transfer of funds. The board's policy statement gave individual Federal Reserve banks the needed approval to research, experiment, and develop systems whereby funds may be transferred with greater speed. Further, on November 19, 1971, the board announced the completion of a computerized national model of how individuals pay their bills. This model was designed principally to study the payments mechanism and to provide the necessary background material for electronic funds transfer systems.

The completion of a nationwide *electronic funds transfer system* (EFTS) using Federal Reserve facilities was announced by the Board of Governors in late 1978. The Board earlier had authorized the use of Federal Reserve facilities to provide such services to *automated clearing house* (ACH) associations.

"The system that has now been completed hooks up for the interchange of electronic payments some 9,400 banks, 1,500 thrift institutions that are currently members of ACH associations, and some 6,000 customer corporations. Any financial institution that is a member of an ACH association can now present payment instructions recorded on magnetic tape to the nearest ACH for transmission nationwide.

Linkage of ACH associations in all parts of the Nation makes possible the electronic transfer of payments to and from virtually any place in the United States. Payments that can be made by check can also be made electronically. At present, most electronically transmitted payments are payroll deposits and payments of recurring bills (such as mortgages) or other recurring amounts (such as U.S. Treasury deposits for social security beneficiaries and the like)."[15]

The automated clearinghouse provides the basis for the electronic funds transfer systems in the United States. The function of the ACH is the same as the traditional clearinghouse except that transfers of funds are accomplished by electronic impulses stored on magnetic computer tapes instead of from paper checks. The development of automated clearinghouses has

---

[14]Based on 1974 volume estimates of 24.4 billion checks with an expected continuing growth rate of 7 percent per year. See R. William Powers, "A Survey of Bank Check Volumes," *Journal of Bank Research,* Winter 1976, pp. 245–256.

[15]"Nationwide EFT Network," *Federal Reserve Bulletin,* October 1978, p. 824.

made it possible to implement a number of kinds of electronic funds transfer systems, including direct deposit of payrolls, preauthorized bill payment plans, automated teller machines, point-of-sale (POS) systems, and check truncation plans. The pioneers in ACH development were the System Committee on Paperless Entry (SCOPE) formed in 1968 by clearinghouses in San Francisco and Los Angeles in conjunction with the Federal Reserve System. SCOPE studied the feasibility of automated clearing houses, developed the computer software necessary to implement them, and assisted in formulation of the necessary rules and legal arrangements. The work of SCOPE was extended by the Committee on Paperless Entry (COPE) in Atlanta, and, in 1973 the Georgia Automatic Clearinghouse Association was organized. By 1974 the National Automated Clearinghouse Association was formed to develop interregional electronic clearing of funds and to promote the automated clearinghouse movement. In late 1976, 21 members were reported to be participating with six more scheduled to join by the end of the year. The Federal Reserve banks have agreed to provide clearing and settlement facilities for members and ACH associations.[16] The new network, announced in 1978, ties together 32 ACH associations and uses computers in 34 Federal Reserve offices.[17]

Paperless entries are now possible for many kinds of recurring transactions that previously have been handled with checks. For example, direct deposit of payrolls can substantially reduce the cost of preparation and clearing of payroll checks. A business firm may enter into an arrangement with a bank, which must have access to an automated clearinghouse, to process the firm's payroll. A few days before payday the firm delivers a magnetic tape containing the bank and account numbers of the various employees and the amount to be deposited to each account. The firm's bank takes from the tape the information for employees having accounts with it. The tape then is utilized by computers at a participating clearinghouse that balances, sorts, and distributes the paperless payroll entry information to the participating commercial banks and to each employee's personal account. In brief, a paperless entry creates a deposit equal to the employee's regular paycheck.

Other examples of electronic funds transfer systems include provision for electronic bill payment services. Preauthorized bill payments for recurring bills are processed on a basis similar to that for direct deposit of payrolls. Or a point-of-sale terminal in a retail store is used to effect a direct transfer

---

[16]Mary G. Grandstaff and Charles J. Smaistrla, "A Primer on Electronic Funds Transfer," Federal Reserve Bank of Dallas *Business Review*, September 1976, pp. 7–14.

[17]"Nationwide EFT Network,' op. cit., p. 824.

of the amount of a sale from a customer's account to the retailer's account.

Electronic transfer of funds is now a reality and is likely to be expanded significantly in the near future. Such a system has some important implications for banking and bank customers. It offers opportunities for the reduction of bank costs and improved efficiency that results in lower costs for bank services and greater conveniences for customers. It might also result in some major changes in banking structure. Retail outlets in some states are in a position to perform many of the services of banks and branches. Retailers might, for example, be willing to dispense currency and coin since no risk would be involved other than the care of money because funds would not be released until an electronic transfer of funds from the customer's account to that of the retailer occurred. Since wages, and possibly other payments in the economy such as dividends, rents, government payments, etc., can be handled electronically, checks will play a smaller role in the payments mechanism. Therefore, frequent visits to a bank could be reduced, which in turn would reduce the need for the number of banks and branches. To further reduce bank visits, borrowers might arrange periodically for the establishment of a line of credit that would permit what might be termed *overdraft banking*.

Such developments do not come about overnight. Before such a utopian arrangement can be attained, many problems may be encountered that must be overcome. A question arises of customer acceptance and cost to the banking industry, which may present monumental hurdles. Although the technology to introduce such a system is available, more hurdles will probably be encountered as we go forward. The electronic transfer of funds, whatever form it takes, will be an interesting development.

Liability Management for Liquidity

Banks have borrowed extensively in recent years to provide liquidity. Such borrowing has become known as liability management. Growth in borrowing has resulted from an increase in the demand for bank credit and the relatively slow growth in demand deposits in recent years. The rise in economic activity and the increase in the inflation rate have meant that business firms need more credit to carry on their activities. Moreover, both business firms and individuals have become more conscious of interest rates which, as already mentioned, have slowed the growth of demand deposits. Increasing expenses have compelled banks to employ their resources fully; this has resulted in a higher loan-to-deposit ratio than existed many years ago.

The Discount Window

Borrowing from a Federal Reserve bank or a correspondent bank is one method of acquiring funds to adjust a bank's reserve position, and consequently its liquidity position. While this method of making reserve adjustments is not common, nonmember banks may borrow from large correspondent banks, while member banks may use the discount window of their Federal Reserve bank. Such borrowing by member banks is subject to regulation by the Federal Reserve System.

Borrowing from the Federal Reserve System is seen as a privilege, not a right that accompanies membership. The central bank cannot be considered a reliable and continuous source of funds. The length of the borrowing period depends on many factors, such as the condition of the bank that wants to borrow and the current economic environment. From recent practices it appears that if large banks wanted to borrow for more than six out of thirteen consecutive weeks, such action would be frowned upon.

Small banks have easier access to the discount window than do large banks. This has been justified on the grounds that small banks are unable to participate in all the markets available to large banks, and because small banks usually experience greater seasonal movements in their loans and deposits than do large banks. In early 1973 a *seasonal borrowing privilege* was introduced by the Federal Reserve System in order to assist small- and medium-sized banks that face substantial seasonal fluctuations in the supply and demand for funds. To qualify for this type of borrowing a bank's seasonal decline in available funds—that is, deposits minus loans—must persist for at least eight weeks and recur at about the same time each year. The length of time funds can be borrowed depends on the duration of the bank's seasonal pattern of needs.

Although borrowing from the Federal Reserve banks is never assured, a bank may reasonably expect to receive access to Federal Reserve credit when its needs are consistent with the objectives of the central bank. Funds made available by Federal Reserve banks must be fully collateralized by eligible commercial or agricultural paper, bankers acceptances, or U.S. government securities. Eligible commercial paper includes a broad category of financial instruments maturing in 90 days or less and agricultural paper with a maturity not in excess of nine months. To qualify, promissory notes must be signed by financially sound and reputable borrowers and arise out of financing current production.

It is fairly obvious that the borrowing privilege was inaugurated when the commercial-loan theory was at its peak. When bank borrowing is secured by commercial or agricultural paper, it must be evaluated by Federal Reserve officials to see that it meets established standards. Since this procedure is time consuming, most borrowing today is secured by pledging U.S. Treasury obligations; consequently, banks that borrow frequently may maintain Treasury obligations at the bank that can be pledged easily and quickly. The Federal Reserve banks closely administer the discount window to assure that the privilege of borrowing is not abused. During periods when money-market rates are above the discount rate, the Federal Reserve's task is complicated by the profit incentive of a bank to borrow. Applications of borrowing banks are reviewed regularly, and those banks found in debt to the Federal Reserve for an excessive time are requested to find other sources of funds.

The banking system has been indebted to the Federal Reserve System since World War II. As would be expected, borrowings have been high during tight money periods. In 1953, for example, member-bank borrowing in one month reached $1.6 billion outstanding. Another high borrowing period occurred in 1969–70 and in 1973–74 when borrowing soared to about $4 billion.

Federal Funds

The purchase of federal funds is one of the most popular methods of using credit to meet liquidity requirements. Federal funds are deposit balances held with Federal Reserve banks. A commercial bank may have excess balances because of an unexpected inflow of deposits or a decline in loans. Since these funds are nonearning assets, banks are willing to make them available to other banks for a short period of time, and those that need funds to comply with reserve requirements or to purchase assets are willing to purchase such balances. Federal funds have long been used by banks to adjust reserve positions, but it has only been since the early 1950s that this source of funds has been widely used to supply bank liquidity. Prior to 1963, federal funds were considered by bank management as a source of one-day funds which could be obtained at a rate no higher than the Federal Reserve discount rate. A bank that needed funds to cover a reserve deficit would purchase federal funds provided the rate was below the discount rate. In the early 1960s, a major New York bank revolutionized the funds market by bidding for federal funds at a rate above the discount rate and was successful in attracting significant amounts of funds. Since that time it has been common for federal funds to trade at rates above the discount rate. Today the large commercial banks view these funds as simply an alternative source that may be obtained at a price to meet liquidity and loan needs.

Federal funds differ from other forms of bank credit in that they are balances at reserve banks; drafts drawn on these balances are available immediately. In contrast, a check drawn on a commercial bank provides funds one or two days later. Since federal funds are recorded as *federal funds bought* rather than as a deposit, the purchasing bank is not required to maintain reserves or pay the FDIC insurance assessment, nor do maximum loan limits apply. On the other hand, except for weekends and holidays, federal funds transactions are usually for one day, which means that the bank relying on this source of funds must enter the market daily in order to replace maturing contracts.

The use of federal funds to meet liquidity requirements has grown significantly in recent years. The volume of trading has increased as a result of the greater number of banks participating in the market. Many medium and small banks, some with deposits as low as $5 million, have become participants in the market in recent years.

A commercial bank wishing to purchase (borrow) or sell (lend) federal funds may deal directly with another bank, contact a federal funds broker, or a correspondent bank. Major New York City stock brokerage firms assist the federal funds market by bringing together buyers and sellers of federal funds. This service may be performed with the implicit understanding that the firm will be allocated part of the bank's stock brokerage business. Instead, a bank might prefer to pay a fee, usually 1/16 of one percent for this service. Many correspondent banks also make a market for federal funds by standing ready to buy or sell funds to other banks without regard to their own reserve position.

Federal funds transactions of the one-day variety are basically unsecured loans and are referred to as *straight* loans. Sometimes the transaction takes the form of a repurchase agreement where one bank sells U.S. government securities to another bank. These agreements usually mature in one day but may be written to mature in one week or even several weeks. The mechanics of trading in federal funds are quite simple. In the typical straight transaction, two banks agree on terms; the bank selling federal funds calls the Federal Reserve bank and requests that the agreed amount be transferred from its reserve account to the reserve account of the purchasing bank. On the following day, at the opening of business, the transaction is reversed. Interest is usually remitted by separate check.

Repurchase Agreements

In addition to the interbank trading in federal funds, similar transactions occur between banks and U.S. government security dealers and other investors. These transactions are referred to as *repurchase agreements,* or more commonly as *RPs* or *repos.* An RP is the sale of a financial asset with an agreement to buy it back on a specified date at a prearranged price. This financial transaction has become an important outlet for temporarily idle funds since it can be tailored to meet the needs of both parties involved. Although it can be made for periods of one day to several months, most such transactions are of a short maturity. An advantage of RPs is that little credit risk is involved since such transactions are usually covered by U.S. government securities. RPs are an excellent method of adjusting the reserve position of a bank. When a bank sells an asset with an agreement to repurchase, it receives payment either by debiting the purchaser's deposit account or by receipt of a check drawn on another bank. If payment is made by debiting an account, the bank's required reserves are reduced; if paid by check, the selling bank receives a claim on the reserves of the bank on which the check was drawn. Although the assets most commonly involved in an RP transaction are securities, loans have also been used.[18]

Eurodollar Borrowing

The Eurodollar loan is a tool of liability management available to large commercial banks in this country and used by banks that may or may not have foreign branches. The Eurodollar may best be defined in terms of the characteristics of the instrument. Eurodollars are U.S. dollar-denominated deposits with commercial banks located outside the United States, including overseas branches of U.S. banks. Eurodollars come into existence when an American or foreign owner of a deposit with a bank in the United States transfers funds to a foreign bank or to a foreign branch of an American bank. In the course of this transaction, ownership of the deposit in the United States is acquired by the financial institution abroad and is offset by that institution's assumption of a liability that is payable in U.S. dollars. In this case, the total bank deposits in the United States remains unchanged, but an additional dollar deposit liability—Eurodollars—has been created abroad.

The bulk of Eurodollar borrowing has been in increases in domestic banks' liabilities to their foreign branches with about 75 percent of the borrowing coming from branches of major New York banks. European banks and branches that accept these deposits pay interest to the depositor at rates generally above those available in the U.S. money market and lend the funds to American and foreign business firms and to U.S. banks. When American commercial banks are unable to attract funds locally in sufficient quantities to meet credit demands, they turn to the Eurodollar market to supplement their resources. The greatest use of Eurodollars has been during periods when banks have recorded a decrease or only a slight expansion in negotiable time certificates of deposits (CDs).

[18]Loans used in RP transactions are subject to Regulations Q and D, except in dealings among banks and thrift institutions.

Levels of Borrowings

Information on selected sources of borrowing by large commercial banks is charted in Figure 6–2. In the aggregate, these banks account for the bulk of bank borrowing. It can be seen that federal funds are an important and growing source of borrowed funds and that Eurodollars were extremely important during the tight money period of 1969–70. The popularity of federal funds results from their many advantages as an instrument of liability management—a highly efficient market, immediate credit, relatively little credit risk, a competitive rate that reflects developments in the money market, and the fact that the transaction can be tailored to meet the needs of both buyers and sellers.

Note that federal funds purchases have increased substantially in recent years. Net interbank federal funds purchases of large commercial banks rose from a level of about $7 billion in mid-1969 to $59 billion in 1978. Gross trading in federal funds is much larger than net purchases. In the week ending October 25, 1978 for example, net purchases of large commercial banks were $59.3 billion, compared to gross purchases by the same banks of approximately $84.4 billion. Gross purchases include all transactions in federal funds including two-way transactions. A two-way transaction occurs

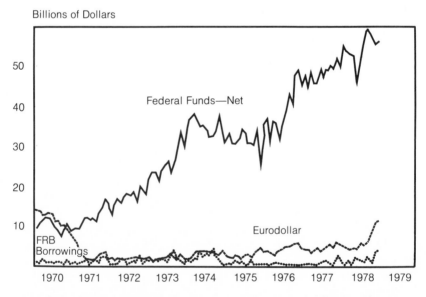

Fig. 6–2 Selected Borrowings of Large Commercial Banks. (Source: Board of Governors of the Federal Reserve System, *Federal Reserve Bulletins.*)

152

when a bank purchases and sells federal funds the same trading day. The deposits of a bank might vary within a business day to warrant such a trade-back. In the morning, for example, a bank might have more than sufficient reserves at the Federal Reserve bank to meet its requirements, but in the afternoon deposits might decline to such a level that it would be forced into the federal funds market to secure funds that had been sold just a few hours earlier. Many banks purchase excess reserves from their correspondent banks and sell them in turn to other banks in need of funds.

Eurodollars were an important source of funds in 1969–70 when the demand for credit and interest rates rose to then unprecedented heights. During the latter part of 1969, Eurodollar borrowing exceeded $14.5 billion. This surge in borrowing from abroad was due in large part to the interest-rate ceilings then required on large CDs, which rendered them unattractive to investors. Eurodollar borrowing has been facilitated by the establishment of branches abroad by large commercial banks.

The amount of borrowed funds derived from the various Federal Reserve banks is not large when compared to other sources. Note, for example, that in the tight money period of 1969–70 the amount borrowed did not vary significantly. The reason was that the Federal Reserve banks simply refused to provide the liquidity desired by commercial banks. As a result of this policy, banks were forced to rely on federal funds and the Eurodollar market to adjust their reserve position.

CDs also play an important role in liability management, as can be seen in Figure 6–3. Note that CDs were around $20 billion in 1967 and 1968, but dropped sharply in 1969 when interest rates rose. Regulation Q ceilings made this instrument unattractive to investors and forced large banks into the Eurodollar market in search of funds. Since the ceiling on CDs of $100,000 and above with maturities in excess of 30 days has been removed, the amount of CDs has increased dramatically, approaching $90 billion in late 1974. CDs rose again during the tight money period of 1978 to about $100 billion. Because of this liberalization in Regulation Q, Eurodollars are likely to play a less significant role as a source of borrowed funds of commercial banks in the future.

Cost of Borrowing

Interest rates on borrowed funds, with the exception of the Federal Reserve discount rate, are highly volatile (see Figure 6–4). The discount rate is really not a market rate. However, it is an administered rate that is changed to conform with market rates. The discount rate is not used by the Federal Reserve System to allocate funds among banks, as the central bank rate is employed in some countries. Since the Federal Reserve bank deter-

Billions of Dollars

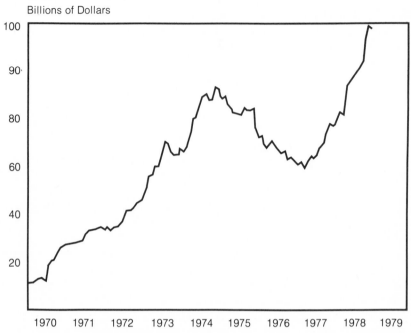

Fig. 6-3 Large CDs held by large commercial banks. (Source: Board of Governors of the Federal Reserve System, *Federal Reserve Bulletins.*)

mines whether a borrowing request is in conformity with the general guidelines of borrowing, rate plays a secondary role.

Although the federal funds rate is determined by supply and demand in the market, several special factors influence it. Since federal funds are used primarily by commercial banks to adjust reserve positions, the supply and demand for funds are influenced by the weekly settlement period. Some banks, mainly smaller ones, try to accumulate needed reserves early in the week, while many large banks tend to wait until near the close of the settlement period. Thus the demand for funds may be concentrated at the end of the week and will be reflected in the rate. The federal funds rate is also affected by the time of day. Most banks do not know their reserve needs before 11:00 a.m. and are not prepared to trade before that time. Moreover, the time differential across the nation subjects the market to the effects of local conditions. For example, most trading by western banks takes place after the New York market is closed; consequently, a substantial part of bank transactions in the San Francisco Federal Reserve district takes place between banks within that district. Because of these factors the federal funds rate is highly volatile and has been known to vary as much as 800 basis points, or 8 percentage points, during a single trading day.

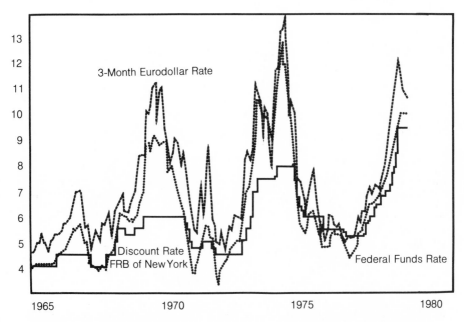

Fig. 6–4 Interest rates: Eurodollar, discount, and federal funds. (Source: Board of Governors of the Federal Reserve System, *Federal Reserve Bulletins.*)

The Eurodollar rate is also highly volatile. While it tends to move together with the federal funds rate, such factors as the strength of the American dollar in international trade, the demand for credit from foreign and American business firms abroad, and, of course, the demand for credit domestically are all important in determining its level.

Rates paid on certificates of deposits are either determined by direct negotiation between the bank and potential depositor or established at a fixed level which a depositor may either accept or reject. Banks have found that depositors are highly sensitive to changes in rates; if a bank needs additional funds to meet loan requests or deposit outflows, it may offer higher rates on CDs to attract funds. It must be remembered that the rate a bank may economically pay on CDs is determined in large part by the earnings it can receive by investing the deposit. To attract deposits, rates offered on CDs must be above competing money market instruments, such as U.S. Treasury bills and bankers' acceptances, to the extent that they can be, since maximum rates are regulated by monetary authorities. In general, commercial banks pay a rate slightly in excess of those that are available on 91-day U.S. Treasury bills to attract CDs. When money market rates increase, banks must post higher rates on CDs or lose time deposits as they mature to competing investments.

Questions

1. What factors have caused about 75 percent of the American families to have a checking account as compared with about 44 percent 25 years ago?

2. Time and savings deposits at commercial banks have outstripped demand deposits in growth since 1945. What factors have contributed to this rapid growth?

3. As vice president for marketing in your commercial bank, what factors would you consider to be important in seeking to increase your share of the local deposit market?

4. Outline and discuss the competitive situation for deposits among commercial banks, mutual savings banks, savings and loan associations, and credit unions.

5. What rationale can justify the imposition of maximum interest rates on time and savings deposits?

6. Why should maximum rates for thrift institutions be higher than those for commercial banks?

7. Discuss recent developments in electronics funds transfer systems. What are their implications for a cashless-checkless society?

8. Discuss the debt instruments that large commercial banks have been using for liability management. What are the advantages and risks of liability management?

9. How do you account for the dramatic growth in volume of negotiable certificates of deposit since 1961?

10. Why do some banks use liability management to take care of deposit fluctuations and rely on asset liquidity to meet increased loan demands?

SELECTED REFERENCES

GILBERT, ALTON, "Effects of Interest on Demand Deposits: Implications of Compensating Balances," Federal Reserve Bank of St. Louis *Review,* November 1977, pp. 8–15.

HIGGINS, BRYON, "Interest Payments on Demand Deposits: Historical Evolution and the Current Controversy," Federal Reserve Bank of Kansas City *Monthly Review,* July–August 1977, pp. 3–11.

HAMMER, FREDERICK S. "Deposit Turnover, Innovations, and Bank Profitability," *The Bankers Magazine,* Spring 1968, pp. 76–82.

LUCAS, C. M., M. T. JONES, and T. B. THURSTON, "Federal Funds and Repurchase Agreements," Federal Reserve Bank of New York *Quarterly Review,* Summer 1977, pp. 33–47.

LOVATI, JEAN M. "The Growing Similarity Among Financial Institutions," Federal Reserve Bank of St. Louis *Review,* October 1977, pp. 2–11.

NIBLACK, WILLIAM C. "Development of Electronic Funds Transfer Systems," Federal Reserve Bank of St. Louis *Review,* September 1976, pp. 10–18.

RHOADES, STEPHEN A. "Sharing Arrangements in an Electronic Funds Transfer System," *Journal of Bank Research,* Spring 1977, pp. 8–15.

SMAISTRLA, CHARLES J. "Current Issues in Electronic Funds Transfer," Federal Reserve Bank of Dallas *Review,* February 1977, pp. 1–7.

———, "Electronic Funds Transfer and Monetary Policy," Federal Reserve Bank of Dallas *Review,* August 1977, pp. 6–12.

WALKER, DAVID A., "Retail EFT Activity by Commercial Banks: A Comparative Analysis," *Journal of Contemporary Business,* Summer 1977, pp. 31–44.

7

Management of Capital Funds and Safety of Banks

The effective management of capital funds may enhance the profitability of a bank while maintaining the traditional and necessary function of safety for depositors. Commercial banks have relied historically on asset management, rather than liability and capital funds management, to attain their profitability and liquidity objectives. Higher profitability has been realized, for example, by shifting funds from short-term government securities to the loan portfolio. Additional liquidity requirements or increases in legal reserves have been met by shifting funds from the loan or investment portfolio to cash. Once deposits have been attracted to a bank, the emphasis of management has been placed on the means to invest or lend the funds that have been attracted, subject to whatever liquidity constraint has been imposed or was desired.

Recent years have seen a shift in the emphasis of management to include adjustments to liabilities and capital funds as ways to meet their objectives of profitability and liquidity. For example, during the late 1960s many banks were able to meet their need for additional funds during a period of tight money by short-term borrowing in the Eurodollar market instead of liquidating some of their investments. Other banks adjusted interest rates to attract (or discourage) additional funds from the sale of certificates of deposit.

Adjustments in short-term liability and deposit accounts can be used to provide liquidity and enhance the profitability of a commercial bank. While similar adjustments in intermediate-term and long-term liabilities and capital accounts are less effective in meeting liquidity objectives, they have been found to be effective in increasing the profitability of commercial banks. Subordinated capital notes issued when interest rates are relatively low may provide low cost funds that can be invested profitably (at higher rates) for many years. These notes may also be considered as capital funds in calculating loan limits and in providing a buffer for the protection of depositors. A dividend policy that results in a rise in the market price of a bank's stock contributes to efficient management of capital funds by making it possible to sell additional stock at higher prices. This approach may be preferable to relying on the retention of earnings to provide equity capital, except where rapid expansion of deposits and loans forces the sale of additional shares at whatever price the market may bring.

Functions and Growth of Bank Capital

Commercial banks normally utilize a much higher degree of financial leverage than do most other business corporations. For a number of years total equity capital of insured commercial banks has accounted for approximately seven percent of total assets, which means that about 93 percent is financed by debt—the funds of depositors and other creditors. In sharp contrast, a typical manufacturing firm might be expected to have only about one-third of its assets financed by borrowed funds.

Protective Function

Because such a high percentage of a bank's assets is financed by depositors —around 85 percent—the primary function of the limited amount of equity capital has been considered to be the protection of depositors. In addition to this important function, bank capital reduces the risks borne by the Federal Deposit Insurance Corporation (FDIC) and bank stockholders. The protective function has been viewed not only as assuring payoff of depositors in case of liquidation, but also as contributing to the maintenance of solvency by providing a cushion of excess assets so that a bank threatened with losses might continue in operation. However, it is important to recognize that current earnings—not capital—actually absorb a majority of bank losses. Also, unlike the situation in most firms, only a portion of the capital account contributes to the maintenance of solvency for a commercial bank. A bank is generally considered solvent only so long as its capital stock is unimpaired: that is, as long as the value of assets is at least equal to the value of liabilities, excluding subordinated capital notes and debentures, *plus* capital stock.

Although the protective function of bank capital has a long history, this role is probably less important to small depositors now because of the protection provided by the Federal Deposit Insurance Corporation in case of liquidation. Recovery of depositors' funds has been received or is available from the FDIC for 99.8 percent of all deposits of insured banks that have failed since the inception of deposit insurance on a national scale.[1] Large depositors, with balances exceeding the maximum for FDIC insurance, have been the losers in recent bank failures when insufficient capital has been available to absorb losses in liquidation. And in deposit assumption cases, where the liabilities of the failed bank are assumed by another bank, even the large depositors have received full credit for their deposits.

Operational Functions

The operational functions of bank capital have been considered secondary, in contrast to the typical nonbanking firm. Operational functions include the provision of funds for the purchase of land, buildings, machinery, and equipment, and providing a buffer to absorb occasional operating losses. At the end of 1977 the total investment of insured commercial banks in buildings, furniture, fixtures, and other physical assets representing bank premises amounted to only $18.3 billion, approximately 20.0 percent of total capital funds and only 1.6 percent of total assets. It should be noted that these physical facilities have become relatively more important, having increased from $3.5 billion in 1961—only 14.0 percent of total capital at that time and 1.2 percent of total assets.

Regulatory Functions

In addition to providing a basis for operations and for protection of depositors, other functions have been attributed to the capital funds of commercial banks. These functions arise only because of the public's special interest in the successful operations of banking firms and the laws and regulations that enable public agencies to exercise some control over these operations. Regulations relating to bank capital include those that have to do with minimum requirements necessary to obtain a charter, establish branch operations, limit a bank's loans and investments, and for acquisitions. Bank capital regulations also impact bank holding companies when acquisitions are being considered. In this sense, a bank's capital helps satisfy the supervisory authorities when they are judging a bank's condition. Moreover, to the extent that a bank's lending and investment activities are limited by the

---

[1]FDIC, *Annual Report of Operations*-1978 (Washington, D.C., Government Printing Office, 1978) p. 14.

availability of capital funds to meet the requirements for such activities, a bank's capital also serves to regulate bank loans and investments.

Growth of Bank Capital

Bank capital has shown considerable growth over the years, but has declined substantially as a proportion of total assets (see Table 7–1). Declining capital ratios are, in part, a function of the rapid increase in bank deposits and earning assets which have outstripped the growth of capital funds. Part of the deposit growth has been due to the aggressiveness of commercial banks in competing with other financial institutions and part has been due to an expansionary monetary policy to provide for the credit needs of the economy. It is important to note that a monetary policy that results in expansion of the money supply is accomplished by encouraging growth of deposits and loans. Growth of capital is subject to different forces from growth in deposits. Traditionally, *equity capital*—preferred and common stock, surplus, undivided profits, and certain contingency reserves—has been the major component of commercial banks' capital accounts. However, reserves for

Table 7–1

Capital Accounts and Reserves for Loan Losses of
Insured Commercial Banks in the U.S. 1951–1977 (in millions of dollars)

Year	*Reserve for Loan Losses* Amount	*Capital notes & Debentures* Amount	*Total Equity Capital* Amount	*Total Capital & Reserves* Amount	% of Assets
1951	$ 814	$ 18	$11,616	$12,429	7.30
1956	1,562	20	15,533	17,115	8.20
1961	2,606	22	22,101	24,729	8.83
1962	2,694	20	23,732	26,446	8.93
1963	2,995	130	25,192	28,317	9.08
1964	3,552	811	26,627	30,990	9.07
1965	4,011	1,653	28,252	33,916	8.94
1966	4,337	1,730	29,963	36,030	8.85
1967	4,733	1,984	32,021	38,738	8.51
1968	5,216	2,110	34,518	41,844	8.28
1969	5,886	1,998	37,578	45,462	8.57
1970	5,999	2,092	40,475	48,566	8.43
1971	6,151	2,956	43,949	53,056	8.29
1972	6,624	4,093	48,275	58,992	8.00
1973	7,527	4,117	53,721	65,365	7.85
1974	8,377	4,260	59,028	71,665	7.85
1975	8,654	4,408	64,309	77,371	8.12
1976	6,187	5,124	72,261	83,572	8.26
1977	6,692	5,739	79,288	91,719	8.06

Source: FDIC, *Annual Reports.*

loan losses and capital notes and debentures have increased significantly in recent years. At the end of 1977, insured commercial banks had earmarked $6.7 billion as valuation reserves against possible bad-debt losses on loans. Capital notes and debentures, subordinated to the claims of depositors, also serve a protective function in the capital structure of commercial banks. The value of these obligations increased from only $20 million in 1962 to more than $5.7 billion at the end of 1977.

Sources of Bank Capital

About 85 percent of the increase in capital funds since 1951 has come from retained earnings and sale of common stock, mostly from retained earnings. Until 1969 substantial amounts were provided by increases in the reserves for loan losses and, since 1964, from the sale of debt securities.

Common Stock

The bulk of the new equity funds was provided by retention of earnings, for several reasons. Some relate to the costs of marketing new issues and the difficulty in finding buyers. Others relate to the likely dilution of earnings and control for existing stockholders. The retention of earnings is often the easiest and least expensive way to provide additional equity capital. Some banks have found, however, that bank stock prices are influenced by the level of dividend payments; consequently, a higher dividend-payment ratio leads to higher stock prices. Thus paying more dividends performs a dual function: increasing the wealth of existing stockholders and making it easier to sell additional stock to provide needed increases in capital.

Furthermore, many dividend-conscious stockholders may prefer their current dividends in the short run to possible future gains, thus making the build-up of capital by earnings retention more difficult.

For most small banks, as for small business in general, no ready market exists for the sale of common stock. Only a few of the largest banks have listed their stock on a national exchange. The stock of many other large banks is readily traded in the over-the-counter market. For most of the country's banks, however, the relatively small number of stockholders and shares outstanding preclude the existence of an active market for their stock. Even where a ready market exists, the cost of distributing relatively small issues of common stock in the over-the-counter market may be substantial.

For a small bank whose stock is closely held, issuing new shares of stock to outsiders may dilute the ability of the existing stockholders to control the bank's operations. In many instances, this factor would cause existing stockholders to veto a sale of new shares of stock.

In a nonfinancial corporation, the bulk of equity funds typically is invested in productive physical assets that enhance the earning power of the firm. This is seldom true for commercial banks, and issuing new shares of stock may not increase their earning power materially. A greater possibility exists that it may affect existing stockholders adversely. When a bank issues new stock, it usually means the earnings will be diluted. While total earnings may be slightly higher, earnings per share may be somewhat less because more shares would be outstanding.

The major way in which additional capital can increase the earning ability of commercial banks substantially is by influencing the lending and investing policy. With an increase in capital, banks can make larger loans to a single borrower and possibly adopt a more liberal lending policy. Banks could also adopt a more liberal investing policy by increasing the amount invested in municipal bonds and in longer maturities of all types of securities.

Sometimes the retention of earnings is considered to be an inexpensive source of funds, but retained earnings must be invested to earn a relatively high rate of return if stockholders are to be as well off as if dividends had been paid. This is because dividends paid to shareholders can be reinvested by shareholders to earn additional returns. If the funds are retained by the bank, the rate that could be earned becomes an opportunity cost to the shareholder. Similarly, funds received by a bank from the sale of new shares must be invested to yield an amount sufficient to maintain at least the same earnings and dividends per share and at least the same stock price as would have been available if the shares were not sold.

Estimating this required rate of return, called the *cost of equity capital,* is difficult because there is no explicit interest cost as with borrowed money. The required rate is, in a sense, an implicit opportunity cost. The cost of retained earnings is the same as the cost of a new issue of common stock, except for the acquisition cost, or flotation charges, associated with the new issue. The cost of equity capital can be considered as the discount rate that will equate the present value of all future dividends to the current stock price. In algebraic terms, k is that rate when

$$P_0 = \sum_{t=1}^{\infty} \frac{D_t}{(1 + k)^t}$$

where P_0 is the current price per share and D_t is dividends per share in time period t. For a bank with a fairly constant rate of growth in dividends this rate can be approximated as

$$k = \frac{D_1}{P_0} + g$$

where g is the rate of growth of the dividend stream, and D_1 is the expected dividend per share for the current year. The cost of capital varies considerably from bank to bank and generally will be higher for the small bank with a limited market for its shares than for a large bank whose stock is traded actively. The cost always will be high enough to provide a return to investors that is commensurate with the return on other investments of similar risk characteristics.

Reserves for Loan Losses

Lending involves risk, and losses do occur; consequently, most banks maintain a reserve for loan losses. This practice has been encouraged by bank regulatory authorities and the Internal Revenue Service. Until 1969, increases in reserves for loan losses contributed substantially to the growth of bank capital. Prior to 1969, banks were permitted to make additions to reserves for loan losses out of pretax income until these reserves reached a maximum of 2.4 percent of the eligible loans. This maximum was reduced to 1.8 percent in 1969 and to 1.2 percent after 1975. It is scheduled to be reduced to 0.6 percent after 1981. After 1987, all banks must use the *experience method;* that is, banks will be permitted to establish reserves only up to the average of actual losses experienced over the most recent six-year period. Until 1969, the amount of pretax earnings permitted to be transferred to loan reserves was far in excess of actual losses. From 1950 to 1968, for example, $8.8 billion was placed in reserve for loan losses, while net loan chargeoff was only $3.2 billion. As a result, reserves for loan losses rose from less than $1 billion to nearly $6 billion during this period. Reserves continued to grow, but at a slower rate, until 1975, when they amounted to about $8.6 billion.

Since reserves for loan losses and bank capital have similar functions, these reserves have been an important source of bank capital over the years. Reserves for loan losses actually have two components—an amount equal to current bad debts plus a tax-free addition to equity capital permitted by the tax laws. The first component should be considered properly as a reduction in the return on loans, whereas the second is a true addition to equity capital and serves exactly the same function as equity.

With the reduction in the amount that can be transferred to loan loss reserves by banks, this source of capital will decline over the years. A study made for the Association of Reserve City Bankers points out that this change may not be in harmony with the public interest:

> At a time when reserves and capital are most needed, public policy will have the effect of reducing reserves from 14.87 percent of capital at year end 1969, to about 2 percent by the close of the century.
>
> When this argument is coupled with the large loan losses which can be

anticipated for a significant number of banks, it seems to us that the level of reserves which may be expected to arise pursuant to the Tax Reform Act of 1969, may not be adequate to enable the country to obtain the maximum of benefits from its banking system.[2]

Should this more restrictive legislation regarding bank reserves for loan losses remain in effect, it will mean that banks will have to rely to an increasing extent on other sources of bank capital.

Preferred Stock, Capital Notes, and Debentures

Preferred stock and subordinated capital debt instruments share some characteristics of common equity capital and some characteristics of savings-type debt instruments, such as promissory notes and certificates of deposit with longer maturities. They provide long-term or permanent additions to a bank's capital structure.

While debt must be repaid at maturity, it often is desirable to refund a long-term issue of capital notes or debentures. A typical issue may provide for a lump-sum repayment at maturity. A growing bank will have continuing needs for long-term capital to finance growth and may prefer to keep debt capital as a permanent part of the capital structure. This can be accomplished by refunding or paying off a maturing debt issue with the proceeds of a new issue of capital notes or debentures.

Many issues of long-term debt have been convertible into common stock. The debenture agreement may provide, for example, that debentures may be exchanged by the holder for a given number of shares of the bank's common stock. The conversion feature would permit the holder to share in the good fortunes of the bank if its stock grew in value, and would permit the bank to obtain funds in effect from issuing common stock at a price somewhat above the market price at the time the debentures were issued. Convertible debentures and capital notes usually carry a lower interest rate than does straight debt because the lenders have an opportunity for a capital gain by converting to common stock.

Senior securities enable a commercial bank to use capital funds to provide additional financial leverage. When the proceeds of a debenture or preferred stock issue can be loaned or invested to earn more than the rate that must be paid to the security holder, the difference will accrue to the benefit of common stockholders. Where such opportunities exist, the earnings on common equity may be increased at the same time as additional protection is made available to depositors. In cases where prudent banking practices dictate obtaining additional capital funds even though the earnings

[2]Carter H. Golembe Associates, Inc., *The Adequacy of Bad Debt Reserves for Banks,* Banking Research Fund, Association of Reserve City Bankers, Chicago, 1972.

Table 7–2
Effect of Alternative Methods of Raising Capital on Earnings Per Share

	Existing Position	*Expand Capital by Issuing*	
		Common Stock	*8% Debentures*
Total assets	$100,000,000	$101,000,000	$101,000,000
Deposits	92,500,000	92,500,000	92,500,000
Debentures	0	0	1,000,000
Common equity	7,500,000	8,500,000	7,500,000
Earnings before interest (2% of total assets)	$ 2,000,000	$ 2,050,000	$ 2,050,000
Interest on debentures (8%)	0	0	80,000
Earnings before tax	$ 2,000,000	$ 2,050,000	$ 1,970,000
Less income tax (50%)	1,000,000	1,025,000	985,000
Earnings after tax	$ 1,000,000	$ 1,025,000	$ 985,000
No. of shares outstanding	50,000	56,667	50,000
Earnings per share	$20.00	$18.09	$19.70
Earnings dilution		9.6%	1.5%

rate may not justify the sale of securities, there still may be an advantage to using senior securities. The use of debt or preferred stock usually will not dilute earnings on common equity as much as will the sale of additional common stock.

The comparative effect on earnings of issuing common stock or long-term debt is illustrated in Table 7–2. In this hypothetical example it is assumed that an additional $1 million of capital should be raised to support the rapid growth of deposits and assets. The existing position of the bank is shown in the first column, with earnings per share of $20 on 50,000 shares. The additional capital funds could be raised by the sale of an additional 6,667 shares at $150 each or by the sale of 8-percent subordinated debentures. The after-tax interest cost on these debentures would be 4 percent, assuming a marginal income tax rate of 50 percent. It is assumed that the capital funds are invested in short-term government securities earning 5 percent to provide additional liquidity. No immediate additional deposit growth is realized. In this illustration, the earnings per share would be diluted by 9.6 percent if common stock were sold, and only 1.5 percent if subordinated debentures were issued. The earnings rate on total assets remains about the same but use of low-cost debt capital instead of selling stock limits the dilution of earnings per share of common equity.

Preferred Stock

The use of preferred stock as a financing instrument has been limited in recent years for financial and nonfinancial corporations alike. At the end of 1977, insured commercial banks in the United States had only $99 million of preferred stock issues outstanding. While this is more than six times as much as in 1961, the total is insignificant in the capital structures of commercial banks.

Commercial banks have shied away from the issue of preferred stock. During the Great Depression, the Reconstruction Finance Corporation made financial infusions to a large number of commercial banks that were in financial distress by purchasing preferred shares in the distressed banks. This type of financing came to have a stigma attached to it because such a distress situation typically was indicated before the management of a commercial bank would consider issuing preferred shares.

The continued association of preferred stock with distress financing in the minds of many bankers and investors is unfortunate. Even though features of the income tax laws make the after-tax-cost of preferred shares a higher-cost financing instrument than debt (because of the deductibility of interest for tax purposes), preferred stock has a legitimate place in the financial structure of a corporation. It may be considered an appropriate alternative to common stock for raising capital funds (rather than a substitute for debt) when equity capital is desired. The existence of fixed-dividend payments may provide additional financial leverage (though at a somewhat higher cost than debt), and dilution of voting rights for common stockholders may be avoided. If the market price of common stock is depressed when the funds are needed, the convertible feature may permit later conversion of preferred securities to common stock when the market price is at a higher level.

Capital Notes and Debentures

Although the issuance of capital notes and debentures by commercial banks also was associated with the need for so-called distress financing in earlier years, bankers' and supervisory authorities' attitudes have changed as to the desirability of long-term instruments in the capital structure of commercial banks. In late 1961, the Comptroller of the Currency ruled that subordinated debentures and capital notes were appropriate financing instruments for national banks, and that they could be considered as a portion of unimpaired capital for purposes of calculating lending limits on unsecured loans to any one borrower. State member banks are more limited in their use of debt as a portion of capital funds. State member banks may not include capital notes and debentures as a part of capital, capital stock, or surplus for purposes of calculating limits on various lending, borrowing, and investment activities according to a ruling by the Board of Governors of the Federal Reserve System. Most states now permit the issue of capital debt by commercial banks, but only about 50 percent of them permit its use when calculating lending limits. Federal Deposit Insurance Corporation approval is required by insured banks prior to repayment of capital debt issues.

Generally such securities must have a minimum of seven years to maturity at the time of issue if they are not to be considered subject to legal reserve requirements. Subordination of capital debt to the claims of depositors generally is required by supervisory authorities when commercial banks issue such debt. Subordination causes debt to serve the same protective function as equity from the viewpoint of depositors. The other functions of bank capital are served by debt as well as by equity. Therefore, subordinated debt, subject to legal requirements and supervisory authority approval, is appropriately considered a portion of the capital funds of a commercial bank. The interest cost of capital notes and subordinated debentures for a large commercial bank is similar to the cost of long-term unsecured debt for a nonfinancial corporation of high credit standing. Smaller banks generally pay higher rates. Although large amounts of subordinated notes and debentures have been issued in recent years, the bulk of new bank capital has been derived from the issuance of new stock and from retained earnings.

The Marginal Cost of Capital

Much of the rest of this book is concerned with various aspects of bank lending and investment. It was suggested in Chapter 5 that the allocation of funds to these earning assets should be done with an expectation of contributing to the profitability of the bank. It is possible now to be more explicit regarding the conditions under which such allocations will be profitable. They will be profitable when the rate of return on the loan or investment is at least equal to the marginal cost of the funds that are invested. The difficulty with this well-known relationship of economic theory is that it must be expressed in operational terms to become a useful tool for a bank manager. In other words, a banker must be able to estimate the marginal cost of funds with some degree of accuracy.

The total (real) marginal cost of any source of debt or equity funds (RMC), say, those obtained by selling negotiable CDs, includes an explicit cost (EXMC) and an implicit cost (IMC). In the case of CDs, the explicit cost is the rate of interest that must be paid for the funds plus the acquisition cost, servicing cost, and deposit insurance premium, all expressed in annual percentage terms. These rates need to be adjusted for the proportion of the funds that must be set aside for legal reserves and liquidity requirements. The explicit marginal cost for any source of bank funds can be expressed in algebraic terms,

$$\text{EXMC}_i = (\text{CP}_i + \text{SRV}_i + \text{ACQ}_i + \text{DI}_i)(\frac{1}{1 - \text{RRF}_i})$$

where each of the terms is expressed as an annual rate:

$EXMC_i$ = the explicit cost of source i

CP_i = cash interest or cost of equity

SRV_i = servicing cost

ACQ_i = acquisition cost (amortized)

DI_i = deposit insurance rate (when applicable)

RRF_i = legal reserve and liquidity requirements and float (when applicable)[3]

In addition to this explicit cost there is an implicit cost (IMC) associated with each source of funds. The IMC arises because an expansion of low-cost borrowings, say, deposits, increases the need for equity and higher-cost capital funds which are needed to maintain constant leverage risk in the mix of funds sources and to satisfy the regulatory authorities and uninsured depositors that the bank has adequate capital. Fortunately, it is not necessary for a bank to estimate this implicit cost individually for each source of funds.

Watson has suggested an estimating method that rests on the premise that the weighted sum of the IMC terms for each source of funds is equal to zero:

> If a bank raises a small block of new funds from all of the sources it is currently tapping in proportions which do not change its funding mix (or leverage risk), the institution's overall cost of funds (RMC_0) will not change. The aggregate cost of the new money will equal the weighted sum of the explicit costs of each source. The vital distinction between a cost of funds estimate based on a single marginal source and one based on the current pool of sources is the elimination of the need to calculate the implicit cost term associated with the single source.[4]

Thus the weighted average of the explicit costs (EXMC) of each source of funds is equal to the real cost (RMC) of each component, including the EXMC and IMC of each. Every allocation of funds to new loans or investments requires a return at least as high as the RMC or the weighted average of the EXMCs. Otherwise the loan or investment should not be made.

To illustrate this estimating procedure, suppose that a bank plans to use

[3]See R. D. Watson, "The Marginal Cost of Funds Concept in Banking," *Journal of Bank Research*, Autumn 1977, pp. 136–147 for the derivation of this and subsequent estimating equations in this section.

[4]Watson, *op. cit.*, p. 141.

the following sources of funds in proportions that do not change its average risk:

Source	Amount
Demand deposits (DD)	$ 400
Savings deposits (SD)	200
Time deposits (TD)	150
Negotiable CDs (CD)	100
Capital notes (CN)	50
Retained earnings (RE)	100
Total	$1,000

Management estimates the following explicit before-tax costs for each source. The cost of retained earnings is estimated on the basis of an after-tax investors' required rate of return of 14 percent with a 50 percent marginal tax rate on bank profits.

Source	RRF	(CP	+ SRV	+ ACQ	+ DI)	$\times \dfrac{1}{1-RRF}$	= EXMC
DD	.15	0	.035	.02	.001	1.176	.066
SD	.05	.05	.015	.02	.001	1.053	.091
TD	.03	.06	.005	.01	.001	1.031	.078
CD	.03	.07	.002	.01	.001	1.031	.086
CN	0	.09	.002	.01	0	1.000	.102
RE	0	.28	0	0	0	1.000	.280

The EXMCs are then weighted according to the mix of funds to be used during the planning period. This mix of funds will keep the leverage risk about the same as before.

Source	Weight	EXMC	Weighted EXMC
DD	.40	.066	.0264
SD	.20	.091	.0182
TD	.15	.078	.0117
CD	.10	.086	.0086
CN	.05	.102	.0051
RE	.10	.280	.0280
Total (RMC)			.0980

Thus the RMC, or weighted average EXMC, equals .098 or 9.8 percent. New loans or investments available that promise a return exceeding 9.8 percent will make a positive contribution to this bank's profit and enhance the wealth of its stockholders. Those loans that are expected to return less than 9.8 percent should not be undertaken, because the return would not be high enough to cover both the explicit and implicit costs of the particular source of funds that would be used to finance it. Notice that the RMC is higher than the EXMC in this illustration for all funds sources except capital notes and retained earnings. This follows if it is recognized that increasing deposits, for example, requires an increase in capital funds to keep depositors' risk about the same. Higher-cost capital funds have a negative implicit cost because they tend to reduce risk and provide the base for more low-cost debt capital.

Adequacy of Bank Capital

Although the capital of commercial banks has increased over the years, the more rapid increase in total assets and deposits continues to focus attention on the adequacy (or inadequacy) of bank capital. Regulatory authorities are expecially concerned with this matter since they have been charged with the responsibility of bank safety. This concern was intensified with the failure of two large banks in 1973 and 1974. The closing of the United States National Bank of San Diego on October 18, 1973, constituted the then largest bank failure in U.S. history. Deposits at the time of closure were $932 million. A year later on October 8, 1974, the Franklin National Bank of New York took the dubious record with deposits of $1.4 billion when it closed. Deposits had declined drastically from $3.7 billion only about nine months earlier.[5]

Then there were more bank failures in 1975 (13) and 1976 (16) than in any other years since 1942. The largest failure in 1975 was American City Bank and Trust Company, N. A. of Milwaukee, Wisconsin, with $98 million of deposits when it closed on October 21, 1975.[6] Three banks that failed in 1976 had deposits exceeding $100 million: the largest being the Hamilton National Bank of Chattanooga, Tennessee (closed February 16, 1976) with $336 million of deposits.[7] Only six banks failed in 1977[8] and seven in 1978. All were small banks, mostly with deposits of less than $22 million.[9]

Even though the number of failures has been relatively small, the greater incidence of failure in the mid-1970s has focused attention on the reasons

[5]J. S. Sinkey, Jr., "The Collapse of Franklin National Bank of New York," *Journal of Bank Research,* Summer 1976, pp. 113–122.

[6]Federal Deposit Insurance Corporation, *Annual Report, 1975,* p. 8.

[7]Federal Deposit Insurance Corporation, *Annual Report, 1976,* p. 19.

[8]Federal Deposit Insurance Corporation, *Annual Report of Operations, 1977,* p. 15.

[9]Federal Deposit Insurance Corporation. *Annual Report of Operations,* 1978. p. 14.

for bank failures and the role that adequate capital funds has in preventing failures. While it may be difficult to determine precisely the amount of capital a bank or the banking system should have, the capital should be sufficient to fulfill the basic functions we have discussed: financing the organization and operation of a bank, providing protection to depositors and other creditors, and inspiring confidence in depositors and supervisory authorities. In this context the protective function is most important of course. Sufficient capital funds to absorb losses and to assure depositors of the safety of their funds often may prevent the failure of a particular bank.

The safety of deposits has been guaranteed by deposit insurance held in most banks through the Federal Deposit Insurance Corporation. Public knowledge that insured deposits will be paid in full (up to $40,000) undoubtedly has prevented mass withdrawals from banks that may have had temporary financial problems. Such "runs" in the early 1930s forced closure of many banks that otherwise would have survived.

The amount of capital funds a bank needs is related to the risks it assumes. If a bank assumes great risk in its loan portfolio, for example, it should have more capital funds than if it were more conservative in its lending policy. Basically, a bank has two choices when establishing the size of its capital account. It can increase its capital as the risks it assumes increase, or invest in assets that are relatively free of risk. This is not to say that banks, to be on the safe side, should follow an ultraconservative loan and investment policy. This, too, has its pitfalls. Such a policy might not result in a bank serving its trade area properly and thus would be openly inviting competition from a new bank, other established banks, or other financial institutions. Determining the size of a bank's capital is not easy, but it is important. And if a bank is to grow, with increased deposits and earning assets, it must expand its capital base but at the same time keep the risk level constant.

Capital Ratios

Many interested parties have wished to establish a set of standards that can be employed to test the adequacy of capital funds of a particular bank or of the banking system, and this has been done. Although a ratio may be helpful as a starting point in analyzing the capital adequacy of an individual bank, it should not be considered an end in itself. A bank does not have adequate capital just because it conforms to some statistical average, nor it is beyond criticism just because it meets some ratio. Ratio analysis of capital adequacy differs very little, if any, from the use of ratio analysis in credit analysis of a bank borrower's financial statement. The inquiry must go beyond the ratio to an examination of the bank's operations and the risks it assumes in its loan and investment portfolio.

Capital funds have been measured in relation to various balance sheet items such as total deposits, total assets, or risk assets. The ratio of a bank's capital funds to these balance sheet items has been thought to indicate the extent to which a bank could suffer losses of one kind or another and still have enough capital to assure the safety of depositors' funds. Various levels of these ratios have been used by supervisory authorities and others as standards of capital adequacy; the bank whose capital ratios were not at least equal to then-current standards has often been considered under-capitalized for the volume of business it was doing or for the volume of assets or deposits it held.

The ratio of capital funds to total deposits has enjoyed the longest use of any ratio devised to measure and determine capital adequacy. The Comptroller of the Currency recommended its use in 1914 when he stated in his annual report that national banks should be required by law to maintain at least one dollar of capital funds for each ten dollars of deposits. Earlier, several states had made use of this ratio, and it was widely used as a standard for capital adequacy until World War II.

The ratio of capital funds to total assets came into use by some supervisory authorities in the late 40s. It was argued that the amount of capital a bank needs is not related to deposits, but to assets. Because a measure of capital adequacy purports to indicate the extent that a bank's capital can absorb loss and still protect the interest of depositors, a valid measure would have to be related to all items in the balance sheet that might be subject to loss. Losses are reflected in the bank's balance sheet by reduced values of assets; therefore, a measure of capital adequacy should logically relate capital funds to those assets and not to deposits.

In 1948, the Comptroller of the Currency announced abandonment of the use of the relationship between capital structure and deposits in determining capital adequacy. At that time he adopted the ratio of capital funds to loans and investments other than U.S. government securities as a rule of thumb for preliminary screening.[10] The ratio of capital funds to total assets, less cash and U.S. Government securities, came into use later under the name of *risk-asset* ratio. While a ratio of one to five was originally considered sufficient, the Comptroller's Office later was reported to have used a standard of one to six, or capital funds equal to at least 16.67 percent of risk assets in determining capital adequacy.

The use of the risk-asset ratio and several variants is based on a refinement of the logic that led to adoption of the ratio of capital to total assets. A ratio that purports to measure the adequacy of capital funds to absorb losses, it is reasoned, must be related to the assets that are subject to

---

[10]U.S. Comptroller of the Currency, *Annual Report, 1948* (Washington, D.C.: Government Printing Office, 1949), p. 4.

shrinkage when loss occurs. The adjusted risk-asset ratio is a further refinement, deducting loans guaranteed by the U.S. government as well as cash and U.S. government securities.

Much discussion regarding the adequacy or inadequacy of bank capital relates to the declining values of these capital ratios over the years. The ratios of capital to deposits and capital to total assets hit a low in the mid-1940s, rose gradually until the early 1960s and declined again until the mid-1970s. The ratio of capital to risk assets peaked in the mid-1940s (after rising through the 1920s and 1930s) and declined until 1974. Capital ratios for the period from 1963 to 1976 are shown in Table 7–3. The definition of total capital that was used to compute these ratios includes reserves for loan losses.

Other ratios have been proposed that make adjustments to capital funds before calculating a ratio. These are the ratios of excess capital funds to deposits, to total assets, and to risk assets.[11] Technically, the funds represented by a bank's capital stock are not available for protection of creditors except in liquidation. A bank becomes technically insolvent if the common stock account is impaired by losses, so these funds cannot serve as a loss absorber to keep a bank open. Therefore, the excess capital funds used to calculate these ratios are total capital funds, less common stock. As noted below, all capital ratios have been poor predictors of bank failures, thus their usefulness as measures to determine capital adequacy is subject to grave reservations.

Formulas for Adequacy

The logical outcome of this type of reasoning was the development of formulas that related capital according to the risk of loss and possible shrinkage of value in each different class of assets. The bank examinations department of the Federal Reserve Bank of New York developed such a formula in 1952 for judging the adequacy of capital funds for an individual bank. The New York formula divided assets into six categories and assigned a different percentage capital requirement for each of the six categories.

[11]These three ratios were proposed after statistical tests with historical data showed them to have been better predictors of bank failures than were the ratios relating total capital to deposits, total assets, and risk assets. See Richard V. Cotter, "Capital Ratios and Capital Adequacy," *National Banking Review*, March 1966, pp. 333–46. Later statistical tests compared the excess capital approach with the formula approach of the Federal Reserve Bank of New York for banks that failed between 1960 and 1969. The excess-capital ratios were found more promising as predictors, but not wholly satisfactory. See Vincent R. Apilado and Thomas G. Gies, "Capital Adequacy and Commercial Bank Failure," *Bankers Magazine*, Summer 1972, pp. 24–30.

Table 7-3
Capital Ratios, Insured Commercial Banks, 1963–1977 (in percent)

Year	Capital to Deposits	Capital to Total Assets	Capital to Risk Assets
1963	10.31%	9.08%	14.05%
1964	10.12	8.98	13.93
1965	10.23	9.03	13.26
1966	10.21	8.94	12.94
1967	9.79	8.60	12.46
1968	9.63	8.36	11.86
1969	10.40	8.57	11.71
1970	10.07	8.43	11.44
1971	9.84	8.29	11.09
1972	9.56	8.00	10.51
1973	9.59	7.85	9.90
1974	9.60	7.85	9.76
1975	9.91	8.12	10.42
1976	10.06	8.26	10.66
1977	9.87	8.06	10.41

Source: Calculated from values reported in FDIC *Annual Reports*.

A more complex formula was adopted in 1956 by the Federal Reserve Board to analyze capital adequacy. The formula required varying amounts of capital for ten different categories of assets, ranging from 0.5 percent for short-term government securities to 100 percent for fixed assets. A liquidity test was incorporated to relate liability structure to asset holdings, with extra capital requirements for banks with higher proportions of less liquid assets. The formula was revised and expanded in 1972 to require separate capital calculations for 29 different categories of assets, total assets, and trust department gross earnings. Separate calculations were made to determine the capital requirement due to credit risk, market risk, and the liquidity available from various assets. In addition, calculations were required for adjusted capital structure ratios to total assets, risk assets, and total deposits, and adjusted equity capital ratios to total assets, risk assets, and total deposits. The formula was reported in 1978 to be no longer in use.

A new approach to definition and measurement of capital adequacy was proposed in 1973 by George Vojta. This approach was based on an explicit recognition that the protective function of bank capital becomes operative only when a bank sustains operating losses or faces possible liquidation. If a bank is to be considered a continuing business, any losses on securities and loans, at least under normal conditions, must be absorbed from operating earnings; that is, operating earnings must be large enough to offset bad debts and losses on the sale of securities and to provide dividends to the stockholders. In addition, earnings retention should provide for at least a portion of raw capital required to finance the growth of a bank. According to Vojta, the functions of bank capital are "to permit a bank to acquire the institutional structure required to maintain a business presence and to protect a bank against unexpected loss."[12]

Accordingly, he proposed a dual capital adequacy test—an earnings test and a capital cushion test. The earnings test would require that current earnings, after taxes and provision for dividends, amount to double the expected loss on loans and securities. The capital cushion test would provide a measure of the bank's ability to meet unexpected losses by requiring capital funds to be at least equal to 40 times the average loss experience over the previous five years.[13]

Criticisms of Ratios and Formulas

Those who have attempted to develop standards of capital adequacy have not been without their critics. All of these ratios and formulas have been judged, at one time or another, to fall short of the requirements necessary for a valid standard of the adequacy of a bank's capital funds. To the extent that adequate capital means enough to absorb losses and prevent failure, all have been poor predictors of bank failures and thus poor measures of capital adequacy.

The *Comptroller's Manual*, until its 1971 revision, provided official guidelines for the determination of capital adequacy that specifically denied reliance on capital ratios. Instead, the following eight factors were listed by the comptroller as those to be considered in assessing the adequacy of capital:

1 The quality of management
2 The liquidity of assets
3 The history of earnings and the retention thereof
4 The quality and character of ownership
5 The burden of meeting occupancy expenses
6 The potential volatility of deposit structure
7 The quality of operating procedures
8 The bank's capacity to meet present and future financial needs of its trade area, considering the competition it faces

Each of these factors relates in some way to the various kinds of risk a commercial bank faces. Most have been mentioned before as being related to the amount of capital funds a bank should have. In addition to these

---

[12]George J. Vojta, *Bank Capital Adequacy* (New York: First National City Bank, 1973), p. 31.
[13]Ibid.

qualitative factors, the regulatory agencies assess the growth rate in earnings and assets when attempting to judge the adequacy of bank capital. If a bank is not growing in earnings and assets, it obviously has more risk than does one that is enjoying a healthy growth. The existence of more risk indicates a need for more capital, other things being equal, than is necessary for a bank with less risk.

Official statements of recent years have been worded very carefully to dispel the idea that reliance is made on capital ratios or formulas to determine capital adequacy. It would appear, however, that all regulatory agencies still make some use of capital ratios or formulas to serve as a rule of thumb for examiners in preliminary screening of the capital positions of banks under their jurisdiction. In late 1972, it was reported that a broad rule-of-thumb standard used by regulatory agencies was a loans-to-capital-funds ratio not exceeding 7.5 times (capital equal at least to 13.33 percent of loans) and a ratio of deposits to capital funds not exceeding 11 times (capital equal at least to 9.09 percent of total deposits). Finally, in 1974, the Comptroller of the Currency reported that his office was considering setting varying standards for the loans-to-capital-funds ratio according to size of bank and to the ratio of classified assets (those which examiners find subject to some type of criticism) to gross capital funds (including loss reserves on securities and loans).[14]

Some shift has been noted in regulatory authorities' attempts to identify banks that appear to be vulnerable to financial deterioration and possible failure. Statistical tests have been used to compare a number of financial ratios of individual banks with those same ratios in other banks in an attempt to find disparities that would provide an early warning to banks likely to be subject to criticism and classification later as problem banks by examiners. Korobow, Stuhr, and Martin have reported, for example, that five ratios have proved to be most useful for this purpose, based on tests of member banks in the Second Federal Reserve District and on limited tests in other districts. These are

1 Total loans and leases to total sources of funds

2 Equity capital to adjusted risk assets

3 Operating expenses to operating revenues

4 Gross charge-offs to net income plus provision for loan losses

5 Commercial and industrial loans to total loans.

The ratio of operating expenses to operating revenues has been found to be a particularly good indicator of management ability and predictor of

[14]James E. Smith, "Assessing the Capital Needs of Banking," *Journal of Commercial Bank Lending*, January 1974, pp. 19–21.

classification of problem banks in conjunction with other ratios.[15] This seems to indicate that adequate capital, by itself, does not prevent bank failure. Operating and investment losses must be absorbed from profits if a bank is to be viable, and narrow profit margins will not indefinitely postpone problems when adverse circumstances occur.

The Federal Deposit Insurance Corporation implemented an integrated monitoring system (IMS) in 1977 to monitor bank performance between examinations. This computerized system was designed to identify banks that merit closer supervisory attention. The IMS utilizes eight factors that "measure a bank's capital adequacy, liquidity, profitability, and asset and liability mix and growth against a predetermined standard."[16] The results of the IMS tests are used as a basis for follow-up activity such as early examination or visitation of the bank.

The ratio of capital funds to deposits continues to show a surprising degree of popularity after having been denounced as a measure of capital adequacy for more than a third of a century. The continued use of this and other ratios for analysis of capital suggests that one of the failures of later formula approaches and of methods of analysis that depend on a great deal of subjective determination of relative factors is their lack of simplicity. It is fairly easy to compute a simple ratio and to compare such a ratio computed for an individual bank with comparable figures for other banks. This is a decided advantage for a banker, so that he can easily compare his position with that of others. It is an obvious advantage, too, for a bank supervisor to be able to make such simple computations.

Simplicity can be a virtue in a measure of capital adequacy, but simplicity is not an adequate guide. Bank management owes, to itself, to the depositors, and to the economy as a whole, a careful appraisal of all the risks facing the bank when ascertaining the adequacy of bank capital. Bank management should not be lulled into a sense of false security by good times. Bank failures result in losses to depositors and stockholders, the inability to meet the legitimate demands of borrowers, and shake the public's confidence in the financial structure of the nation. The depression of the 1930s was the last period in which our commercial banking system suffered great losses. Losses on loans approached $2 billion during the 1930–1936 period, an amount equal to 22 percent of the capital of all operating commercial banks in 1929, and an average loss of 1.76 percent on loans. Losses on securities for the period 1931–34 were a little in excess of $800 million.

[15]L. Korobow, D. P. Stuhr, and D. Martin, "A Nationwide Test of Early Warning Research in Banking," Federal Reserve Bank of New York *Quarterly Review*, Autumn 1977, pp. 37–51. See also J. F. Sinkey, Jr., "A Multivariate Statistical Analysis of the Characteristics of Problem Banks," *Journal of Finance*, March 1975, pp. 21–38.

[16]Federal Deposit Insurance Corporation, *Annual Report of Operations, 1977*, p. 9.

Safety of Commercial Banks

The safety of commercial banks has always been of concern to stockholders, depositors, and supervisory and regulatory authorities, since bank failures probably have a more adverse effect on the economy than do failures in any other type of business. Safety is important to stockholders because bank losses, if of serious proportions, may involve a loss of their investment. Losses in deposits represent the life savings of many depositors and the working capital of many business firms. Bank losses have a detrimental effect on public confidence, which is transferred to other segments of the economy.

Although bank suspensions and failures have been a serious problem in some periods of our history, they have not been since 1934. Since then we have had very few bank failures, and losses to depositors have been minimal. Since its formation in 1934, the FDIC has made disbursements in 541 cases involving deposits of $6.43 billion. Of this amount only $17.2 million had not been returned to the depositors at the end of 1977. The total losses of the FDIC through 1977 amounted to only $308 million, and 99.8 percent of depositors in failed banks had received or were assured of payment of their deposits in full.[17] When this amount is placed in the context of total deposits of the commercial banking system, it is a near-perfect record. The failure rate per 10,000 insured banks has ranged between 0.8 and 11.1 since 1942. In only six of those years did the rate exceed 5.0.[18] The number of failures and the amount of losses occurring in nonbanking enterprises are considerably greater. Dun & Bradstreet, Inc. reports, for example, that the average *annual* failure rate among nonbanking business firms was 40 per 10,000 listed companies during the 1974–77 period and that the total liabilities of these firms averaged about $3.4 billion *each year*.[19]

The history of bank failures in the United States shows that economic conditions are an important contributing cause. For example, the recession of the early 1920s was quite sharp and especially serious in agricultural areas of the nation. Although bank suspensions occurred throughout the nation, the rate was unusually high in rural areas and small towns. The Great Depression of the 1930s was no respecter of any area or economic sector of the nation. Gross national product (in constant dollars) plummeted nearly 31 percent from 1929 to 1933, the largest drop ever experienced; unemployment rose from 3.2 percent to 24.9 percent during the same period. Obviously, banks as well as all other financial institutions encoun-

[17]FDIC, *Annual Report of Operations,* 1977, p. 17.

[18]C. Herzig-Marx, "Bank Failures," Federal Reserve Bank of Chicago *Economic Perspectives,* March/April 1978, pp. 22–31.

[19]Dun & Bradstreet, Inc., *The Business Failure Record,* New York, 1978.

tered difficulties in remaining solvent in an economic environment of this kind.

Since 1934, economic conditions have not been a major contributor to bank failures as they were in the 1920s and 1930s. Although it is difficult to identify the causes of bank failures, in recent years managerial weakness and illegal practices rather than economic conditions have been the greater contributors to bank failures.

In discussing 1973 bank failures, the FDIC *Annual Report* stated:

> In two of the six cases, one of which involved by far the largest failing insured bank in the Corporation's history, there had existed self-serving, unsafe, and unsound loan practices and policies. Two cases involved check kites and other manipulations. One failure resulted from embezzlement or other manipulations, and another from managerial weaknesses in loan portfolio management.[20]

Banks that have failed since 1934 have generally been small banks with limited resources and income, which placed them in a difficult position in attracting good management. For example, 70 percent of the banks that failed had deposits of less than $1 million, 92 percent had deposits of less than $5 million, and in 96 percent of the banks deposits did not exceed $10 million. Through 1973, only four banks failed that have had deposits in excess of $50 million.[21] The failure of several larger banks between 1974 and 1977 brought this number to twelve.

The present federal deposit insurance plan, which became effective January 1, 1934, at first provided for the insurance of each account up to $2,500. The maximum insurance coverage has been increased several times and now amounts to $40,000. The insurance plan was adopted for three basic reasons: to restore public confidence in our banking system that had been ravaged by bank suspensions and failures, to provide protection to depositors who were not in a position to judge the quality of a bank, and to provide for improved supervision and examination of banks that were not members of the Federal Reserve System. At the end of 1978, the deposit insurance fund, which is derived from an annual assessment on insured banks and from earnings on the investments of the fund, amounted to nearly $8.8 billion, having increased by $3.2 billion, or 57 percent, since 1973.[22] Of this increase in the fund, $1.6 billion occurred when the FDIC was supervising the increased number of bank failures from 1974 to 1976.[23] In addition to

[20]FDIC, *Annual Report*, 1973, p. 5.

[21]FDIC, *Annual Report*, 1973, p. 231.

[22]FDIC, *Annual Report of Operations, 1978*, p. 118.

[23]FDIC, *Annual Report*, 1976, p. 35.

the insurance fund, the Federal Deposit Insurance Corporation has the authority to borrow up to $3 billion from the U.S. Treasury.

In protecting depositors' funds, the Federal Deposit Insurance Corporation may follow one of three avenues in case of a bank failure: 1) It may act as a receiver and provide direct payoff to insured depositors; 2) it may provide aid in facilitating the merger or consolidation of a bank in financial difficulties with another stronger bank; 3) the FDIC may organize a Deposit Insurance National Bank to operate for a period of two years. This has been done in a few cases where a community would have ended up without banking services. During the two-year period there is opportunity for those in the community to consider organizing a new bank before final disposition of the assets is affected and the deposits are transferred from the old bank. The FDIC may also make loans to, purchase assets from, or make deposits in an insured bank that it considers to be on the verge of closing because of financial difficulties if that bank's operation is essential to the functioning of its community. In recent years the FDIC has often followed the practice of facilitating the merger of insured banks in financial difficulties with sound banks, rather than acting as receiver or making loans and purchasing the assets of banks in trouble.

The safety of commercial banks has been greatly improved by external controls that arise outside the banking system and are the responsibility of the various regulatory and supervisory agencies. These agencies exercise their controls by requiring periodic reports that reflect a bank's condition and operation and by the examination of banks. The objectives of these reports and examinations are to ascertain a bank's financial progress, its soundness and solvency, whether banking laws are being violated, the competence and integrity of bank management, and whether any unsafe and unsound banking practices and policies are being followed, in order that corrections may be made.

Internal controls, too, are important in maintaining efficiency and safety. In the structural organization of relatively large commercial banks, the responsibility of the audit function rests with the auditor or the audit department. Their job is improving accounting methods and systems to produce accurate and complete records of bank transactions in an efficient and economical manner and in conformity with the various regulations applicable to the bank. Many visualize auditing in a bank as a process of searching out would-be embezzlers of the depositors' and stockholders funds. This is one function, but the greater part of the audit department's work is to create an environment that discourages dishonesty and misapplication of funds. The objective is to lock the barn door before rather than after the horse is stolen.

Although the consensus at times seems to be that our knowledge of depressions, our so-called built-in stabilizers, and our antidepression monetary and fiscal powers and other techniques are of such quality and abundance that a serious recession accompanied by bank failures cannot recur, this is extremely doubtful, and few people, if any, are willing to believe it. Even though the commercial banking system is strong, stronger in fact than it was in the past, the citizenry must not become complacent or procrastinate in making improvements that would result in greater strength.

Bank capital should be increased in those banks that have capital weaknesses; bank management must continue to increase its alertness in regard to the management of bank funds; capable and educated personnel must be attracted to banking; bank auditing should become more widespread and efficient; and regulatory and supervisory authorities must continue to secure and train capable people to examine and supervise banks. Inefficient banks must go by the way, and banks should not rely on the deposit insurance fund to furnish protection to depositors.

Questions

1. What are the functions of bank capital? How do they differ from the capital functions in a manufacturing firm?

2. Usually one thinks of regulation being accomplished by people who are regulators. How does bank capital serve to perform a regulatory function?

3. How can a small bank increase its capital to support deposit growth if there is no active market for its shares?

4. How can an increase in reserves for loan losses be considered an addition to equity capital? A reduction in assets?

5. The text suggests a method for estimating the cost of equity capital that utilizes a formula incorporating the current share price and expected dividend. How would you estimate the cost of equity capital (required rate of return) for a bank whose stock is not publicly traded and which pays no dividends?

6. Table 7–2 provides an illustration of how issuing debentures can minimize the dilution effect on earnings of new capital funds. Under what conditions could the sale of debentures or capital notes make a positive contribution to bank earnings?

7. Support the argument that capital ratios have little value in judging the capital adequacy of commercial banks.

8. What statistical techniques would you use to isolate ratios that might be good predictors of "problem bank" status? Review the studies referred to in the text and evaluate their statistical methodology.

9. It has been said that the existence of deposit insurance serves in itself to reduce the frequency of loss by depositors. Develop arguments to support this position.

SELECTED REFERENCES

BURGESS, B. G., and J. MCCABE, "Capital Notes and Debentures," Federal Reserve Bank of Richmond *Monthly Review,* December 1971, pp. 8–10.

CAREY, G. V., "Reassessing the Role of Bank Capital," *Journal of Bank Research,* Autumn 1975, pp. 165–169.

GAMBS, C. M., "Bank Failures—An Historical Perspective," Federal Reserve Bank of Kansas City, *Monthly Review,* June 1977, pp. 10–20.

HEMPEL, G. H., "Bank Capital Needs in the Coming Decade," *Journal of Contemporary Business,* University of Washington, Summer 1977, pp. 77–93.

KOROBOW, L., D. P. STUHR, and DANIEL MARTIN, "A Nationwide Test of Early Warning Research in Banking," Federal Reserve Bank of New York *Quarterly Review,* Autumn 1977, pp. 37–52.

MAYNE, L. S., "Impact of Federal Bank Supervisors on Bank Capital," *The Bulletin,* New York University, Nos. 85-86, September 1972.

SINKEY, J. F., JR., 'Adverse Publicity and Bank Deposit Flows: The Cases of Franklin National Bank of New York and United States National Bank of San Diego," *Journal of Bank Research,* Summer 1975, pp. 109–112.

SINKEY, J. F. JR., "Identifying Large Problem/Failed Banks: The Case of Franklin National Bank of New York," *Journal of Financial and Quantitative Analysis,* December 1977, pp. 779–800.

VOJTA, G. J., *Bank Capital Adequacy.* (New York: First National City Bank, 1973).

WATSON, R. D., "The Marginal Cost of Funds Concept in Banking," *Journal of Bank Research,* Autumn 1977, pp. 136–147.

8

Profitability of Banks

Gross income of commercial banks is determined by the rate of return on loans and investments, by the level of various fees and charges imposed for the performance of services, and by the size and composition of assets. Bank assets, as we have learned, have increased substantially in recent years and so has the return. Although service fees have increased and will probably do so in the future, interest on earning assets, from loans and investments, provides almost 90 percent of bank income.

Banking is a highly personalized service industry; consequently, the expenses of commercial banks are to a great extent fixed, especially in the short run. Banks, like public utilities, bear a certain degree of public interest, and the capacity to serve the public must be available at all times. Banks are not in a position to produce for inventory, suspend operations, or reduce their labor force appreciably as are some industries; therefore, expenses in the short run are not closely correlated with the volume of business conducted. This is not to say that bank management has no control over expenses in the long run. Over the years banks have improved their organizational structures, expanded their services, and automated many activities, all of which have reduced the cost of operation.

Income from Bank Loans

The lending function is the single most important source of gross income for commercial banks (see Table 8–1). In recent years, approximately 65 percent of bank operating income has been comprised of interest on loans.

As Table 8–1 shows, interest on loans increased significantly during the 1970s. This is due primarily to the greater volume of loans outstanding (see Figure 1–1), but higher interest rates on loans are factors also.

Interest earned on "balances with banks" comes primarily from Eurodollar redeposits and is most significant to large banks which have foreign operations. Although not classified as such by the Federal Reserve, interest on balances with banks is essentially interest on loans.

Another item of income that is in reality interest on loans is "income on federal funds sold and securities purchased under resale agreement." Although bankers use the terms "buy" and "sell" when discussing federal funds transactions and repurchase agreements, these are, in fact, loans. A bank earns interest when it lends (sells) some of its excess balances in a Federal Reserve bank to another bank. It also earns interest when it buys securities from another bank or a bond dealer whereby the seller has agreed to buy the securities back at the same price plus interest for the period. Since none of the risks of investment go with either transaction, both are technically loans.

Factors Affecting Bank Loan Rates

Interest rates on bank loans differ from rates on money-market instruments, such as Treasury bills and commercial paper, in that they are negotiated between borrower and bank rather than determined in an organized market. As a result of this negotiated method of establishing the price for credit, interest rates on bank loans are not uniform. They reflect both the characteristics of the individual loan and supply of and demand for credit in the money and capital markets. Rates vary also with the degree of credit risk associated with the loan, its maturity, the size of the loan, the cost of making and supervising the loan, the deposit balances of the borrower, and security. In addition, rates are influenced by habit and custom, competition between banks and other sources of funds, legal maximum rates, and the attitudes that bankers and borrowers may have regarding future economic conditions.

In general, the ability of banks to lend is dependent on the level of excess reserves in the banking system. If the demand for bank credit remains relatively stable and excess reserves increase, interest rates on loans fall as banks search for earning assets. However, if a strong demand exists for bank credit and excess reserves remain constant or rise more slowly than the demand for credit, the interest rates rise. Attitudes also influence bank interest rates. If the economic outlook is pessimistic, bankers may not lower the rate as much as the supply of loanable funds might warrant. If the attitude is optimistic—feeling that the Federal Reserve System will make additional funds available—rates may not be raised appreciably even though the level of excess reserves is relatively low.

Table 8-1
Report of Income for All Insured Commercial Banks
Amounts shown in millions of dollars

Item	1970	1971	1972	1973	1974	1975	1976	1977
Operating income—Total	34,574	36,204	40,065	52,794	67,872	66,285	80,388	90,069
Interest on:								
Loans	22,859	22,954	25,498	35,213	46,942	43,197	51,471	58,811
Balances with banks	n.a.	n.s.	n.a.	n.a.	n.a.	n.a.	4,459	4,860
Federal funds sold and securities purchased under resale agreement	1,004	870	1,023	2,474	3,695	2,283	1,979	2,471
Securities (excluding trading accounts)—								
Total interest income	*6,523*	*7,660*	*8,329*	*9,138*	*10,344*	*12,201*	*14,333*	*15,140*
U.S. Treasury securities	3,069	3,384	3,376	3,436	3,414	4,415	5,952	6,369
U.S. Government agencies and corporations	686	914	1,144	1,469	2,014	2,343	2,410	2,466
States and political subdivisions	2,617	3,124	3,490	3,861	4,449	4,911	5,116	5,338
Other bonds, notes, and debentures	151	238	319	372	467	532	750	858
Dividends on stock	(1)	(1)	(1)	(1)	(1)	(1)	105	109
Trust department	1,132	1,258	1,366	1,460	1,506	1,600	1,795	1,980
Direct lease financing	n.a.	n.a.	n.a.	n.a.	n.a.	n.a.	534	699
Service charges on deposits	1,174	1,226	1,256	1,320	1,450	1,547	1,629	1,797
Other changes, fees, etc.	839	981	1,079	1,247	1,405	1,647	2,175	2,404
Other operating income	1,043	1,256	1,512	1,942	2,530	3,811	2,011	1,903
On trading account (net)	348	344	257	341	430	508	717	420
Other	695	912	1,255	1,601	2,100	3,303	1,205	1,350
Equity in return of unconsolidated subsidiaries	n.a.	n.a.	n.a.	n.a.	n.a.	n.a.	89	133
Operating expenses—Total	**27,465**	**29,511**	**32,836**	**44,113**	**58,645**	**57,313**	**70,466**	**78,484**
Salaries, wages, and employee benefits	7,683	8,355	9,040	10,076	11,526	12,624	14,686	16,276
Interest on:								
Time and savings deposits	10,444	12,168	13,781	19,747	27,777	26,147	34,894	38,701

Interest on time CD's of $100,000 or more issued by domestic offices	n.a.	n.a.	n.a.	n.a.	n.a.	n.a.	7,083	6,732
Interest on deposits in foreign offices	n.a.	n.a.	n.a.	n.a.	n.a.	n.a.	8,745	10,216
Interest on other deposits	n.a.	n.a.	n.a.	n.a.	n.a.	n.a.	19,066	21,753
Federal funds purchased and securities sold under repurchase agreements	1,396	1,093	1,425	3,883	5,970	3,313	3,305	4,536
Other borrowed money	464	139	115	499	912	374	665	816
Capital notes and debentures	104	142	212	253	280	292	343	391
Occupancy expense	1,547	1,721	1,915	2,141	2,424	2,739	3,247	3,587
Less rental income	299	318	340	367	383	427	494	551
Net	1,249	1,403	1,575	1,774	2,041	2,312	2,752	3,036
Furniture and equipment	905	1,014	1,083	1,196	1,355	1,525	1,712	1,923
Provision for loan losses	695	860	964	1,253	2,271	3,578	3,650	3,244
Other operating expenses	4,525	4,337	4,640	5,432	6,514	7,149	8,456	9,561
Minority interest in consolidated subsidiaries	......	......	1	1	......	......	29	24
Other	4,525	4,337	4,639	5,431	6,514	7,149	8,427	9,537
Income before taxes and securities gains or losses	7,109	6,693	7,229	8,681	9,227	8,973	9,922	11,585
Applicable income taxes	2,173	1,688	1,708	2,120	2,084	1,790	2,287	2,829
Income before securities gains or losses	4,936	5,005	5,522	6,560	7,143	7,182	7,635	8,756
Net securities gains or losses (−) after taxes	−105	210	90	−27	−87	35	190	95
Extraordinary charges (−) or credits after taxes	−13	−1	18	22	12	32	24	47
Net income	4,818	5,213	5,630	6,555	7,068	7,249	7,849	8,898
Cash dividends declared	2,036	2,227	2,191	2,423	2,760	3,025	3,029	3,299
MEMO:								
Number of banks	13,502	13,602	13,721	13,964	14,216	14,372	14,397	14,397

[1] Included in income from other bonds, notes, and debentures.

n.a. not available.

Source: Board of Governors of the Federal Reserve System, *Federal Reserve Bulletin*.

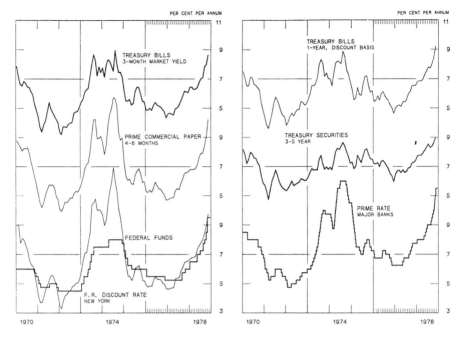

Fig. 8–1. Yields on various securities

Income from Securities

Interest on securities is the second most important source of income for commercial banks. The amount of income from this source depends on the size and composition of the investment portfolio and the rates of return on the various classes of securities. In 1964, for example, interest on securities held by banks accounted for 22.2 percent of operating income, but for only 16.7 percent in 1977. This decline occurred primarily because investments comprised a steadily smaller portion of total assets.

Yields on all classes of securities increased substantially in the late 1960s and 1970s. (see Figure 8–1). The return on municipal securities, which had not exceeded 4.0 percent for 30 years, rose beyond this level in 1966 and by year-end 1974 averaged about 7.0 percent. Yields on three- to five-year U.S. government securities exceeded 5.0 percent by 1966, and at times in 1974 were above 8.6 percent. The market yield on three-month U.S. Treasury bills, which is quite volatile, rose above the 4.6-percent level in 1964 for the first time since their introduction by the Treasury in 1929, and at times in 1974 exceeded 9.0 percent. All of these yield levels declined after late 1974, turned up again in mid-1977, and continued to climb throughout 1978· (see Figure 8–1).

The considerations in choosing the various investment securities are discussed in Chapters 16 and 17. Banks continuously balance the income possibilities offered by securities against their own periodic liquidity needs. Funds for securities investments usually are made available only after the liquidity needs of the bank are met. This subordinated positon of the investment account adds to the complexity of bank securities management and to the variations in income from securities from year to year. Even greater complications result from the fact that securities income is in two forms: interest income and capital gains (with, of course, frequent capital losses as well).

Securities Gains and Losses

Gains and losses on securities do not appear as items of operating income on the income statement as does interest on securities. The reason is that gains and losses are considered as not arising from normal operations but occurring at irregular intervals, resulting from forces not entirely within the control of bank management. Therefore, gains and losses appear after deduction of "applicable income taxes" in Table 8–1. Securities losses can be sizeable. In 1970, for example, gross (before-tax effects) losses on securities for insured commercial banks equalled $224 million, an amount equal to about 2/3 of 1 percent of operating income.

At first such losses might give the feeling that banks do a poor job of investing. One must be aware, however, that banks tend to have more funds to invest when interest rates are low and securities prices are high, but are frequently forced to sell securities to raise funds to meet loan demands when interest rates are high and securities prices are down. Those conditions existed in 1970, but by 1971 and 1972 interest rates had moved lower (see Figure 8–1) and banks had net gains on securities sales. Interest rates rose again in 1973 and 1974, and losses again resulted. Most rates peaked in late 1974 and moved lower in 1975, 1976, and 1977, all years which produced gains (see Table 8–1). Securities losses are somewhat illusory. True enough, showing the loss recognizes the decline in the value of an asset; but such a loss was taken usually in order to switch from bonds to higher-yielding loans during a high interest rate, tight money period. The loss is thus partially offset by higher earnings.

Other Sources of Income

Although other sources of bank income are important, they are not large when compared to the income from loans and investments. Other sources include trust department income, direct lease financing, service charges on deposit accounts, other charges and fees, etc., and other operating income, etc., (see Table 8–1).

Trust Department Income

Trust income amounted to $1.98 billion in 1977, an increase of 75 percent over the amount earned seven years earlier. However, this increase lagged behind that of total operating income, which rose more than 160 percent during that period. Trust income accounted for only 2.2 percent of operating income in 1977, compared to 3.2 percent in 1970. Trust departments vary from extremely profitable to extremely unprofitable. Trust departments provide services, and do not utilize bank funds. The assets with which they work belong to trust customers. Therefore, if a trust department has a good list of profitable accounts, its earnings relative to expenses can be very high. However, many trust departments, particularly small ones, do not have sufficient numbers of profitable accounts to be profitable themselves. Much of what these trust departments do is the result of the desire to be *full-service banks;* that is, to provide services to customers who are valued for their commercial business (for example, taking the small trust of a businessman for the benefit of a grandchild when the trust department would prefer to refuse such small accounts).

Direct Lease Financing

This source of income results when commercial banks lease assets to businesses and individuals. Leasing as a form of financing has become popular in recent years, so this category of bank income should grow rapidly in the future. In 1977, it accounted for only 0.8 percent of bank operating income, however.

Service Charges on Deposit Accounts

To help cover the cost of handling demand deposit accounts, most banks impose a service charge. Service charges normally are not imposed on time deposit accounts since the interest paid on such accounts takes into consideration the cost of handling the account. The income derived from service charges on deposit accounts has declined in recent years as a percentage of operating income. It accounted for 3.4 percent in 1970, but only 2.0 percent in 1977. The reasons for this declining percentage are twofold. First, demand deposits, the source of almost all service charges on deposit accounts, constitute a much smaller percentage of total deposits than was true in earlier years. During the 1960s and 1970s, most deposit growth was in time and savings deposits. Second, many banks have eliminated service charges on demand deposit accounts if balances do not drop below some established minimums such as $200 or $300. A few banks do not have any service charge on checking accounts. These practices do not necessarily mean that it is becoming less expensive for banks to maintain checking accounts; instead, it is a way of competing for deposits. These banks are assuming that the extra income generated by the use of new deposit funds will more than offset the cost of maintaining the accounts. This assumption may prove false. If all banks eliminated service charges, the competitive edge would no longer exist, and bank income would be reduced. Further relative declines in service charges can be expected as a result of introduction of automatic transfer service accounts in late 1978.

Other Charges and Fees

This category includes a multitude of items, including commissions on the sale of insurance policies; charges for the collection of domestic checks, notes, and bills of exchange; the sale of bank drafts; the acceptance of bills of exchange in domestic trade; servicing real estate mortgages or other loans held by others; equipment leasing and rental fees; data processing services; gross rentals from other real estate and safe deposit boxes; net trading-account profits; any recoveries on securities previously charged off when no securities reserve exist; and loan commitment fees. This final item is a charge banks frequently make in return for the commitment to have loan funds available at some later date: for example, the permanent financing on a building to be constructed. To have such funds available may mean keeping a higher proportion of assets in liquid form than would otherwise be necessary. Since liquid assets usually produce low returns, the commitment fee is charged to offset the income lost as a result of the commitment.

Other Operating Income

This category provided 2.1 percent of operating income in 1977. It is a catchall category for everything not included in the more specific categories. Its major components are income from managing municipal underwritings, and income from securities held in trading accounts.

Bank Expenses

In the long run all costs are variable, and this is as true of banking as it is of any other industry. Thus bank management has been able to reduce many costs in recent years, most notably by using computers. This automation program has partially offset the tremendous increase in interest expense for time and savings deposits. Largely because of this increased cost, expenses rose faster than income during the past several years. For example, operating income increased 160 percent from 1970 to 1977, while operating expenses increased 185 percent.

Salaries, Wages, and Employee Benefits

Salaries, wages, and fringe benefits once comprised the largest category of bank expenses. Every year since 1963 interest on time and savings deposits has been larger, however. In 1977, salaries, wages, and fringe benefits comprised 21 percent of operating expenses; this compares with 28 percent in 1970 and 41 percent in 1962. These figures show that a relatively declining salary expense has at least partially offset the rise in the interest expense of time and savings accounts. The reduced salary expense is due largely to the fact that the number of employees has increased less rapidly than have assets. From 1970 to 1977 total assets almost doubled, while total employees rose by only one-third.

Interest on Time and Savings Deposits

The largest expense item by far is interest on time and savings deposits. In 1977 it comprised over 49 percent of operating expenses. This was up from 38 percent in 1970 and 33 percent in 1962. There are two reasons for this very large increase. First, interest rates have gone up tremendously during this period. In 1962, the average rate paid on time and savings deposits was 3.18 percent—in 1977 it was 5.72 percent. Secondly, time and savings deposits have become a much larger percentage of total deposits. In 1977 they comprised 59 percent of total deposits, while in 1962 they made up only 37 percent.

Other Interest Expenses

Other interest expense items of commercial banks as shown in Table 8–1 are the expense of federal funds purchased and securities sold under repurchase agreements, interest on capital notes and debentures, and interest on other borrowed money. These items have been a growing category of expense in recent years, totaling 7.4 percent of operating expenses in 1977. The largest portion, 79 percent, of other interest expense is for federal funds and repurchase agreements. It must be remembered, however, that banks also earn from lending (selling) federal funds and buying securities under repurchase agreements.

Occupancy Expense of Bank Premises, Net, Furniture, and Equipment

These expenses, although individually not relatively large, collectively accounted for approximately 6.3 percent of operating expenses in 1977. Occupancy expenses include the salaries of officers and employees concerned with the management and operation of bank buildings, depreciation, maintenance and repairs, fire and other insurance, parking lots, leasehold improvements, and taxes on bank premises.

Provision for Loan Losses

Since lending involves risk, banks normally maintain a reserve for loan losses. The amount that can be transferred from income for this purpose is closely regulated by the Internal Revenue Service and has a long history. This subject was discussed in Chapter 7. With changes in the legislation regarding the amount that can be transferred to the reserve for loan losses, we can expect this item to become less important in the future. In 1977, the amount transferred was equal to 4.1 percent of operating expenses.

Other Operating Expenses

Other operating expenses include all those not classified previously, but nonetheless necessary for the successful operation of commercial banks. Some major expenses included in this classification are the assessment for federal deposit insurance, insurance coverage for a variety of risks and bonding, advertising, supplies, cost of examination by supervisory authorities, retainers' fees, expenses related to the use of automobiles for bank business, and some minor taxes. Other operating expenses amounted to 12.2 percent of total operating expenses in 1977.

One of the major items in this classification is the assessment made by the Federal Deposit Insurance Corporation for the insurance of deposits.

The annual rate of assessment, which has been in effect since 1935, is 1/12 of 1 percent of assessable deposits. Beginning in 1950, however, a credit was allowed against assessments, which amounted to 60 percent of the prior year's net assessment income. This credit was increased to 66 2/3 percent in 1961, which reduced assessment payments to 1/27 of 1 percent of assessable deposits by 1977. In 1977, the amount paid was $319 million.

Premiums for insurance other than on deposits is a relatively important expenditure made by commercial banks. An adequate insurance program is important to banks, since probably no other business is exposed to as many risks. In addition to the usual risks associated with the ownership of property such as fire, flood, windstorm, riot, and civil commotion, banks are subject to additional risks inherent in the nature of banking. Since banks deal in a medium of exchange, the possibility of embezzlement and defalcation is ever present. Other important banking risks include burglary, robbery, and the loss of notes, checks, drafts, securities, and other important documents carried by messengers or in transit. Many risks are associated with the safe-deposit function. Losses also occur from forged checks and other documents.

Banks usually carry insurance that protects them from losses arising from the loss of securities. Protection against errors and omissions in various documents is needed also. Commercial banks follow a policy of eternal vigilance as a means of protecting themselves against such risks, but the risks are so great that the sharing of them through insurance is a necessity. The American Bankers Association, in cooperation with insurance representatives, has studied the risks of banking and has made recommendations, which many banks have followed, regarding the type, kind, and amount of insurance that banks of various sizes should carry. As a result, it is probably correct to say that commercial banks are relatively well insured.

Advertising has become a sizeable expense item in commercial banking, especially in areas where considerable competition exists among banks and between banks and competing financial institutions. As banks have attempted to reach lower economic levels of income-receivers who need banking services, advertising expenditures have tended to increase.

Another major expense is for printing and office supplies. Commercial banks and their customers use large amounts of printed forms and documents—checks, drafts, notes, deposit books and slips, mortgage forms, loan applications, and the like.

Income Taxes

In 1977, commercial banks paid more than $2.8 billion in state and federal income taxes. Banks are subject to the standard corporate income tax rates. For years there have been differences in the tax rules that apply to various financial intermediaries. The Commission on Financial Structure and Regulation recently recommended uniform and nondiscriminatory tax treatment for all financial institutions except credit unions. Credit unions do not pay income taxes at present. Apparently the commission felt that this advantage would not give them sufficient competitive superiority to be damaging to other financial institutions.

Commercial Bank Profits

Several methods can be used to measure bank profitability, all of which have some advantages as well as shortcomings. A popular method is to relate profitability to total bank assets. The rate of return on assets is a valuable measure when comparing the profitability of one bank with another or with the commercial banking system. A low rate might be the result of conservative lending and investment policies or excessive operating expenses. If time and savings accounts comprise an unusually large proportion of total deposits, interest expense may be higher than average. Banks could, of course, attempt to offset this by adopting more aggressive lending and investment policies to generate more income. A high rate of return on assets may be the result of efficient operations, of a low ratio of time and savings deposits to total deposits, or of high yields earned on the assets. If the latter is true, the bank may be assuming a high level of risk; for the higher the returns yielded by assets, the more likely they are to embody higher degrees of risk. This is not necessarily bad, for the bank may be doing a good job of managing its assets, although it may be subjecting itself to large potential losses.

Rate of return on total assets does not show how well the bank is performing for its owners. For this reason, bankers and bank stockholders look closely at earnings per share. This is an excellent way to see how well a bank has done compared to previous years or to management's expectations. Earnings per share divided by book value per share shows the rate of return earned on owners' equity; that is, how effectively the owners' contributions were employed during the year. It is difficult to use earnings per share to compare banks, however, because dividend-payout ratios may differ. If one bank has a high payout ratio and another a low payout ratio, the percentage growth in earnings for the first, all else remaining equal, would not be as great as for the second because of the smaller increase in the first bank's capital base in the previous year. A second weakness of the earnings-per-share method of comparing banks is evident in the case of a rapidly growing bank which must add outside equity capital in order to maintain an adequate equity base. The new shares will dilute earnings per share so that for two or three years after the new issue is sold, earnings per share will not be a fair indicator of the bank's performance.

The third commonly used measure of profitability is rate of return on capital which is calculated by dividing net income by the total of the capital accounts. This is the same as rate of return on owners' equity in the case of a bank whose capital consists entirely of ownership accounts: common stock, preferred stock, surplus, undivided profits, and capital reserves. Many larger banks raise part of their capital through the sale of capital notes and debentures, however; so, for such banks, the rate of the return on capital would differ slightly from the rate of return on the owners' equity. Debt issues comprised 6.7 percent of bank capital in the United States as of the end of 1977.

For a given bank, the rate of return on total assets may be relatively low, yet the rate of return on capital may be very high. Should this be the case, such a bank would be heavily leveraged; that is, its capital would be small relative to its deposits. A heavily leveraged bank may be risking the safety of deposits and may also be criticized by the regulatory authorities, although from the owners' standpoint it appears to be performing well because of the high rate of return on capital. A financial arrangement of this kind highlights a shortcoming of the return-on-capital method of measuring bank profitability.

Each method of measuring profitability has its good and bad points, but the earnings-per-share method has no applicability to measuring the profitability of the banking system. Either of the other methods is appropriate, depending on the answers sought. The results of both methods are given in Table 8–2 for the years 1956 through 1977. As the table shows, the relationship between the two sets of rates was quite stable over the years, with the return on capital rates about 13 times as large as the return on total asset rates in most years. Note that both sets of rates were generally higher

Table 8–2
Rate of Return on Capital and Rate of Return on
Total Assets of Insured Commercial Banks, 1956–1977

Year	Rate of Return on Capital	Rate of Return on Total Assets	Year	Rate of Return on Capital	Rate of Return on Total Assets
1956	7.82	.58	1967	9.56	.74
1957	8.30	.64	1968	9.70	.72
1958	9.60	.75	1969	11.48	.84
1959	7.94	.63	1970	11.89	.89
1960	10.03	.81	1971	11.85	.87
1961	9.37	.79	1972	11.60	.83
1962	8.83	.73	1973	12.14	.85
1963	8.86	.72	1974	11.67	.81
1964	8.65	.69	1975	10.97	.78
1965	8.73	.70	1976	10.66	.70
1966	8.70	.69	1977	10.99	.83

Source: FDIC, *Annual Reports* and *Federal Reserve Bulletins*.

after 1968. This was due to increased revenue per dollar of assets held— higher returns on both loans and investments—and a greater proportion of assets made up of high-yielding loans.

Although the net income of banks has varied over the years, the trend has generally been upward. Normally banks have followed a policy of retaining a relatively large portion of their profits after income taxes. The percentage paid out in the form of dividends by banks has been less variable than for all corporations, a reflection of the relative stability of bank profits and the consistent policy of bank management to "plow back" a sizeable amount of profits annually. In 1977, for example, banks retained 63 percent of net income, paying out only 37 percent in the form of cash dividends.

The dividend payout ratio varies from bank to bank, but almost any profitable, growing bank strongly prefers to build equity capital through retained earnings rather than through the issuance of new shares. This is because of the dilution effect on earnings per share that results when new shares are issued. This dilution effect is much greater for banks than for corporations in most other industries because such a small proportion of bank assets is financed with equity capital. As of the end of 1977, equity capital of insured banks comprised only 7 percent of "total liabilities and equity capital." Since net income as a percent of total assests is much less for a profitable bank than net income as a percent of equity capital, the assets financed with the proceeds of a new stock issue cannot produce net income sufficiently high to sustain the rate of return on equity capital that existed prior to the new stock issue. The precise impact of the dilution depends on a number of factors, including the price received for the new shares in relation to book value of the previously outstanding shares, and any actions the management might take to cushion the impact. Nonetheless, bank stockholders usually view the announcement of a new stock issue as a negative event. Of course, the main function of equity capital in a bank is to provide a cushion of safety for depositors and not to finance assets, so if a new stock issue allows more rapid growth of assets than would have otherwise been expected, the dilution effect may decline in importance.

To summarize recent trends in bank profitability and the reasons for changes that have occurred, it is useful to consider first the operating income and expenses of banks. Operating income has been rising in recent years (see Table 8–3). This increase reflects two factors: 1) higher interest rates on loans and investments, and 2) an increasing proportion of assets consisting of higher yielding loans. Operating expenses have been rising even faster, with higher interest payments on time and saving deposits and other borrowed money accounting for most of the increase. The higher payments are due to higher interest rates and a rapid growth of time and savings deposits. Salaries and wages have not increased as rapidly as have other expenses and thus have offset some of the effect of higher interest

Table 8–3
Operating Income and Expenses, Insured Commercial Banks,
1970–1977 (in millions of dollars)

Year	Operating Income	Operating Expenses	Income before Income Taxes	Profit Margin (%)
1970	35,574	27,465	7,109	19.98
1971	36,204	29,511	6,693	18.49
1972	40,065	32,836	7,229	18.04
1973	52,794	44,113	8,681	16.44
1974	67,872	58,645	9,227	13.59
1975	66,285	57,313	8,973	13.54
1976	80,388	70,466	9,922	12.34
1977	90,069	78,484	11,585	12.86

Source: Board of Governors of the Federal Reserve System, *Federal Reserve Bulletin*.

payments. With expenses rising more rapidly than income the profit margin for all commercial banks has been falling; income before taxes and securities gains or losses declined from 19.98 percent of operating income in 1970 to 12.86 percent in 1977.

While profit margins have been falling, operating income has been rising faster than the value of assets (see Table 8–4). This has somewhat increased the productivity of assets for the banking system due mostly to the allocation of an increasing proportion of funds to higher-yielding loans rather than lower-yielding securities investments and to a smaller proportion of funds held in cash.

The increasing productivity of assets has not offset the declining profit margins, however. A well-known analytical model relates profit margins and asset productivity in the following manner:

(Profit margin) X (Asset productivity) = (Operating return on assets)

Table 8–4
Productivity of Assets, Insured Commercial Banks, 1970–1977
(dollar values in millions)

Year	Operating Income	Total Assets	Productivity of Assets (%)
1970	$35,574	576,351	6.17
1971	36,204	639,903	5.66
1972	40,065	737,699	5.43
1973	52,794	832,658	6.34
1974	67,872	912,529	7.44
1975	66,285	952,451	6.96
1976	80,388	1,011,329	7.95
1977	90,069	1,129,712	7.97

Source: FDIC, *Annual Reports*; and Board of Governors of the Federal Reserve System, *Federal Reserve Bulletins*.

This relationship, for the commercial banking system, can be expressed as follows:

$$\text{Profit margin} = \frac{\text{Income before income taxes and securities gains or losses}}{\text{Total operating income}}$$

$$\text{Asset productivity} = \frac{\text{Total operating income}}{\text{Total assets}}$$

Operating return on assets =

$$\frac{\text{Income before income taxes and securities gains or losses}}{\text{Total assets}}$$

These values are shown in Table 8–5 and reflect a decline in the operating return on total assets from 1.23 percent in 1970 to 1.02 percent in 1977. Interestingly, while commercial banks suffered a declining operating return on total assets, the after-tax return, after allowing for securities gains and losses, was down only slightly from 1970 to 1977 (see Table 8–2). During this period, before-tax income increased from $7.1 billion to $11.6 billion while interest income on obligations of states and political subdivisions increased from $2.6 billion to $5.3 billion. Income from this source generally is exempt from federal income taxation and often from state taxation as well. Thus, the effective rate of income tax on net operating income (including tax-exempt income) fell from 30.6 percent in 1970 to 24.4 percent in 1977. It should be stressed, however, that all of the factors discussed above helped contribute to maintaining after-tax profits at relatively constant rates—including several that contribute to a higher level of

Table 8–5
Operating Return on Assets, Insured Commercial Banks,
1970–1977 (Percent)

Year	Profit Margin	X	Productivity of Assets	=	Operating Return on Assets
1970	19.98		6.17		1.23
1971	18.49		5.66		1.05
1972	18.04		5.43		.98
1973	16.44		6.34		1.04
1974	13.59		7.44		1.01
1975	13.54		6.96		.94
1976	12.34		7.95		.98
1977	12.86		7.97		1.02

Source: FDIC, *Annual Reports*; and Board of Governors of the Federal Reserve System, *Federal Reserve Bulletins*.

financial risk in the banking system—declining liquidity, increased loan risk, and increased risk due to relatively lower levels of capital.

The Need for Adequate Profits

It is essential that commercial banks earn adequate profits. Bank profits are necessary to attract new capital to make possible the expansion and improvement of banking services. If the return on existing capital is not comparable to the returns on other investments, capital will be attracted to other more profitable pursuits. An important function of profits in banking is to provide reserves for contingencies and losses that may occur incident to the business of banking. Finally, profits in banking, just as in other businesses, act as a stimulant to management to expand and improve the business, reduce costs, and improve services.

Bank profits are important to every group in the economy. Stockholders are interested in profits since they represent their return on invested capital. Bank profits result in benefits to depositors by producing a stronger, safer, and more efficient banking system through the increase in reserves and improvements in services. Borrowers also have an indirect interest in adequate bank profits since the lending ability of a bank depends on the size and structure of the bank's capital accounts, and bank profits constitute the major source of equity capital. Even those economic groups who may not directly use the services of commercial banks are benefited indirectly by adequate bank profits, inasmuch as a strong banking system, in part the result of bank profits, results in the safety of deposits and the availability of credit to the economy on which business firms and consumers depend.

Are commercial bank profits adequate to serve all these needs? Table 8–6 lists the recent history of the rates of return on stockholder's equity for durable and nondurable manufacturing and for insured commercial banks. Banks earned lower returns than did manufacturing firms for the first two years listed in Table 8–6, but the gap narrowed in 1967 and 1968, and by 1969 banks were at least as profitable as manufacturing corporations, if not more so. By the late 1970s, however, bank profitability was again trailing that of manufacturing industries. Also, it must be remembered that the levels of profitability attained by banks in the 1970s were accompanied by a general increase in the risk character of banking. The changes that brought about the increased risk exposure include the relative decline in capital, in investments as a portion of total assets, and in U.S. government securities as a portion of the total investment portfolio. These trends resulted from opportunities to increase earnings and the need to compete in providing financial services in a rapidly expanding economy.

In a very real sense, however, banks had little choice except to attempt to earn higher rates of income as returns on capital otherwise employed

Table 8-6
Rate of Return on Stockholder's Equity,
Durable and Nondurable Manufacturing Corporations
and All Insured Commercial Banks, 1965–1977

Year	Total Durable	Total Nondurable	Insured Commercial Banks
1965	13.8	12.2	9.2
1966	14.2	12.7	9.2
1967	11.7	11.8	10.1
1968	12.2	11.9	10.3
1969	11.4	11.5	12.0
1970	8.3	10.3	12.4
1971	9.0	10.3	12.4
1972	10.8	10.5	12.3
1973	13.1	12.6	12.9
1974	12.6	17.1	12.5
1975	10.3	12.9	11.8
1976	13.7	14.2	11.4
1977	14.5	13.9	11.7

Source: FDIC, *Annual Reports*, and Economic Reports of the President.

increased. Had their returns not increased, banks would have been unable to expand capital as much as they did. Neither retaining earnings nor issuing new stock would have provided adequate expansion of banks' capital to enable them to serve our country so well. So the crux of the question of the adequacy of bank earnings—as we find ourselves with the record-high interest rates of recent years—is whether these earnings will enable banks to maintain adequate capital. If so, we will continue to be served in an ever-improving and more efficient manner by our commercial banks.

Questions

1. By examining Table 8-1 we see that total operating income of banks declined from 1974 to 1975. Why did this decline occur?

2. Table 8-1 also shows that bank net income increased modestly from 1974 to 1975 even though total operating income declined. Which income and/or expense items contributed most to producing the higher profits in the face of declining operating income?

3. Also in Table 8-1 we see that applicable income taxes were little more than one-fourth as large as net income in 1977. Why was the amount paid in taxes so low relative to net income when the prevailing corporate income tax rates would otherwise suggest net income and income tax would be approximately equal?

4. If a bank has a higher than average rate of return on capital but a lower than average rate of return on total assets, what is indicated about the bank's capital position?

5. Banks with assets of less than $1 billion earned a return on assets of 0.9 percent in 1977, while those with assets of $1 billion or more earned 0.56 percent. Also in 1977 the less-than-$1 billion group earned a return on equity capital of 12.2 percent while the return on equity for those of $1 billion and more was 11.3 percent. What does the smaller spread of equity returns versus total asset returns indicate about the relative equity capital positions of the two groups? Why would the return on assets be so much lower for the large banks?

6. In what ways did the risk character of banking change in the 1970s?

7. Assume that a bank which has $100 million of total assets and $7 million of equity capital and earning 0.7 percent on total assets issues new shares which increase the total shares outstanding by 10 percent. Assume further that the sale of the new shares nets the bank $700,000 which, on a per share basis, is the same as the book value of the previously outstanding shares. What would be the rate of return on equity capital in the year after the new shares are issued if all else remained constant? How much would issuing the new shares dilute earnings per share?

SELECTED REFERENCES

ADAMS, E. SHERMAN, "Are Bank Dividend Policies Too Conservative?" *Banking*, November, 1967, pp. 37–40, 116–17.

BAUGHN, WILLIAM H., and CHARLES E. WALKER, (eds.), *The Bankers Handbook*, Revised Edition, 1978, Dow Jones-Irwin, chs. 23, 24, 25.

CATES, DAVID C., "Bank Capital Management: Interest Sensitivity in Banking," *The Bankers Magazine*, January–February, 1978, pp. 23–27.

HESTER, DONALD D., and JAMES L. PIERCE, *Bank Management and Portfolio Behavior*, New Haven, Yale University Press, 1975.

LEVINE, SUMNER N., (ed), *Financial Analysts Handbook II*, Homewood, Ill., Dow Jones-Irwin, 1975, ch. 7.

PAYNE, C. MEYRICK, "Profitability Management: Banking's Next Generation," *The Bankers Magazine*, Spring, 1977, pp. 51–57.

ROBINSON, ROLAND I., *The Management of Bank Funds*, McGraw-Hill, 1962, chs. 22, 23.

SHICK, RICHARD A., and JAMES A. VERBRUGGE, "An Analysis of Bank Price-Earnings Ratios," *Journal of Bank Research*, Summer, 1975, pp. 140–49.

9

Credit Analysis

The numerous and varied risks in lending stem from the many factors that can lead to the nonpayment of obligations when they come due. Losses sometimes result from "acts of God" such as storms, droughts, fires, earthquakes, and floods. Changes in consumer demand or in the technology of an industry may alter drastically the fortunes of a business firm and place a once profitable borrower in a loss position. A prolonged strike, competitive price cutting, or loss of key management personnel can seriously impair a borrower's ability to make loan payments. The swings of the business cycle affect the profits of many who borrow from banks and influence the optimism and pessimism of businesspeople as well as consumers. Some risks arise from personal factors that are difficult to explain. In the process of lending, commercial banks must investigate factors that may lead to default in the repayment of a loan. This investigation is referred to as *credit analysis.*

Objectives of Credit Analysis

The principal purpose of credit analysis is to determine the ability and willingness of a borrower to repay a requested loan in accordance with the terms of the loan contract. A bank must determine the degree of risk it is willing to assume in each case and the amount of credit that can be prudently extended in view of the risks involved. Moreover, if a loan is to be made, it is necessary to determine the conditions and terms under which it will be granted. Some of the factors that affect the ability of a borrower to repay a loan are very difficult to evaluate, but they must be dealt with as realistically as possible in preparing financial projections. This involves looking into the past record of the borrower as well as engaging in economic forecasting. Thus, the bank lending officer attempts to project the borrower and the environment, including all possible hazards that may affect them, into the future to determine whether the loan will be repaid in the ordinary course of business. Loans should not be based entirely on a borrower's history and reputation—they may be contracted today, but are paid in the future.

The work of the credit department is basically the same in all banks, but certain functions may be emphasized to a greater extent in some banks than in others. In general, they include the collection of information that will have a bearing on credit evaluation, the preparation and analysis of the information collected, and the assembling and retention of information for future use. In some banks the credit department may make recommendations regarding a credit application, but the final decision regarding a loan is left to the lending officer and/or the loan committee. In addition to these important functions, the credit department serves as a training ground for future loan officers.

Factors Considered in Credit Analysis

Many factors are considered by bank credit people in analyzing a loan request. They are the ingredients that determine the lending officer's faith in the debtor's ability and willingness to pay the obligation in accordance with the terms of the loan agreement. For years credit people have referred to the three C's of credit—capacity, character, and capital. Over the years two more have been added—collateral and conditions—making five C's in all. For purposes of discussion, we shall classify the essential factors in credit analysis as capacity, character, ability to create income, ownership of assets, and economic conditions.

Capacity to Borrow

Banks are interested not only in the borrower's ability to repay but also in his legal capacity to borrow. Banks make few loans to minors, since they can disaffirm at a later date unless the proceeds of the loan are used for essential purposes. When a loan is made to a minor, a parent, guardian, or other person of legal age is usually asked to co-sign the note.

In lending to a partnership, it may be advisable to require that all members of the partnership sign for the loan. If that is not feasible, the lending officer should determine whether the signing partners have authority to borrow for the partnership. A verified copy of the partnership agreement or power of attorney may be used for this purpose. When such evidence of authority is not received, the lender may find it difficult to collect from nonsigning partners if they establish that the borrowed funds were not used to further the business of the partnership. In general, every partner has authority to execute instruments for the partnership, but if the nonsigning partners can show that the partner(s) who purportedly acted on behalf of the partnership did not have such authority and that the lender knew this or, in some cases, should have known it, they may avoid any responsibility for the loan.

In lending to a corporation, it is advisable to examine the charter and bylaws to ascertain who has authority to borrow in its behalf. In many cases, banks also follow the practice of requiring a corporate resolution signed by the members of the board of directors setting forth the borrowing authority and designating the person or persons who have the authority to negotiate for loans and to execute borrowing instruments. Banks may also require a resolution to borrow from cooperatives and other associations, such as churches and other nonprofit associations.

Banks sometimes find it inadvisable to make a loan unless certain other creditors of the borrower agree to subordinate their claims to that of the bank. This occurs frequently in lending to small corporations where the corporation has borrowed sizeable amounts from its major stockholders. In such cases, the bank may be willing to loan to the corporation only on the condition that the lending stockholders, and perhaps other creditors as well, agree to permit the corporation to pay the bank first in the event of liquidation of the business. Through this process of subordination, the bank becomes a preferred creditor and is assured of a prior claim on the assets of the business as against all who have agreed to subordinate their claims.

Character

The concept of character, as it relates to credit transactions, means not only the willingness to repay debts but also a strong desire to settle all obligations within the terms of the contract. A person of character usually possesses attributes such as honesty, integrity, industry, and morality, but character is a difficult thing to evaluate. It is entirely possible for a person not to have all of these qualities but to still wish to repay financial obligations. The Mississippi River gambler may have paid his debts as agreed even though he was unacceptable as a whole to society because of certain socially undesirable traits. Character worthy of credit is largely a function of a person's honesty and integrity, and is just as important in lending to business firms as in consumer credit. The past record of a borrower in meeting his obligations is usually weighed heavily in evaluating his character for credit purposes.

Ability to Create Income

If a loan is to be repaid from earnings, it is essential to evaluate the borrower's ability to earn a sufficient amount to make the payments. The borrower's honesty and integrity are very important, but an ability to obtain funds with which to make payment is also essential. Debts are paid from four sources—income, sale of assets, sale of stock, and borrowing from another source. A loan may be repaid from the proceeds of the sale of assets pledged by the borrower as security for the loan, but banks do not favor this method of repayment since it may be expensive and time-consuming and damaging to the bank's public relations. Neither do banks generally favor being repaid with funds borrowed from another lender, unless this was contemplated by the parties at the time the loan was made. Except when it has been prearranged, borrowing from another source cannot be depended on, since the borrower may find it impossible to locate another lender if his financial condition has deteriorated greatly.

An individual's power to generate income depends on such factors as education, health and energy, skill, age, stability of employment, and resourcefulness. For a business firm, generating income depends on all factors that affect sales volume, selling prices, costs, and expenses. These include the location of the firm, the quality of its goods and services, the effectiveness of its advertising, the amount of competition, the quality and morale of its labor force, the availability and cost of raw materials, and the quality of its management. Many credit people rank the quality of management as the chief factor in deciding whether to extend credit. They refer to it as the *management factor*—the ability of a firm's managers to assemble manpower, raw materials, and capital assets to produce a satisfactory flow of goods, services, and profits. Some businesses rise while others fall, and the difference is often attributable to management. Effective management sees and takes advantage of new opportunities, makes timely adjustments in production in response to changes in demand for the firm's products, replaces inefficiency with efficiency, and provides products and services with strong customer appeal because of their quality and/or pricing. It is difficult to evaluate the managers of a firm, particularly when they have not been on the job very long, but it is nevertheless important.

Ownership of Assets

Ownership of assets is similar to capital and collateral in the five C's of credit. Manufacturers must have modern machinery and equipment if they are to be competitive producers. Retailers must have a stock of merchandise and attractive buildings and fixtures if they are to attract customers. Credit will not be supplied to business concerns unless capital has been supplied by the owners to support the debt. The net worth of a firm (the capital supplied by the owners) is one measure of its financial strength. It is often one of the principal determinants of the amount of credit a bank is willing to make available to a business borrower. The amount and quality of the assets held by a firm reflect the prudence and resourcefulness of its management. Some or all of these assets may serve as security for a loan and thus as insurance that the loan will be repaid should the borrower's ability to create income not be sufficient to retire the loan. It should be emphasized, however, that while security does reduce the risk, banks prefer that borrowed funds be repaid out of income.

Consumer loans are frequently secured by assets of the borrower. Most cars, for example, are purchased on credit, and the automobile serves as collateral for the loan. The same is true for houses and, to a lesser extent, for household furnishings and appliances. If the value of the pledged assets has not depreciated below the unpaid balance of the loan, the borrower has a strong incentive to continue his payments.

Economic Conditions

Economic conditions affect the ability of the borrower to repay financial obligations but are beyond the control of the borrower and the lender. Economic conditions are the environment within which business units and individuals operate—the stage on which the actors perform. Borrowers may have good character, an apparent ability to create income, and sufficient assets, but economic conditions may render the extension of credit unwise. It is here that the loan officer must become an economic forecaster. The longer the maturity of the loan, the more important economic forecasting becomes, since there is a greater possibility of an economic downturn before the loan has been fully repaid. The economy is subject to short- and long-run fluctuations which vary in intensity and duration. These movements are never the same, conform to no definite pattern, and may affect different industries and areas of the country differently.

Many borrowers fare well in periods of prosperity, but in periods of recession capital may be dissipated, income may decline, and even character may be undermined. These factors give rise to the nonpayment of debts. A bank lending officer must, therefore, keep informed as to the economic pulse of the nation, the community, and the industry or industries in which s/he makes loans.

In extending credit to business borrowers, a bank is interested in the economic function performed by the business and its importance in the industry. A knowledge of what is happening in the industry is very important —changes in competitive conditions, technology, the demand for products, and distribution methods. If a loan applicant is not performing a function basic to the operation of the economy, the lender will be less likely to act favorably on the credit application than if the opposite situation prevails.

Relative Importance of the Credit Factors

Although all the factors mentioned earlier are important in credit analysis, most bankers agree that the collateral available for a loan is generally the least important. Credit is granted with the expectation that the funds will be repaid as agreed, not that the pledged assets will have to be sold to provide the funds needed for repayment. Security is taken in most instances to strengthen a weakness found in one or more of the credit factors, such as the ability to create income.

Every loan application is unique. One credit factor may be most important in one situation while another one is in a second situation. Over the entire spectrum of credit analysis, however, character emerges as the most important factor. If a borrower is of poor character, the probability is high that at some time he will not comply with the terms of a loan agreement.

Scope of Credit Investigation

The scope of a credit investigation will vary depending on such determinants as the size and maturity of the loan, the operating record of the business, the security offered, and previous relations with the borrower. No definite routine is followed since each applicant for credit may have some peculiar features that should be investigated more thoroughly than others. The objective is to accumulate information that can be used to evaluate the applicant's character, ability to create assets and income, and the probable economic environment for his business. In the investigation of a business loan application, banks like to know something about the history of the business—the firm's operating record, labor relations, experience in the development and marketing of new products, and sources of growth in sales and earnings. Since management is of great importance, information about the executives of a firm is a necessity. Information about their experience, background, outside affiliations, and interests is of value, as are the opinions of others concerning their integrity and capabilities. It is also important to know whether adequate provision has been made for management succession in the firm.

Banks should know about the nature and operation of the business; what type of products are handled or produced, what type of services are rendered. Whether the goods are staple or styled, consumer or capital, luxury or necessity would be worthwhile information. The source and stability of raw materials and labor as well as the proximity to markets are important. Buying and selling terms, distribution methods, extent of fabrication, hazards in the business, and the importance of the business in the economy are important facts that will place the business in proper perspective.

The bank would certainly want information on the concern's financial condition. This necessitates reviewing financial statements, investigating the possibility of contingent liabilities, and examining the insurance coverages. Since the condition and efficiency of the firm's physical facilities are very important, the lending officer may wish to examine them personally. It may also be helpful to contact other banks with which the firm has done business, as well as suppliers and customers of the firm. Information about competitive conditions in the industry and the trends of sales and profits may be of considerable importance also in evaluating the firm's future.

Sources of Credit Information

The many sources of credit information include interviews with loan applicants, the bank's own records, a variety of external sources, inspection of applicants' places of business, and applicants' financial statements.

Interview of Loan Applicant In the interview with the applicant, the lending officer learns the reason for the loan and whether the loan request meets various requirements established in the loan policies of the bank. Even if the loan request is not in harmony with bank policy or violates some regulation established by law or a bank regulatory agency, the lending officer may offer the applicant advice regarding other possible sources of funds. From the interview, the lending officer can also get some idea as to an applicant's honesty and ability and may form an opinion as to whether security will be necessary. Information about the history and growth of the business, the backgrounds of key personnel, the nature of the products and services, sources of raw materials, competitive position, and plans for the future can be obtained through the interview and, if desired, checked later against other sources. In the interview, the lending officer will also advise the applicant as to what additional financial information will be needed for evaluating the proposed loan.

Bank's Own Records

A bank may maintain a central file of all its depositors and borrowers from which credit information can be obtained. For example, it will show the payment record on previous loans, the balances carried in checking and savings accounts, and whether the applicant has a habit of overdrawing his account. Even if the applicant has never been a customer of the bank, the central file may contain some information if the applicant has been solicited by the new-business department.

External Sources of Credit Information

Dun & Bradstreet, the most widely known credit-reporting agency, collects information on approximately three million businesses in the United States and Canada and makes it available on a subscription basis. Brief information and credit ratings on each firm are published in national and regional reference books. More detailed information on individual firms is supplied in the form of credit reports, the most common of which is the Business Information Report (see Figure 9-1).

The first of the six sections in the report is a summary showing the name and address of the firm; the Standard Industrial Classification Number and the D-U-N-S (Data Universal Numbering System) number; the type of business; ownership; composite credit rating; promptness with which payments are made by the firm; sales, net worth, and number of employees; and the general condition of the firm and the trend of the business. The composite credit rating for a firm consists of two parts—two letters (or a number and a letter) followed by a number. The first part indicates the firm's estimated financial strength, and the second its composite credit appraisal. The rating of DD1 for Arnold Metal Products Company, for example, indicates that the firm's estimated net worth is $35,000 to $50,000 and its credit rating is high.

The second section of the report contains information from the firm's suppliers as to how promptly it has been paying its bills and the highest credit granted during the year. The third section contains a recent balance sheet and information as to the firm's sales and profits, if available. This section may also include information regarding insurance coverages, leases, trends of sales and profits, and important recent developments such as major asset acquisitions and new financing. The fourth section provides information as to the usual size of the firm's deposit balances and its payment record under loan agreements. The fifth section contains significant biographical information about the principals or owners of the business, including their previous experience, outside business affiliations, and past financial difficulties, if any. The final section of the report describes in some detail the nature of the firm's business, the kinds of customers to whom it sells, and its physical facilities. It may also give the approximate number of customers served by the firm and the numbers and types of its employees.

Dun & Bradstreet issues several kinds of reports in addition to the Business Information Report. One of the most useful of these is the Key Account Report, which contains considerably more detailed information about a firm. Several credit agencies in addition to Dun and Bradstreet are generally classified as special mercantile or trade agencies. These agencies usually limit their coverage to a single trade or industry or to a limited number of

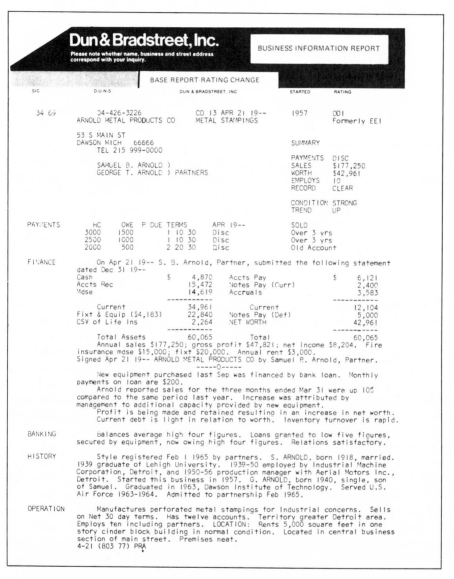

Fig. 9–1. Example of a business information report. (Names and figures are wholly fictitious.)

allied trades or industries, in contrast to the comprehensive coverage of Dun and Bradstreet. An example is the Lyon Furniture Mercantile Agency, which limits its services to the fields of furniture, home appliances, department and general stores, funeral parlors, and interior decorators.

Banks sometimes check with other banks that have had relationships with the loan applicant. They may also check with various suppliers and customers of the firm. Suppliers can give information on how the firm's bills have been paid, whether discounts have been taken, the high and low credit outstanding, and whether unjust claims are made and discounts deducted to which the firm is not entitled. Checking with the firm's customers can provide information as to the quality of its products, the reliability of its service, and the amount of merchandise that has been returned. Such checkings with the trade and with other banks may also reveal something about the character and ability of the firm applying for the loan, or its managers.

Another source of information is the Credit Interchange Service of the National Association of Credit Management, an organization that provides information about the credit experience of the suppliers of a firm on a nationwide basis. This organization provides its members with an answer to the question: How well does the firm pay? However, it only presents the facts and does not provide an analysis or interpretation or offer any recommendations. Other sources of information on business firms, especially large ones, include trade journals, newspapers, directories, public records, and statistical reporting services such as Standard and Poor's and Moody's. Some banks even check with the competitors of a business firm. Such information must be used with great discretion, but it can be very helpful.

Sources of consumer credit information have changed recently in several important ways. For many years banks and other lenders relied heavily on retail credit bureaus that specialize in gathering credit information on consumers. These agencies are either privately owned or owned and operated mutually by the firms they serve in the community, including the banks. Information on an individual's employment, income, number of dependents, indebtedness, paying habits, and other facts that have a bearing on his or her credit is gathered and made available to members or customers, either by telephone or in a written report. Because federal legislation has placed restrictions on the distribution of consumer credit information in recent years, this source has declined in importance and may decline even further.

The basic objectives of the Credit Reporting Act of 1971 are to protect consumers from inaccurate and obsolete information in credit reports about them and to safeguard their privacy. The act places heavy responsibilities on consumer reporting agencies and users of consumer credit information. Consumer reporting agencies, as defined in the legislation, include any person or business firm who, for profit or on a cooperative nonprofit basis, regularly engages in the practice of assembling and disseminating consumer credit information in written or oral form. The act states that a consumer reporting agency may furnish a consumer report only:

1 In response to a court order
2 In response to the consumer's written instructions

3 In connection with a credit transaction

4 For employment purposes

5 For the purposes of writing insurance for the consumer

6 To determine the consumer's eligibility to obtain a license

7 For some other legitimate purpose

The act states that no consumer report may contain any information on the following:

1 Bankruptcies more than 14 years old

2 Suits and judgments more than 7 years old

3 Paid tax liens more than 7 years old

4 Accounts placed for collection more than 7 years old

5 Record of arrest, indictment, or conviction more than 7 years old

6 Any other adverse information more than 7 years old

These restrictions do not apply, however, in the event one of the following is involved:

1 A credit transaction in excess of $50,000

2 Life insurance of more than $50,000

3 Employment at an annual salary of $20,000 or more

A consumer has several rights under the act. With a few exceptions, the law gives the consumer the right to know the nature, substance, and sources of the information collected by a consumer reporting agency. Also, the consumer has a right to be told who has received a consumer report containing this information and to have the agency correct any incorrect information relating to the consumer and to notify those to whom the incorrect information has been distributed. Should a dispute develop between the consumer and the credit reporting agency, the consumer has the right to request that his or her version of the dispute be placed in the file and included in subsequent reports. The act also provides that a consumer is entitled to be notified when a party is seeking information from a credit reporting agency of such a nature that it would constitute an "investigative report," and has a right to request that additional information about him or her be disclosed. An investigative credit report pertains to a consumer's character, general reputation, personal characteristics, or mode of living and is obtained generally through personal interviews with friends, neighbors, and associates.

The act is not concerned with the practices of persons and firms other than credit reporting agencies who give reports based solely on transactions between consumers and themselves. This is known as *direct checking*. If a consumer has been delinquent in his payments on a personal loan, for example, it is perfectly all right for the lender to report this information to a retail dealer where the consumer has asked for an extension of credit. It is not acceptable, however, for the lender to report the financial relationship as "unsatisfactory" or "poor," or by some similar description. Direct checking is much more expensive than obtaining similar information from a credit bureau. Therefore, the cost of consumer credit information and thus the cost of consumer credit are likely to be increased in the future. Moreover, because of the work and exposure to liability involved, it would appear that few banks will elect to become credit reporting agencies under the law.

Financial Statements

Financial statements are required of most borrowers, especially if the amount involved is relatively large. Even in consumer credit, where loans are usually quite small, an applicant may be asked to list what s/he owns and owes, income and expenses, current bills outstanding, dependents, and other information that will reflect his or her financial condition. The proper evaluation of information contained in financial statements is of great importance in the credit analysis process. The remainder of this chapter is devoted to the discussion of methods of financial statement analysis.

Analysis of Financial Statements

Financial statements of borrowers and prospective borrowers are among the most important sources of credit information available to bank lending officers. In dealing with business borrowers in particular, banks find that historical financial statements, pro forma statements, and cash projections provide not only a good basis for evaluating a loan applicant's financial condition and profitability but also a knowledge of the applicant's ability to generate cash flows for operating purposes and making loan payments. The usefulness of historical financial statements in making credit decisions depends, of course, on the timeliness and quality of the statements themselves. The extent to which lending officers actually use financial reports and projections in evaluating loan proposals depends on such factors as the size, purpose, and maturity of the loan, and the amount of security being furnished.

Lenders use financial statements and budgets to estimate the extent of the borrower's need for funds, evaluate the probability of loan repayment, estimate the potential loss if the borrower does not pay, and decide on the terms of the financing if a loan is to be made. Loan officers must avoid placing too much reliance on historical balance sheet information, since a firm's financial condition can deteriorate rapidly if it begins to incur operating losses. Information provided by prior income statements must also be used with discretion in view of the fact that past profits are often a poor indicator of future earnings. This is not to deny the importance of evaluating as accurately as possible the borrower's current financial condition and examining the level and trend of past earnings; nevertheless, lending officers should also examine pro forma financial statements and cash projections that show what the borrower's financial condition, profitability, and cash requirements are expected to be in the future. A major value of historical financial statements is the help they provide in appraising the soundness of the borrower's cash and profit projections. For example, if a borrower's pre-tax profit margin had averaged approximately 5 percent in recent years and never exceeded 6 percent, a projection showing a margin of, say, 8 percent, would need to be questioned.

The validity of any conclusions drawn from financial statements can be no better than the information contained in the statements. Often it is necessary to work with audited statements many months old, supplemented by unaudited interim statements. In that case, the loan officer should consider carefully the quality of the interim statements even if they have been prepared by persons who appear competent. Even audited statements must be used with discretion. Many judgments are required in determining the book values of a firm's assets and the amount of its earnings. Lenders are interested in the degree of conservatism with which these judgments have been made. It is not enough that the firm has been following generally accepted accounting principles, since those principles often permit a great deal of latitude in the recognition of income and expenses. In the early 1970s, for example, it became all too clear that a number of computer-leasing firms had overstated their income for several years in financial statements that were certified as having been prepared in accordance with generally accepted accounting principles. If reliance is to be placed on a borrower's cash forecasts and pro forma financial statements, the loan officer must examine critically the underlying assumptions that have been made with respect to important profit determinants such as sales volumes, selling prices, wage rates, and selling and administrative expenses. Many of the same techniques used in analyzing historical statements can also be used in analyzing profit projections and pro forma financial statements.

Evaluation of Items on the Financial Statements

One method of analyzing financial statements is to evaluate each significant item to determine its accuracy and reasonableness. This method often involves trimming down various items to more reasonable and conservative figures. A thorough analysis is made of each item that appears in the financial statement in an effort to appraise its fair value, but no reference is made to proportions, relationships, or ratios. Obviously, a bank credit analyst must have some knowledge of the business and statement items in order to appraise them properly.

Evaluation of Asset Items

Accounts receivable should be analyzed carefully because they represent the nearest thing to cash and may be the principal source of debt repayment of short-term loans. Information about the size, age, and sources of the accounts is important. If receivables are concentrated in a few large accounts, the inherent risk of nonpayment may be greater than if they are distributed over many accounts. In some cases an investigation into the financial strength and paying habits of the debtors is in order. If the bank credit analyst finds evidence that some accounts are not being paid in accordance with the credit terms of the business, s/he may ask for an aged trial balance. If many accounts are past due, they must be evaluated accordingly, and an adequate reserve for bad debts must be established. In the investigation of accounts receivable, it is also important to determine whether any of the accounts have been factored or assigned to others; usually the better accounts are disposed of in this manner. Also, the possibility exists of a contingent liability if the accounts were assigned with recourse, that is, the assignee promises to pay in the event the accounts receivable are not paid.

In many instances notes receivable arise because customers of the business are not paying their accounts according to the credit terms, and notes are obtained in an effort to strengthen the firm's position. If notes receivable appear large in relation to accounts receivable, a thorough investigation should be made to determine the soundness and liquidity of the notes. If notes receivable have been discounted with a lending institution, there is the possibility of a contingent liability, as in the case of accounts receivable. When notes receivable have been discounted with recourse, they should remain on the balance sheet as an asset item, and the amount of the loan should appear as a liability.

A bank credit analyst is interested in the age, liquidity, and price stability of the inventories, the degree to which they are free of risks of obsolescence and deterioration, the adequacy of insurance coverage, and the firm's method of inventory accounting. One must also know whether the inventories are based on a physical count, whether the firm uses the first-in, first-out (FIFO) or the last-in, first-out (LIFO) method of valuation, and whether the quantities on hand are excessive. If one is thinking in terms of the probable liquidation value of the firm, then goods in process and supply inventories should be largely discounted because of their limited marketability. And since raw materials usually have a broader market than do finished goods they are more likely to maintain their value. And if one is looking to the inventories as security for a loan, some control must be maintained over them.

Normally, banks do not look to the sale of fixed assets as a source of funds for repayment of a loan. However, if the debt is intermediate- or long-term, fixed assets are likely to take on more significance. This is especially true when fixed assets are taken as security for the loan. Usually, however, the principal importance of fixed assets in credit analysis is due to their ability to produce income. The credit analyst should be certain that the firm is taking adequate depreciation, is maintaining the properties in good condition, and has adequate insurance coverage. With respect to liquidation values, the analyst would consider whether the properties are general purpose or special purpose, since this would affect their marketability.

Intangible assets such as goodwill, trademarks, copyrights, patents, leaseholds, and franchises are usually accorded little value by bankers. Patents, copyrights, franchises, and leaseholds which have substantial value are occasional exceptions. However, as a general rule, bank credit analysts are interested principally in tangible assets and tangible net worth.

When the balance sheet shows that the firm owns stock in one or more companies, the analyst is interested not only in the value of the investment but also in any interrelationships between the companies. The financial relationships or commitments that may affect the debt-paying ability of the borrowing firm are of particular interest. If the assets of the firm include amounts due from officers and employees or affiliates and subsidiaries, these will be investigated very closely. Bankers take a dim view of amounts due from officers and employees of a firm. And, in the case of accounts receivable from affiliates and subsidiaries, a careful evaluation must be made of their ability to pay. If any sinking funds appear on the borrower's balance sheet, the banker is concerned with their adequacy. Sinking funds for repaying other obligations are not available for repayment of bank loans of course, but the banker wants to be certain that all sinking fund provisions have been complied with.

Evaluation of Liabilities and Net Worth

There are three types of creditors—secured, preferred, and general—and the amount owed each may influence the amount of credit a business can obtain from a commercial bank. Secured creditors are those that hold a lien on specific property, such as a mortgage on plants and equipment. Preferred creditors have a preference over all others by operation of law. Preferred claims include taxes owed to governmental bodies and wages due employees. General creditors are those who have been provided with no security and have no preference in the event of liquidation. They usually share proportionately in any assets remaining after the preferred and secured creditors have been paid.

Commercial banks are quite interested in the amounts and maturities of all liabilities for which a loan applicant is responsible. If a firm's accounts payable are large relative to its scale of operations, it may need additional equity capital or borrowed funds. Careful investigation is usually made if there are notes payable to suppliers since this may indicate that the firm has been slow in paying its trade obligations and has been asked or compelled to give notes to evidence the indebtedness. If the firm has obligations under conditional sales contracts, an investigation may be made to determine if any payments are past due, and if so, the penalties that are likely to be involved. If the firm owes a significant amount to its shareholders or officers on notes payable, the bank may ask that such liabilities be subordinated as a condition to granting the firm a loan. In many cases the analyst will want to review the amounts accrued for taxes and other expenses to evaluate their adequacy.

Long-term liabilities consist of mortgage loans, debentures (senior and subordinated), notes, term loans, and all other forms of indebtedness that do not mature within one year. The credit analyst is concerned with the nature and maturity of these obligations and the provisions that have been made for meeting the required payments. The default provisions of the various agreements and whether the loan applicant is in full compliance are of interest also. For example, failure to pay interest on bonds or term loans can cause the entire unpaid balance to become due and payable immediately.

The owner's equity, or net worth, is an item on which bankers place great value in extending credit. In the case of proprietorships and partnerships, where the owners are individually responsible for the debts of the firm as well as for any debts they have contracted outside the business, it is important to consider not only the income and net worth of the firm itself but also the owners' earnings, assets, liabilities, and net worth outside of the business.

The possibility of contingent or undisclosed liabilities is always a matter of concern. Such liabilities may arise, for example, from borrowing on the security of notes and accounts receivable, endorsing or guaranteeing the obligations of others, guaranteeing products or services, injuring third parties or damaging their property, and under-reporting taxable income. Liabilities of this nature may arise without any warning and can easily impair the debt-paying ability of the firm; to the extent possible, they should be insured against. However, the banker will want to be certain insofar as possible that the exposure to noninsurable potential liabilities is not very great.

Evaluation of the Income Statement

A firm's earnings tell us something about the quality of the assets reported on the balance sheet as well as the effectiveness of the management. The importance of income statement analysis increases with the maturity of the loan. Bankers may place more emphasis on balance sheet items in negotiation of short-term loans, but with longer maturities the income statement takes on a greater significance. Analysis of the firm's income statements will reveal the degree of stability in its operations and the efficiency with which it is being managed. The firm's accounting practices should be examined carefully to see that no changes have been made that would cause the figures to be noncomparable from year to year.

Income statement analysis is facilitated by developing a common-size statement in which all items are expressed as a percentage of sales. The percentage figures are easily compared then with similar figures for previous periods and with the percentages of other firms in the same type of business. For example, if an analyst were to find that the selling expenses of a firm had been increasing steadily as a percentage of sales over a period of years and that the percentage figure for the latest year was considerably above that of other firms, reasons for this apparently unfavorable situation must be determined. The fact that certain expenses appear to be out of line in comparison with other firms does not necessarily mean that they are too large. But if the firm is spending either too much or too little in a particular category, the banker should review the situation with the borrower to help find ways of improving operations, particularly if the banker has special competence in the area involved.

Extraordinary income and expenses are given particular attention if they are substantial items. Extraordinary expenses might include losses on the sale of fixed assets, uninsured losses from natural causes, inventory shortages, and abandonment losses. Extraordinary income often consists of profits on the sale of operating assets or land. Such profits are likely to be nonrecurring.

Ratio Analysis

Figures on a firm's balance sheet and income statement are often much more informative when related to other figures on those statements or to averages for comparable firms in the same industry. While it may be interesting to know that a firm's profits were $5 million last year, it may be considerably more helpful to know that those profits were earned on sales of $500 million, assets of $400 million, and net worth of $200 million. Lending officers are interested in relationships that shed light on the direction in which a firm appears to be moving, as well as on its current financial condition and recent profitability. In analyzing trends, the lending officer is concerned not only with the year-to-year and possibly month-to-month changes in aggregate quantities such as sales and profits, but also with the trends of such important ratios as net income to sales, current assets to current liabilities, and total debt to total assets.

The ratios that could be computed with the figures in a firm's financial statements are almost limitless, but logic and experience tell us that only a handful are really useful. In general, ratios based on historical statements are used in searching for answers to questions such as the following:

1 Will the firm be able to continue to meet its obligations as they come due?

2 Are the firm's accounts receivable and inventories reasonably current and liquid?

3 Is the firm achieving a satisfactory volume of sales in relation to its investment in current and fixed assets?

4 Is the firm earning a reasonable rate of return on sales, assets, and net worth?

5 How much could the firm's profits decline before it would be unable to meet fixed charges such as interest, rentals, and principal payments?

6 If the firm were to fail, how much could the assets shrink in value from the balance sheet figures before unsecured creditors would sustain any losses?

7 Is the firm's financial condition generally strong, weak, or something in between?

The reader will note that none of these questions relates directly to the firm's future profitability—a matter of great importance to a lender, particularly a lender of intermediate- or long-term money. In one way or another, it is necessary to estimate the probability that the borrower's profits will decline to levels that would make it impossible to comply with the repayment schedule of the proposed loan. The probable duration of any such periods of low profitability or losses should also be considered. This kind of forecasting usually requires a study of the competitive conditions, demand and supply conditions, and future prospects of the borrower's industry or industries. It also requires a careful analysis of the strengths and weaknesses of the borrowing firm itself: the quality of its management, the efficiency of its production organization, the effectiveness of its marketing, the healthiness of its employee relations, the condition of its physical facilities, the availability and cost of labor and raw materials, the value of any

Table 9–1
Commonly Used Financial Ratios

Type of Ratio	Name	Numerator	Denominator
1. Liquidity	Current ratio	Current assets	Current liabilities
2. Liquidity	Acid test	Current assets minus inventories	Current liabilities
3. Activity	Turnover of total assets	Net sales	Total assets
4. Activity	Turnover of fixed assets	Net sales	Net fixed assets
5. Activity	Collection period	Accounts receivable	Daily credit sales
5.* Activity	Turnover of receivables	Credit sales	Accounts receivable
6. Activity	Inventory turnover	Cost of sales	Inventories
7. Financial leverage	Debt/asset ratio	Total debt	Total assets
7.* Financial leverage	Debt/net worth ratio	Total debt	Net worth
8. Financial leverage	Fixed charges coverage	Earnings before fixed charges and taxes	Fixed charges
9. Profitability	Operating profit rate of return	Earnings before interest and taxes	Total tangible assets
10. Profitability	Net profit margin	Net profit	Net sales
11. Profitability	Return on assets	Net profit	Total assets
12. Profitability	Return on common equity	Net profit minus preferred dividends	Common stock equity

Note: Ratios 5* and 7* are alternates to 5 and 7.

intangibles such as patent rights and licensing agreements, and the possibility of contingent liabilities.

We will examine the ratios customarily found most useful in financial analysis to gain an appreciation of the insights ratio analysis can provide, as well as an awareness of its limitations. Basically, there are four types of ratios: liquidity, activity (or turnover), financial leverage, and profitability (see Table 9–1). Each of these four aspects of a firm's financial health can be measured in more than one way by the use of ratios, and it is often useful to consider more than one measurement. In some instances, two similar ratios provide essentially the same information in different form, as in the case of the ratios of debt to total assets and debt to net worth, both of which are measures of the proportion of the firm's total financing that has been supplied by creditors. In other instances two ratios of a given type provide essentially different information, as in the case of the current ratio and the acid test or quick ratio, both of which are measures of liquidity. If the firm has a significant amount of inventories, the acid-test ratio is a far more stringent test of liquidity than is the current ratio, since inventories are included in the numerator of the current ratio but not in the acid-test ratio.

In working with financial ratios, it is important to keep in mind that proportionate increases in the numerator and denominator leave the ratio unchanged. For example, if the current assets of a firm increase from $400,-

Table 9–2
Balance Sheets December 31, 1980 (in thousands)

	Company A	Company B
Assets:		
Cash	$ 200	$ 25
Accounts receivable	400	125
Inventories	600	500
Total current assets	1,200	650
Fixed assets (net)	2,100	750
Other assets	100	100
Total assets	3,400	1,500
Liabilities and net worth:		
Accounts payable	400	175
Notes payable	100	10
Accrued liabilities	100	15
Total current liabilities	600	200
Deferred income taxes	400	50
Long-term debt	1,000	100
Common stock	400	300
Retained earnings	1,000	850
Total	3,400	1,500

000 to $600,000 and current liabilities from $200,000 to $300,000, the current ratio remains unchanged at 2 : 1. In this case, if one were to consider the current ratio alone, one would conclude that the firm's financial condition had not changed. But this conclusion could be very much in error. A more thorough investigation might reveal that current assets and current liabilities had both increased to levels that were too high in relation to the firm's sales, and that some of the firm's current assets were becoming quite illiquid. In this case the current ratio is misleading. Generally, it is unwise to consider a single financial ratio by itself without reference to other aspects of the firm's financial condition and profitability.

The use of ratios in financial analysis will be illustrated by comparing two business firms assumed to be operating in the same industry (see Tables 9–2 and 9–3). Company A is about twice as large as company B in terms of assets and sales. The 1980 financial statements and ratios for the two firms in the tables that follow reveal a number of differences and highlight certain areas that seem to merit further investigation.

Liquidity and Activity Ratios

Looking at the liquidity ratios for companies A and B (Table 9–4), we see that A is less liquid than B in terms of the current ratio but more liquid in terms of the acid-test ratio. This reflects the substantial differences in the

Table 9-3
Income Statements Year 1980 (in thousands)

	Company A	Company B
Sales	$4,200	$2,000
Cost of goods sold:		
Cash costs, except rentals	2,470	1,280
Depreciation	200	125
Total	2,670	1,405
Gross profit	1,530	595
Selling and administrative expense	800	355
Operating profit	730	240
Interest expense	100	10
Earnings before taxes	630	230
Income taxes (48 percent)	302	110
Earnings after taxes	328	120

proportions of cash, accounts receivable, and inventories in the current assets of the two firms. Cash and accounts receivable are 50 percent of total current assets for company A but only 23 percent of current assets for company B. In that respect, company A appears to be more liquid than B. However, we must also consider the quality of the receivables and inventories of the two firms, and neither the current ratio nor the acid-test ratio provides any information on that. One indicator of asset quality is the speed with which the asset appears to be turning over as measured by its relationship to sales in the case of accounts receivable, or cost of sales in the case of inventories.

In considering activity ratios, we will assume that operations for both firms were essentially level throughout the year, exhibiting little in the way of seasonal, cyclical, or secular influences. With that assumption, it is appropriate to relate year-end accounts receivable to sales for the year, and

Table 9-4
Liquidity, Activity, and Leverage Ratios

	Company A	Company B
Current ratio	2:1	3.25:1
Acid-test ratio	1:1	.75:1
Turnover of total assets	1.24	1.33
Turnover of fixed assets	2.00	2.67
Accounts receivable turnover	10.50	16.00
Collection period (360-day year)	34.3 days	22.5 days
Inventory turnover	4.45	2.81
Debt/asset ratio	.59:1	.23:1
Debt/net-worth ratio	1.43:1	.30:1

Note: Deferred income taxes have been considered as debt in computing the leverage ratios.

year-end inventories to cost of sales for the year. Otherwise, it might be more appropriate to relate receivables and inventories to sales and cost of sales for the last few months of the year. When inventories vary widely from month to month, analysts sometimes relate the average month-end inventories for the year to cost of sales for the year to get an average turnover figure. However, this computation obviously does not indicate whether inventories at year-end were at a reasonable level. If it is the level of year-end inventories with which we are concerned, then it is the year-end inventories that should be related to a cost of sales figure. Such a turnover figure can then be compared with similar figures for other firms and with prior years' figures for the same firm.

The turnover figures for accounts receivable and inventories show that here, too, are significant differences between the two companies (Table 9–4). The turnover rate for the accounts receivable of company A is only about two-thirds that of company B. Or, in terms of collection periods, the 34.3 days for A is about 50 percent longer than the collection period of 22.5 days for B. With respect to inventories, the turnover rate of 4.45 for A is considerably faster than B's rate of 2.81. These differences in turnover rates appear large for two firms in the same industry. An analyst would want to know why such large differences exist.

A number of things could cause A's collection period to be 50 percent longer than B's. For example, A's credit and collection policies may simply not be as tight as B's, and this could mean that A's receivables are inferior in quality to B's. To determine whether a quality difference exists in the receivables, it would be a good idea to compare the credit terms of the two companies and to examine aged trial balances of their accounts receivable to see the amounts that are past due and for what periods. It might be found that A has different credit terms from B or that A gives special credit terms to a number of its customers. Another possibility is that the two firms sell largely to different types of customers. Or, it could be that company B sells a substantial part of its receivables to a factoring firm, in which case the receivables remaining on B's books might actually be lower quality than A's, even though the reverse appears true at first glance. These are some of the more common reasons for differences in collection periods among firms.

The large difference in inventory turnovers for the two firms (A's turnover being more than 50 percent greater than B's) would also seem to merit investigation. The turnover figures may indicate that A's inventory management is considerably better than B's, but there are a number of other possible explanations. The two firms may sell to different classes of customers and use different channels of distribution, or have a different product mix. Or perhaps company B sells a substantial part of its total output on a consignment basis and finds itself with large inventories held by its consignees. Another possibility is that B is carrying large safety stocks in anticipation of interrupted shipments from one or more of its suppliers. These, again, are only examples of the many things that could account for the difference in the turnover ratios. Ratio analysis is useful principally in locating areas of possible difficulty or weakness. Once such areas have been discovered, it is necessary to investigate further to determine why the firm's ratios are out of line with those of other firms or with its own past norms.

Looking next at the total asset and fixed asset turnover ratios (Table 9–4), we find the first of these about equal for both companies, but the turnover of fixed assets is considerably higher for B than for A. This could be due to B's having a more modern and efficient manufacturing facility than A. It could be due to differences in methods of calculating depreciation, or it could be the result of B's utilizing its plant for more hours during the year by working crews at night or on weekends.

Financial Leverage

The financial ratios in Table 9–4 show A's greater dependence on borrowed capital. It should be noted that in computing these ratios deferred income taxes have been treated as debt, even though it is possible that such taxes will not have to be paid for a very long time, if ever.

A third measure of financial leverage, in addition to the debt/asset and debt/net-worth ratios, is the ratio of earnings before taxes and fixed charges to fixed charges, known as the fixed-charges coverage. Although we will use the 1980 figures to compute the coverage of fixed charges, it should be recognized that a bank lending officer's real concern is with the extent to which the future fixed charges of a firm, including those associated with any loan the bank is considering for the firm, will be covered by future earnings. In computing the fixed-charges coverage, we will assume that the annual principal payments are $100,000 for A and $10,000 for B. Fixed charges include rentals, interest expense, and principal payments. Principal payments must be converted to a before-tax basis (since they are not deductible for tax purposes), and this is done by dividing the payments by one minus the income tax rate. With an income tax rate of 48 percent, the principal payments are divided by .52. So we find that A must earn approximately $192,000 before taxes, and B, $19,000, to make their principal payments of $100,000 and $10,000. As shown in Table 9–5, the coverages of fixed charges for the two firms are very different.

Assuming that all of the earnings are available to pay fixed charges, the earnings of company A would still cover fixed charges if a decline of 60 percent were experienced, but B would still be able to cover fixed charges if its earnings dropped 88 percent. Although coverage of fixed charges is widely used as a measure of financial condition, it is important to recognize the limitations of this ratio. The numerator of the ratio (earnings before

Table 9–5
Fixed Charges Coverage, Year 1980 (in thousands)

	Company A	Company B
Operating profit	$730	$240
Interest expense	100	10
Principal payments (before-tax basis)	192	19
Total fixed charges	292	29
Fixed charges coverage	2.50	8.28

taxes and fixed charges) is a very crude measure of a firm's capacity to make required payments, and the denominator does not include all payments a firm may be required to make. Nevertheless, the ratio is useful because cash inflows do depend to a considerable extent on earnings, and because payments under loan agreements and non-cancellable leases do in many cases represent a firm's most significant financial obligations. A projection of the coverage of fixed charges, however, is not an adequate substitute for detailed forecasts of cash inflows and outflows. The fixed-charges coverage ratio is not in terms of cash flows and does not take into account, for example, the cash required to finance an increase in net working capital or an increase in net fixed assets. To evaluate properly a firm's ability to make future loan payments, cash forecasts should be prepared using various plausible assumptions as to sales volumes, selling prices, and costs. In this way it is possible to estimate the probability that the borrower will be able to comply with the repayment provisions of the proposed loan.

Profitability

The profitability ratios of the two firms are set forth in Table 9–6. Company A emerges as the most profitable under all profitability ratios. It is performing particularly well for its stockholders in comparison to B. In addition to

Table 9–6
Profitability Ratios and Fixed Charges Coverage

	Company A	Company B
Operating profit rate of return	21.5%	16.0%
Net profit margin	7.8	6.0
Return on assets	9.6	8.0
Return on common equity	23.4	10.4
Fixed charges coverage	2.50	8.28

Note: Computation of the fixed charges coverage is based on the assumption that annual principal payments for A and B (in thousands) are $100 and $10, respectively. See details in Table 9.5.

looking at these ratios, the analyst will want to determine whether there are any significant differences in the accounting practices of the two firms that affect the profit comparisons. If so, it might be wise to explore the possibility of adjusting the earnings so as to place them on the same basis. The analyst will also want to examine the profit trends of the two firms over a period of years.

While company A is clearly more profitable, company B is much less dependent on debt, as is shown by its strong leverage ratios and high fixed-charges coverage. Which is the preferred loan applicant? This depends on the answers to a number of questions, including the purposes of the requested loans and each firm's potential within its market. However, A has demonstrated its ability to earn high rates of profit. The banker should be convinced that B can improve its profitability before advancing that firm extensive amounts of credit.

Ratio Trends

Significant developments often come to light through an examination of the trends of a firm's financial ratios over a period of years. Just as it is helpful to compare the ratios for one firm with those of other firms or with industry averages, it may also be helpful to see whether a firm's financial condition or profitability is improving or deteriorating and, if so, in what respects. Based on the 1980 figures, company A appears to be more profitable than B, but if A's return on assets has been declining steadily for the last few years and B's has been improving, an investigation of the reasons for the profit trends might indicate that B's return will soon be as high as or higher than A's. In any event, the directions in which a firm's financial condition and profitability have been moving are matters of great interest, since they may provide an indication as to what the future will be. Of course, sales and profit trends often change direction, sometimes quite abruptly, so it is never wise to forecast earnings by simply extrapolating from past trends. Often it is desirable to examine in depth the strengths and weaknesses not only of the loan applicant but also of the industry in which the firm is operating. This involves a study of the demand and supply conditions in the industry. In the final analysis, a bank lending officer wants to know where the firm's sales and profits have come from in the past and where they can be expected to come from in the future.

Use of Financial Ratios to Predict Bankruptcy

In recent years considerable research has been conducted in the use of financial ratios as predictors of the insolvency of business firms. Most of the research in this area has been univariate in nature and designed to identify those ratios that, individually, are the best indicators of bankruptcy. But with a multiple-discriminant analysis model it is possible to select the best set of ratios for predicting the insolvency of business firms. One study using such a model selected five ratios that jointly provided the best predictive powers. These ratios were:

1 Net working capital/total assets. When a firm experiences financial difficulties, this ratio usually declines. It was found to be more useful in the multiple discriminant model than either the current ratio or the acid test ratio.
2 Retained earnings/total assets. This is a measure of cumulative profitability over time. The ratio tends to be small for young and unprofitable firms, where bankruptcy frequently occurs.
3 Earnings before interest and taxes/total assets. This is a good measure of the true productivity of a firm's assets before the impact of taxes and financial leverage.
4 Market value of equity/book value of total debt. This ratio has been found to be a better predictor of bankruptcy in the discriminant model than the ratio of debt to net worth based on book values. The presence of this variable in the model, however, limits it to the analysis of firms whose stocks are publicly held.
5 Sales/total assets. This ratio shows the sales-generating ability of the firm's assets. Taken alone, it is a very poor predictor of bankruptcy, but when combined with the other four ratios it ranks second in its contribution to the overall discriminating power of the model.[1]

Although additional research is probably needed in the use of models to predict bankruptcy, the findings thus far are very encouraging. It has been found, for example, that it is possible to predict bankruptcy accurately up to two years prior to the failure of the firm, but the degree of accuracy diminishes rapidly when the lead time is increased to more than two years. This would indicate that the greatest deterioration in a firm's financial condition tends to occur about two to three years prior to bankruptcy. A multiple-discriminant analysis model can be very helpful to bank lending officers in screening out undesirable candidates for business loans. It might be even more useful in helping to identify existing borrowers whose financial condition is becoming critical, perhaps soon enough to take protective action.

[1]Edward I. Altman, "Financial Ratios, Discriminant Analysis and the Prediction of Corporate Bankruptcy," *Journal of Finance* 23 (September 1968): 589–609.

Sources of Comparative Financial Information

Financial ratios for various industries can be found in a number of places, one of which is the *Annual Statement Studies* published by Robert Morris Associates. This volume contains composite financial data for almost 300 different lines of business, based on the financial statements of approximately 40,000 different firms. The figures are presented for four size-groups of companies within each industry and for the industry as a whole. The number of business firms in each group is shown along with the financial data, which consists principally of eleven financial ratios and a common-size balance sheet and income statement for each group. In the common-size statements, each balance-sheet item is shown as a percent of total assets and each income-statement item as a percent of sales. Three values are reported for each of the ratios for each group of firms: the upper quartile, the median, and the lower quartile. This method of reporting the ratios avoids distortions that could be caused by a few extreme ratios if an arithmetic mean were used, and it gives a good indication as to the dispersion of the ratios within each group of companies. For example, if a credit analyst finds that some ratios for a particular firm are either substantially above the upper quartile or below the lower quartile, it can readily be seen that they are unusual. The editors of the *Annual Statement Studies* point out to the reader that the figures contain several inconsistencies. First, the sample of companies is not selected in a scientific manner. Second, many companies operate in more than one industry, yet they are placed in the industry of their primary product line. The editors recommend, therefore, that the figures be used as general guidelines rather than as absolute norms for a given industry.

Dun & Bradstreet is a second source of financial ratios for a large number of industries. Fourteen ratios are published annually in *Dun's Review* (three fall issues) for 22 types of retail firms, 32 types of wholesalers, and 71 types of manufacturing companies. With a few exceptions the number of firms represented in each of the 125 categories ranges from about 50 to 250. The reporting is similar to the *Annual Statement Studies* in that the upper quartile, median, and lower quartile are reported for each ratio, but the firms are not grouped by size class within each industry. It is interesting to observe, as shown in Table 9–7, that only six of the 14 ratios reported by Dun & Bradstreet are the same as those in the *Annual Statement Studies*.

Cash Budgets and Pro Forma Financial Statements

In evaluating a proposed business loan, it is not only important to consider how funds will be obtained for repayment of the loan but also to forecast what the borrower's financial condition will be at various times over

Table 9–7
Financial Ratios Reported in *Annual Statement Studies* and *Dun's Review*

	Annual Statement Studies	Dun's Review
Liquidity:		
1. Current ratio	Yes	Yes
2. Quick (acid-test) ratio	Yes	No
3. Inventory to net working capital	No	Yes
4. Current debt to inventory	No	Yes
5. Fixed assets to tangible net worth	Yes	Yes
Activity:		
6. Turnover of net worth	Yes	Yes
7. Turnover of net working capital	Yes	Yes
8. Turnover of receivables	Yes	No
9. Collection period	No	Yes
10. Turnover of inventories	Yes	Yes
Financial leverage:		
11. Current debt to tangible net worth	No	Yes
12. Funded debt to net working capital	No	Yes
13. Total debt to tangible net worth	Yes	Yes
14. Unsubordinated debt to capital funds	Yes	No
Profitability:		
15. Net profit margin	No	Yes
16. Profit before taxes on net worth	Yes	No
17. Return on tangible net worth	No	Yes
18. Profit before taxes on total assets	Yes	No
19. Return on net working capital	No	Yes

Note: In ratio no. 14 "capital funds" consists of equity capital and subordinated debt.

the life of the loan. Information of this kind is developed in cash budgets and pro forma financial statements. Although such statements will often be quite wide of the mark, their preparation and use is necessary when planning for the future. The accuracy of pro forma statements depends heavily on the assumptions made about future developments, so bank lending officers are interested in the reasonableness of such assumptions. A forecast of a substantial increase in income, for example, based on an unprecedented rise in sales or a sharp decline in unit costs, would certainly be questioned. All borrowers do not provide lending officers with pro forma financial statements. Many are not accustomed to making such projections, and in some cases they are not necessary. If the maturity is short and the loan well secured, elaborate statements are not required. The longer the maturity, the greater the need for pro forma statements in making a proper analysis of a loan request.

Cash budgets for larger firms are typically prepared for the most part from the information contained in projected income statements and balance

Table 9-8
Company A Cash Budget

	Year 1981 (in thousands)
Sources of cash:	
Earnings after taxes	$338
Dividends	218
Earnings retained in the business	120
Depreciation provision	280
Increases in liabilities:	
Accounts payable	70
Deferred income taxes	70
Accrued liabilities	10
Decrease in other assets	15
Total	565
Uses of cash:	
Capital expenditures	350
Increases in assets other than fixed assets:	
Accounts receivable	40
Inventories	30
Decreases in liabilities	
Notes payable (current)	20
Long-term debt	100
Total	540
Increase in cash balance	25

sheets. A satisfactory analysis of the projected sources and uses of cash can usually be prepared from the income statement and comparative balance sheet information. Sources of cash include decreases in assets and increases in the liabilities and net worth of the firm. Uses of cash include increases in assets and decreases in liabilities and net worth. Reference to projected income statement figures makes it possible to show some of the more important details underlying the balance sheet changes. Net profit and non-cash charges (principally depreciation) can be shown as sources of cash, while dividends and the net addition to gross fixed assets can be shown as uses of cash.

An example of a simple cash budget for a business firm is presented in Table 9-8. This budget was prepared from the comparative balance sheets and projected income statements in Tables 9-9 and 9-10. From the cash budget it can be seen that most of the company's cash requirements are expected to be supplied by retained earnings and depreciation, with the remainder being accounted for by increases in accounts payable, accrued liabilities, deferred income taxes, and a small decrease in other assets. The principal uses of cash are capital expenditures and a reduction in long-term debt. Other uses are increases in accounts receivable and inventories (most

Table 9–9

Company A Comparative Balance Sheets (in thousands)

	1981 *(Projected)*	*1980* *(Actual)*	*Increase* *(Decrease)*
	December 31		
Assets:			
Cash	$ 225	$ 200	$ 25
Accounts receivable	440	400	40
Inventories	630	600	30
Total current assets	1,295	1,200	95
Fixed assets			
Cost	3,850	3,500	350
Depreciation reserve	(1,680)	(1,400)	(280)
Net fixed assets	2,170	2,100	70
Other assets	85	100	(15)
Total assets	3,550	3,400	150
Liabilities and net worth:			
Accounts payable	470	400	70
Notes payable	80	100	(20)
Accrued liabilities	110	100	10
Total current liabilities	660	600	60
Long-term debt	900	1,000	(100)
Deferred income taxes	470	400	70
Common stock	400	400	—
Retained earnings	1,120	1,000	120
Total	3,550	3,400	150

likely attributable to the higher level of sales projected for 1981) and a small decrease in notes payable due within one year. If the lender were considering a five-year term loan to company A, it would be important to have cash budgets similar to this for each of the five years. In addition, if the company's outside financing requirements were expected to vary widely within a given year, the lender should be provided with quarterly, and perhaps monthly, pro forma balance sheets for the borrowing firm.

Besides serving as a source of information from which cash budgets can be prepared, pro forma financial statements can be used directly in appraising the level of risk in a proposed loan. For this purpose they can be subjected to ratio analysis in the same way as historical statements. The usefulness of cash budgets and pro forma statements does not end with the approval of the loan. The borrower's actual performance and financial condition in future periods can be compared with the earlier projections. Such comparisons may give an indication as to why the borrower's profits and financial condition are either better or worse than expected, and this may

Table 9-10

Company A Projected Income Statement (in thousands)

	Year 1981
Sales	$4,500
Cost of goods sold:	
Cash costs, except rentals	2,540
Rentals	55
Depreciation	280
Total	2,875
Gross profit	1,625
Selling and administrative expenses	830
Operating profit	795
Interest expense	90
Earnings before taxes	705
Taxes (federal and state)	367
Earnings after taxes	338
Dividends	218

be helpful in deciding whether any action should be taken to protect the interests of the bank.

Questions

1. Why does analysis of the balance sheet receive relatively more emphasis than the income statement in the case of short-term loans, while the reverse is true in the case of long-term loans?

2. The credit analysis performed by your bank shows that a potential business borrower does not quite qualify for a loan from your bank. You are the loan officer who must tell the applicant his firm does not qualify for a loan. How do you tell him?

3. What does it mean if the current ratio is rising and the quick ratio is falling?

4. What would it mean if the return on assets was declining but the return on equity was rising?

5. Certain ratios vary widely from industry to industry. For example, in comparing the retail grocery industry to most other industries, would you expect the current ratio to appear high or low? Why? What about turnover of total assets and net profit margin?

6. A high inventory turnover ratio would normally be considered to indicate efficient inventory management. However, an exceptionally high ratio could carry negative implications. Why?

7. Which of the five C's would you consider to be the most difficult to evaluate? Why?

SELECTED REFERENCES

BAUGHN, WILLIAM H., and CHARLES E. WALKER (eds.),   *The Bankers' Handbook.* Homewood, Ill., Dow Jones-Irwin, 1966, Part III.

BERNSTEIN, LEOPOLD,   *Understanding Corporate Reports.* Homewood, Ill., Dow Jones-Irwin, 1974.

Duns Review. Fall issues, annually.

FAULKE, ROY A.,   *Practical Financial Statement Analysis.* 6th ed. New York, McGraw-Hill Book Co., 1968.

HELFERT, ERICH A.,   *Techniques of Financial Analysis.* Homewood, Ill., Richard D. Irwin, Inc., 1972.

LEV, BARUCH,   *Financial Statement Analysis; A New Approach.* Englewood Cliffs, New Jersey, Prentice Hall, Inc., 1974.

LEVINE, SUMNER, (ed.),   *Financial Analysts Handbook.* Homewood, Ill., 1975, Section 4, Richard D. Irwin, Inc., 1975.

Robert Morris Associates, *Annual Statement Studies.* Philadelphia, Pa., annually.

O'MALIA, THOMAS J.,   *Banker's Guide to Financial Statements.* Boston, Bankers Publishing Company, 1976.

10

Lending Practices and Policies

Loans are the most important asset held by banks, and bank lending provides the bulk of bank income. Although bank loans fluctuate with the economy, they have increased significantly over the years (see Figure 1–1). Loans of all insured banks doubled from 1950 to 1960 and have increased over fourfold since then. Obviously, inflationary pressures had much to do with this phenomenal increase, but the gain was very large, even when adjusted for the rise in prices.

Classification of Loans

Bank loans can be classified in a variety of ways, including purpose, the type of security if any, maturity, method of repayment, and origin. Other classifications exist, but these are sufficient to give us an understanding of the lending activities of commercial banks.

Purpose

A common classification of loans is by purpose or use of the borrowed funds. We have, for example, such categories as commercial and industrial, real estate, consumer, etc. Table 10–1 shows the commonly employed classifications used by regulatory authorities and the amount of loans in each category as of year-end 1977. Note that commercial and industrial loans, the term used to include credit extended to business firms, accounted for the

235

Table 10-1

Loans of Insured Commercial Banks

December 31, 1977 (in millions of dollars)

	Amount	*Percent*
Commercial and industrial loans	197,092	32.2
Real estate loans—total	178,607	29.2
Construction and land development	*21,395*	
Secured by farmland	*7,732*	
Secured by 1- to 4-family residential properties:		
Insured by FHA and guaranteed by VA	*7,868*	
Conventional	*88,897*	
Secured by multi-family (5 or more) residential properties:		
Insured by FHA	*405*	
Conventional	*4,506*	
Secured by nonfarm nonresidential properties	*47,803*	
Loans to individuals—total	141,252	23.1
To purchase private passenger automobiles on instalment basis	*49,864*	
Credit cards and related plans:		
Retail (charge account) credit card plans	*14,695*	
Check credit and revolving credit plans	*3,779*	
To purchase other retail consumer goods on instalment basis:		
Mobile homes (excluding travel trailers)	*9,126*	
Other retail consumer goods	*8,378*	
Instalment loans to repair and modernize residential property	*7,321*	
Other instalment loans for household, family, and other personal expenditures	*20,151*	
Single-payment loans for household, family, and other personal expenditures	*27,937*	
Loans to financial institutions—total	36,816	6.0
To real estate investment trusts and mortgage companies	*9,074*	
To domestic commercial banks	*3,152*	
To banks in foreign countries	*7,245*	
To other depository institutions	*1,747*	
To other financial institutions	*15,597*	
Loans to farmers	25,714	4.2
Loans for purchasing or carrying securities—total	17,111	2.8
To brokers and dealers in securities	*12,781*	
Other loans for purchasing or carrying securities	*4,330*	
All other loans	16,115	2.6
Loans, gross	612,706	100.0

Source: FDIC *Annual Report*, 1977.

largest percentage, followed by real estate and consumer. These three categories comprised nearly 85 percent of the total.

Secured and Unsecured Loans

Secured loans involve the pledge of specific collateral. An example is a loan that is secured by a chattel mortgage on an automobile or some other form of personal property. Pledged collateral for secured loans may consist of a variety of assets such as real estate, warehouse receipts, accounts receivable, plants and equipment, trust receipts, negotiable bills of lading, oil runs, corporate stocks, and bonds. The basic requirement of such assets is marketability. The main reason for requesting that a loan be secured is to reduce the bank's risk of loss in the event the borrower is unwilling or unable to repay the loan at maturity. Security does not assure that the loan will be repaid; however, it does reduce the risk, since the bank becomes a preferred creditor in the event of liquidation, and takes precedence over general creditors in the liquidation of any assets pledged to the bank as collateral.

The value of the assets securing a loan may deteriorate, and this deterioration, coupled with a forced sale, may not furnish sufficient funds to cover the indebtedness. In arranging security for a loan, it is imperative that the bank obtain the primary claim to the collateral and that its value be as great as, or greater than, the amount of the loan. Should the value of the collateral exceed the amount of the loan, and the bank be forced to liquidate it because of default on the part of the borrower, the excess is returned to the borrower. In the event the security is not sufficient to cover the loan, the bank can in some instances obtain, through court proceedings, a deficiency judgment for the difference. This entitles the bank to a claim on additional property or income, should the borrower have any. In recent years some states have enacted legislation limiting the use of deficiency judgments in the area of consumer lending. In most instances this has taken the form of eliminating the deficiency judgment when the loan is reduced below a certain level. The objective of limiting deficiency judgments was to reduce overcharging on consumer durable goods at the retail level. The limitation was later extended to lenders as well. Limiting the use of the deficiency judgment has increased the risk of lending and will eventually reduce the availability of credit to certain borrowers. Consumer credit will, to an increasing extent, be made available only to those borrowers who have a good, well-established credit record.

Security is required on loans for several reasons. One of the most common is probably the borrower's financial weakness. Such weakness may be indicated by several factors, including heavy obligations to creditors, poor management, and insufficient income. Borrowers in this financial condition can strengthen their credit by pledging certain assets. Having a secured loan may also be a psychological advantage for a bank. As long as the borrower has greater equity in the pledged assets than does the bank and the bank is in a preferred position and can foreclose in the event the loan agreement is broken, the borrower has a strong incentive to repay the obligation. The length of a loan also has a bearing on whether it will be secured. As the term of the loan lengthens, the risk of nonrepayment increases. Loans for purchasing real estate are nearly always secured, especially if the funds are borrowed for long periods of time, because of risk of nonrepayment.

Several federal agencies have been created by Congress since the 1930s that, as one of their functions, guarantee loans granted by commercial banks and certain other lenders. The guarantee of loans by these agencies may be a direct guarantee, insurance, or commitments to assume a portion of the loan after it is granted. For example, the Federal Housing Authority insures real estate and modernization loans, and the Small Business Administration enters into an agreement with a commercial bank to participate in a portion of a loan granted to a small business.

Unsecured loans are based more exclusively on the borrower's integrity and financial condition, expected future income, and past record of repayment. Contrary to popular belief, the largest loans and the greatest dollar volume of loans made by some banks are often granted on an unsecured basis. The largest commercial borrowers are able to borrow on an unsecured basis. Some companies are considered by banks to be prime borrowers, and in many cases they receive the most favorable interest rate. Such companies have competent management, products and services that are well accepted in the marketplace, relatively stable profits, and a strong financial condition. They provide their banks with financial statements from which it is relatively easy to determine their financial condition and keep track of their progress.

Business firms are not the only ones who borrow on an unsecured basis —many individuals enjoy this privilege. Persons who own their own homes, have a steady job which they have held for years, and have a record of prompt payment both at the bank and at retail stores are commonly in a position to borrow on an unsecured basis. An applicant's ability and willingness to pay are projected into various situations. The question as to how the bank would fare as a general creditor in periods of adversity and liquidation would certainly be considered, as would the claims of other creditors, secured or unsecured, and whether the bank could collect without being a preferred creditor.

Maturity

Bank loans can be classified according to the maturity of the loan contract as short, intermediate, and long-term. Short-term loans are usually defined as those with maturities of one year or less, intermediate loans mature in more than one year and up to seven or eight years, and long-term loans have still longer maturities. Short-term loans may be made for a specific period of time—up to a year—or on a demand basis. A demand loan is one that has no stated maturity and, since it is payable on demand, repayment can be requested at any time. The granting of a demand loan often implies that the borrower is in a relatively liquid position and that the assets in which the borrowed funds have been invested can be liquidated in a very short time.

A great deal of vagueness surrounds the definition of an intermediate loan. It is not uncommon to find a loan made for a period of ten years considered an intermediate loan. Many consumer loans may be classified as intermediate. Business term loans, which have increased greatly in recent years, usually have maturities of ten years or less. Real estate loans for the purchase of houses and for the financing of industrial and commercial buildings are the most common type of long-term loans.

Method of Repayment

Bank loans may be repaid in one lump sum or on an instalment basis. Lump-sum loans are usually referred to as *straight loans,* which means that the contract calls for repayment of the entire principal on one final maturity date. Interest payments, however, might be due at various intervals or when the loan matures. Instalment loans require periodic payments of principal, usually of equal amounts. Payments may be monthly, quarterly, semiannually, or annually. Instalment lending recognizes the principle of amortization, whereby the principal amount is amortized over the life of the contract. In this manner repayments do not become as great a burden on the borrower as if the total loan were due at one time. The repayment schedule, especially in real estate lending, is comparable to the rent a person would pay if he were renting rather than buying a house. Instalment loans serve as a budgeting instrument for many people. Repayment of loans on an instalment basis is not reserved exclusively for consumer and real estate loans. Many term loans to businesses are made on this basis, with payments closely tied to the amount of income generated by the borrower.

Origin

The loan portfolio of commercial banks is derived principally from three major sources: directly from borrowers, by the purchase of notes from dealers of automobiles and other consumer goods, and by purchasing notes from commercial paper dealers. By far the largest number of loans are made directly to borrowers who apply for loans at the banking office. Such loans are evidenced by a promissory note signed by the borrower or by notes payable to the borrower which are endorsed over to the bank with recourse. Many banks derive a large portion of their loan portfolio by purchasing notes from dealers of various products. A final source of loans, less important than those already discussed, is the purchase of commercial paper and banker's acceptances. Because these credit instruments are of short maturity and high quality, which contribute to their marketability, they are usually considered a part of the bank's secondary reserve.

Regulation of Bank Lending

Bank lending is highly regulated for a number of reasons. One is to protect the safety of banks, an example of which is a limitation placed on the amount of credit that can be extended to a single borrower. The objective of such a rule is to avoid undue concentration and reduce risk. In recent years Congress has enacted several statutes designed to protect borrowers which are applicable to all lenders including commercial banks. These include the Truth-in-Lending Act (1968), which is intended to insure that prospective borrowers will be advised of the effective costs of the credit for which they are applying; the Fair Credit Reporting Act (1971), one of whose principal purposes is to protect borrowers from being denied credit because of erroneous information in their credit files; and the Equal Credit Opportunity Act (1974) which prohibits lenders from discriminating on the basis of sex, marital status, race, color, religion, national origin, or the receipt of public assistance benefits.

Another reason for regulating bank lending is to encourage or limit particular kinds of lending because of the expected impact on the economy. The Community Reinvestment Act (1977), for example, is intended to encourage lending in low and moderate income neighborhoods. Regulation U of the Federal Reserve Act, issued pursuant to the Securities Exchange Act of 1934, limits the amount that can be loaned to purchase or hold securities and is designed to reduce speculation.

Probably the most important limitation placed on bank lending is the amount of credit that can be extended to any one borrower. This limitation is commonly referred to as the *ten percent rule*, and it generally limits the amount of credit extended to one borrower to 10 percent of a bank's capital and surplus. Capital notes and debentures may be included as a part of a bank's capital and surplus for the purpose of determining its lending limit. This rule is more restrictive on small than on large banks of course. Large banks are in a position to handle the loan requests of many large borrowers; in the event they are not, a loan can be shared with other banks through a participation arrangement.

Several exceptions to the 10 percent rule reduce its restrictive effect. Obligations in the form of drafts or bills of exchange drawn in good faith against actual existing values are completely exempt; this includes the financing of foreign trade and a large portion of the domestic movement of goods. Obligations that arise out of the discount of commercial or business paper are also exempt. This includes the indirect financing of consumer goods, which in the area of consumer lending is quite large. An important exemption, or at least a partial exemption, involves the financing of goods secured by shipping documents, warehouse receipts, or other such documents of title covering readily marketable staples when such property is insured, if insurance is customary. For example, if the market value of the collateral securing a loan is 115 percent, a bank could make a loan equal to 25 percent of its capital and surplus. The size of this loan could be increased depending on the increase in the market value of the security. In fact, it is possible to make a loan equal to 50 percent of a bank's capital and surplus for a period of ten months if the market value of the security is 140 percent. The reason for what might appear to be a liberal interpretation of this 10 percent rule is based on the fact that loans collateralized by such security have a minimum risk. The 10 percent restriction is designed to limit the amount of risk concentrated in credit extended to any one borrower. Exceptions to the rule are justified on the grounds that the loans are well secured or are secured by collateral that will maintain its value and marketability during the life of the loan. The rule limits the small bank in making loans to relatively large borrowers and, as a result, encourages them to seek larger banks to participate in loans that exceed the small bank's legal limit. It also encourages banks to increase their capital stock and surplus accounts so that they will be in a position to make larger loans. The lending limit has encouraged the merger of banks for the same reason.

Real estate lending has been closely regulated since the adoption of the National Bank Act of 1864, but in recent years the regulations have been liberalized. Both the amount of loans that a bank can make and the maturity of individual residential loans have been increased. These limitations will be discussed more fully in the chapter on real estate lending. Since 1974 commercial banks have been permitted to make real estate loans secured by second mortgages, but the amount is limited to 20 percent of the bank's capital and surplus.

Loans to executive officers are closely regulated in amount and purpose, and loans to bank examiners are prohibited. In general, banks are prohibited from making loans secured by their own stock. If lending on this type of security were permitted, it would be possible for bank owners to borrow from the bank the equity that is necessary for the protection of the depositors. The reason for this law is obvious—the practice would be contrary to the public interest. However, national banks are permitted to make loans secured by the bank's own stock in cases where it is necessary to prevent loss on a debt previously contracted in good faith. If such a loan is made and defaulted, the stock must be sold at public or private sale within six months.

Loans to affiliates and bank holding companies are closely regulated. In general, a bank cannot invest in or purchase the securities of these organizations. However, it can lend to them under certain conditions. The securities pledged for such loans must have a market value of at least 20 percent more than the amount of credit extended unless they are securities of governments, in which case the margin may be less. These provisions do not apply to affiliates such as those engaged in holding bank premises or conducting a safe deposit business.

Secured bank loans must meet various requirements established by regulatory and supervisory authorities to assure that the bank has a valid and enforceable claim. Real estate loans made by national banks, for example, must be secured by a mortgage, trust deed, or other instrument which constitutes a first lien in fee simple. Loans on leaseholds can be made only if the lease has a maturity of at least ten years beyond the maturity of the loan. In general, banks are not permitted to accept second mortgages as security unless trouble develops with a loan and the taking of additional security is advisable. If warehouse receipts are taken as security, the commodities they represent must be in the exclusive possession and control of a genuine independent public warehouseman. Loans secured by the cash value of an insurance policy must be recognized by the life insurance company. Unsecured loans, and even relatively large loans that are secured, should be supported by adequate credit files. If they are not, they may be classified as substandard by bank examiners.

Loan Policy

The restrictions imposed by statutory law and administrative regulations do not provide answers to many questions regarding safe, sound, and profitable bank lending. Questions regarding the size of the loan portfolio, desirable maturities, and the type of loans to be made are left unanswered. These questions and many others about lending must be answered by each individual bank. Thus, it is desirable to have explicit lending policies to establish the direction and use of the funds from stockholders, depositors, and others, to control the composition and size of the loan portfolio, and to determine the general circumstances under which it is appropriate to make a loan. More and more banks have developed formal, written lending policies in recent years. The Comptroller of the Currency now insists that national banks have such policies. Although written lending policies serve a number of purposes, the most important is that they provide guidance for lending officers and thereby establish a greater degree of uniformity in lending practices.

Factors That Influence a Bank's Loan Policies

Since lending is important both to the bank and to the community it serves, loan policies must be worked out carefully after considering many factors. For the most part, these same factors determine the size and composition of the secondary reserve and the investment account of a bank. Many of these factors have been discussed elsewhere and will only be mentioned briefly here. The most important are:

1 Capital position
2 Risk and profitability of various types of loans
3 Stability of deposits
4 Economic conditions
5 Influence of monetary and fiscal policy
6 Ability and experience of bank personnel
7 Credit needs of the area served

The capital of a bank serves as a cushion for the protection of the depositors' funds. The size of capital in relation to deposits influences the amount of risk that a bank can afford to take. Banks with a relatively large capital structure can make loans of longer maturities and greater risk.

Since earnings are necessary for the successful operation of a bank, all banks consider this important factor in formulating a loan policy. Some banks may emphasize earnings more than others. Banks with a greater need for earnings might adopt a more aggressive lending policy than those that do not consider earnings to be paramount. This aggressive policy might be making a relatively large amount of term or consumer loans, which normally are made at a higher rate of interest than short-term business loans.

The fluctuation and type of deposits must be considered by a bank in formulating its loan policy. After adequate provisions have been made for the primary and secondary reserves, banks can then engage in lending. Even though these two reserves are designed to take care of the predictable deposit fluctuations and loan demands, unpredictable demands force banks to give consideration to the stability of deposits in formulating loan policy.

The economic conditions of the area served by a bank are influential in determining its loan policy. A stable economy is more conducive to a liberal loan policy than one that is subject to seasonal and cyclical movements. Deposits of feast or famine economies fluctuate more violently than do deposits in an economy noted for its stability. Consideration must also be given to the national economy. Factors that adversely affect the nation as a whole may, if they are of serious magnitude, eventually affect local conditions.

The lending ability of banks is influenced by the monetary and fiscal policies. If additional reserves are made available to the commercial banking system, the lending ability of banks is increased. Under these conditions banks can have a more liberal loan policy than if the opposite situation exists wherein expansion of bank reserves is being curbed or reduced.

The expertise of lending personnel is not insignificant in the establishment of bank loan policy. For example, officers may have considerable ability and experience in business lending but practically none in making real estate loans, while in other banks their specialty may be consumer lending. One of the probable reasons banks were slow in entering the consumer lending field was the lack of skilled personnel. Some banks may be so specialized in certain fields of lending that their presence may influence the loan policy of other banks.

An obvious factor influencing a commercial bank's loan policy is the area it serves. The major reason banks are chartered is to serve the credit needs of their communities. If this cannot be done, there is little justification for their existence. Banks are morally bound to extend credit to borrowers who present logical and economically sound loan requests. Banks in areas where the economy is predominantly one of cattle raising, for example, cannot turn their back on this type of lending, but must tailor policy to fit the needs of this economic activity.

Items Included in a Loan Policy

Loan Territory

The territory to be served by a bank will depend on many factors, including the amount of its resources, competition, the demand for loans, and the bank's ability to supervise or keep in close contact with the borrowers. Banks may have no territorial limitations for certain classes of loans. For example, very large banks make loans to large national business firms no matter where their principal offices may be located.

Types of Loans to Be Made

Bank management must decide what types of loans would be best for the bank. Some of the more important considerations in making this decision are the risks associated with various kinds of loans, the need for diversification to spread the risk, the need for liquidity, the types of customers the bank wants to serve, the capabilities of bank personnel, and, certainly, the relative profitability of various kinds of loans. To the extent that it is practicable, banks diversify their loan portfolios among the various broad categories of loans such as business, consumer, and agricultural, and strive also for considerable diversification within each of these broad categories.

Acceptable Security and Credit Worthiness

To facilitate lending, reduce risks, and maintain standard practices, a bank's loan policy should deal with the question of what is considered acceptable security and credit worthiness. If certain loans are to be secured, the lending officers should have some indication of what is acceptable security. For example, some banks may not want to accept accounts receivable as security, except on a notification basis, or household goods for consumer loans. Furthermore, a bank may frown on accepting consumer loans that are endorsed by the borrower's friends or relatives. Banks may not wish to make real estate loans on single-purpose buildings. Construction loans may be made only in cases where the work is being supervised by a competent architect and the contractor has provided a completion bond and acceptable security. Banks may not want to lend more than a certain percent of the fair-market value of farm chattels or a certain percent of the retail price of automobiles. Some collateral may not be acceptable at all, such as cars over five years old, or highly perishable commodities. Banks may wish to limit the amount of individual consumer loans to a certain percentage of a borrower's annual disposable income. For acceptable collateral, an indication should be given as to the amount of funds that will be advanced on such security.

Banks receive many requests for loans from applicants who do not have acceptable credit worthiness. To save the time of the credit department and lending officers, it might be well to outline what is considered acceptable. Consumer loans might be restricted to persons who are presently employed and have been for a minimum period, and who have an assured income and a satisfactory credit record. Loans to businessmen may be restricted to those who have been in business for a certain length of time and have demonstrated an ability to produce a commodity or render a service profitably.

Maturity

A comprehensive loan policy would certainly cover loan maturities. The maturity of a bank's loan portfolio will affect bank liquidity as well as its risk exposure. Term loans to businesses are apt to be less liquid than 30-, 60-, or 90-day business loans, and the 20-year real estate loan lacks the liquidity of one made for a period of ten years. As loan maturities increase, money and credit risks also have a tendency to increase. Some banks may not wish to make loans on real estate for exceptionally long periods, and some may not want to make many business loans on a term basis. Moreover, some banks may wish to limit loans for the purchase of automobiles to 24 or 30 months rather than longer periods. To serve as a guide for the loan officer, the policy regarding maturities should be definite.

Excess Lines

One problem confronting many banks is that of loan requests exceeding their legal lending limit. The applicant may be a customer of the bank who is entitled to the credit requested, and the loan would be satisfactory from the standpoint of security and maturity. The bank is then faced with the choice of either working out a satisfactory arrangement with a correspondent bank to carry the excess portion of the loan, or of refusing the request and running the risk of losing the applicant's account, which may be valued highly. Some banks may not handle such requests or even lend up to their limit. Others may have a policy of arranging for a correspondent bank to carry the excess loan.

Loan Liquidation

To maintain an acceptable degree of loan quality and liquidity, a bank must have an adequate policy of loan liquidation. Numerous renewals of a loan impair the liquidity of the loan portfolio and increase the risk. Moreover, a *slow* loan becomes subject to an unfavorable classification by bank examiners. Some banks may want all business borrowers to liquidate their loans, other than term loans and revolving credits, once each year and to stay out of debt to the bank for a reasonable period of time. Missed payments are frowned upon, and after a few occur, corrective steps—even legal action—may be taken.

Compensating Balances

Banks require borrowers to carry a deposit balance with them; after all, borrowers must carry a deposit somewhere, and the most logical place is with the lending institution. Moreover, loans cannot be made unless banks have deposits. The term compensating balance is used to describe a deposit balance primarily of a business firm that is required and is part of the consideration for the extension of credit. In this manner the effective rate on a loan is increased. Compensating balances may also be used as a protective device for a lending bank. If the borrower experiences financial difficulties and it appears that default is imminent, the bank may be able to apply the borrower's deposit to the balance of the loan.

Compensating balance requirements vary among banks and are influenced by conditions in the money market. A common requirement is referred to as ten plus ten, meaning that the deposit balance required is 10 percent of the unused portion of a loan and another 10 percent once the loan is made for a total of 20 percent of the unpaid balance. Under such an arrangement, a borrower who has a commitment for $1,000,000 would carry a deposit of $100,000 during the time the loan was committed until it was used, and once the funds were drawn down would carry an average deposit of $200,000.

Although compensating balances are looked upon with favor by commercial banks and are required, they have lost some popularity in recent years. The growing emphasis on commercial bank profitability analysis has caused banks to become increasingly aware of all the costs and benefits associated with a borrower's account. Two disadvantages in requiring a compensating balance rather than a higher lending rate are that legal reserves must be carried against the balance and an FDIC assessment of three-tenths of one percent must be paid. Because of these factors, the benefits received by the bank from the borrower's balances are apt to be less than their cost to the borrower. Thus, in some cases it is better to charge a higher lending rate than to require a compensating balance.

Loan Commitments

Many bank customers, especially large business borrowers, plan their borrowing needs with the bank in advance of the time the funds will be actually needed. Therefore, banks adopt a policy regarding the types of commitments that will be made, the types of enterprises to which they will be made, the amounts that will be made available, and the charge for such commitments. Such planning is of value to the bank in that it gives some indication as to the demand for credit during certain periods of the year, and plans can be made regarding the maturity of other loans and of the secondary reserve.

A commitment is an agreement, oral or written, between a bank and a borrower whereby the bank stands ready to extend an agreed amount of credit for a specified period of time. A commitment may have no restrictions attached or may be subject to a number of conditions such as compensating balances, security, fixed-asset limitations, officer's salary limitations, etc. Normally, loan commitments do not exceed one year and may take several forms. Probably the simplest form is an oral commitment that a certain amount of credit will be available at a certain time in the future. Many loan commitments take this informal arrangement and are frequently referred to as open lines of credit. It is not uncommon for such a statement to be in written form, however. An even more formal commitment would be what is commonly referred to as a *standby commitment.*

A standby commitment is usually a more binding and exacting financial arrangement than is a line of credit. The bank and the borrower enter into a formal contract in which the bank agrees to lend a certain amount to the borrower and the borrower agrees to borrow. The agreement includes a statement regarding the time the funds will be available and such lending terms as security, interest rate, and liquidation of the loan. The borrower pays a fee for this commitment that is usually based on the unborrowed amount of the commitment.

A revolving credit is usually of longer maturity than is a line of credit. It firmly obligates the bank to lend a certain amount to a borrower for a stated period. The terms of the agreement are written out in detail since the agreement usually runs from one to three or more years. Under a revolving credit the borrower agrees to borrow in accordance with the terms set forth and to pay a fee that is usually computed on the unborrowed portion of the established maximum. A revolving credit agreement can become quite detailed and can include such items as the use of the borrowed funds; the rate of interest; the maturities of the notes; submission of financial statements and other financial and production data; security; and, in case of default, provisions regarding termination of the agreement and repayment of the loans outstanding.

Size of Loan Portfolio

The appropriate size for the loan portfolio is a question that constantly faces bank management. Since loans are the most profitable assets of commercial banks, bank management is under constant pressure to increase the loan account. Banks must maintain sufficient liquidity to meet the depositors' demands, however. They also have a social responsibility to the local community and the nation as a whole. Banks cannot withdraw from this responsibility and simply invest their resources in other assets such as bonds, and provide liquidity for the depositor. Competition prohibits activity of this kind—other lending institutions may take up the slack. Further, if a bank is not performing its lending responsibility, the bank chartering authorities would be justified in permitting an increased number of banks to operate in competition with it. Banks should not expand credit too liberally to the point of violating prudent banking.

No categorical answer exists as what is the optimum size of a bank's loan portfolio. Every bank operates within an environment of its own. The credit demands of the community, the depositors' demands for funds, capital funds, the abilities of bank personnel, and the liquidity needs are all different for different banks. It is as difficult to say how large the loan portfolio should be as it is to determine the amount of liquidity a bank should maintain. The size of a loan portfolio must be computed by analysis of the various needs or priorities for bank funds. Since priorities vary, it is impossible to establish hard and fast rules regarding the size of the loan portfolio of an individual bank or the banking system as a whole.

Bank loan portfolios have increased over the years as measured by the loan/deposit ratio. In general, large money center banks have higher loan to deposit ratios than do smaller rural banks. Several factors have contributed to these higher ratios. In addition to the desire to increase income, the ability to maintain liquidity has contributed greatly to this trend. The federal funds market and improvements in both asset and liability management have contributed greatly to a rise in the loan/deposit ratio as well as an improvement in credit analysis and the evaluation of credit risk. Finally, an expanding economy without many serious downturns has also contributed to a favorable lending market.

Loan Pricing

The pricing of bank loans involves the setting of interest rates, the establishment of a compensating balance requirement—especially for business firms—and in some cases, the imposition of loan fees. Interest rates may be either fixed or variable. As the term implies, a fixed rate is one that remains the same during the loan contract. A variable rate is one that may change during the term of the loan. The *prime rate*—the rate banks charge their most creditworthy business customers—is the most popular variable rate and varies with changes in money market conditions. Banks may also make loans, the interest of which is tied to the prime rate. A loan might be made at a rate of one or two full percentage points above the prime rate. For example, if the prime rate were 8 percent and the rate were set at 10, the interest would change automatically as the prime rate increased or decreased. The reason for this type of arrangement is the belief on the part of both borrowers and bankers that it is more equitable than negotiated rates, especially in an environment characterized by a considerable amount of inflation. Loan fees are sometimes imposed, depending on the amount of work involved in making a loan; these are found especially in the granting of term loans and in real estate lending.

The numerous factors that are considered in pricing loans include:

1 The cost of funds
2 The degree of risk in the loan
3 The maturity of the loan
4 The costs of originating and administering the loan (These costs, as a percentage of the loan, are a function of the size of the loan, the amount of credit investigation required, the cost of acquiring and maintaining control of the collateral, and the expense of collecting the loan.)
5 Rates available to the borrower from competitive sources of funds, including other banks and the commercial paper and bond markets
6 The overall relationship between the bank and the borrower (This includes income earned on the borrower's deposit balances as well

as expenses incurred in performing services such as paying checks and collecting deposited items for the borrower.)

7 The rates of return that can be earned on alternative investments.

Rates on Business Loans

Rates on business loans are generally the lowest of all bank rates, primarily because of their relatively short maturities. This is especially true for loans referred to as *commercial* and *industrial* loans because of their comparatively low credit risk. Business loans for current production usually have a maturity of less than one year and are frequently secured by highly marketable products. Because of these characteristics, they are among the most liquid and sought-after loans made by commercial banks.

Large businesses with the highest credit standing are able to borrow short-term from commercial banks at the prime bank rate. Since many businesses have a choice of borrowing from commercial banks or issuing commercial paper, the prime rate is generally close to, but a little above, the rate on prime commercial paper (see Figure 10–1).

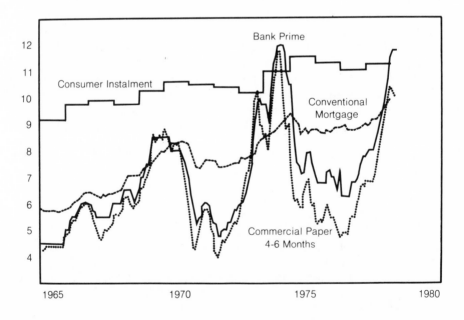

Fig. 10–1 Selected Interest Rates [Source: Board of Governors of the Federal Reserve System, *Federal Reserve Bulletin* and "Interest Rates on Selected Consumer Instalment Loans at Reporting Commercial Banks," Statistical Release (G. 10)].

Until the early 1970s, changes in the prime rate were relatively infrequent and were usually initiated by one of the major money center banks. Once initiated, a change was promptly adopted by other major banks throughout the country. Many bankers had come to believe that the prime rate should be even more responsive to movements in other short-term rates. They were also concerned about growing criticism when there was an increase in the rate. The result was the adoption by a number of large banks of formula approaches to setting their prime rates. The term *floating* was given to this new concept, implying that the prime would move freely with other money market rates. The formulas were first keyed to short-term money market rates, particularly the rate paid on commercial paper. Later the floating prime rate was tied to the average rate paid by large banks on certificates of deposits due in 90 days. However, banks that have adopted a formula-based prime rate do not feel compelled to follow their formulas if there are good reasons for not doing so.

Although the adoption of floating prime rates by some major banks has caused more frequent rate changes and more variation among banks, there is still a strong tendency for the various banks' rates to move together. All major banks are affected by essentially the same demand and supply conditions, and they are in competition with one another in making loans. Thus, when a bank lowers its prime rate and others do not follow, it will soon find itself with more loan requests than it can handle. If it raises its prime rate and others do not raise theirs, it will soon have a shortage of borrowers.

The prime rate has been slightly below the rate charged on business loans generally, but the spread is not significant. Large business loans normally carry a lower rate than do smaller loans. This is primarily because of the cost of administration, although credit worthiness would also be a factor. Rates on business loans also differ among various geographical areas of the country. Normally the lowest rates are found in New York City, followed by the West Coast. The highest rates during some periods have been found in the Northeast and North Central. Although these slight differences may be due in part to the credit rating of borrowers and the economic outlook for the area, probably the most influential factor is the difference in the availability of bank funds. All areas of the nation do not expand uniformly; therefore, the intensity of demand for business loans is not the same. Moreover, bank deposits do not expand at the same rate; consequently, the geographical differences in business loan rates result from of an imbalance in the supply-demand relationship.

Interest Rates on Farm Loans

Rates on farm loans are usually higher than those on business loans primarily because of their greater risk and smaller size. Farming is a risky enterprise because of such factors as weather, disease, infestation, oversupply, and changes in consuming patterns. Farm loans also have a long maturity. Most operating loans, which are considered the shortest of all farm loans, have a maturity of six months to one year normally. The extension of farm loans for another season or year is not uncommon as a result of some unforeseen development that adversely affects production or harvesting.

In addition to being higher, interest rates on farm loans are less variable than on business loans. The difference in rates for small and large loans reflects the cost of making and supervising loans and the bargaining power of the borrower. Although large farm borrowers may not have as many sources of credit available to them as do large business borrowers, some alternative sources are the Federal Land Bank, Intermediate Credit Bank, individuals, and life insurance companies. This fact is recognized by commercial banks; if the loan is desired, competitive rates must be met.

Interest Rates on Consumer Loans

Interest rates on consumer loans are higher than on most other bank loans because of their small size and the risk involved. Banks have costs to meet just as do other businesses, and in consumer lending the costs are greater per dollar of loan than in any other type of lending. The major reason for this is that a large number of people are required in the process. Applications must be taken and credit evaluations made, and after a loan is consummated an expense occurs in servicing it. Although a consumer-lending officer might make twenty $500 loans in one day, a commercial-lending officer might make a business loan of $100,000 or $1 million in less than an hour. The break-even point on consumer loans varies from bank to bank, but many bankers discourage instalment loans below $300 to $400 with maturities of less than two years. The cost of making small loans has prompted many banks to avoid loans for household items such as televisions, radios, refrigerators, and other appliances. Those banks with credit card programs have encouraged customers to use them for such purchases.

Consumer lending involves risks which contribute to the relatively high cost of consumer credit. The borrower's ability to pay may be interrupted by unemployment, sickness, accident, or some other unforeseen development. Unfortunately, in some instances the borrower's intention to repay may deteriorate after the loan is made, and a loss is then incurred by the bank. Maturity also influences the level of consumer loan rates, just as it does in other types of lending. All these factors contribute to a relatively high and sticky rate when compared to other types of bank loans.

Although interest rates on consumer loans vary among banks and among different parts of the country, in general, consumer loan rates are higher than other bank rates. There are some exceptions to this general rule, however, especially during tight money periods. In periods of restrictive credit, consumer loan rates tend to increase less than do rates on business loans. In mid-1974, for example, the interest rate on new car loans with a maturity of 36 months averaged 10.8 to 11.1 percent, and on other consumer goods loans with a 24-month maturity the rate was 13.0 to 13.1 percent. At this time, the prime rate reached 12¼ percent.

Residential Real Estate Interest Rates

Interest rates on residential real estate loans are influenced particularly by the maturity of the loan, the loan-to-value ratio, the availability of loanable funds, the need for liquidity, and whether the loan is guaranteed or insured by an agency of the federal government. In general, the higher the loan-to-value ratio, the higher the rate of interest, since the credit risk is obviously greater. This is especially true of conventional loans and, to some extent, of those underwritten by the various government agencies. The maturity of the loan is a very important factor since the longer the maturity, the greater the money-rate risk to the bank. The guarantee and insurance of real estate mortgages provided by various government agencies influence rates in that the credit risk involved in such loans is reduced. Since commercial banks have a greater need for liquidity than do other major lenders of real estate funds, their liquidity needs influence the interest rate that they will charge. As liquidity needs increase, interest rates usually increase; if not, banks at least become less eager to make real estate loans.

The movement of four significant interest rates that are especially important to banks is presented in Figure 10–1. Note that the bank prime rate has changed frequently as has the commercial paper rate. These changes are in response to fluctuations that occur in the money markets which are influenced by supply and demand and by monetary and fiscal policies. Although the conventional mortgage rate changes also, it is a more stable rate than the bank prime rate. The consumer instalment rate presented in Figure 10–1 is the average for the year rather than monthly. Consumer loan rates show less volatility than do other rates, due to a difference in the elasticity of demand. Many, if not most, consumer loan borrowers seem more concerned with the size of the down payment and the amount of the monthly payment than with the interest rates. Unless it is very substantial, an increase or decrease in interest rate does not have much effect on the size of the monthly payment. For example, if the effective annual percentage rate were reduced from 12 percent to 11 percent on an $8,000, three-year loan, the monthly payment would be reduced by less than $4. Thus it would probably take a substantial decrease in interest rates to cause an appreciable increase in demand for instalment loans. Recognizing this, bankers are not inclined to reduce their rates on instalment loans when there is a decrease in money market rates and the marginal cost of funds.

Usury

A factor that must be given consideration in loan pricing, especially in some areas of lending, is the usury laws of the various states. Usury laws limit the amount of interest that can be charged on loans and are found in all states, except Massachusetts and New Hampshire. The ceilings imposed by such laws are of ancient origin and stem from the belief that loans are unproductive and, in fact, immoral. Although this view does not prevail today, most legislators adhere to the belief that charging "excessive" interest on a loan should be prohibited.

Most state usury laws establish a number of ceiling rates that vary according to the type of lender and the nature of the transaction. Many of these laws exempt loans to corporations; some exempt large loans (e.g., loans over $100,000) to individuals on the notion that a usury law is to protect borrowers who are in a weak bargaining position and perhaps lack knowledge of financial matters. Generally, the statutes establish higher ceilings for consumer instalment loans and consumer revolving credits than for other types of loans because of the higher costs involved in such lending.

Frequently, the usury statutes not only establish different ceiling rates for different kinds of loans but also provide different methods of calculating the interest (declining balance, add-on, or discount) for the various kinds of loans. Sometimes they also permit additional charges for investigation and for processing the loan. Even in the absence of statutory provision for such additional charges, they may be allowed by the courts in reasonable amounts. Although one state limits interest on loans to individuals to 6 percent in amounts below $50,000 and a few permit a rate of 18 percent or more, the most common rates range from 8 to 12 percent.

In some states usury ceilings have seriously impeded the financing of real estate. For example, if the ceiling rate for home loans is 8 percent and market conditions call for a higher rate, lenders might charge points on their mortgage loans. The amount of funds actually supplied will be less than the amount of the loan in order to increase their yields. For each point, the lender reduces the proceeds of the loan by 1 percent, thereby increasing his yield by approximately 1/8 of 1 percent. The points are supposed to be paid by the seller of the house, and to the extent that builders absorb this cost, they may be discouraged from entering the market. Moreover, during periods of high interest rates, usury ceilings on mortgage loans make it more difficult for mortgage lenders to sell their loans in the secondary market, thus shutting them off from sources of funds for making additional loans.

A federal law provides that national banks may charge interest at the same rate as allowed by the laws of the state or district where the bank is located or at a rate 1 percent in excess of the Federal Reserve discount rate in effect at the Federal Reserve Bank in the Federal Reserve District in which the bank is located, whichever may be greater.

Administration of the Loan Policy

After the loan policy of a bank has been formulated, provision for its proper execution must be made. Certain individuals must carry out the loan policy, and some provisions should be made for its periodic review and evaluation in order to make any necessary changes. It should be remembered that a loan policy serves as a guide to lending, not as a straitjacket. Economic conditions change and so should a loan policy. Periodically, the loan portfolio and lending practices should be compared with the loan policy to determine whether it is being followed and if changes should be made.

The person in charge of the overall lending organization should be in charge of supervising the bank's loan policy. In small banks this may be the president or one of the vice presidents. In banks that rely to a great extent on a loan or discount committee to supervise lending, this body would be responsible for effecting the lending policies of the bank. In larger banks the responsibility would probably be assigned to the senior vice president in charge of lending, who would explain the provisions of the loan policy to the lending officers and secure their cooperation in carrying it out, which is necessary for a loan policy to be successful. Lending officers cannot consider what is desirable to them; they must consider what is good for the bank. The purpose of a lending policy is to promote the objectives of the lending function, not to serve as an end within itself.

Organization of Bank Lending

The organization of the lending function depends on numerous factors, including the character and quality of the lending officers, the size of the bank, the size of the loan portfolio, the type of loans made, and the board of directors' attitude toward the amount of authority delegated. The legal responsibility for bank lending rests with the board of directors, and some boards play a more important role in lending than do others. In general, larger banks delegate lending authority and specialize in lending more than do smaller ones.

The lending officer usually makes personal contact with the borrower, receives applications for loans, interviews the applicants, decides whether the applications are worthy of consideration, and may obtain all the necessary information about the applicant, or part of it may be obtained by the credit department. The lending officer may make the decision to grant the loan request, or this may rest with a committee or the board of directors, depending on the size of the request. Once the loan has been made, s/he usually supervises the loan: that is, keeps in close contact with the borrower during the life of the loan. This may include plant visits, occasional visits with the borrower in the bank, and requests for financial and other credit information from the borrower and from other sources. In the event of difficulty with the loan, the lending officer will exert every effort to collect the amount outstanding. If renewals or additional funds are requested, s/he handles these requests.

In small unit banks, all the officers may perform lending functions along with their other activities. Each officer may handle all types of loan requests, whether they are for consumer, business, or real estate purposes. Little formal specialization prevails. However, one officer may specialize in some type or types of loans because of special interest or experience. Each officer must secure the necessary credit information and maintain the credit files, since few small banks have a separate credit department. Each officer may have a lending limit within which decisions can be made regarding loan requests. Loans above a certain amount may be submitted to a loan or discount committee which will make the decision or, in smaller banks, refer the request to the board of directors for further consideration if the loan is extremely large or in any way unusual.

In medium-size unit banks, there is more delegation of authority and specialization regarding lending. Many medium-size banks have credit departments. Each officer may have an established lending limit, which is usually higher than in the small bank. Sometimes a loan committee composed of senior loan officers may exist within the bank to handle loan requests above the lending officer's limit. Members of the board of directors may be on this committee. If this is the case, only those requests requiring special attention would be referred to the discount committee and the board of directors. As in the small bank, supervision of the loans would be the responsibility of the lending officers.

The lending organization in large unit banks differs considerably from that in small banks and, to some degree, in medium-size banks, in the departmentalization and specialization of lending activities. Large banks may have such lending departments as real estate, business or commercial, consumer, and agricultural. Some of these departments are broken down further. Business loans, for example, can be divided according to industry, with a lending officer in charge of each industry or related industries. One large bank, for example, has separate loan divisions for iron and steel, automobiles, machinery, agricultural implements, electrical products, radio, and manufacturing sundries. Many banks divide their lending activities on a territorial basis.

Lending officers in large banks have lending limits, but they are usually higher than those in smaller banks. Larger banks make greater use of officer loan committees than do small- and medium-size banks. They may be organized on a formal or informal basis according to departments. For example, a request for a real estate loan larger than the lending officer's established limit would be referred to an officer's loan committee composed of real estate lending officers, rather than of officers from several departments. With an organization of that kind only the very large requests are referred to a loan or discount committee, and probably few, if any, requests are referred to the board of directors for action.

In larger banks, the credit department plays a much more important role in the lending process than it does in smaller banks. The lending officer turns over to the credit department all the information received from the applicant that would be used in the preparation of a formal loan request. Additional credit information on the applicant would be secured from many sources and assembled in one folder for the use of the lending officer, who in turn may discuss it with some colleagues or the officers' loan committee. The report of the credit department may include such items as financial statements (with balance sheets and profit and loss statements for a period of years arranged on one sheet so they can be evaluated at a glance), various financial statement ratios that have been calculated by the credit department, credit agency reports, pictures of the applicant's place of business, budgets, analysis of the industry's prospects as well as the applicant's, and many other details of value in making a decision on whether to grant the credit request.

The lending organization in branch banks varies considerably. Branch managers and officers may have limited loan authority, just as in a unit bank. Loan requests above this limit might be referred to the head office where consideration would be given to the request by the regional supervisor of that particular branch and a decision reached. The regional supervisor may also have a lending limit. Loans exceeding this limit would be referred to a loan or discount committee. In very small branches, the lending organization may be very similar to a small unit bank, but in large branches it may be more like the lending organization found in large unit banks, with a great deal of specialization and departmentalization. From a practical standpoint, it is not desirable to have a great deal of centralization of lending authority in the head office. Borrowers do not like to wait for credit decisions, and much of the personal touch important in credit evaluation is lost if many requests must be directed to the head office. When there are many branches, the head office usually performs general policy supervision and permits branch managers considerable discretion in lending. This, in fact, is about the only way branches can be operated efficiently.

Questions

1. What are the reasons for the regulation of bank lending? Comment on them. What is the purpose of the legal lending limit?

2. What are the reasons for usury laws? Comment on their effect on the mortgage market. Would you prefer reliance on the free market?

3. What are the advantages of having formal, written lending policies? What variables influence bank lending policies?

4. What considerations are involved in determining the appropriate size for a bank's loan portfolio? Comment on them.

5. How is an open line of credit similar to yet different from a revolving credit?

6. How do rates in the money and capital markets influence bank lending rates? Discuss the importance of the prime rate in bank lending.

7. Why are rates on consumer instalment loans generally more stable than money market rates?

8. What variables influence lending rates for commercial and industrial loans?

9. What should a bank use as the cost of its funds in setting the interest rate on a loan?

SELECTED REFERENCES

CLEW, HARRY T. JR., "Monitoring the Quality of a Loan Portfolio," *The Journal of Commercial Bank Lending*, February 1977, pp. 2–9.

HANNA, PAUL J., and PAUL S. NADLER, "Pricing Commercial Bank Business Loans," *The Bankers Magazine*, Winter 1971, pp. 12–20.

HAYES, DOUGLAS A., "Commercial Loan-Pricing Policies," *The Bankers Magazine*, January–February 1978, pp. 45–52.

————, *Bank Lending Policies*, 2nd ed., Ann Arbor, Michigan, The University of Michigan, 1977.

MERRIS, RANDALL C., "Loan Commitments and Facility Fees," *Economic Perspectives*, Federal Reserve Bank of Chicago, March/April 1978, pp. 14–21.

————, "The Prime Rate Revisited," *Economic Perspectives*, Federal Reserve Bank of Chicago, July/August 1977, pp. 17–20.

————, "Prime Rate Update," *Economic Perspectives*, Federal Reserve Bank of Chicago, May/June 1978, pp. 14–16.

MILLER, RICHARD B., "Everybody's Floating the Loan Rate," *The Bankers Magazine*, Spring 1975, pp. 42–45.

MOTT, HUBERT C., "Establishing Criteria and Concepts for a Written Credit Policy," *The Journal of Commercial Bank Lending*, April 1977, pp. 2–16.

MUELLER, P. HENRY, "The Most Challenging Issues Facing Bank Lending," *The Journal of Commercial Bank Lending*, March 1977, pp. 16–24.

WATSON, RONALD D., "How Good are Your Marginal Cost Estimates?", *The Bankers Magazine*, Winter 1977, pp. 57–62.

11

Short-Term Business and Farm Loans

Short-term loans account for more than one-third of the dollar amount of all bank loans, and more than half of the loans to businesses are short-term. In addition, commercial banks do a substantial amount of short-term lending to farmers, brokers, dealers, and nonbank financial institutions. Loans of this kind are highly regarded by commercial bankers. They have less credit and money-rate risk than do longer maturities and, in general, have more liquidity than do many other types of loans.

Short-term loans are widely used in financing seasonal increases in working capital and in the temporary financing of capital expenditures and other long-term commitments pending negotiation of a long-term loan or the flotation of a stock or bond issue. Commercial banks also commonly grant short-term loans with the understanding that if the borrower's financial condition and profitability continue to be satisfactory the loans will be renewed at maturity and thus become a source of longer-term debt capital.

Businesses That Borrow on a Short-Term Basis

Retail firms, food processors, and manufacturers with seasonal operations are among the most important users of short-term bank loans. Many retail firms borrow heavily during Christmas and Easter seasons to carry increased inventories and accounts receivable. Food processors often require short-term funds when crops are brought in for processing. Manufacturing firms may require short-term financing when seasonal factors impact on either their production or their sales. For example, firms in the forest products industry find it necessary to build up large inventories of logs to keep their manufacturing plants supplied with raw materials during seasons when logging operations cannot be carried on. Manufacturers of items such as lawn mowers and lawn furniture may produce in anticipation of a seasonal increase in demand and rely on short-term loans to finance a temporary increase in working capital. Steel mills located on the Great Lakes usually accumulate inventories of iron ore during the summer months to supply their needs during the winter when lake freighters are unable to transport the material because of inclement weather. Fish canneries must do their processing as the fish are caught, which often results in the accumulation of substantial inventories. Building contractors achieve higher levels of production when the weather is favorable. These industries and many others look to commercial banks as a source of funds during their busy seasons.

Commercial banks are major suppliers of funds for home builders and mortgage companies. Most home builders must borrow at least part of the funds required for carrying inventories of materials and houses. Short-term construction loans granted to home builders are usually repaid, as the homes are sold, with funds obtained by the home buyers from long-term lenders. Mortgage companies often serve as connecting links between the home buyer and the supplier of the long-term funds. They originate the loans with home buyers and arrange with investors for the long-term financing. In performing these functions, they sometimes find it necessary to carry loans on inventory for a short period of time before turning them over to a permanent investor such as a life insurance company. A bank loan obtained to finance such an inventory of mortgage loans is known as a *mortgage warehousing loan.* The security for a mortgage warehousing loan includes the mortgage loans themselves plus the forward commitment of the permanent investor to take over the loans.

Securities firms, many of which perform three major functions—investment banking, commission brokerage, and security trading—are large borrowers of short-term funds from commercial banks. As investment bankers, they need short-term funds for the underwriting and distribution processes since it is often necessary to make payment to the company issuing the securities before the entire issue has been sold and the proceeds received by the underwriters. If a firm elects to operate as a dealer in securities it must be prepared to carry inventories, which often require bank financing. Securities held by the dealer are provided as collateral for such loans. In performing as a broker, a securities firm makes loans to customers who buy and hold securities on a margin. The investments of the customer can serve as collateral not only for the broker's loan to the customer but also for a loan obtained by the securities firm from a commercial bank. Typically, loans to brokers and dealers for the purpose of financing margin accounts and dealer inventories are "callable" by the bank, or repayable by the borrower, at any time on one day's notice and so are known as *call loans.* The rates on call loans are among the lowest granted by commercial banks, and they are announced daily by the major money-market banks in New York City. Dealers in government securities borrow from many sources, including other commercial banks, especially the large New York banks, corporations, and the Federal Reserve. Much of their borrowing is by means of repurchase agreements with sources other than the large money-market banks. Since rates on these loans tend to be lower than the New York call-loan rate, the dealers borrow from New York banks only when they are unable to obtain their required financing elsewhere.

When borrowers need long-term financing, banks frequently provide them with temporary financing in the form of a short-term loan with the understanding that the loan will soon be repaid with funds from another prearranged source. For example, when a corporation has a commitment from an investment-banking firm to purchase a certain amount of its securities, it may borrow from a commercial bank on a short-term basis, use the funds to pay for fixed assets and possibly increased working capital, and repay the loan when its securities have been sold. This type of bank financing is often referred to as a *bridge loan,* and it may involve a high degree of risk if the borrower does not have a firm commitment from a substantial investment-banking firm to buy its securities. In the absence of such a commitment, the commercial bank will want to evaluate the loan as it would any other, recognizing that it may turn into an intermediate- or longer-term credit. Businesses may borrow from banks on a short-term basis to construct manufacturing plants, warehouses, and office buildings, having arranged for permanent financing with some investor such as an insurance company or a pension fund. The agreement of the long-term investor to take over the loan after the facility has been constructed is known as a *take-out commitment.* In many situations commercial banks are better prepared than are long-term investors to handle efficiently the initial, piecemeal financing that often leads to a long-term financial commitment.

Finance companies of all types depend heavily on commercial banks for both short- and intermediate-term credit. For short-term funds they look to commercial banks and the commercial-paper market, and thus find it necessary to maintain large open lines of credit with their banks. Some of the larger finance companies have lines with as many as several hundred banks around the country. It has been customary for commercial banks to require finance companies to maintain a 10 percent compensating balance for the unused portion of an open line of credit and a 20 percent balance for any portion of the line in use. The larger companies generally borrow a high proportion of their short-term funds in the commercial-paper market and obtain lesser amounts from their banks. The amount borrowed from each source depends in part on the comparative rates and availability of funds. Typically, the cost of borrowing through the issuance of commercial paper is a fraction of a percentage point less than the cost of a bank loan, even before taking into account compensating balances. However, in times of extreme credit tightness the commercial-paper market can be an uncertain source of funds.

Unsecured Short-Term Business Loans

A survey of bank lending to business, conducted many years ago but still fairly reliable in its general findings, showed that approximately one-half of all short-term business loans of commercial banks are made on an unsecured basis.[1] The chance that a bank will be willing to make a loan without requiring security is enhanced if the funds are to be invested in current assets that are likely to be converted into cash within a reasonably short period of time. If the principal purpose of the loan is to permit the borrower to accumulate inventories, the salability of those inventories becomes an important factor. In some cases the cost and inconvenience of providing security for a loan are so great as to make it prohibitive. The banker must then decide whether it would be wise to make the loan on an unsecured basis.

Firms that borrow on an unsecured basis are those that are properly financed, have adequate capital and net worth, competent management, stable earnings, a record of prompt payment of obligations, and a bright future. A business firm that meets these criteria would have little trouble obtaining an unsecured loan for 90 days. Business firms that borrow on an unsecured basis are the prime borrowers of the business community—the elite from the standpoint of credit worthiness. The mechanics of making an unsecured loan are quite simple. In deciding to make an unsecured loan, the banker relies heavily on the borrower's financial statements. If they are satisfactory, the most important document involved in the extension of this type of credit is the signing of a promissory note.

Secured Short-Term Business Loans

Businesses that borrow on a secured basis are usually either financially weak as indicated by a high debt/net-worth ratio, for example, or have not established a record of satisfactory and stable earnings or generated enough

---

[1] *Federal Reserve Bulletin,* September 1959.

sales in relation to their capital. Also of importance are the record of the management, the competitive environment in which the firm operates, and the size and maturity of the loan. Sometimes when security is not required the borrower provides it in order to receive a lower rate of interest. When security is needed, it is necessary to decide what type of security would be acceptable and how much margin would be required. In making such judgments, the bank must consider the financial condition and profitability of the firm, and the marketability and probable liquidation value of the various assets. Staple commodities, for which there is a relatively steady demand, can be sold more promptly in the event of liquidation than can specialized machinery, for which the demand is quite limited. Many types of collateral serve as security for short-term business loans.

Endorsed or Co-maker Loans

Many short-term business loans are secured by the endorsement or guarantee of parties other than the borrower. When the borrower is a corporation, the principal shareholders may be required to endorse or guarantee the loan so as to commit, to some degree, their personal assets outside the business to repayment of the loan. The lender should consider not only the amount of assets outside the firm (present as well as probable future) held by the shareholders but also the extent to which the shareholders have given, or can be expected to give, similar guarantees to others. A loan may be endorsed or guaranteed by a corporation as well as by an individual. For example, a corporation may guarantee a loan to one of its subsidiaries or to a firm that supplies it with essential materials or serves as an important outlet for its product.

When a loan is guaranteed, the lender can usually assume that the guarantor will attempt to use his influence to see that the borrowing firm is operated in such a manner that the loan will be repaid. It is sometimes said that the best collector is the endorser or guarantor of a loan. In making such loans, banks try to satisfy themselves that those who are offering to be secondarily liable on the loan would be willing to make payment and have sufficient funds to do so if necessary. An assessment of the guarantor's willingness to make payment, if need be, is important since banks do not like to be in the position of having to force payment. Experience has shown that guarantors are sometimes reluctant to pay a loan on behalf of the borrower even though they were quite willing to issue the guarantee in the first place. Bankers evaluate requests for loans of this kind very carefully, not only to see that the security is adequate but also to advise the guarantor or endorser of the risks associated with the loan.

Assignment of Contracts

Construction companies and firms that supply materials under contract often find it necessary to borrow for their operations pending the receipt of payments under their contracts. In such cases they may assign the contract to the lending banks as security for a short-term loan. Then, as they perform under the contract, payments are made directly to the bank by the other contracting party. Sometimes the borrowing firm is a subcontractor, in which event, payments may be made to the bank by the prime contractor. It is not unusual for both the prime contractor and the subcontractors to be borrowing from commercial banks to finance their particular activities.

Assigned contracts can be attractive collateral, but they are not without hazards. The value of an assigned contract as security for a loan depends on the ability and willingness of the other contracting party to make payments as well as the ability and willingness of the borrower to perform under the contract so that he will be entitled to payment. For example, if the borrower is supplying a product under the contract that is inferior and not up to specifications, payment will probably not be forthcoming and the contract may be cancelled. Prior to making the loan, the lending banker must know the terms of the contract and assure himself that the borrower will perform according to the conditions set forth. The banker must also evaluate the financial capacity of the party for whom the work is being performed or the products supplied. In construction contracts, performance by the borrower is often encouraged by a provision for withholding a percentage of payment until performance is completed. This is known as a *retainage*.

Assignment of Accounts Receivable

Accounts receivable financing by commercial banks has grown substantially in the past 25 years, particularly at larger banks. Receivables are frequently used as collateral for both short-term seasonal loans and revolving credits. When a loan is secured by receivables, the amount of credit available to the borrower tends to increase as the need for credit grows. Typically, a seasonal loan is paid off as inventories and receivables are reduced following a period of high production and sales. With revolving credit, on the other hand, the lending may be more or less continuous; if the borrower is a growing firm, the size of the credit may continue to grow over a considerable period of time.

When commercial banks lend on the security of accounts receivable, it is usually—but not always—on a nonnotification basis, with the customers of the borrower not being advised that their accounts are being pledged as security for a loan. Borrowers often prefer this because of a feeling that borrowing on the security of receivables may be viewed as a sign of financial weakness. With nonnotification financing the borrower agrees to forward directly to the bank all payments received from customers whose accounts have been assigned. On the other hand, when financing is on a notification basis, the borrower's customers are advised to make all payments directly to the bank instead of to the borrower. The bank notifies the borrower of their receipt and applies the payments to the loan. Some bankers who prefer nonnotification financing contend that if a borrower cannot be trusted to abide by an agreement on a nonnotification basis, credit should not be extended at all.

The decision of whether to make an accounts receivable loan, and if so, the amount of funds that will be advanced on a given amount of receivables, rests not only on the credit worthiness and integrity of the borrower but also on the nature and quality of the receivables themselves. The credit standing of the borrower's customers is another important factor. The size of the individual accounts, the type and quality of the borrower's merchandise, the number of merchandise returns, and the age of the receivables are also important considerations. The sales and credit policies of the borrower should be considered: if the borrowing firm sells to nearly everyone who applies for credit in order to achieve high sales volume, troubles may develop. However, if the borrower has a policy of selling only to firms that pay their bills promptly and have good management and a high credit rating, the lender will be exposed to little risk.

The type and quality of the merchandise sold by the borrowing firm are factors to consider in deciding whether to lend on accounts receivable. The higher the quality of the goods, the fewer the returns and refusals to pay. Banks review carefully the amount of merchandise returns in relation to sales before agreeing to loan on a firm's accounts receivable, and they continue to watch the returns closely after a lending relationship has been established. They also investigate the age of the borrower's accounts receivable to evaluate the paying habits of its customers.

The maximum that a bank will loan on a given amount of accounts receivable usually ranges from 50 to 90 percent of the face value of the accounts. If the borrower's bad debt losses have been large, the bank may decide not to grant any loan at all, or the amount of the loan may be limited to a relatively small percentage of the total accounts. The sizes of individual accounts and the degree to which the borrower's receivables are concentrated in a relatively few accounts are also considered. Banks favor lending on larger accounts because it involves less paperwork and may involve fewer returns and disputed items. On the other hand, banks do not like to see receivables heavily concentrated in a few accounts unless they are with customers having high credit ratings. Typically, the maximum loan is 75 to 80 percent of the total receivables pledged.

Some important items usually covered by a loan agreement for accounts receivable financing follow:

1 The duration of the lending arrangement

2 The right of the bank to screen the accounts presented to it by the borrower to determine which are acceptable as security

3 The procedure by which accounts held by the bank are to be replaced or the loan reduced, if they become past due

4 The percentage that the bank will loan against the face amount of the receivables

5 The maximum dollar amount of the loan

6 The evidence required from the borrower to show the amount owed by each customer (As additional sales are made, the borrower may be required to submit copies of invoices or other evidence of shipment.)

7 The responsibility of the borrower to forward directly to the bank payments received on assigned accounts

8 Authorization for the bank to inspect the borrower's books and to verify, through confirmation by a public accounting firm or other agency, the accounts receivable

9 The frequency with which the borrower can submit evidence of additional sales and must deliver to the bank any payments received from customers (Often this is done on a daily basis, with daily adjustment of the security base and the loan balance.)

When a firm is borrowing on accounts receivable, it can quickly fall into serious difficulty if some of the pledged receivables become delinquent. The problem is apt to be serious if previously pledged receivables are rejected at a time when the borrower has no surplus funds and no other means of raising money. Instead of supplying the borrower with additional funds as new sales are made, the banker may substitute the new receivables for those no longer acceptable as collateral until the deficiency has been eliminated. If the amount of delinquent receivables is large, the borrower may be faced with the prospect of having to operate for a considerable period of time without receiving any cash from either its customers or its bank. Sometimes this is an impossibility.

The cost of borrowing on the security of accounts receivable tends to be higher than the cost of an unsecured loan. There are two reasons for this: firms that borrow against receivables tend to be weaker financially than firms that can borrow without security, and accounts receivable financing requires a great deal of clerical work for the bank as well as careful supervision. In addition to charging an interest rate that is usually two or three percentage points above the prime bank rate, it is customary to impose a service charge amounting to one or two percent of the borrower's average loan balance.

Factoring

The *factoring* or buying of accounts receivable is more than a method of financing. Typically, the factor buys the accounts of his clients on a non-recourse basis, and performs a number of services in addition to the advancement of funds before the accounts have been collected. These services include credit analysis, bookkeeping, the collection of accounts, and the assumption of the credit risk. The factor evaluates the credit of his client's present and prospective customers and establishes credit limits in advance. The client's customers are instructed to remit directly to the factor, who receives copies of the invoices. The client's drawings against uncollected receivables are usually limited to 80 or 90 percent of the invoice value, net of discounts and the factor's commission. The 10 to 20 percent reserve is retained by the factor for protection against merchandise returns, shortages, and other claims by the client's customers. Usually at the end of each month the factor calculates the fees earned and the amount of the holdback on uncollected receivables and makes any excess funds available to the client.

The factor's compensation is in the form of a commission (for credit analysis, bookkeeping, collection of accounts, and assumption of the credit risk) plus an interest charge on the daily balance of drawings against uncollected receivables. Interest is earned from the date of the advance to the due date of the receivables. The commission usually runs from 1 to 2 percent of the gross amount of the accounts factored, depending on the client's volume of business, the level of risk, and the amount of work required of the factor in relation to the volume of business. The amount of risk assumed by the factor depends largely on the credit standing of the client's customers, while the amount of work required for a given volume of business depends primarily on the average size of the invoices. The commissions tend to be a considerably larger source of income for the factor than is the interest on advances. If the rate is 1.5 percent, for example, and the accounts turn over in 30 days, the commission amounts to 18 percent of the receivables on an annual basis.

A few major banks, including Bank of America, the First National Bank of Boston, and the Trust Company of Georgia, have been factoring for many years. However, it was not until 1963, when the Comptroller of the Currency ruled that factoring was a legitimate banking activity, that banks began to move strongly into this field. A number of major banks have entered the factoring business in recent years, mostly by acquiring factoring companies rather than by starting up factoring departments de novo. A few banks have set up factoring operations on a joint-venture basis with Walter E. Heller & Co., a major finance company.

Factoring has been used mostly in the textile and furniture industries, but in recent years it has spread to a number of other industries, including shoes, toys, and floor coverings. With factoring operations, major banks are finding it possible to expand significantly their customer relationships in a number of industries. Moreover, they are able to perform a service for correspondent banks whose customers need factoring services. The entry into factoring represents another move by major banks into the area of high-risk, high-return commercial financing. Banks are becoming more and more competitive in areas of commercial lending that were once dominated by independent factoring companies and the major finance companies.

Assignment of Oil Runs

Commercial banks make two major types of oil loans—production loans and oil-payment loans. Production loans are made to oil operators for purchasing machinery and for other purposes that will improve operations; they are usually payable out of the monthly proceeds of the operator's share of the production. The collateral for a production loan is the operator's interest in the oil produced, often together with a security interest in some of his other assets. Successful lending on oil and gas production depends on proper evaluation of these minerals in the ground and of the operator's ability to bring them to the surface efficiently and economically. Although oil and gas in the ground may be good collateral for a loan, the value is considerably decreased if they are not produced properly. Banks are therefore vitally interested in the managerial capabilities of the operator, his financial capacity, and his ability to produce competitively.

Lending on oil and gas in the ground is quite technical and requires the specialized services of a petroleum engineer. The value of the collateral must be determined before the loan is consummated and the funds are released. Many banks in oil and gas areas have petroleum engineers on their staffs to perform this very important function. Others rely on the appraisals of independent engineers.

An oil-payment loan is secured by a contractual arrangement providing for payments at designated intervals and arises from the sale of an economic interest in oil and gas properties. The payment is assigned to the bank, and the loan is paid off as the oil payments are received. Although some oil loans are for a period of one year, many are for longer periods.

Loans Secured by Inventories

The desirability of inventories as security for a bank loan depends on the nature of the inventories, as well as the effectiveness with which they can be controlled or policed by the lender or an independent third party. In general, to be acceptable as security, inventories must be readily marketable, nonperishable, and insurable. A reasonable degree of price stability is also desirable. The amount a bank will loan against inventories depends in large measure on these characteristics. Commodities and products such as grain, cotton, wool, coffee, sugar, logs, lumber, canned foods, baled wood pulp, automobiles, and major appliances tend to be very acceptable as collateral. Not so attractive, for obvious reasons, are such items as special-purpose machinery, fresh produce, and advertising materials. One of the requirements for inventory financing is that the inventory be insured at all times, with a loss-payable clause in favor of the bank.

When a loan is made on the security of inventories, the lender is concerned whether the inventories will actually be there to satisfy the loan if the borrower should default in his payments. When pledged inventories are left in control of the borrower, there is a definite risk that they will be liquidated before the loan is repaid if the borrower gets into serious financial difficulties. Operating losses often lead to a shortage of cash, which in turn leads to slowness in the payment of suppliers and a problem in keeping adequate inventories on hand. Inventories that may seem to provide ample security when a loan is made can disappear rapidly. Sometimes the disappearance results from fraudulent acts on the part of the borrower. Banks find it advisable, therefore, either to remove the inventories from the borrower's control or to police them very carefully if they are to be accepted and relied on as collateral.

Warehouse Receipts   For the lender's protection, inventories are best controlled by placing them in the custody of a warehouse company. When this practice is followed, warehouse receipts are issued and serve as security for a loan. Warehouse receipts may be negotiable or nonnegotiable. Negotiable warehouse receipts are used to finance inventories in which trading is active, such as corn, cotton, and wheat. The major disadvantage of negotiable warehouse receipts is that they are easily transferred, are usually in large denominations, and must be presented to the warehouseman each time a withdrawal is made. Banks therefore prefer the use of nonnegotiable receipts issued in the name of the bank, which provides better control of the inventory they represent. The bank is thus in a position to permit the borrower to withdraw inventory only as it is sold, and the funds derived from the sale applied to the loan at the bank. When nonnegotiable receipts are used, withdrawals can be made with a prepared form known as an *order for warehouse release* or simply by writing a letter.

In a situation where the use of a public warehouse would be too costly or too inconvenient for the borrower because of the space required or the need to move goods in and out at frequent intervals, a field-warehousing arrangement may be used. In field warehousing, the goods are stored on the premises of the borrower but they are under the control of a person employed by the warehouse company. Sometimes that person is an employee of the borrower who is engaged by the warehouse company on a part-time basis to take custody of the inventories. The storage facility can be a building, a portion of a building, an oil tank, a log pond, an outside area where products such as lumber, coal, or wood pulp can be stored, or almost any other kind of space or container that can be kept under control. Signs are posted around the storage area to show that the goods located there are in the custody of the warehouse company, and the custodian is instructed to keep the inventories under lock and key. Except for the fact that storage is on the premises of the borrower, a field-warehousing arrangement operates the same as does a public warehouse—receipts are issued by the warehouse company to the lender and goods are released only at the direction of the lender. Field warehousing is widely used to provide security for business loans. Warehoused inventories range from small, high-valued items such as jewelry to large and bulky items such as logs, lumber, wood pulp, and coal. Food canners were among the first to use field warehousing, and their products generally make very good security.

When a loan is made on the security of warehouse receipts, the lender places great reliance on the competence and integrity of the warehouse company itself. He assumes that the company will issue receipts only against actual physical inventories and will not release inventories without his authorization. Usually it operates that way, but notable exceptions have occurred. In certain instances lenders have sustained large losses when the warehouses failed to contain the property for which warehouse receipts had been issued, and the warehouse companies were incapable of making good the deficiencies. By far the largest and most notorious case of this kind was the great salad oil swindle of the early 1960s, perpetrated by Anthony De Angelis and his associates in the Allied Crude Vegetable Oil Refining Corporation. Total losses in the salad oil case were over $100 million, and among the losers were a dozen of the country's leading banks, two brokerage houses which were bankrupted, and the American Express Field Warehousing Company—the company that issued warehouse receipts against well over $100 million of nonexistent salad-oil inventories. It was found that many of the storage tanks existed only on paper, and others, which were real, contained mostly water. The deception occurred primarily because both the warehouse company and the lenders disregarded some very basic principles of credit evaluation and loan administration. Thorough inspections of warehouse facilities did not take place, and apparently a weak link developed in the issuance of warehouse receipts.

In making loans secured by warehouse receipts, banks are concerned perhaps above all with the honesty and integrity of the borrower, particularly if field warehousing is used and the custodian is an employee or former employee of the borrower. Banks are also interested in the suitability of the warehouse. Goods that must be kept refrigerated require a warehouse that will maintain the desired temperature. If the goods must be kept dry, the warehouse must be constructed to keep dampness out. Warehouses do not guarantee the quality of the goods that are warehoused unless the grade is definitely stated in the warehouse receipt. If the bank has agreed to loan funds only on goods that meet a certain standard of quality, a certificate of quality or grade may be required from the borrower. Such a certificate would be issued by a qualified third party. Generally, loans secured by warehouse receipts should not exceed 85 percent of the market value of the collateral.

Warehouse receipt financing is relatively expensive to the borrower. In addition to the interest charge, there is the cost of warehousing, typically from 1.5 to 2 percent of the amount of the loan. Costs tend to be higher when inventories are small or the number of deposits and withdrawals from the inventory is large. In field warehousing there may be an additional charge for establishing the warehouse.

Trust Receipts Retail firms seldom find it practical to use warehouse receipt financing because of the need to display products for sale and have them available for immediate delivery. The same is probably true for most wholesalers. Thus, in lending to retailers and wholesalers it is generally feasible to use inventories as security only if they are left in the possession of the borrower. If inventories consist of items that can be specifically identified by description and serial number, trust receipt financing, commonly known as *floor planning,* is appropriate. When trust receipts are used, the lender buys the items from the firm that supplies them to the borrower. Delivery is made to the borrower, and he agrees to hold the inventories in trust for the lender. The lender holds legal title to each item he has financed until it is sold, at which time the borrower is obligated to remit the amount loaned against it. The borrower's obligation is normally in the form of a demand note, that is, a note that the lender can ask the borrower to repay any time. Trust receipts are used extensively in financing the inventories of automobile dealers, heavy equipment dealers, and retailers of major applicances.

From a lender's standpoint, one advantage of trust receipt financing over unsecured lending is that he owns the property and can reclaim it if the borrower becomes bankrupt or for any other reason defaults the agreement. In addition, if the property has been sold and the proceeds are still held by the borrower, they are deemed to be held in trust for the lender. However, the lender's protection is far from perfect—he does not have the right to recover the property from someone who has purchased it from the borrower in good faith. Thus it is important to use trust receipt financing only with borrowers who are deemed completely trustworthy. In any case, it is good policy to make periodic checks of the borrower's inventories to see that all items for which the lender has not yet received payment are still on hand.

Trust receipt financing can be attractive to a bank not only for the revenues it produces directly but for the consumer paper it develops for the bank as a result of the relationship with the dealer. This does not mean that banks always find it necessary to provide dealers with financing to obtain an adequate amount of retail instalment loans.

Uniform Commercial Code and Floating Liens

Prior to the Uniform Commercial Code, which has now been adopted in all states except Louisiana, a lender could obtain a security interest in the inventories of a borrower by such legal devices as chattel mortgages, conditional sales contracts, trust receipts, and factor's liens. Under the Uniform Commercial Code these devices have been merged, technically, into one called a *security interest,* which is created through a security agreement. However, the names of the old security devices are still used to a considerable extent in agreements between borrowers and lenders even though they may no longer be mentioned in the statutes.

A *floating lien* applies to the borrower's more or less constantly shifting stock of inventories and/or receivables. This security agreement gives the lender a security interest in after-acquired assets of the borrower as well as in those existing at the time the agreement is made. The floating lien may also provide security for future advances of money and may cover proceeds from the sale of inventories, as well as the inventories themselves. When the agreement covers the proceeds of sales, the lender has a security interest in any accounts receivable arising from sale of inventories. Proceeds also include cash received from sale of inventories, so long as such cash can be separately identified.

There are various ways by which a lender can obtain a security interest in at least a portion of the borrower's current assets if another creditor has already obtained an interest in them by means of a security agreement. For example, if a lender wants to extend accounts receivable financing to the firm, he can ask the first creditor to subordinate his interest in the receivables to the lender. Or if the lender wants to obtain a security interest in certain new items to be purchased by the borrower with funds advanced by the lender, he can arrange to become a purchase-money financier. This can be accomplished by perfecting a security interest in new items before they are delivered to the borrower. The floating-lien holder must be notified by registered mail that these particular new items are being financed by the lender.

Under the Uniform Commercial Code, as before, the lender must decide what controls over the collateral and proceeds from the sale of the collateral are needed for his protection. Since loans secured by inventories and receivables are usually made to the less credit worthy firms, the lender normally wishes to take all reasonable precautions to prevent loss of the collateral. It is important to recognize that the lender does not exercise control over the borrower's inventories with a floating lien; for that reason, it is likely to be inferior to either trust receipt financing or warehouse receipt financing in the protection it affords. Some believe that a floating lien should be viewed only as a secondary or supplemental source of protection and not as primary collateral. It is also thought that little, if any, reliance should be placed on the value of a floating lien unless the management of the borrowing firm is of high integrity and the outlook for the firm is good; it is not good policy to rely heavily on the protection of a floating lien in any situation where the degree of risk indicates that security is important.

Loan Secured by Plants and Other Real Estate

By offering a mortgage on plants and other real estate, business firms are sometimes able to borrow larger amounts than they could otherwise obtain, especially if their earnings have been low. The amount that banks will lend on land, buildings, and equipment varies considerably, depending on such factors as location, type of construction, marketability, and the debt-paying ability of the borrower. Legal restrictions may also come into play. The type of construction and location are extremely important since they influence the marketability of the property. Single-purpose buildings have a more limited market and are generally less attractive as security than are buildings with more versatile potential uses. If a factory building, for example, can be remodeled inexpensively and adapted to another use, its marketability will be improved.

In loaning money on the security of plants, equipment, and other real estate, banks are interested in more than just the marketability of the property and the probability that it can be sold at a price equal to or greater than the loan. No banker or appraiser can be sure that the property will sell for its estimated market value or how long a time will be required to sell it. Thus, banks are concerned that the firm has the ability to generate sufficient income to repay the loan, so it will not be necessary to sell the security. Banks must also take into account legal restrictions that relate to lending on real estate. National banks are limited to 50 percent of the appraised value of the property if the loan is not to be amortized over a period of years. This rule also applies to most state banks.

Loans on Securities

Many firms hold substantial amounts of securities, especially issues of the United States government, which can be pledged to secure business loans. Nonfinancial corporations held $19 billion in United States government securities in late 1978. Some business firms also own securities of other corporations and these are also eligible as security for bank loans.

Several factors are considered by bankers before making a loan secured by stocks or bonds. One of the most important is marketability. The credit rating of the governmental unit or corporation that issued the securities is also important. Securities issued by business concerns and governments with a record of prompt payment of principal and interest or a record of stable dividends have greater price stability and broader acceptance in the market than do those that fail to meet these qualifications. If there is an indication that the issuer of bonds will be unable to meet the interest payments or retire the securities when they mature, or that an issuer of stock will be unable to maintain a stable dividend, the securities will probably not be acceptable as collateral for a commercial bank loan.

The amount that a bank will loan on securities also depends largely on their credit rating and marketability. United States government securities, which have no credit risk and are easily sold, are highly acceptable for bank loans; it is not unusual for banks to loan from 90 to 95 percent of the market value of such securities pledged. On stable, marketable securities of large and financially strong corporations a bank may advance funds equal to 80 to 85 percent of the market value. In general, more will be advanced on bonds than on stocks. Stocks of small, closely held companies do not make attractive security, and a bank will not lend money to a stockholder of a small business firm on the security of that company's stock if the bank already has a loan outstanding to the company itself.

When the collateral for a bank loan consists of securities, periodic checks are made to ascertain their marketability, the financial soundness of the issuer, and the market price of the collateral. Banks prefer securities that are listed on an exchange or traded actively in the over-the-counter market. Stocks closely held and not traded actively may be difficult to sell, so the price received for a large block may be substantially less than the latest published quotations.

In making business loans secured by stocks and bonds, banks must take precautions that the funds will be used for business purposes, not for the purchase of additional stock. If the latter is the purpose, the loan must comply with Regulation U of the Federal Reserve Board relating to margin requirements. Banks must also be sure that the securities are assignable. United States Savings Bonds, for example, are nonmarketable and therefore cannot be assigned or transferred to another person. Another important factor is ownership: if the securities are owned jointly, both owners must jointly pledge them. Bonds may be in either bearer or registered form. When the securities are bearer bonds (as distinguished from registered bonds, where the owner's name appears on the face of the security), banks must take reasonable precautions to establish that the person pledging the bonds is the legal owner.

When registered bonds or stocks are accepted as collateral, a *stock* or *bond power* is usually obtained for each separate issue assigned by the owner. Stock and bond powers are *powers of attorney* that authorize the bank to sell the pledged securities in the event of default on the loan. Instead of executing powers, the owners could endorse the certificates if they wished, but this is not the most desirable procedure usually since the endorsement would remain on the certificate after the loan was repaid. Also, if a certificate is endorsed in blank, a financial loss may be sustained if the certificate is either lost or stolen. Stock certificates are sometimes carried in the name of the broker through whom the owner purchased the stock, and, if so, are referred to as being in *street name.* When that is the case, the bank requests that the stock be transferred to the name of the borrower.

Loans Secured by Life Insurance

Loans to small business firms are sometimes secured, in whole or in part, by the assignment of the cash surrender value of life insurance policies. Generally speaking, this is a very desirable type of security because of its liquidity, definite value, and ease of handling. However, certain precautions should be taken when accepting the assignment of a life insurance policy as security for a loan. It is important to determine whether the insurance company is strong financially and can be depended on to pay the cash surrender value if necessary. The bank must ascertain whether the insurance policy is assignable. If the insured has irrevocably designated his beneficiary, he cannot assign the policy without the beneficiary's consent. For that reason, some banks have a standard practice of requiring the beneficiary to join in the assignment. The bank must also verify that the policy has not already been assigned to a third party. And, finally, a loan should not be made on the security of a policy until the insurance company has been given a copy of the assignment and the bank has received written communication from the insurance company acknowledging receipt of the assignment.

Loans to Farmers

Although farm loans are considered separate and distinct from business loans, they are similar in nature. The same fundamental principles of credit analysis are employed in making such loans. Both businessmen and farmers are motivated by the same basic forces and are interested in the same objectives. Even though the economic resources of each may be different, they are employed for the same purposes—to produce goods and/or services and generate earnings and, hopefully, profits; consequently, credit serves the same purpose.

Farm loans for current expenses include loans made by commercial banks for financing recurring seasonal expenses of crop and livestock production, such as feed, seed, fertilizer, labor, and fuel; for family-living outlays; and to purchase feeder livestock. These loans are comparable to short-term business loans. Most current-expense loans to farmers are secured, and most have been relatively small in the past. However, with inflation and the continuing growth in the size of the average farm, these loans are becoming larger. A security interest may be taken therefore in growing and harvested crops, machinery, and livestock. For operators who have a limited net worth, real estate and endorsements are also relied on as security.

Farm loans for intermediate-term purposes include loans to purchase assets that will last several years. Such loans make possible the purchase of livestock (other than feeder livestock), machinery and equipment, automobiles, other consumer durable goods, and the improvement of land and buildings. Because of the increased maturity of these loans as compared to current expense loans, a larger portion is secured. In most cases the security consists of chattel mortgages on the items purchased with the funds. Farm real estate is commonly used as security for loans, especially if the funds are used to improve land and buildings. A large percentage of intermediate-term farm loans is repayable in instalments.

The risk in farm lending has been increasing as debt-asset ratios have risen, operating costs have risen, and prices of farm products have remained relatively low. Prices for farm products are extremely volatile, and falling prices can drastically reduce the value of the lender's collateral. To reduce their risk in agricultural lending, bankers sometimes encourage their customers to diversify operations and produce more than one crop, thereby reducing the risk of losses from price declines in one commodity. Bankers may also urge farmers to sell their products three or four times a year, instead of when the crop comes in or instead of waiting for a higher price, to avoid the risk of selling at the bottom of the market.

In periods of declining prices, bankers often find that farmers do not wish to sell at reduced prices to pay off the loans. However, if the loans are renewed, which is often the case, the borrowers may need additional credit to cover operating and storage costs. Periods of low prices or poor crops, or both, are characterized by decreased rates of loan repayment, large numbers of loan renewals, and refinancings. As an alternative to a loan extension or refinancing, borrowers may be urged to sell commodities, or land, or equipment, even at depressed prices, to raise funds for making repayment. Sometimes hard pressed borrowers can refinance through one of the emergency plans of the Farmers Home Administration (FmHA); in some cases they are able to take advantage of the appreciation in land values and convert short- or intermediate-term debt into long-term real-estate debt.

In periods of poor crops or low prices, loan demands by farmers are especially heavy, and loan-deposit ratios of rural banks are apt to rise sharply, in some cases to well over 80 percent. Banks respond to these conditions in a number of ways: by raising their credit standards and turning down more loan requests; by requiring larger down payments on equipment loans; by sharing their loans through participation with larger correspondent banks; by encouraging borrowers to take advantage of one or more of the Farmers Home Administration programs or a loan guaranteed by the Small Business Administration; and by increasing their own resources in various ways, including selling loans and borrowing federal funds.

Many banks have had excellent experience with agricultural lending for many years. To assure continuance of this favorable experience, banks have become more insistent on good financial planning by their borrowers, frequently requiring their borrowers to supply historical financial statements as well as detailed plans for their future operations along with budgets, cash flow projections, and pro-forma financial statements showing the expected results of those operations.

Indirect Lending

Indirect lending to farmers is done by purchasing notes of dealers in agricultural machinery and equipment and by purchasing the bonds of various federal agricultural lending agencies. Arrangements between commercial banks and implement dealers are similar to the arrangements with automobile dealers in consumer financing. In general, indirect financing through dealers involves less risk for the bank, since the dealer usually endorses the paper purchased by the bank.

Banks are large purchasers of the bonds of three important federal agricultural lending agencies—Federal Intermediate Credit Banks, Federal Land Banks, and Banks for Cooperatives. This method of lending is sometimes referred to as the *bond system*. The purchase of these bonds is in reality a form of indirect lending to farmers.

Government-guaranteed Loans

The Farmers Home Administration administers several programs under which it can guarantee 90 percent of a loan made by commercial banks and other lenders. These include, among others, farm ownership loans that are secured by land and have a maximum repayment period of 40 years, and operating loans that are secured by collateral other than land and have a maximum maturity of 7 years. The maximum amount for a guaranteed farm ownership loan is $300,000; the maximum guaranteed loan for operating purposes is $200,000; and the ceiling on total FmHA indebtedness for an individual or farm unit is $650,000. One attraction of FmHA guaranteed loans to commercial banks is the bank's ability to sell the federally guaranteed portion in secondary markets to raise additional funds.

The Small Business Administration also has authority to guarantee loans to farmers and ranchers so long as their gross income does not exceed $275,000. One advantage of an SBA loan guarantee over an FmHA guarantee is that it covers loans to farm corporations. The SBA lending ceiling is $500,000.

Questions

1. Comment on precautions that should be taken when lending on the security of an endorsement or guarantee.

2. What precautions should be taken when lending on the security of accounts receivable?

3. Under what circumstances are inventories satisfactory collateral for a business loan?

4. Explain how a field warehousing arrangement operates.

5. Explain how trust receipt financing operates. Compare the lender's protection in trust receipt financing with the protection in warehouse receipt financing.

6. What is a floating lien? How good is the protection it affords?

7. What precautions should be taken in lending with pledged securities as collateral?

8. What precautions should be taken in lending on the security of pledged life insurance policies?

9. Comment on the risks involved in non-real-estate farm loans.

10. What are the various responses of banks to an increase in the demand for farm loans when farm prices or crop yields are declining?

SELECTED REFERENCES

ANDERSON, CARL G. JR., "Farm Debt—A Problem for Some," Federal Reserve Bank of Dallas, *Review.* June 1977, pp. 10–14.

ARBINI, JOHN, "Small Business Administration: Answer to the Small Business Term Loan?" (Thesis, Pacific Coast Banking School, University of Washington, 1971).

BARUCH, H., "Risks in Loans Collateralized by Securities," *Journal of Commercial Bank Lending,* June 1977, pp. 29–40.

BENJAMIN, GARY L., "The Farmers Home Administration," Federal Reserve Bank of Chicago, *Business Conditions,* December 1975, pp. 3–8.

——, "Concern for Growing Farm Debt," Federal Reserve Bank of Chicago, *Business Conditions,* June 1974, pp. 8–13.

BOWLES, H. C., "Beyond Financial Analysis," *The Bankers Magazine,* Spring 1972, pp. 52–58.

COOPER, P. J., "Short Maturities Alone Do Not Enhance Loan Liquidity," *Journal of Commercial Bank Lending,* February 1971, pp. 19–22.

GEE, EDWARD F., "Constructive Lending in Constrictive Times," *Journal of Commercial Bank Lending,* March 1971, pp. 9–19.

HAYES, DOUGLAS A., *Bank Lending Policies,* 2nd ed., Ann Arbor, Michigan, The University of Michigan, 1977.

QUILL, G. D., J. C. CRESCI, and B. D. SHUTER, "Some Considerations About Secured Lending," *Journal of Commercial Bank Lending,* April 1977, pp. 41–56.

"Special Report: Commercial Lending," *Banking,* February 1978, pp. 31–54.

STRISCHEK, DEV, "Solvency: The Concept and an Approach for the Analysis of Long-term Borrowers," *Journal of Commercial Bank Lending,* February 1973, pp. 30–47.

12

Business Term Loans

In addition to serving as a primary source of short-term credit for business firms, commercial banks have become important suppliers of intermediate-term credit. The principal medium used for extending such credit to business borrowers is the *term loan,* which is defined by the Federal Reserve as "a commercial and industrial loan with an original maturity of more than one year or a loan granted under a formal agreement—revolving credit or standby—on which the original maturity of the commitment was in excess of one year."

Real estate mortgage loans to business firms are not considered term loans even though they have a relatively long maturity. Although not considered term loans by most bankers, instalment equipment loans usually qualify as term loans. An instalment equipment loan is similar to a conventional term loan in that both are usually amortizable over a period of years, but it differs from a term loan in certain significant respects. In the first place, the loan agreement for an instalment loan is typically much less elaborate than that for a term loan and does not place similar obligations and restrictions on the borrower. Secondly, the effective interest rate on an instalment equipment loan tends to be much higher than the rate on a term loan. And third, instalment equipment loans are for the purchase of specific items of equipment, whereas the proceeds of term loans are often used for general corporate purposes, including, for example, working capital, the acquisition of land and buildings, and the purchase of equipment.

Reasons for the Growth of Terms Loans

Banks have traditionally favored short-term loans because of their liquidity and because they make possible the time-honored practice of an *annual clean-up*, which requires business borrowers to pay off their loans once each year. Bankers believed that by requiring the borrower to pay off his entire loan at least once each year, they were assured that the proceeds were not being used for the acquisition of fixed assets or for other relatively long-term commitments. Thus the loan was considered highly liquid and relatively free of risk. Also, by lending with short-term notes, the bank had an opportunity to decide at least once a year whether it wanted to continue with the borrower.

This attitude changed over the years, and the making of term loans became an accepted and desirable form of lending by commercial banks. Several factors were responsible for this change. Increased lending capacity and higher operating expenses prompted banks to seek other outlets for loanable funds to increase their income. The advent of deposit insurance brought greater confidence in the stability of bank deposits and thus a greater willingness on the part of banks to give up some liquidity. Also, examining authorities changed their attitude toward bank lending; instead of singling out term loans and classifying them as "slow" on the basis of maturity, they began to place greater emphasis on collectibility.

Term loans are of great benefit to business borrowers. Firms that need funds in excess of the amount that can be retained from current earnings or that can be obtained from the capital markets at reasonable cost often find term loans the best means of acquiring outside financing. The maturities of term loans are easily adapted to the duration of the borrower's need for funds. For example, firms that can pay for fixed assets in a short period of time may find term loans more advantageous than long-term bonds or equity capital. With a term loan, they can reap the benefits of financial leverage without surrendering control of the firm or being faced with the problem of calling bonds or preferred stock when the funds are no longer needed. Also, with a term loan, in contrast to a renewable short-term loan, the firm does not face the possibility of having to pay the total loan at one time; instead, payments are made according to a schedule that is based on a projection of the firm's cash flows at the time the loan is made.

Another reason for the growth in term lending has been the borrowers' increased demand for longer-term loans. Among the users of term loans are business firms too small to secure funds economically from the capital markets. In many cases, large corporations also find substantial benefits in term-loan financing. For example, they may turn to their banks for funds rather than float new securities when conditions in the securities markets are unfavorable for new issues. However, as conditions in the capital market improve, they may issue securities to the public and use the proceeds, or a portion of them, to repay term loans negotiated at an earlier date. High corporate income tax rates have provided further impetus for the increase in term borrowing since high taxes make it difficult for business firms to retain sufficient earnings to take care of the financial requirements for expansion. Also, with high income tax rates, the tax benefits accruing from interest deductions provide a strong incentive for using borrowed money instead of equity capital. The rapid technological improvements in industry combined with higher prices for equipment and other fixed assets have provided further reasons for business firms to turn to commercial banks for term loans. In addition, higher wage rates have served as an incentive for acquiring labor-saving equipment, with term loans providing much of the financing.

Banks have discovered through experience that term loans are desirable earning assets when properly made and supervised. Banks have been encouraged to make term loans to smaller firms by the activities of the Small Business Administration. Many banks now make many term loans to small business firms, with and without SBA participation.

The growth of term lending over the years has been impressive. Although current data are not available on the amount of term loans held by all commercial banks, information is available on the amount of term loans held by approximately 160 large banks whose commercial and industrial loans amount to about 70 percent of those held by all commercial banks. The term loans of these 160 banks on December 27, 1978 accounted for 39 percent of their commercial and industrial loans and totaled 55 billion (see Table 12–1). It has been estimated that about one-half of all lending by large New York City banks is in the form of term loans.

Businesses Using Term Loans

Although term loans are made to all classes of business, they are most prevalent in certain industrial classifications characterized by heavy fixed capital requirements such as durable goods manufacturing, chemicals and rubber, petroleum refining, mining, transportation, and public utilities (See Table 12–1). However, a significant portion of the total term lending is to firms in industries such as trade and services where the demand for funds is primarily for working capital.

The loan size varies considerably among industries, with larger loans being made, as one would expect, to firms with heavy investments in plants and equipment. A greater part of the total dollar amount of term lending is to large business firms. However, most term loans are made to small

Table 12–1
Commercial and Industrial Loans of Large Commercial Banks
December 27, 1978 (in millions of dollars)

Industry	Total Loans	Term Loans	Term as a Percent of Total
Durable goods manufacturing:			
Primary metals	2,659	1,624	61
Machinery	5,355	2,771	52
Transportation equipment	3,066	1,663	54
Other fabricated metal products	2,464	1,119	45
Other durable goods	3,984	1,902	48
Nondurable goods manufacturing:			
Food, liquor, and tobacco	4,676	1,918	41
Textiles, apparel, and leather	3,766	1,050	28
Petroleum refining	2,626	1,895	72
Chemicals and rubber	3,457	2,181	63
Other nondurable goods	2,377	1,184	50
Mining, including crude petroleum and natural gas	10,582	7,940	75
Trade:			
Commodity dealers	1,916	314	16
Other wholesale	9,371	2,342	25
Retail	8,437	3,202	38
Transportation	5,456	3,789	69
Communications	1,770	1,158	66
Other public utilities	5,858	4,221	71
Construction	5,092	2,375	47
Services	14.783	7,270	49
All other domestic loans	8,538	2,866	34
Bankers' acceptances	3,817		
Foreign commercial & industrial loans	5,589	2,658	48
Total classified loans	115,639	55,442	
Total commercial & industrial loans	141,981	55,442	39

Source: "Commercial and Industrial Loans Outstanding by Industry," Statistical Release H.12. January 3, 1979 and "Commercial and Industrial Term Loans Outstanding by Industry," Statistical Release H.12(B) January 10, 1979.

businesses, which rely on term loans partly because of their limited access to the capital markets.

Large firms use term loans for the flexibility they provide, among other reasons. By negotiating directly with the lender, the borrower may obtain terms better suited to his needs than those available with a public bond issue. Also, with a term loan, some terms may be renegotiated with the lender at a later date if need be. Bank term loans are more flexible than a public bond issue in another respect: they can usually be prepaid without penalty, except where the funds used for prepaying are obtained by borrowing at a lower interest rate from another commercial bank. The shorter maturity of a term loan, as compared to the usual public bond issue, may in itself be considered an advantage in a period of high interest rates. The borrower may use a term loan with a view to replacing it in a few years with proceeds from a public bond issue at a lower interest rate. Another advantage of term borrowing over the issuance of bonds is that the costs of arranging for the financing are almost sure to be less, and the interest rate may be lower. With a term loan, the borrower avoids the costs of registration, underwriting, and selling that are usually incurred with a public issue of securities.

Use of Term Loan Funds

Funds derived from term loans are used for a number of purposes. One of the most important is the purchase of buildings and equipment needed by the borrower to maintain his competitive position and keep pace with the demand for his products. In addition, increased sales usually call for increased working capital, which may be financed through term borrowing. Term loans are used to finance new ventures, as when a firm adds a new product or integrates vertically to produce some portion of the raw materials needed in its operations. Term borrowing is also used to refinance existing obligations.

Frequently, the borrower needs to draw down the funds over a period of many months, as in the case of a major plant expansion or the acquisition of a fleet of aircraft. In such cases it is common practice to combine the term-loan agreement with a commitment agreement or revolving credit. The lender agrees to make funds available to the borrower as they are needed over a period of, say, two years up to a specified total amount. The agreement also provides that at the end of the commitment period the entire amount borrowed to that date shall be incorporated in a term loan. For an arrangement of this kind the borrower is normally required to pay a commitment fee of from one-fourth to one-half of one percent on unborrowed amounts during the period of the bank's commitment.

Maturity, Security, and Method of Payment of Term Loans

The maturities of term loans vary considerably, but they usually range from two to six years. Although some are for longer periods, few are for more than ten years. The maturity of a term loan is in part a function of the purpose for which the funds are being borrowed. For example, if the funds are to be used to purchase short-lived fixed assets, the maturity would also be short. It is not unusual for term loans to be repaid before their maturity date. Since an early repayment usually means that the customer has fared well and is in a strong financial condition, banks are generally not averse to early payments if the funds are derived from the firm's operations. However, they do not look with favor on repayments made with funds borrowed elsewhere at a lower rate of interest, and may impose a penalty for this kind of prepayment. In general, commercial banks require security on a larger proportion of term loans than short-term loans. This, of course, is because of the greater risk associated with longer-term loans. Also, term loans to small firms are secured more often than are loans to larger businesses.

Most term loans are amortized, which means that instalment payments are required on a monthly, quarterly, semiannual, or annual basis. Repayment provisions sometimes provide for a larger, balloon payment at the end, in which case a new loan may be negotiated prior to the final payment date for some portion of the balloon payment. Some lenders favor this type of arrangement when the borrower's needs are for a longer period than the lender would like to grant. It is believed that the balloon provision gives the bank an opportunity to take a fresh look at the credit when the balloon payment is due. In some cases, however, the purpose of a balloon payment is simply to give the borrower more flexibility during the early years of the loan, and both parties fully expect that the borrower will be able to make the payment when it is due.

Instalment terms extend to a high portion of agricultural loans, too, but sometimes with different provisions regarding size and timing of payments. Repayment on an instalment basis does not mean that instalments are of equal size or due monthly. They are usually unequal in size and irregular in time since agriculture does not permit any other method of payment. Only in poultry, egg, and dairy operations are equal and regular payments comparable to the consumer credit field.

Interest Rates

Interest rates on term loans depend on the general level of interest rates, the amount and maturity of the loan, and the credit standing of the borrower. The rate for a term loan is generally higher than the rate the same borrower would pay on a short-term loan, because it is less liquid and involves more risk. Rates on large term loans are generally lower than on small loans because the costs of originating and administering a loan do not increase proportionately with an increase in the amount of the loan, and because larger loans are usually made to larger business firms. It is generally assumed that larger borrowers have less risk of failure. The borrower's financial condition and profit prospects also have an important influence on the interest rate. It can be expected, for example, that firms with high debt–asset ratios will be required to pay higher rates than firms with low debt–asset ratios because of a greater risk of failure and a smaller equity cushion for the creditors in the event of failure.

Given the prime bank rate, the range of interest rates on term loans tends to be quite small. Typically, the rates on loans granted during a period when the prime rate remains unchanged will fall within a range of about .25 to 2.5 percentage points above the prime rate. This rather narrow spread confirms that banks generally are willing to make term loans only to borrowers whose credit ratings are quite high. The differences in risk among term loans are generally not very great.

The rates on most small term loans are fixed for the life of the loan. Large loans, on the other hand, often have provision for a variable rate—that is, a rate that is adjusted upward or downward with changes in the prime bank rate. Variable-rate provisions often include a ceiling and a floor (sometimes referred to as a *collar*) so that the rate cannot move outside a specified range. For example, if a loan were made when the prime rate was 6 percent, the initial rate might be 6.5 percent with provision for subsequent adjustments to keep the rate one-half percentage point above the prime rate, but never above 7.5 percent nor below 5.5 percent.

Borrowers of term loans are sometimes required, either by the loan agreement itself or by informal understanding with the lender, to maintain a compensating balance. When that is the case, the effective cost to the borrower will exceed the stated rate if the required balance exceeds the amount the borrower would otherwise have on deposit. In some cases it is required that the compensating balance be carried as a time deposit, which may or may not draw interest. Small borrowers are seldom required to carry compensating balances, but they are usually expected to deal exclusively with the lending bank and not maintain deposits elsewhere.

Loan Participations and Guaranteed Loans

Commercial banks sometimes participate with insurance companies, pension funds, and other long-term lenders in making term loans. Participations with insurance companies are usually in the form of large loans, and the banks take the shorter maturities. On a fifteen-year loan the banks would probably take the amount repayable in the first five to seven years, and the insurance companies would take the rest. Because of their relatively slight need for liquidity and their preference for long-term lending, insurance companies usually impose more severe prepayment penalties on the borrower than are normally imposed by commercial banks.

Two government agencies, the Small Business Administration and the Farmers Home Administration, have important programs for promoting term loans to small and, in the case of the FmHA, moderate-sized business firms. The SBA works closely with commercial banks in administering several lending programs, including regular business loans, minority business loans, economic opportunity loans, real estate development company loans, revolving lines of credit for small contractors, and loans to displaced businesses. The law intends that the proceeds of such loans be used for productive purposes—to create employment and increase the flow of goods and services within the economy. The SBA is not in competition with private lenders and is allowed to make or guarantee loans only if the borrowers cannot obtain funds from commercial banks or other private lenders on a reasonable basis. In a large majority of the SBA regular business loans the funds are supplied by commercial banks, with a 90 percent guarantee by the SBA.

SBA-guaranteed loans can be very attractive to commercial banks, partly because of the ease with which the guaranteed portion of the loan can be sold in the secondary market. At one time, the secondary market was largely local, consisting of state development funds and others interested in the economic development of an area. Now a broad secondary market has been developed in which more than 20 investment banking firms arrange for the sale of SBA-guaranteed loans to insurance companies, pension funds, trust funds, credit unions, and others. By selling the guaranteed portion of a loan, the lending bank recovers most of the funds it has loaned out; yet it continues to service the loan and receives a fee for doing so. Approximately two-thirds of all banks in the country now participate in SBA loans, and the annual volume exceeds $2 billion. Annual sales of the guaranteed portion of SBA loans in the secondary market are approximately $500 million.

The Farmers Home Administration's lending program for business firms provides up to a 90 percent guarantee on loans obtained by corporations for investment in rural cities of less than 50,000 population. The objective is to maintain and create employment in rural areas. As with SBA-guaranteed loans, the lender has the privilege of selling the guaranteed portion of the loan. In contrast to the SBA program, however, FmHA-guaranteed loans can be made to larger firms, and the borrowing corporation is not required to demonstrate that it would be unable to borrow the funds at a reasonable rate without the guarantee. Some loans guaranteed by the FmHA have been larger than $5 million. The interest rate on the guaranteed portion of FmHA loans is usually from 1 to 1-½ percentage points less than the borrower would have to pay otherwise.

Sources of Repayment for Term Loans

Term loans are ordinarily repaid from different sources than are short-term bank loans. A common purpose of short-term borrowing is to obtain funds for seasonal increases in accounts receivable and inventories. After inventories have been sold and receivables collected, the loan is repaid. Thus the inventories and receivables for which financing was required, provide the funds for repayment when they are liquidated. Conversely, term loans are used primarily to acquire fixed assets and working capital that will be needed for relatively long periods; the usual source of funds for repayment is retained earnings, which requires good prospects for profitable operations over an extended period. The use of funds derived from profitable operations to repay loans means that a business firm substitutes equity funds for debt funds in its capital structure. This relative increase in equity may make it easier to borrow additional funds at a later date. Banks therefore look on term loans and short-term loans quite differently.

It is sometimes said that in making term loans a bank can look to the borrower's total cash flows (earnings plus noncash charges) as a source of funds for loan repayment. However, this is often not true, especially in the case of a growing business where a portion of the cash flows must be used to finance increases in net working capital and fixed assets. The borrower's future growth must be taken into consideration in planning repayment schedules. And, even where little if any growth is involved, business firms are often compelled to make large capital expenditures to keep up with new technological developments and maintain their position in the market. For example, many manufacturing firms find it necessary to make annual investments in fixed assets that exceed their provision for depreciation. In addition, firms may find it necessary to carry increased inventories and allow longer credit terms to their customers. Such possibilities should be considered in reviewing a borrower's loan proposal.

Factors Considered by Banks in Term Lending

Since term lending involves greater risk than does short-term lending because of the need for profitable operations over a relatively long period, banks take added precautions when committing themselves to term loans. Economic conditions can change drastically from the time a loan is made until its final maturity. The borrowing firm's position within the industry is also subject to change during the term of the loan.

Internal Factors

In entering into a program of term lending, commercial banks must make a careful appraisal of their own present and future financial condition. Such a self-evaluation includes an appraisal of the nature and fluctuation of deposits; the type, quality, liquidity, and diversification of earning assets; and an analysis of the capital account. Much has already been said about the importance of deposits in influencing the decisions of bank management. But it should be emphasized again that the type and fluctuation of deposits have much to do with the extension of term loans.

If deposits, whether demand or time, are concentrated in the hands of a few customers, the chances of fluctuation are greater than if they are held by many customers in moderate amounts. Banks in agricultural areas, where deposits normally fluctuate greatly, are less likely to engage extensively in term lending than are banks in industrial areas where a more balanced economy ordinarily results in relatively stable deposits.

The type, quality, liquidity, and diversification of a bank's assets influence the extent to which it will engage in term lending. A bank that has a relatively large amount of assets in the form of long-term real estate loans is not in as favorable a position to engage in term lending as one that has few long-term real estate loans and a large proportion of short-term commitments. Banks whose loan portfolios consist largely of loans to high-quality borrowers can engage in term lending to a greater extent than can those with a larger number of marginal borrowers who may be slow in meeting their obligations and may request an extension on their loans when they come due.

Banks that have a highly liquid secondary reserve and investment account are also in a better position to meet requests for term loans than those that have securities with longer maturities or a more restricted market. Banks with active demand for seasonal loans must move slowly when considering term loans. Banks with loans that may be discounted at the Federal Reserve are often in a good position to engage in term lending. During periods of high deposit withdrawals or an increase in seasonal lending, this factor could be quite important. Banks often request other banks to participate in some of their term loans, either because the loan exceeds their legal limit or because they desire to spread the risk. This means that banks find it advantageous to have correspondent bank relations that are favorable to participation and pool arrangements in lending.

In addition to having some loans eligible for discounting at the Federal Reserve, banks with large amounts committed to term loans should have securities that can be pledged for short periods in the event funds are needed on short notice. Banks may also find participation in the federal funds market a desirable backstop in their program of term lending. Finally, it is important to have loan personnel and legal counsel trained in term lending. This kind of lending requires skills that are not necessarily acquired through experience with short-term lending or the making of real estate and consumer loans. Term loan agreements frequently require the services of attorneys, engineers, and people who have extensive knowledge about the industry or industries in which the borrower is operating.

The proportion of a bank's loan portfolio that may appropriately consist of term loans is influenced by many factors that vary considerably from bank to bank. A few banks have adopted policies limiting their total term lending in relation to their time deposits or their capital, or the sum of the two. In such cases the limitations are usually placed on the total of term loans and real estate loans combined. A review of the bank's liquidity needs and the condition of the term loan portfolio, in terms of both quality and liquidity, must be a continuous process for sound and profitable term lending.

Credit Worthiness of the Borrower

Credit analysis for term lending is similar to that for short-term lending, but because of the longer maturities involved, considerably more emphasis must be placed on the borrower's profitability. In term lending the bank is, in a sense, becoming a partner of the borrower and may remain one for several years. There must be no doubt as to the character and management ability of the principals involved in the business. There is no place for those who must be watched and doubted continuously for the duration of the loan.

The success or failure of a business is largely dependent on the abilities of those who direct its affairs, so banks must have confidence that the firm has good management before a term loan is granted. Economic conditions, competition, and technological factors may change after a term loan is established, making it imperative that basic changes be effectuated in the borrower's operations. Determining what those changes should be and putting them into effect are functions of management. Banks want to be assured that the term loan applicant has a management that can adapt to a changing environment, accept new ideas, and adopt new practices. Businesses dominated by one person that have no new managers "coming up the ladder" are not favored as candidates for term loans.

In evaluating an application for a term loan, banks place great emphasis on conditions in the industry and the applicant's competitive position and relative stability. Businesses that are very cycle-sensitive or that operate in a feast or famine industry are not good candidates for a term loan. The bank should make a study of the trends in the industry, including technological changes, new processes, and changes in customer demands. Technological change, for example, might completely alter the economic importance of an industry.

If the applicant's management is capable of meeting the changes that occur, chances of survival and continued success are certainly enhanced. If a firm's past growth and financial success have been the result of a monopolistic position based, for example, on patents or control of the supply of raw materials, which may change with the passage of time, these factors must be considered before entering into a term loan agreement. A firm that has sound labor policies, an effective research and development program, and an ability to keep in touch with changes in consumer demand has a greater chance of survival and success than does one that neither projects its position into the future nor plans for improvements to meet the competitive challenge from other business firms. Political considerations and potential governmental controls and taxes must also be taken into account. Bankers are primarily interested in the borrower's ability to repay the loan as agreed. Estimating this involves investigating the firm's past record carefully as well as projecting its cash flows into the future.

Evaluating the many factors that will be responsible for a borrower's economic and financial success may require the knowledge and experience of technicians in addition to that of bank lending officers. Petroleum engineers maintained on the staff of many large banks specializing in oil loans are trained to appraise the oil reserves of oil producers. Specialists in chemical production, aviation, public utilities, forest products, and food processing may be invaluable in presenting information about an applicant for a term loan. New processes and products may appear attractive, but they must be economically feasible when sizeable funds are being advanced for long periods. Banks must look to the applicant's ability to generate sufficient income to repay the loan. Security is probably of less significance in term loans than in short-term lending. For many reasons, then, term loans are generally reserved for borrowers who can be classified as high quality in every respect.

The Term Loan Agreement

Loan agreements have been designed to offer a considerable amount of protection for banks involved in term lending. Sometimes the agreement is incorporated in the note, but usually it is prepared as a separate document which is referenced to the note. The loan agreement is normally prepared by the bank's legal counsel and is reviewed by the borrower's attorney. The provisions of term loan agreements are tailored to each specific situation but usually contain provisions under each of the following headings:

1 Preamble
2 Amount and term of the loan
3 Representations and warranties
4 Conditions of lending
5 Description of collateral
6 Covenants of the borrower
7 Events of default
8 Miscellaneous

Preamble

The preamble sometimes does nothing more than name the parties and state that they are entering into an agreement; however, it may also contain a statement of the purpose of the loan.

Amount and Term of the Loan

This portion of the agreement sets forth the amount of the loan, the manner in which the borrower may take down the funds, the interest rate, the maturity dates, the amount of fees, if any, and the provisions relating to prepayments. The usual arrangement is for equal periodic instalment payments. As mentioned previously, provision is sometimes made for a balloon payment at maturity. In this case, a provision is sometimes included in the loan agreement to the effect that if additional income above a certain amount is derived from operations or from the sale of assets, a certain portion will be applied to the reduction of the balloon portion of the note.

Banks do not generally impose a fee for prepayment of an instalment or for early retirement of the entire loan if the funds are derived from current operations, from funding the debt, or from the sale of assets. However, if the early payments are made possible by borrowing from another bank, a penalty is imposed.

As mentioned previously, a commitment fee may be charged if the loan is a revolving credit with provision for converting the credit into a term loan. The bank is justified in imposing a fee for unused but committed funds since they must be readily available for the borrower's use. The bank will not feel free to invest these funds in high-earning assets such as other loans of intermediate maturities.

Representations and Warranties

It is here that the borrower represents and warrants that the financial statements on which the credit decision was based are correct and truly reflect the borrower's financial condition. Other representations commonly made by the borrower include the following:

1 The company is duly incorporated and in good standing.

2 The company has the power to make the agreement and execute the notes and to perform thereunder.

3 The properties of the company are free and clear of all liens and encumbrances other than those set out in the agreement.

4 No actions or suits are pending or threatened against the company other than those described in the agreement.

5 The company possesses adequate licenses, patents, copyrights, trademarks, and trade names to conduct its business substantially as now conducted.

6 The consummation of the transaction and performance of the agreement will not result in the breach of, or constitute a default under any other agreement of the company.

7 The business and properties of the company have not been materially affected in an adverse way since the date of the latest audited financial statements.

8 The company has no federal income tax liability in excess of the amount shown on its balance sheet.

Conditions of Lending

This article, like the previous one, is legalistic in that it is concerned with the conditions that must exist, the representations that must be made, and the documents that must be delivered to the lender before the loan is made. Here, a legal opinion is in order. Before disbursing any monies under the loan, the legal counsel for the bank must be satisfied with the documents submitted by the borrower. If the agreement provides for a revolving credit followed by a term loan, it is further provided that before each disbursement an officer of the borrower shall provide the bank with a certificate stating that all previously made representations and warranties are still accurate, and that no event has occurred which would constitute default under the loan agreement.

Description of Collateral

When the loan is a secured loan, the agreement sets forth a detailed description of the collateral and how it is to be handled. If the collateral consists of securities, the agreement normally specifies who is to receive the interest or dividends, who is to have the right to vote the stock, under what conditions the securities are to be sold, and if sold, who is to receive the proceeds from the sale.

Covenants of the Borrower

This is a very important part of the loan agreement. The number and detail of the covenants will depend somewhat on the financial strength of the borrower and the quality of management. If the borrower is strong financially and has excellent management, the number of covenants will be less than if the borrower's financial condition and management are only moderately strong.

Affirmative Covenants

The affirmative covenants are obligations imposed on management. One of the most common is the requirement that the bank be furnished with financial statements at periodic intervals and with such other relevant information as may be reasonably requested. In this manner, the bank is kept informed of the borrower's financial condition; if trouble appears to be developing, steps may be taken to prevent it. It is common practice to require unaudited statements for the first three quarters of the borrower's fiscal year, in addition to audited statements at year-end. Term-loan agreements generally require, also, that the borrower carry insurance satisfactory to the bank to reduce those risks that are insurable.

Many term loan agreements require the borrower to maintain working capital above some stated minimum amount. Some bankers consider this one of the most important provisions of the loan agreement since its purpose is to have the borrower maintain a certain amount of liquidity. The working-capital requirement provides a measure of protection for other creditors as well as for the bank. However, this provision may not provide as much protection as some people think, inasmuch as the composition and quality of a borrower's current assets can change to the lender's detriment. It would be possible for a business to maintain the requirements established in the term-loan agreement but not be very liquid simply because of having too much invested in slow-moving inventories or inferior receivables. Therefore, a close check should be kept on the quality of items that make up the working capital. Nevertheless, the working-capital requirement is a potent force, since it gives the bank the right to declare the borrower in default should the working capital drop below the agreed minimum.

An affirmative covenant, which is sometimes incorporated in term-loan agreements, requires the borrower to maintain management satisfactory to the bank. This is another important provision since the management is closely tied to the success of a business firm. This provision means that if the management should change due to resignation, death, or other causes, the bank must give its blessing before new personnel can be employed. Banks often require, also, that *key-man* insurance be carried on those people in responsible positions who cannot be readily replaced.

Negative Covenants

Negative covenants are the things a borrower agrees not to do during the life of the loan unless prior consent is obtained from the lending bank, usually by an amendment to the term-loan agreement or by letter. The objectives of negative covenants are to prevent a dissipation of assets that would weaken the firm's financial strength, and the assumption of obligations (definite or contingent) that might reduce the borrower's ability to repay the loan. A common negative covenant is the *negative pledge clause,* usually found in unsecured loans, by which the borrower agrees not to pledge any of his assets as security to other lenders, and not to sell receivables. Even though this clause may be included if the loan is secured, its importance is probably lessened since other lenders would be reluctant to loan sizeable amounts to a firm that has already pledged most of its assets. Such a covenant assures the bank that other lenders will not be placed in a more favorable position than it occupies.

Prohibitions regarding merger and consolidation, except with the approval of the bank, are also generally included for the bank's protection. To assure that the productive ability of the concern remains intact, a prohibition is usually included against the sale or lease of substantially all of the borrower's assets. Term-loan borrowers also usually agree not to make loans to others or to guarantee, endorse, or become surety for others. Such a prohibition reduces the possibility of cash withdrawals, a weakened financial position, and the assumption of contingent liabilities, which can become a heavy responsibility.

Restrictive Clauses

Restrictive clauses seem similar to negative covenants but are basically different. Negative covenants prohibit certain acts of management in general, while restrictive clauses permit certain acts but restrict their latitude. For example, a negative covenant may prohibit a term-loan borrower from mortgaging plant and equipment during the life of the loan, whereas a restrictive clause may limit the amount of dividends the borrower is permitted to pay. The bank recognizes that the borrower must have some latitude in management but that certain acts must be limited or restricted if the bank is to be protected.

To assure that the borrowing firm will retain a portion of its earnings in the business so as to strengthen its financial condition, restrictions are usually placed on the amount of dividends that may be paid. Limitations may also be placed on salaries, bonuses, and advances to officers and employees, as well as to others. The objectives of such restrictions are to encourage, if not force, the borrower to be less dependent on borrowed funds and to increase the amount of equity in the business. The limitation on salaries and bonuses is a way of forcing a borrower to "tighten his belt" until he has adequate capital funds. The restriction on dividends may be in terms of a certain percentage of earnings, or it may be specified that dividends not be allowed to reduce earned surplus below a certain level.

Banks realize that the borrowing firm may need short-term funds to take care of seasonal needs. Such borrowings are permitted, but usually a limit is placed on total borrowings, both long- and short-term. The amount that will be permitted varies, of course, with the nature and needs of the business.

A restriction may be placed on the amount of funds that a term-loan borrower can invest in fixed assets such as plant and equipment. The purpose of this limitation is to prevent the firm from over-extending itself. The amount that can be invested may vary considerably and may be limited to the company's annual depreciation charges. To prevent a weakening of the firm's financial strength, a restriction may also be placed on the amount of funds that can be used for the purchase of its capital stock.

If a borrower owes long-term debts to others, a limitation may be placed on the amount that may be retired annually without also retiring a portion of the term debt owed to the bank. The purpose of such a provision is to prevent the bank from being the last to be repaid. It also prevents the firm from using the bank's funds to pay off some other lender. Finally, a restriction may be imposed on the purchase of securities, with the usual exception of United States government obligations. This limitation is designed to prohibit speculation in securities.

Default Provisions

All term loans have default provisions to make the entire loan immediately due and payable under certain conditions. This is done through an *acceleration clause* which provides that if certain conditions are not met, the total loan is immediately due. If such a clause were not included in the agreement, the bank would be forced to wait until each instalment was due before legal action could be taken against the borrower. This would certainly be more expensive, troublesome, and risky than suing for the entire amount at one time. Usually when default is in the offing, the liquidation value of the firm declines rapidly, and it is desirable to act immediately.

Several default provisions are ordinarily included in term loan agreements. Probably the most important act of default is failure to pay principal or interest according to the terms agreed on. When this happens, the firm is not necessarily in a serious financial condition but it is at least a signal that trouble may be developing. If such is the case, steps can be taken to collect the loan. Another act of default is the misrepresentation of information presented in financial statements. This is an indication not only of financial trouble but also of the management's lack of integrity. Since financial statements are one of the principal means by which management can be evaluated, misrepresentation is a clear indication that the borrower is not of high moral character and that it would be best for the bank to dissolve the relationship. Failure to perform or observe any of the terms of the agreement is also a default. This is indeed a broad provision. Evidence of insolvency or bankruptcy is also included as an act or event of default.

Term-loan agreements may appear burdensome and strict, but the terms and conditions are an expression of sound financial principles. True, they are designed to protect the bank, but they also have as their objective the continued financial health of the borrower. One of the difficulties in drawing up a term-loan agreement is that conditions change after the loan is consummated, and some may become obsolete and too restrictive. This is recognized, of course, and it is not uncommon for the parties to negotiate a change in some terms after the agreement is in effect.

Questions

1. Why is is unwise to assume that a borrower's total cash flows will be available to repay a term loan?
2. What aspects of a bank's financial condition determine the amount of term lending it should do?
3. How would you evaluate the credit worthiness of a term borrower?
4. List eight representations and warranties commonly found in term loan agreements. How do representations and warranties differ from affirmative covenants, negative covenants, and restrictive clauses?
5. List five affirmative covenants that may be found in a term loan agreement.

Which of these are not likely to be found in an agreement with a major corporation? Why?

6. List four negative covenants and five restrictive clauses often found in term-loan agreements. How do restrictive clauses differ from negative covenants?

7. What are the usual acts or events of default under a term-loan agreement? What is an acceleration clause and why is it important?

SELECTED REFERENCES

See Chapter 11.

13

Leasing

In recent years, lease financing has become one of the most dynamic areas in commercial banking. Direct participation of commercial banks in lease financing began in the early 1960s, and in 1971 the Federal Reserve Board ruled that bank holding companies could establish subsidiaries to lease personal property and equipment. In 1974 the authority of bank holding-company subsidiaries was broadened to include the leasing of real property under certain conditions. The finance leasing of equipment ranges from small items of office equipment to commercial aircraft and ocean-going tankers. Banks and bank-affiliated leasing companies are limited in their leasing authority to *full-payout net leases,* also known as finance leases, financing leases, or capital leases. A full-payout lease is one from which the lessor expects to realize a return of its full investment in the leased property plus the estimated cost of financing during the base term of the lease. The lessor's expected return is derived from rentals, plus estimated tax benefits, plus either the estimated residual value of the property at the expiration of the base term of the lease or a guarantee of the residual value by the lessee or a third party.

In finance leasing, the leased asset is purchased by the lessor at the request of the lessee, and the lessee assumes virtually all the responsibilities of ownership, including maintenance of the property and payment of all property taxes and insurance. One major New York bank sees its market as being composed of the following three types or sizes of leases: multimillion-dollar, tax-sheltered leases for items such as commercial airliners and off-shore oil well drilling equipment; so-called middle-market leases, which range from $500,000 to $5 million and are for periods of up to ten years; and *marketing leases,* in which the bank consolidates several pieces of relatively inexpensive equipment produced by a manufacturer into a single master lease.[1] For many banks the leasing of motor vehicles has become the most important leasing activity, however.

Advantages of Leasing

The reasons for the fast rate of growth in finance leasing are to be found in the advantages it affords, in certain circumstances, over buying assets with money borrowed under a conventional loan. The advantages claimed for finance leasing, not always appropriately, include the following:

1 Provides financing at a lower cost
2 Gives greater flexibility
3 Requires a lower down payment—provides more financing
4 Requires no capital expenditure authorization or bond issue
5 Releases funds for more profitable investment in other assets
6 Offers a tax advantage

Cost Savings through Leasing

To make a proper comparison of leasing costs with the cost of borrowing and owning, it is necessary to base all calculations on the after-tax cash flows, as in a capital expenditure evaluation. The usual method of analysis is to compute the annual net cash outflows for the leasing and borrowing alternatives and then reduce these outflows to present values by discounting them at an appropriate rate. Other things being equal, the lower the present value of the net cash outflows the more attractive the financing plan. Variables that determine the relative costs of leasing and borrowing include:

1 Residual value of the equipment at the end of the lease period
2 Rate at which the cash flows are discounted
3 Number of years by which the duration of the lease exceeds the maturity of the loan

[1]*Fortune,* October 1972, p. 147.

4 Number of years by which the expected useful life of the asset exceeds the maturity of the loan

5 *Implicit interest rate* for the lease compared to the rate for the loan[2]

To illustrate how changes in certain of these variables can alter the relative costs of leasing and borrowing, two simplified examples are presented in Tables 13–1 and 13–2. In both examples, it is assumed that a business firm wants to obtain the use of a piece of equipment costing $100 —an unrealistically low price for this kind of problem but convenient for illustrative purposes—and is considering two methods of financing, a lease and a term loan. In Table 13–1 the expected useful life of the equipment is six years, the final maturity of the loan is four years, and the lease period is also four years. In Table 13–2 the expected useful life of the equipment is increased to eight years, the base period of the lease to six years, and the final maturity of the loan is maintained at four years. In both examples the loan bears interest at 8 percent on the unpaid balance, and the principal is repayable in equal annual instalments. The lease rentals are also based on an interest rate of 8 percent and are payable at the end of each year—$30.20 a year for the four-year lease and $21.63 a year for the six-year lease. If the firm borrows and buys the asset instead of leasing, it will use the sum-of-the-years-digits method of depreciation for tax purposes. The effective income tax rate (state and federal combined) is 52 percent, and there is no investment tax credit. If the asset is leased, the lessee will exercise an option (or first right of refusal) to buy at the end of the lease period for a price equal to the estimated fair market value—$20 in the case of the four-year lease or $15 in the case of the six-year lease. After buying the asset, the lessee will depreciate it down to a salvage value of $5, using the straight-line method.

To show how much difference a change in the rate used for discounting cash outflows can make, the two examples are worked out in three different ways: by applying the firm's approximate after-tax borrowing rate (4 percent) to all the cash outflows; by applying a rate equal to the firm's assumed after-tax cost of capital (10 percent) to all cash flows; and by discounting the residual value and the tax benefits from depreciation of the residual value at 10 percent and all other cash flows at 4 percent. The choice of a discount rate in a problem of this kind is important since one method of financing may look better at a relatively low discount rate, and the other may look better at a higher rate because of differences in the time patterns of the outflows. A high discount rate tends to favor a financing method whose

---

[2]The implicit interest rate for a finance lease is the rate that will discount the minimum lease payments (including the amount of any residual value guarantee by the lessee) plus the unguaranteed portion of the expected residual value to a present value equal to the fair value of the leased property at the inception date minus any investment tax credit retained and expected to be realized by the lessor.

Table 13-1
Comparison of Leasing with Cost of Borrowing and Buying
(assuming an asset life of 6 years)

Loan amortization schedule

Year	Beginning Balance	Payments Total	Payments Principal	Payments Interest	Ending Balance
1980	$100.00	$ 33.00	$ 25.00	$ 8.00	$75.00
1981	75.00	31.00	25.00	6.00	50.00
1982	50.00	29.00	25.00	4.00	25.00
1983	25.00	27.00	25.00	2.00	0
Total		$120.00	$100.00	$20.00	

Depreciation schedule

Year	Basis for Depreciation[a]	Depreciation Rate[b]	Depreciation
1980	$100.00	.2857	$28.57
1981	100.00	.2381	23.81
1982	100.00	.1905	19.05
1983	100.00	.1429	14.29
1984	100.00	.0952	9.28
1985	100.00	.0476	
		1.0000	$95.00

Cost of leasing

	A	B	C	D	E	F
		Payment for	Tax Deductions		Tax Benefit	Net Cash Outflows
Year	Rentals[c]	Residual Value	Rent	Dep'n[d]	$(C + D) \times 52\%$	$(A + B - E)$
1980	$ 30.20	$	$ 30.20	$	$15.70	$14.50
1981	30.20		30.20		15.70	14.50
1982	30.20		30.20		15.70	14.50
1983	30.20	20.00	30.20		15.70	34.50
1984				7.50	3.90	(3.90)
1985				7.50	3.90	(3.90)
Total	$120.80	$20.00	$120.80	$15.00	$70.60	$70.20
Salvage						(5.00)
Total						$65.20

	F	G	H	I	J	K
	Net Cash Outflows	Interest Factors		Present Value of Outflows		
Year	$(A + B - E)$	4%	10%	$4\% (G \times F)$	$10\% (H \times F)$	$4\% \& 10\%^c$
1980	$14.50	.962	.909	$13.95	$13.18	$13.95
1981	14.50	.925	.826	13.41	11.98	13.41
1982	14.50	.889	.751	12.89	10.89	12.89
1983	34.50	.855	.683	29.50	23.56	26.06
1984	(3.90)	.822	.621	(3.21)	(2.42)	(2.42)
1985	(3.90)	.790	.564	(3.08)	(2.20)	(2.20)
Total	$70.20			$63.46	$54.99	$61.69
Salvage	(5.00)		.790	.564	(3.95)	(2.82)
Total	$65.20			$59.51	$52.17	$58.87

[a] Federal tax law provides that if the estimated salvage value does not exceed 10 percent of the cost of the asset, it need not be deducted from the cost in arriving at the basis for depreciation. Note, however, that the total amount of depreciation cannot exceed cost minus salvage value. In this example $100 is the basis for depreciation since the $5 salvage value is only 5 percent of the cost.

[b] First year, 6/21; second year, 5/21; etc.

[c] Based upon implicit rate of 8 percent.

Table 13–1 (continued)

Cost of borrowing and buying

	A	B	C	D	E	F
			Tax Deductions		Tax	Net Cash
	Loan				Benefit	Outflows
Year	Payments	Dep'n.	Int.	Total (B + C)	(D X 52%)	(A – E)
1980	$ 33.00	$28.57	$ 8.00	$ 36.57	$19.02	$13.98
1981	31.00	23.81	6.00	29.81	15.50	15.50
1982	29.00	19.05	4.00	23.05	11.98	17.02
1983	27.00	14.29	2.00	16.29	8.47	18.53
1984		9.28		9.28	4.83	(4.83)
1985						
Total	$120.00	$95.00	$20.00	$115.00	$59.80	$60.20
Salvage						(5.00)
Total						$55.20

	F	G	H	I	J	K
	Net Cash	Interest Factors		Present Values of Outflows		
	Outflows					
Year	(A – E)	4%	10%	4% (G X F)	10% (H X F)	4% & 10%[f]
1980	$13.98	.962	.909	$13.45	$12.71	$13.45
1981	15.50	.925	.826	14.34	12.80	14.34
1982	17.02	.889	.751	15.13	12.78	15.13
1983	18.53	.855	.683	15.84	12.66	15.84
1984	(4.83)	.822	.621	(3.97)	(3.00)	(3.97)
1985						
Total	$60.20			$54.79	$47.95	$54.79
Salvage	(5.00)	.790	.564	(3.95)	(2.82)	(2.82)
Total	$55.20			$50.84	$45.13	$51.97

Summary

	Costs at Various Discount Rates		
	4%	10%	4% & 10%
Leasing costs	$59.51	$52.17	$58.87
Borrowing costs	50.84	45.13	51.97
Excess of leasing costs over borrowing costs	$ 8.67	$ 7.04	$ 6.90
Percentage by which leasing costs exceed borrowing costs	17.1%	15.6%	13.3%

[d]Federal tax law provides that if the estimated salvage value exceeds 10 percent of the cost of the asset, then cost less salvage value must be used as a basis for depreciation. In this example $15 is the basis for depreciation since the $5 salvage value is 25 percent of the cost of the asset to the lessee.

[e]All cash flows except the salvage value, the payment for the residual value, and tax benefits from depreciation of residual value are discounted at 4 percent.

[f]All cash flows except estimated salvage value are discounted at 4 percent.

outflows are heavy in the later years. Some writers believe that in evaluating two or more competing financial plans, the cash flows should be discounted at the firm's estimated cost of capital, the rate normally used for evaluating proposed capital expenditures. However, in a lease-or-borrow problem where most of the cash flows can be easily predicted, depending as they do on the terms of the borrowing and leasing contracts, this is not a sound position. With the risk being much less than for a typical capital expenditure proposal, it is inappropriate to use the cost of capital as the discount rate since it reflects the average risk relating to the firm's activities. A better procedure is to use the firm's after-tax borrowing rate for discounting all cash flows except the estimated residual value, the salvage value, and the tax benefits from depreciation of the residual value, all of which can be appropriately discounted at the cost of capital because of their uncertainty.

In the first example (Table 13–1), the present value of the cost of leasing is substantially larger than the present value of the cost of borrowing and owning, no matter which discount rate is applied to the cash outflows. A change in the discount rate alters the relative costs very little because most of the cash flows occur in the comparatively short period of only four years. Leasing is more costly than borrowing and owning even though the two proposals are based on the same interest rate. This, of course, is because of the payment of $20 by the lessee for the residual value of the equipment at the end of the four-year lease period.

In the second example (Table 13–2), where the expected useful life of the asset and the lease period are both increased by two years, the amount by which the cost of leasing exceeds the cost of borrowing and owning is substantially reduced, and the size of the discount rate becomes considerably more important because the cash flows extend over longer periods. Lengthening the lease period reduces the annual rentals and causes some of them to be more remote and therefore discounted more heavily. Assuming no change in the implicit rate of interest, lengthening the lease period will always reduce the present value of the cost of leasing when the discount rate is higher than the after-tax implicit rate of interest. The longer lease period also causes heavier discounting of the residual value, substantially reducing its importance. There are a number of rather obvious ways in which the cost of leasing could be still further reduced relative to the cost of borrowing and owning without lowering the rentals. These include a further reduction in the residual value, a further increase in the expected useful life of the equipment, a further increase in the lease period, and an increase in the discount rate. An increase in the expected useful life of the equipment would increase the present value of the costs of owning because of a decrease in the present value of the tax benefits from depreciation— the decrease resulting from spreading such benefits over a greater number of years. An increase in the lease period would decrease the present value of the costs of leasing if the discount rate were higher than the after-tax implicit interest rate in the lease. An increase in the discount rate would reduce the cost of leasing more than it would the cost of borrowing and owning because the cash outflows are spread over a longer period under the lease. Leasing is often shown to be less costly than a conventional loan simply by making the loan maturity considerably shorter than the lease period, then discounting all cash outflows at a rate substantially higher than the implicit interest rate for the lease.

Table 13-2

Comparison of Leasing with Cost of Borrowing and Buying

(assuming an asset life of 8 years)

Loan amortization schedule

| Year | Beginning Balance | Payments | | | Ending Balance |
		Total	Principal	Interest	
1980	$100.00	$ 33.00	$ 25.00	$ 8.00	$75.00
1981	75.00	31.00	25.00	6.00	50.00
1982	50.00	29.00	25.00	4.00	25.00
1983	25.00	27.00	25.00	2.00	0
Total		$120.00	$100.00	$20.00	

Depreciation schedule

Year	Basis for Depreciation[a]	Depreciation Rate[b]	Depreciation
1980	$100.00	.2222	$22.22
1981	100.00	.1944	19.44
1982	100.00	.1667	16.67
1983	100.00	.1389	13.89
1984	100.00	.1111	11.11
1985	100.00	.0833	8.33
1986	100.00	.0556	3.34
1987	100.00	.0278	
		1.0000	$95.00

Cost of leasing

| | A | B | C | D | E | F |
Year	Rentals[c]	Payment for Residual Value	Tax Deductions Rent	Tax Deductions Dep'n[d]	Tax Benefit $(C + D) \times 52\%$	Net Cash Outflows $(A + B - E)$
1980	$ 21.63	$	$ 21.63	$	$11.25	$10.38
1981	21.63		21.63		11.25	10.38
1982	21.63		21.63		11.25	10.38
1983	21.63		21.63		11.25	10.38
1984	21.63		21.63		11.25	10.38
1985	21.63	15.00	21.63		11.25	25.38
1986				5.00	2.60	(2.60)
1987				5.00	2.60	(2.60)
Total	$129.78	$15.00	$129.78	$10.00	$72.70	$72.08
Salvage						(5.00)
Total						$67.08

| | F | G | H | I | J | K |
| | Net Cash Outflows | Interest Factors | | Present Value of Outflows | | |
Year	$(A + B - E)$	4%	10%	4% $(G \times F)$	10% $(H \times F)$	4% & 10%[c]
1980	$10.38	.962	.909	$ 9.99	$ 9.44	$ 9.99
1981	10.38	.925	.826	9.60	8.57	9.60
1982	10.38	.889	.751	9.23	7.80	9.23
1983	10.38	.855	.683	8.87	7.09	8.87
1984	10.38	.822	.621	8.53	6.45	8.53
1985	25.38	.790	.564	20.05	14.31	16.66
1986	(2.60)	.760	.513	(1.98)	(1.33)	(1.33)
1987	(2.60)	.731	.467	(1.90)	(1.21)	(1.21)
Total	$72.08			$62.39	$51.12	$60.34
Salvage	(5.00)	.731	.467	(3.66)	(2.34)	(2.34)
Total	$67.08			$58.73	$48.78	$58.00

[a] See footnote (a), Table 13-1.

[b] First year, 8/36; second year, 7/36; etc.

[c] See footnote (c), Table 13-1.

Table 13-2 (continued)

Cost of borrowing and buying

	A	B	C	D	E	F
		Tax Deductions			*Tax*	*Net Cash*
	Loan				*Benefit*	*Outflows*
Year	*Payments*	*Dep'n.*	*Int.*	*Total (B + C)*	*(D × 52%)*	*(A − E)*
1980	$ 33.00	$22.22	$ 8.00	$ 30.22	$15.71	$17.29
1981	31.00	19.44	6.00	25.44	13.23	17.77
1982	29.00	16.67	4.00	20.67	10.74	18.26
1983	27.00	13.89	2.00	15.89	8.27	18.73
1984		11.11		11.11	5.78	(5.78)
1985		8.33		8.33	4.33	(4.33)
1986		3.34		3.34	1.74	(1.74)
1987						
Total	$120.00	$95.00	$20.00	$115.00	$59.80	$60.20
Salvage						(5.00)
Total						$55.20

	F	G	H	I	J	K
	Net Cash					
	Outflows	*Interest Factors*		*Present Values of Outflows*		
Year	*(A − E)*	*4%*	*10%*	*4% (G × F)*	*10% (H × F)*	*4% & 10%*[f]
1980	$17.29	.962	.909	$16.63	$15.72	$16.63
1981	17.77	.925	.826	16.44	14.68	16.44
1982	18.26	.889	.751	16.23	13.71	16.23
1983	18.73	.855	.683	16.01	12.79	16.01
1984	(5.78)	.822	.621	(4.75)	(3.59)	(4.75)
1985	(4.33)	.790	.564	(3.42)	(2.44)	(3.42)
1986	(1.74)	.760	.513	(1.32)	(.89)	(1.32)
1987						
Total	$60.20			$55.82	$49.98	$55.82
Salvage	(5.00)	.731	.467	(3.66)	(2.34)	(2.34)
Total	$55.20			$52.16	$47.64	$53.48

Summary

	Costs at Various Discount Rates		
	4%	*10%*	*4% & 10%*
Leasing costs	$58.73	$48.78	$58.00
Borrowing costs	52.16	47.64	53.48
Excess of leasing costs over borrowing costs	$ 6.57	$ 1.14	$ 4.52
Percentage by which leasing costs exceed borrowing costs	12.6%	2.4%	8.5%

[d]See footnote (d), Table 13-1.

[e]See footnote (e), Table 13-1.

[f]See footnote (f), Table 13-1.

Implicit Interest Rate, Lessor's Yield, and Cost to Lessee

On a before-tax basis, the lessee's cost will often be the same as the implicit interest rate, which is the rate that will discount the rental payments plus the residual value to a present value equal to the cost of the asset net of the investment tax credit. However, on an after-tax basis, the lessee's cost may be considerably less than the lessor's yield. Herein lies one of the principal reasons for the rapid growth in finance leasing: leasing can be very attractive for both parties when the lessor's yield is substantially higher than the cost to the lessee. This seeming paradox results entirely from the impact of income taxes. When leasing makes tax benefits available to the lessor without a corresponding decrease in benefits to the lessee, both parties may be better off than if the transaction were handled as a straight loan. If the lessor's tax status and profitability are such that full advantage can be taken of accelerated depreciation and any investment tax credit, but the lessee's tax status is such that if he were to borrow and then buy the property he would not be able to take full advantage of these benefits, there is a net advantage in the lessor rather than the lessee buying and owning the property. In those circumstances, the lessor usually passes at least a portion of the tax benefits on to the lessee; because of this, it is not uncommon for leases to be negotiated at rentals that imply an interest rate considerably lower than the lessee's normal rate for borrowing. As a general rule, however, the implicit interest rates on equipment leases are somewhat higher than the rates on straight loans of similar maturities, probably because of higher servicing costs.[3]

A cost sometimes associated with borrowing and owning that has been ignored to this point is that of maintaining compensating balances. This is likely to be a consideration only for large borrowers since compensating balances are not usually required of smaller bank customers. Certainly, to the extent that a firm is required to carry higher balances if it borrows, the cost of carrying those additional balances should be included.

Several studies have examined the cost of finance leasing. Their findings indicate that on average the cost of leasing is higher than the cost of conventional debt. However, as previously observed, the reverse is often true in one important class of cases—where the lessee would be unable to benefit from the investment tax credit or accelerated depreciation if he were to buy the asset and the lessor is willing to pass some of those tax benefits on to the lessee through lower rental rates.

Flexible Financing

An advantage claimed for lease financing is greater convenience and flexibility than is available with conventional borrowing. Leasing can provide financing on a piecemeal basis at precisely the time when the assets to be financed are needed. This feature may be particularly attractive to small borrowers, who may find it impossible to get similar convenience and flexibility through loan commitment agreements or revolving credits, which are more likely to be made available to larger firms. Revolving credits—often

[3]Merle K. Buck, "The Financing of Personal Property Leasing Companies by Commercial Banks" (Thesis, Pacific Coast Banking School, University of Washington, 1967), p. 27; Gilbert A. Scherzinger, "Direct Equipment Leasing by the Commercial Bank" (Thesis, Pacific Coast Banking School, University of Washington, 1971), p. 38.

combined with term loans—have been used extensively, for example, in lending to commercial airlines and trucking companies.

Lower Down Payment————More Financing Provided

It is said that leasing provides 100 percent financing. This is often true, but for many business firms conventional borrowing can do the same. For such firms the relevant question is whether the total capacity to acquire assets with debt capital—finance leasing being counted as debt capital—can be increased by using lease financing. Earlier leasing studies indicated that many financial analysts and bankers believed that by using long-term non-cancellable leases a company could obtain a greater amount of financing than with straight loans alone. More recent evidence indicates, however, that members of the financial community have rejected the idea that a company can improve its apparent financial condition and increase its total debt capacity by leasing instead of borrowing in a conventional manner.

One principal reason for the rapid growth in leasing of motor vehicles is the low down payment required of the lessee. The willingness of lessors to accept smaller down payments in leasing than in instalment lending is often due to the fact that leasing is more profitable.

No Capital Expenditure Authorization or Bond Issue Required

Formal differences between a lease and a purchase often make it possible to lease when it would be inconvenient, if not impossible, to buy. Rentals are normally classified as operating expenses and, because of this, leases are sometimes not required to be included in capital expenditure budgets. When that is true, operating managers may find it easier to lease equipment than to buy it. However, as more and more people come to recognize that the acquisition of assets through financial leasing really differs very little from borrowing and buying, this loophole in capital budgeting procedures will no doubt become rare.

Local governments and departments of the federal government some-times use leasing as a way around budgetary restrictions and the legal authorizations required for capital expenditures and borrowing. By leasing, local governments may find it possible to avoid bond issues and the need for approval by the voters. Even the United States Navy has found leasing a convenient way to avoid the need for capital expenditure authorizations. For example, in the early 1970s, the navy leased a number of tankers from a consortium consisting of an investment banking firm, a bank-affiliated leasing company, and a shipping company.[4]

[4]*Forbes,* July 15, 1972, p. 18.

Releases Funds for Investment in Other Assets

It is often stated that leasing is advantageous because it conserves capital or releases funds that can be invested more profitably in other assets. This is a valid argument for leasing only if lease financing is not essentially equivalent to conventional borrowing. If leasing is the same as borrowing, it is just as appropriate to say that borrowing conserves working capital or releases funds for more profitable investment in other assets as it is to say that leasing accomplishes these things.

Offers a Tax Advantage

It is often stated that leasing is advantageous because rental payments are fully tax-deductible as an operating expense, and the lessee thus pays for the use of the equipment out of current, untaxed income. This ignores the fact that a finance lease is a substitute for conventional borrowing and that if the asset is purchased by a business firm with borrowed funds, it can deduct interest expense as well as depreciation. If the firm uses accelerated depreciation, the present value of the tax benefits may actually be greater with borrowing and buying than with leasing.

As previously discussed, leasing may have a tax advantage in two situations, one of which occurs when the lessee would be unable to take full advantage of the investment tax credit or accelerated depreciation if the asset were purchased instead of leased. The other is where some of the leased property consists of land. By leasing land instead of buying it, the lessee may, in effect, be able to deduct the cost of the land over a period of years. For this privilege he gives up the possibility of building up an equity, however. Furthermore, since the lessor cannot depreciate the land, the rentals (other things equal) will be higher than on depreciable property.

Motor Vehicle Leasing

Motor vehicle leasing has become important enough and different enough from other leasing to merit special attention. For individuals and some business firms the attractions of leasing are a lower down payment and lower monthly payments than with instalment buying. For these benefits, however, an individual who is not using the leased car for business proposes gives up a possible tax deduction for interest expense. Leasing is attractive to automobile dealers because it encourages people to acquire automobiles, and the dealer may receive the benefit of the investment tax credit and accelerated depreciation.

In motor vehicle leasing the lessee is usually required to guarantee (in full or to some lesser extent) that the vehicle will have a certain residual value at the expiration of the lease. Leases containing such a guarantee are called *open-end* leases, while leases without a guarantee are known as *closed-end* leases. Often the lessee's guarantee is limited, quite commonly to an amount no greater than three monthly rental payments. In both open-end and closed-end leases the lessee is responsible for any damage to the car, and may be required to pay an additional charge of several cents a mile for any miles in excess of, say, 15,000 miles a year.

The finance leasing of motor vehicles by commercial banks usually arises out of leases generated by automobile dealers. A bank will agree to be the lessor in such a transaction only after it has reviewed the terms of the lease and is satisfied as to the amount of the down payment, the size of the rental payments, the estimated residual value, and the credit worthiness of the lessee. When the estimated residual value in an open-end lease is a significant fraction (30 to 40 percent or more) of the value of the leased property, the lease is similar to a term loan with a large balloon payment. Rental payments are based on the excess of the initial value of the asset over the estimated residual value rather than on the full value of the asset. Thus a 36-month lease is like a 36-month loan with a balloon payment, which reduces monthly payments to the level of a five or six year ordinary loan. In many cases, banks become involved in the finance leasing of motor vehicles by lending to lessors on the security of leases rather than becoming lessors themselves. However, because of the low down payments in leasing, the amount loaned is often based on the cost of the asset to the lessor rather than on its retail value.

Leveraged Leasing

It is estimated that over 85 percent of all full-payout leasing is in the form of leveraged leases, also known as third-party equity leases or investor leases. A *leveraged lease* is one where the lessor borrows up to 80 percent of the cost of the leased property from one or more long-term lenders. In a typical leveraged-lease transaction the lessor receives a fee for originating the financing, in addition to interest income and rapid recovery of his investment by virtue of heavy tax deductions for depreciation and interest expense in the early years. The long-term money is usually borrowed by the lessor on a nonrecourse basis, with the rentals and equipment pledged as collateral for the loan. For tax purposes, the lessor reports the rentals as gross income and is allowed to deduct accelerated depreciation on the leased equipment as well as interest on the long-term borrowing. As a consequence, the lessor has substantial tax losses and large cash inflows in the early years of the lease period, followed by cash outflows in the later years. In the final year of the lease, cash may come in from the residual value of the equipment and from the tax benefit that results from disposing of the asset at a loss, if that is the case.

Leveraged leasing is often used on large transactions with lessees who are unable to take advantage of the investment tax credit or accelerated depreciation. This may be because they have inadequate profits or their income is largely or entirely tax-exempt, as in the case of producer cooperatives. By leasing instead of buying, the lessee is able to transfer valuable tax benefits to the lessor in return for financing at interest rates often substantially below the lessee's ordinary borrowing rate. For example, in the late 1960s and early 1970s the five largest airlines leased most of their new equipment, primarily because their poor earnings made it impossible for them to take full advantage of accelerated depreciation and the investment tax credit. By the end of 1971 they had over $2 billion of aircraft on lease. At the same time, most of the smaller, more profitable airlines were not using lease financing.

Leveraged leases are originated by a wide variety of firms, including commercial banks, investment banks, independent leasing companies, commercial finance companies, and so-called lease-originating companies or brokers. Larger commercial banks sometimes originate leases in which they take no equity position but derive a profit from the origination fees. Investment-banking firms are frequently called on to arrange for the long-term portion of the financing, although commercial banks sometimes perform this function for themselves by going to institutional lenders, industrial corporations, other commercial banks, and individuals for the longer-term money. Some banks have found that leveraged leasing can be used effectively on transactions as small as $300,000 and for terms as short as five years.

Negative cash flows in the later years of a leveraged lease make the problem of measuring the lessor's yield a rather complicated one. When two changes occur in the signs of the cash flows during the lease period, two rates of return will discount the cash flows to a present value that equals the investment. And even if only one change occurs in the cash flows (from inflows in the early years to outflows in the later years), the question still remains whether it is appropriate to find the rate of return in the same way as when all the cash flows are inflows after the initial investment has been made. That is, should the rate of return be determined by simply finding the rate of interest that will discount the cash flows (positive and negative) to a present value equal to the investment? Inherent in this approach is an assumption that all inflows from the early years will be reinvested at the rate of return that is found for the investment. Such an assumption may not be appropriate if a substantial portion of the inflows in the early years is needed to cover the outflows in the later years. To deal with this problem, many

Table 13–3
Leveraged Lease—Computation of Yield

Year	A Lease Receipts	B Dep'n.	C Interest Expense	D Taxable Income A – (B + C)	E Income Tax D × 48%	F Earnings after Taxes D – E	G Payment on Principal	H Cash in (out)[b]
1/1/80								$(20.00)
1980	$ 9.20	$ 15.36	$ 6.40	$(12.56)	$(16.03)[a]	$ 3.47	$ 2.95	15.88
1981	9.20	14.08	6.16	(11.04)	(5.30)	(5.74)	3.19	5.15
1982	9.20	12.80	5.91	(9.51)	(4.56)	(4.95)	3.44	4.41
1983	9.20	11.52	5.63	(7.95)	(3.82)	(4.13)	3.72	3.67
1984	9.20	10.24	5.34	(6.38)	(3.06)	(3.32)	4.01	2.91
1985	9.20	8.96	5.02	(4.78)	(2.29)	(2.49)	4.33	2.14
1986	9.20	7.68	4.67	(3.15)	(1.51)	(1.64)	4.68	1.36
1987	9.20	6.40	4.29	(1.49)	(.72)	(.77)	5.06	.57
1988	9.20	5.12	3.89	.19	.09	.10	5.46	(.24)
1989	9.20	2.84	3.45	2.91	1.40	1.51	5.90	(1.55)
1990	9.20		2.98	6.22	2.99	3.23	6.37	(3.14)
1991	9.20		2.47	6.73	3.23	3.50	6.88	(3.38)
1992	9.20		1.92	7.28	3.49	3.79	7.43	(3.64)
1993	9.20		1.33	7.87	3.78	4.09	8.02	(3.93)
1994	9.20		.68	8.52	4.09	4.43	8.56	(4.13)
Total	$138.00	$ 95.00	$60.14	$(17.14)	$(18.22)	$ 1.08	$80.00	$(3.92)
Writeoff[c]		5.00		(5.00)	(2.40)	(2.60)		2.40
Total	$138.00	$100.00	$60.14	$(22.14)	$(20.62)	$(1.52)	$80.00	$(1.52)

[a]The income tax credit (benefit) of $16.03 in the year 1980 includes an investment tax credit of $10.00.
[b]Individual amounts in column H = B + F – G. Total of column H = B + F – G – $20.00.
[c]Undepreciated balance of $5.00 written off at end of 15 years; asset assumed to be worthless at that time.
[d]See Tables 13–4 and 13–5.

lessors now use the sinking fund method for computing the yield on leveraged leases. With this approach, the cash outflows of the later years are viewed as a deferred liability of the lessor that must be paid from inflows received in the early years. A sinking fund is created, in theory, from a portion of the early cash inflows to cover the later cash deficiencies. The remaining inflows are then related to the investment to determine the yield. Measurement of the yield from the lease thus depends heavily on the rate of earnings assumed for the sinking fund. The higher the assumed-earnings rate, the less cash required from the early inflows to cover the later outflows, and the higher the lessor's yield. The yield is of course particularly sensitive to the assumed-earnings rate when the cash outflows in the later years are large.

A typical leveraged-lease transaction (using small numbers for convenience) is shown in Tables 13–3, 13–4, and 13–5, with the yield computed by the sinking-fund method. The annual rentals are $9.20 for a period of 15 years, and the assumed earnings rate for the sinking fund is 3 percent

Table 13–3 (continued)

I	J	K	L	M	N	O	P
	Cash		Interest	Ending			Present Value
Cumulative	to (from)	Beginning	Earned	Fund	Cash	Interest	of Cash Flow
Cash	Sinking	Fund	on Fund	Balance	Flow to	Factors	to Investment
in (out)	Fund[d]	Balance	K × 3%	J + K + L	Investment	(6.0%)	N × O
$(20.00)					$(20.00)		$(20.00)
(4.12)					15.88	.943	14.97
1.03	$ .59			$ .59	4.56	.890	4.06
5.44	4.41	$ .59	$ .02	5.02			
9.11	3.67	5.02	.15	8.84			
12.02	2.91	8.84	.26	12.01			
14.16	2.14	12.01	.36	14.51			
15.52	1.36	14.51	.43	16.30			
16.09	.57	16.30	.49	17.36			
15.85	(.24)	17.36	.52	17.64			
14.30	(1.55)	17.64	.53	16.62			
11.16	(3.14)	16.62	.50	13.98			
7.78	(3.38)	13.98	.42	11.02			
4.14	(3.64)	11.02	.33	7.71			
.21	(3.93)	7.71	.23	4.01			
(3.92)	(4.13)	4.01	.12	0.00			
$(3.92)	$(4.36)		$4.36		$ .44		$(.97)
2.40					2.40	.417	1.00
$(1.52)					$ 2.84		$ .03

after taxes, or 6.25 percent before taxes. The lessor borrows 80 percent of the cost of the asset from a long-term lender on a 15-year, 8 percent loan which is repayable in 15 equal annual instalments of $9.35, principal plus interest. The estimated useful life of the asset is 15 years. However, depreciation is based on a 12-year life under the Asset Depreciation Range System. Since the salvage value need not be deducted from the cost in computing the annual depreciation, the asset is actually depreciated down to the estimated salvage value of $5.00 in the tenth year, using the sum-of-the-years-digits method.

In this example the lessor recovers his investment in less than two years and, except for the initial investment, cash inflows exceed outflows in each of the first eight years. However, in the ninth year the cash flows become negative and remain so until the end of the fifteenth year when a tax benefit is received from writing off the remaining book value of the asset. Over its full life, the lease produces a cash loss of $1.52, yet the lessor's after-tax rate of return is approximately 6 percent or a pretax return of 11.5 percent. The sensitivity of the lessor's yield to the assumed-earnings rate for the sinking fund is indicated by the fact that if it were assumed that the sinking fund would earn nothing, the lessor's yield would be negative. And if the assumed after-tax earnings rate for the fund were increased from 3 percent to 5

Table 13–4
Amount of Sinking Fund Required at the
Beginning of Cash Outflow Period (present value of cash outflows)

Year	Cash Outflow	Interest Factor (3%)	Present Value
1988	$ .24	—	$ .24
1989	1.55	.971	1.51
1990	3.14	.943	2.96
1991	3.38	.915	3.09
1992	3.64	.889	3.24
1993	3.93	.863	3.39
1994	4.13	.838	3.46
Total	$20.01		$17.89

percent, the lessor's pretax yield would be increased to nearly 22 percent.

The most optimistic way of looking at the earnings rate for the sinking fund is to assume that it should be the same as the lessor's estimated investment-opportunity rate for those funds. Some writers contend that the use of the investment-opportunity rate would not be appropriate because it assigns to the sinking fund the profit from future investment opportunities. A more conservative and perhaps better approach is to base the assumed-earnings rate for the sinking fund on the lessor's estimated cost of funds, recognizing that the so-called negative investment phase of the lease provides only a temporary source of funds to the lessor because the excess funds must be used later to cover the cash deficiencies under the lease. On this basis an assumed-earnings rate of 4 or 5 percent before taxes is perhaps reasonable over the long run.

Table 13–5
Accumulation of Sinking Fund Required to Cover Cash Flows

	A	B	C	D	E	F
						Sinking
			Amount in Fund		Fund Required	
	Cash[a]	Interest	Annual			Remainder
Year	Inflows	Factor (3%)	(A × B)	Cumulative	Total	(E–D)
1987	$ .57	1.030	$ .59	$ .59	$17.89	$17.30
1986	1.36	1.061	1.44	2.03	17.89	15.86
1985	2.14	1.093	2.34	4.37	17.89	13.52
1984	2.91	1.126	3.28	7.65	17.89	10.24
1983	3.67	1.159	4.25	11.90	17.89	5.99
1982	4.41	1.194	5.27	17.17	17.89	.72
1981	.59	1.230	.72	17.89	17.89	0.00

[a] All cash inflows for the years 1982 to 1987 are required for the sinking fund. In addition, $.59 of the 1981 cash inflow of $5.15 is needed for the sinking fund; the remaining $4.56 is included among the cash flows to the investment, column N of Table 13–3.

Legal and Tax Problems

Lease financing involves a number of legal complications usually not present in other bank lending activities. These include the problem of structuring the agreement so that it will be accepted as a true lease for tax purposes; the need to be concerned with and evaluate the legal and tax implications of owning property and doing business in states other than that in which the bank's principal office is located; and the various problems arising out of the bank's ownership of the leased assets, including the need to evaluate the rights of the bank as owner of the property and lessor in the event of the lessee's bankruptcy.

Income Tax Considerations

A lessor is entitled to receive the expected tax benefits from accelerated depreciation and the investment tax credit only if the agreement meets the Internal Revenue Service requirements for a lease. If the agreement is not a true lease, the transaction will be treated as though the property had been sold to the lessee and pledged to the lessor as security for a loan with the following consequences: the lessee is denied a deduction for rental expense but is allowed, as owner of the property, to deduct depreciation and interest expense instead; the lessor, because he is not considered owner of the property, is denied a deduction for depreciation expense but needs to report only the interest portion of the "rentals" as income, the remainder being considered as repayment of principal. As a result, the lessor's income will be greater and the lessee's smaller during the early years of the lease, with the opposite occurring in the later years. Thus, if the lessee happens to be a tax-exempt organization or a corporation that lacks sufficient earnings to receive the full benefit of an early reduction in taxable earnings, the failure of the agreement to stand up as a true lease can mean an increase in the lessor's taxes during the early years without a corresponding decrease for the lessee.

An agreement will be recognized as a lease for tax purposes only if it is evident that the parties intended it to be a lease. Designating the agreement as a lease is not enough. It must be clear that the lessee is not in effect buying the property and using a portion of the rental payments to build up an equity. The lessor must retain the risks of ownership, including the possibility that the residual value at the end of the lease will be substantially less than expected. Probably the most difficult restriction is the requirement that the lease period, including all extensions provided for in the agreement, be substantially less than the expected useful life of the asset. This means that over a period perhaps 15 to 20 percent shorter than the expected useful life of the asset the lessee must pay rentals large enough in aggregate to cover the cost of the asset and provide a return on the lessor's investment. It is also required that the rental payments be reasonable in relation to the value of the property during all periods of the lease. And, finally, the lease agreement must not contain any provision giving the lessee the right to buy the property at the end of the lease period by payment of an amount less than the fair market value of the property, nor may it give the lessee a right to renew the lease at rentals that are nominal in relation to the value of the property.

For tax purposes, one of the most important things for the lessor to determine is the minimum number of years over which the leased assets can be depreciated. The shorter the depreciable life, the more valuable the tax benefits to the lessor and the more attractive the agreement can be made for the lessee without sacrificing yield. In any case, the lessor will want to avoid either overestimating or underestimating the minimum useful life for tax purposes. If the life used for computing the tax-deductible depreciation is too long, the lessor may quote rental rates too high and thereby lose attractive business; if the asset life is too short and later disallowed by the Internal Revenue Service, the rentals may be too low and give the lessor a disappointing yield.

Rights of the Lessor

Finance leases generally contain a provision under which the lessee agrees to indemnify the lessor against all liabilities, except income taxes, arising out of the lessor's ownership and leasing of the equipment. If the investment tax credit is involved, the lease may also require the lessee to give full indemnification for loss of the credit if that should occur. Similar indemnification may be required for the loss of depreciation deductions. The lessor's primary protection against physical loss of the property, its damage, or destruction is provided by insurance, the premiums for which are paid by the lessee. The lessee is also required to insure the lessor against public liability and passenger liability where appropriate.

The rights of equipment lessors in the event of a lessee's reorganization or bankruptcy are substantially better under the Uniform Commercial Code than they were previously. Under the provisions of the code, if the lessee defaults and the trustee in bankruptcy decides that no further rental payments shall be made because they are unduly burdensome, the lessor is generally entitled to the return of the equipment; reimbursement for expenses resulting from the default, for example, costs of repossessing and selling or re-leasing the equipment; and contract damages in the amount of the difference, if any, between the present value of the rentals and other payments that were to be received during the remainder of the lease and the fair market value of the property or price received for it through sale or re-lease. To the extent that the proceeds from the sale or re-lease are not sufficient to cover the unpaid rentals and expenses caused by the default, the lessor takes a position as a general creditor. Provisions for liquidated damages in lease agreements are generally sustained only if the actual loss is approximately equal to the specified damages, which of course leaves the lessor with the burden of proving the amount of actual damages and largely defeats the purpose of including such a provision.

Qualification to Do Business in Other States

When a corporation is doing business in more than one state, it is often difficult to determine whether its activities in a particular state are such that it must get a license to conduct business there. To be on the safe side, corporations often qualify to do business in states where they have very little activity, since failure to qualify can be very costly in terms of penalties and in being denied access to the courts of the state. The problem of qualifying to do business may not be as serious for national banks as for state banks, however, since a number of court cases appear to exempt national banks from state qualification statutes, either because they are considered federal instrumentalities or are not considered "foreign corporations" inasmuch as they are incorporated under federal law. Presumably, these decisions would apply to leasing as well as to the other activities of national banks. But again, to be on the safe side and to avoid the expense of qualifying in foreign states and paying taxes on an allocated portion of their total revenue there, national banks often elect to avoid any direct ownership and leasing of assets outside the state of their principal office. This is sometimes done by handling leasing transactions in foreign states through trustees, often correspondent banks, who hold title to the equipment and are principal parties to the leasing agreement. Another way for banks to avoid any direct involvement in foreign states is through the organization of a leasing subsidiary owned either by a bank or by a one-bank holding company. A number of major banks have adopted this course of action.

Accounting for Leases

Statement No. 13 of the Financial Accounting Standards Board prescribes the proper methods of accounting for leases. If a lease meets any one of the following four criteria, it is considered a capital lease and should be capitalized by the lessee:

1 Ownership of the property is to be transferred to the lessee by the end of the lease, or

2 The lease contains a bargain purchase option, or

3 The term of the lease is 75 percent or more of the property's estimated economic life, or

4 The present value of the minimum lease payments required by the lease is 90 percent or more of the fair value of the leased property, less any investment tax credit retained by the lessor

All other leases are considered operating leases and need not be recorded as assets and liabilities.

The discount rate used to determine the present value of the minimum lease payments for the purpose of applying criterion number 4 is the lessee's incremental borrowing rate or the lessor's implicit interest rate, whichever is lower. Minimum lease payments include, along with rentals, the maximum amount of the lessee's obligation to make up any residual value deficiency at the expiration of the lease.

The amount to be recorded as an asset and a liability by the lessee of a capital lease is the lower of the present value of the minimum lease payments at the beginning of the lease term, or the fair value of the leased property at the inception of the lease. The lessee is required to allocate lease payments between a reduction of the lease obligation and interest expense in a manner that will produce a constant periodic interest rate on the balance of the obligation. Generally, a capital lease asset should be amortized down to the value of the asset to the lessee at the end of the lease period.

Lessor accounting for capital leases is generally parallel to that of the lessee. For lessors other than manufacturers or dealers of the leased property, capital leases are classified as either direct financing leases or leveraged leases. Lessors account for direct financing leases as follows:

1 The minimum lease payments (that is, rental payments plus the amount of the lessee's guarantee of the residual value) plus any unguaranteed residual value to the lessor are recorded as the gross investment

2 The excess of the gross investment over the cost of the leased property is recorded as unearned income

3 The net investment is the gross investment less the unearned income.

Unearned income is amortized over the lease term using the interest method, which results in a constant periodic rate of return on the net investment. The interest method leaves a net investment balance at the end of the lease term equal to the amount of any bargain purchase option or residual guarantee.

Lessor accounting for leveraged leases is somewhat more complicated. The net investment shown on the balance sheet consists of rentals receivable, net of the portion applicable to principal and interest on the lessor's debt to the long-term lenders, plus a receivable for the investment tax credit until it is realized, plus the estimated residual value of the property, plus unearned income, which is the remaining amount of estimated pretax income and investment tax credit to be allocated to income over the term of the lease. Typically, the net investment is positive in the early years of a lease, negative in the middle years, and positive again in later years. The net investment is decreased in any year when cash flows are positive (a portion being allocated to reduction of the investment and a portion to income) and increased in years when cash flows are negative. Over the full term of the lease enough cash flows are allocated to the investment to cover the lessor's beginning net investment; the remainder of the cash flows are allocated to income. The allocations each year are made in such a way that the rate of return on the net investment is the same each year. A trial-and-error process (usually programmed on a computer) is used to find the rate of return that will allocate just enough cash flows to the investment to cover the lessor's initial investment and at the same time provide a constant rate of return on the lessor's net investment. This method of calculating the rate of return on a leveraged lease differs from the sinking fund method illustrated earlier in the chapter. The sinking fund method is widely used by lessors in pricing leveraged leases.

Organizing and Administering a Leasing Program

The size and nature of the staff required to operate a leasing program depend on the volume of business, the size and complexity of the leases granted, and the extent to which assistance is obtained from leasing experts in other organizations. It is one thing to handle leases of short duration on equipment costing no more than a few thousand dollars, for which standard leasing agreements can often be used with little or no modification, and quite another to grant leases with maturities of eight to twenty years on airliners, ocean tankers, nuclear cores, railroad cars, or the principal equipment of a major manufacturing plant. Large leases of this kind typically involve the participation of outside investors, stiff competition from other lenders, and an elaborate agreement tailored to the specific circumstances of the transaction.

One way to participate directly in finance leasing without setting up an extensive organization is to employ another bank or leasing company to handle all lease negotiations, arrange the necessary documentation, and provide administrative services. For example, the United States Leasing

Company, handles the leasing operations for a number of important regional banks whose assets average close to $1 billion. In this program, the bank originates the lease and provides all the funds, while United States Leasing or one of its subsidiaries is the lessor and holds title to the equipment. The lease is made only with the bank's approval, and the bank receives an assignment of the lease receivable and a security interest in the equipment. Another way of participating in lease financing without having a special leasing staff is to buy participations in leases originated or underwritten by others. Typically, this occurs only with large leases negotiated by major banks, investment-banking firms, or leasing companies. Of course the underwriter must structure the lease so that it will be attractive both to the investors and the lessee. The underwriter's compensation is principally in the form of front-end fees for arranging the transaction and sometimes an additional fee for disposing of the equipment at the end of the lease. When the lease is handled through a trust arrangement, the underwriter may also receive a small fee for trustee services.

Setting Up a Leasing Organization

Although leasing is similar to term lending in many respects, the structuring and documenting of a lease can be considerably more complex; because of this, special training and experience are required to run a leasing operation. Determining the yield on a finance lease is a rather complicated problem, as we have already observed, since it is a function of a number of variables, including the implicit interest rate, income tax rates, the depreciation method, the estimated useful life of the asset, expected residual value, the amount of leverage, the rate of interest paid to outside investors, the investment tax credit, and the method by which the yield is computed. Because of the many variables involved, the negotiation and structuring of a large lease may require many calculations. Therefore it is essential to have access to a time-sharing computer system if the bank has a significant volume of large leases. Leasing is appropriate only where it provides an advantage, on balance, for both the lessor and the lessee; this usually requires that the terms of the lease be carefully tailored to the situation. With the aid of a computer and appropriate computer programs, the bank can readily develop leasing plans to offer its prospective customers. The computer output includes the terms of the proposed lease, the yield to the lessor, and the cost to the lessee. Through sensitivity analysis, it is possible to determine how the bank's yield and the cost to the customer will vary with changes in rental rate, residual value, and other key variables. If it appears that the initial plan would be unattractive to the prospective lessee, the bank can determine how much it might be necessary to lower the payments to make leasing attractive and what the bank's probable yield would be at such lower rentals. By this process, the upper and lower limit for the rental can be established before negotiations are commenced. By adding a subroutine, the bank can make a probabilistic simulation of the lessee's performance, find the expected yield, the probability of default, and the yield under various assumptions as to when default may occur.

Some large regional banks have employed leasing companies or other firms as consultants to help them get started in the direct-leasing business. Banks also call on their attorneys and public accountants for advice relating to the legal, accounting, and tax problems associated with leasing. The services performed by leasing consultants usually include furnishing a comprehensive set of legal documents, computer programs, and procedure manuals. The consultants may also provide assistance in selecting and training personnel, developing new leasing business, and raising funds from outside investors. A significant commitment of time, effort, and money is required to institute a direct-leasing program, but the rewards can make it well worthwhile.

Questions

1. To what extent does finance leasing provide a tax advantage for the lessee?
2. Five variables determine the relative costs of leasing and borrowing. How do each of these variables affect the relative costs?
3. Is leasing advantageous because it releases funds for investment in other projects? Explain.
4. What is the difference between open-end and closed-end motor vehicle leases?
5. Why are monthly payments on a motor vehicle lease usually lower than the payments on a loan?
6. What is a leveraged lease? Why are such leases attractive to banks and bank leasing companies?
7. What variables determine the lessor's yield on a leveraged lease? Explain why each is important.
8. Explain how to calculate the lessor's yield on a leveraged lease using the sinking fund method.

SELECTED REFERENCES

ANDERSON, P. F., and J. D. MARTIN, "Lease vs. Purchase Decisions: A Survey of Current Practice," *Financial Management,* Spring 1977, pp. 41–7.

BERNHARDT, A. B., and D. C. GRANESKO, "Tax Implications of Bank Leasing," *The Bankers Magazine,* Winter 1977, pp. 46–52.

BIERMAN, H. JR., "Leveraged Leasing: An Alternative Analysis," *The Bankers Magazine*, Summer 1974, pp. 62–5.

BLACK, S. H., "How to Obtain a Ruling on Leveraged Lease Property and Avoid the Limited Use Rules," *Journal of Taxation*, June 1977, pp. 354–7.

DEMING, J. R., "Analysis of FASB No. 13," *Financial Executive*, March 1978, pp. 46–51.

DYL, E. A., "Sinking Fund Assumptions in Leveraged Leasing," *Journal of Commercial Bank Lending*, March 1978, pp. 47–52.

——— and S. A. MARTIN, JR., "Setting Terms for Leveraged Leases," *Financial Management*, Winter 1977, pp. 20–7.

PACKHAM, E. R., "An Analysis of the Risks of Leveraged Leasing," *The Journal of Commercial Bank Lending*, March 1975, pp. 2–29.

SCHACHNER, L. "New Accounting for Leases," *Financial Executive*, February 1978, pp. 40–7.

SORENSON, J. W., and R. E. JOHNSON, "Equipment Financial Leasing Practices and Costs: an Empirical Study," *Financial Management*, Spring 1977, pp. 33–40.

VAN HORNE, J. C., "Cost of Leasing with Capital Market Imperfections," *The Engineering Economist*, Fall 1977, pp. 1–12.

14

Real Estate Lending

Commercial banks make a variety of real estate loans that provide funds for all sectors of the economy—consumers, farmers, and businessmen. Commercial banks hold approximately 18 percent of mortgage debt outstanding and are exceeded only by savings and loan associations, which specialize in residential real-estate lending. Of the broad categories of real-estate loans held by commercial banks (see Table 10–1), one- to four-family residential properties accounted for nearly 54 percent of the total. Banks were also large lenders for construction and land development and for nonfarm, nonresidential properties, a broad category that includes commercial and industrial properties. Only 4.3 percent of the real estate loans of banks at year-end 1977 were secured by farmland, and banks were not large lenders for the development of multi-family properties.

Because of regulations and the fact that real estate loans are not as liquid as some other types of loans, commercial banks have not always been important real estate lenders. Prior to amendments to the National Bank Act in 1916, national banks were not permitted to make urban (residential) real estate loans. Although state banks generally were not restricted by regulations from making such loans, they simply chose not to participate heavily in real estate lending. For several years the amount of real estate loans a national bank could make was limited to an amount equal to the capital and surplus of a bank or to 70 percent of the time deposits, whichever was greater. With the insurance of residential real estate loans, their improved liquidity, and the creation of a secondary market, real estate loans became much more popular, and the rules and regulations applied to this area of lending were relaxed or eliminated.

Residential Real Estate Loans

Bank loans on one- to four-family residential properties have increased fourfold since 1960 (see Table 14–1). Several factors have been responsible for this increase, one of which is the recognition that mortgagees tend to carry their checking and savings accounts at the bank that extends them credit for the purchase of a house. Moreover, interest rates on residential real estate loans have usually been moderately attractive and are, therefore, a desirable source of income. Although considerable time is involved in making a residential real estate loan, once it is made, the effort required for administration is relatively little.

The activities of several agencies of the federal government have contributed to the growth of residential real estate lending. Because home ownership is regarded as a desirable aspect of American life, the federal government has fostered several programs to promote the flow of funds into housing and to ease the terms under which mortgages are made. The Federal Housing Administration (FHA) was created in 1934 and charged with the responsibility of insuring residential real estate mortgages to encourage housing and home ownership.

FHA insurance is provided for loans on homes and apartments based on specific criteria concerning the nature of the property and the qualifications of the borrower. The maximum amount of the loan, the required down payment, the maturity limits of the loan, the amount charged for mortgage insurance, monthly prepayment of taxes, appraisal, inspection, and maximum interest rate are stipulated by FHA. In general, the conditions of an FHA mortgage are similar to those of conventional loans except that the rate of interest tends to be lower than rates on comparable conventional loans. In addition to issuing mortgage insurance, FHA has in recent years been

Table 14–1

Types of Residential Real Estate Loans Made by

Insured Commercial Banks Selected Years (amounts in millions of dollars)

		Conventional		FHA		VA	
	Total	Amount	Percent	Amount	Percent	Amount	Percent
1960	20,257	11,245	55.5	5,979	29.5	3,033	15.0
1965	32,519	21,930	68.1	7,952	24.5	2,637	8.1
1970	42,187	32,322	76.6	7,302	17.3	2,563	6.1
1977	96,765	88,897	91.9	7,868	8.1	*	*

*VA included with FHA.

Source: FDIC *Annual Reports.*

directly concerned with mortgage and rent-subsidy programs, which have also played a significant role in housing. The Veterans Administration (VA) guarantees loans of war veterans and operates under many of the same conditions as FHA. On defaulted loans the VA may pay a portion or all of the loan outstanding.

Secondary Mortgage Market

One desirable development that has occurred in real estate finance is a secondary mortgage market for residential mortgages—a market in which previously originated mortgages are bought and sold. This secondary market has facilitated the flow of funds from investors to home buyers and has made possible the adjustment of mortgage portfolios of mortgage holders. Two types of transactions take place in the secondary mortgage market. One market involves the buying and selling of mortgages; another involves what is commonly referred to as *mortgage pools.* The mortgages bought and sold in the secondary market may be either federally insured or conventional loans. A mortgage lender, such as a bank or mortgage company, owned by a one-bank holding company might sell as many as a hundred or more mortgages with a value of several million dollars to an insurance company. Often a bank or mortgage company will enter into a contract with the insurance company to service the loans for an established fee. This kind of financing would be very beneficial to a bank because it would be providing funds for the community, increasing its income, and attracting deposits as well.

Mortgage pools involve the issuance of securities that represent shares in a pool of mortgages. The originator of the pool who moves these mortgages from its balance sheet issues securities and the buyers of these securities become joint owners of the pool of mortgages. Mortgage payments are distributed to the holders of the securities. The creator of the pool would assume the responsibility for servicing the mortgage—collecting and distributing payments.

The Federal National Mortgage Association (FNMA) has been responsible for a secondary market for FHA and VA mortgages. Fanny Mae, as FNMA is commonly called, fulfills this function by buying, servicing, and selling loans. In the 1960s, Fanny Mae was limited to FHA and VA loans; the Housing Act of 1970 further enabled the corporation to operate a secondary market in conventional loans. In brief, Fanny Mae buys mortgages when loanable funds are in short supply and sells mortgages when mortgage funds are abundant. The effect of this action is to assist in stabilizing residential construction and thus contribute to the overall objective of encouraging home ownership. As a private, government-sponsored organization, Fanny Mae is profit-oriented with its profits dependent on the spread between the yield earned on mortgages purchased and the cost of funds. Commercial banks have utilized the service of FNMA, both as a supplier and a purchaser of mortgage securities.

Another corporation involved in stabilizing the residential mortgage market is the Government National Mortgage Association (GNMA), often referred to as Ginny Mae. GNMA was given the responsibility of issuing guarantees of securities backed by a pool of FHA and VA mortgage loans. Such mortgage-backed securities, when guaranteed by GNMA, bear the full faith and credit pledge of the federal government. These securities are sold in the market and have been purchased by pension funds, individuals, banks, and other financial institutions. GNMA securities can be originated by any mortgage company or mortgage lender that is authorized to make FHA loans. Banks, therefore, participate in this type of lending either directly or indirectly.

GNMA offers three basic securities: straight pass-through securities that pay the investor actual principal and interest collected on pooled loans in an amount proportionate to the investor's share in the pool, modified pass-through securities that pay monthly to the investor an instalment on the underlying mortgages and a fixed rate of interest on the mortgage balance unpaid, and the bond type of security that pays semiannually a specified rate of interest and returns the principal at maturity of the security. The effect of the guarantee is that these payments to the investor are made whether or not they are collected from the issuer.

The addition of FNMA and GNMA has made real estate mortgages more liquid in that the market for such instruments has been broadened. Commercial banks have been relatively large suppliers of capital to FNMA as well as purchasers of GNMA securities. Both these investments provide good rates of return to the investing commercial bank. The guaranteed aspects of GNMA securities plus their high yield make them an excellent investment for intermediate liquidity requirements and trust department investments.

The Federal Home Loan Mortgage Corporation, or Freddy Mac, is another federal agency created recently to provide support for the conventional portion of the secondary market. The FHLMC buys conventional mortgages mainly from savings and loan associations; the agency then sells some of the mortgages by creating pools and selling shares or participations in these pools. Although of minor importance, two other federal agencies —the Farmers Home Administration and the Federal Land Bank System— are involved in one- to four-family housing in mortgage markets in rural areas.

The significance of the secondary market is illustrated in Table 14–2, which shows the originations and holdings of one- to four-family residential mortgages. Note that practically all of the mortgages were originated by the private sector, and the yearly average was $72 billion during the 1970–76 period. This was 1.7 times the new issues of stocks and bonds by nonfinan-

Table 14-2
Originations and Holdings 1-4 Family Residential Mortgages 1970-76

Lender Group	Originations Yearly Average: 1970-76 Billions of Dollars	Percent	Holdings Dec. 31, 1976 Billions of Dollars	Percent
Federal Credit Agencies	2.2	3.1	36.6	7.5
Federally Sponsored Pools	0.0	0.0	41.9	8.6
Private Sector:	69.8	96.9	411.4	84.0
Commercial Banks	15.6	21.7	77.5	15.8
Mutual Savings Banks	4.5	6.2	52.4	10.7
Savings and Loan Associations	35.8	49.7	253.5	51.7
Life Insurance Companies	0.4	0.5	15.5	3.2
Mortgage Companies	12.8	17.8	4.2	0.9
Others*	0.7	1.0	8.4	1.7
Total	72.0	100.0	489.9	100.0

*Private Pension Funds, Mortgage Investment Trusts, State and Local Retirement Funds, State and Local Credit Agencies. Other groups not included here due to lack of data also make or hold small amounts of mortgage loans.

Source: Federal Reserve Bank of Kansas City, *Monthly Review*. September/October, 1977.

cial corporations during the same period. It can be seen from these data that mortgage companies specialize in originating and servicing mortgages and do not hold them for extended periods. Banks also were sellers of mortgages in the secondary mortgage market during this period. However, savings and loan associations were net buyers. Several banks have followed the lead of Bank of America, which in 1977 offered the first private mortgage pool and pass-through certificates issued by commercial banks. These certificates were offered in accordance with the rules and regulations of the Securities and Exchange Commission. These certificates are not obligations of the bank but represent partial ownership of mortgages in a pool. In arrangements of this kind, the pool of conventional mortgages that are privately insured backs the certificates, and all payments to holders of the certificates are made out of mortgage payments from the underlying pool just as is the practice in GNMA-guaranteed pass-throughs. An increase in this type of financing is likely for, if done properly and accepted by investors, it will add breadth and liquidity to the secondary mortgage market.

Types of Real Estate Loans Made by Commercial Banks

Commercial banks have three basic mortgage types or plans available to them: FHA, VA, and conventional. FHA loans are insured by the Federal Housing Authority, VA loans are guaranteed by the Veterans Administration, and conventional loans are neither insured nor guaranteed by the federal government. Private mortgage insurance may, however, be required by some banks on certain conventional loans. Table 14–2 shows the types of loans made by commercial banks. Note that nearly 90 percent are conventional loans.

Several factors are responsible for the rapid increase in conventional loans relative to FHA and VA loans over the years. From the investor's standpoint, FHA and VA residential loans have some disadvantages. First, bank officers do not look favorably on the low down payment and long maturity. The owner's lack of equity and a distant maturity are conducive to nonpayment and default during periods of financial stress. Another reason some commercial banks favor conventional residential real estate loans over FHA and VA mortgages is the minimum of red tape in making, supervising, and foreclosing on the loans in the event such a step must be taken. Probably the most important reason has been the comparatively low rate of interest allowed on FHA and VA loans. The rate of interest on FHA and VA loans has not kept pace with other market rates. Banks, as well as other lenders, can sometimes compensate for this spread between rates by charging *points,* that is, purchasing the FHA loan at a discount. For example, if the FHA rate were 8.75 percent and an effective rate of 9.75 percent were necessary, since this is the rate dictated by the free market, a lender would discount a mortgage in the amount of $40,000 by approximately 8 points or 8 percent.[1] However, when this is done, the discount must be absorbed by the seller of the house, which means that he will suffer a reduction in his profit margin. Another factor contributing to the increase in conventional loans is the availability of private mortgage insurance similar to FHA. This type of insurance is available on that portion of the loan that exceeds the legal limit of a lending institution. Banks cannot make loans in excess of 80 percent of the appraised value of the property with the exception of FHA and VA loans. However, a conventional 90 percent loan can be made if the 10 percent excess over the normal 80 percent limit is insured by an eligible insurer. Finally, VA loans were a product of World War II, and with the decline in the number of eligible veterans over the years the demand for such loans has declined.

Significant Steps in Residential Real Estate Lending

Because of their long maturity, residential real estate loans are subject to a significant amount of interest rate risk and, since many things can happen to the borrower before the loan is fully repaid, they are also subject to a considerable amount of credit risk. These risks have prompted many banks

---

[1]Based on an average maturity of 12 years.

to develop expertise in this area and to establish real estate loan departments.

Credit Analysis of the Borrower

The first concern of a commercial bank in making a residential real estate loan is the credit worthiness of the borrower. The borrower must have the ability and the determination to pay. In this respect, credit analysis of real estate loan customers does not differ materially from the analysis of other types of borrowers. In real estate lending, however, a more thorough analysis is made because of the nature of the loan; it is larger and its maturity is longer than in short- and intermediate-term consumer loans. The size of the loan in relation to the value of the property should also be considered in a thorough credit analysis. Many years ago a loan equal to 50 percent of the appraised value of the property was normal, but in recent years a loan equal to 80 percent of the appraised value and sometimes even more is quite common. When the loan-to-value rate was relatively small, greater reliance could be placed on the value of the property as a source of repayment in the event of a default. Now it is necessary to rely more heavily on the borrower's ability to meet the terms of the loan agreement.

Banks are interested in the amount and stability of an applicant's income and his previous experience in caring for a house. Monthly payments on a 25-year mortgage are sizeable and due with regularity for a large portion of a borrower's working years. In fact, monthly housing expenses are normally the largest single item in the family budget. A person who has a reputation of not keeping a house in a neat condition, attractive, and in good repair is not as acceptable as one who is noted for being a good "housekeeper." The market value of a house that has suffered from poor maintenance is much less than one that has been well cared for.

Appraisal of Property

A very important step in residential real estate lending is the appraisal of property offered as security for a loan. This is important since the ability of the borrower to pay may not continue as hoped and predicted, and the bank may have to look to the value of the house for repayment. The objective of such an appraisal is to arrive at the market value of the property—a difficult task since many factors influence the value.

Appraisal of residences is difficult because some qualities are intangible. For example, the architecture or style can cause one house to have a higher value than another even though they are quite similar in other respects. Location, type of construction, and arrangement of rooms influence the value. A split-level house has less appeal to some purchasers than does a house on one level; houses far from the traffic flow are demanded by more buyers than are those located on a thoroughfare.

The neighborhood in which a house is located also influences its market value. Houses near an industrial area appeal less to some than do those in a residential district where all the houses are similar in appearance and construction and are occupied by middle-income families. Houses located near schools, churches, parks, and playgrounds are especially appealing. The availability of services such as police and fire protection, sewers, and street lighting is a factor that must be considered in arriving at the marketability of residential properties.

Although real estate appraising is not an exact science, it must be done to carry out a real estate lending program effectively. Its success depends on the ability and experience of the appraiser and the use of such tools of appraising as adequate records of residential sales, new construction permits, sales prices of existing and newly constructed houses, population movements, depreciation and obsolescence factors, the supply of houses, and potential demand for housing. The appraiser must examine all the factors that influence market value and convert them into an estimated valuation expressed in dollars.

Small banks frequently rely on the members of their board of directors to perform this function. Some banks permit the officer or officers concerned with real estate loans to do the appraising; others may employ independent professional appraisers, especially if appraising a particular piece of property presents unique problems. Many large banks that make sizeable amounts of real estate loans have professional appraisers on their staffs.

Several methods of appraisal are employed by residential real estate appraisers, the most common of which are cost and market data. In the cost method, the appraised value is the product of the reproduction cost of a house less depreciation. The value of the land or lot is arrived at by comparing it to similar parcels of land in the area. The appraiser estimates the cost of constructing the house, usually on a square- or cubic-foot basis, then subtracts from this figure the "used up" portion of this value. Consideration is also given to the intangible factors mentioned earlier. The market-data method compares the house being appraised with similar houses sold recently whose actual market price is known. This method, like the cost method, is not easy since all houses are not alike and other factors must be considered. Both methods have limitations and can be used successfully only by persons who have had considerable training and experience.

It is essential to make the appraisal as accurate as possible, for this is the basis of the mortgage loan. For example, if a bank agreed to loan an amount equal to 80 percent of the appraised value of a house appraised at $50,000 but worth only $42,000, it would be lending $40,000 or approximately the full current market value of the house. Should a default occur, assuming stable real estate prices, it would be doubtful that the bank could avoid some loss by the time all the costs of foreclosure and sale were considered. If the house were appraised at $35,000, however, the borrower might go to another lender, since the bank would be willing to lend only $28,000 on a house that was entitled to a loan of $33,600. Poor appraising can be expensive to a bank or any other lender. If appraisals are too high, the bank's risks are increased; if too low, borrowers will seek their loans elsewhere.

Terms of Residential Real Estate Loans

Real estate loan agreements and security instruments differ significantly from other types of bank loans. This is largely because of the maturity and size of real estate loans. Consequently, a considerable amount of investigation and document preparation is necessary in real estate lending.

Enforceable Lien

Since the property that secures a real estate loan may have to be sold to satisfy the loan if the borrower is not able to pay it in later years, an enforceable lien is absolutely essential. Securing such a lien may involve considerable time, effort, and expense both to the lender and to the borrower. Real estate is transferred by a legal document called a *deed,* and an enforceable lien can only be given by a person who has legal title to the property. The bank, as lender, must be sure that no prior liens on the property exist, such as unpaid taxes and mechanics' liens, which take precedence over a mortgage. This requires either the services of an attorney or the acquisition of a title insurance policy. From an examination of an abstract, which is a recorded history of the property, an attorney can usually determine the lawful owner. He will give what is known as an attorney's opinion, which identifies the legal owner and sets forth any outstanding claims or encumbrances against the property.

If there is any cloud on the borrower's title, it must be cleared up satisfactorily before a loan will be made. In some areas, lenders rely on title companies to investigate the property and determine who is the legal owner and whether any liens exist, and to insure the lender against loss should some person later prove that he has title to the property or that there were liens or claims against it.

Mortgage

In commercial bank lending on residential real estate, a loan is evidenced by a note and a real estate mortgage, or, in some areas, by a trust deed. Some states regard the mortgage as a document that transfers legal title of the property to the mortgagee or lender as security for a debt. If the debt is paid as agreed, the transfer becomes void. Other states regard the mortgage as a document that gives the mortgagee a lien on the property to secure the debt. This lien can be exercised by the mortgagee only if the borrower defaults on the debt. Whatever the mortgage concept, however, the mortgage is the basic security for real estate loans in this country.

A real estate mortgage usually includes several covenants that the borrower agrees to fulfill and that, basically, are similar to those found in term loan agreements employed in business lending. First, the mortgagor agrees to repay the principal sum with interest as set forth in the note. Another covenant states that the borrower will pay all taxes, special assessments, and other charges levied on the property. In many cases these special tax funds are held in escrow by the bank. However, recent class-action suits against banks and other financial institutions for nonpayment of interest on escrow funds could result in changes in the handling of such funds. Further, the mortgage generally requires the borrower to keep the property in good repair and not use it for any unlawful purpose. It may also prohibit making substantial alterations or additions to the property without the express permission of the lender. The mortgagor is required to keep the property fully insured against such risks as fire and windstorm, and to assign the policies to the bank.

These covenants are important and, in many instances, have proved necessary to maintain the lender's economic interest in the property. They can be invoked if they are being violated by the mortgagor. Covenants are defensive devices in that they are designed to protect the lender against excessive wear and tear on the property, undue hazards, the possibility of claims being levied against the property, and changes that will decrease its market value. If they are not complied with, the lender's interest in the property may be lessened; in the event foreclosure and sale of the property are necessary, the lender may sustain substantial loss.

Mortgages usually contain an *acceleration clause:* if the borrower fails to make principal and interest payments or to comply with any of the covenants, the full amount of the loan becomes immediately due and payable. The need for such a clause is obvious. Finally, the mortgage must be recorded in the proper public office to protect the lender's interests from subsequent claims by third parties. The cost of consummating a real estate loan is quite high and is usually borne by the borrower.

From what has been said it may appear that, in the event of nonpayment, the foreclosure and sale of property is a relatively simple process. This is not the case. Each state follows the principle that every mortgage carries a *right of redemption* before foreclosure can be effected. This borrower's equitable right of redemption permits a mortgagor to redeem the mortgaged property by paying the debt within a certain period of time prior to the foreclosure sale. It is designed to temper the harshness of the law that permits the taking of a borrower's property.

Statute also gives the mortgagor a right to redeem after the sale. The redemption time varies from two months to two years after the foreclosure sale. During this period, depending on state law, the borrower may occupy the property if the rent is paid to a court-appointed receiver, and the purchaser of the property does not receive a deed until after the statutory term has expired. Since foreclosure proceedings are time consuming and the property may decline in value, banks are reluctant to foreclose, except as a last resort. The mortgagor is given every opportunity to pay or to transfer the property to another buyer.

Repayment Provisions

Most residential real estate loans are payable on an amortized basis with principal and interest combined in a single, uniform monthly payment. An example of a portion of an amortization schedule for a 30-year loan in the amount of $40,000, at 9.5 percent interest, is presented in Table 14–3. In this example the monthly payment of $336.35 consists of two parts, principal and interest. At the end of the first month, most of the payment, $316.-67, is for interest and only $19.68 is allocated to the reduction of the principal. As additional payments are made, the amount allocated to interest declines because the amount of the loan is constantly being reduced, and

Table 14–3
Terms on an Amortized Mortgage Loan
Amount of Loan–$40,000   Time outstanding–30 years   Interest rate–9.5 percent

| . Time | | | Monthly Payment | | |
Year	Month	Payment	Interest Portion	Principal Payment	Balance Due on Loan
0	1	$336.35	$316.67	$ 19.68	$39,980.32
0	3	336.35	316.35	20.00	39,940.48
0	9	336.35	315.39	20.96	39,817.15
5	6	336.35	303.49	32.86	38,302.44
10	3	336.35	284.84	51.51	35,928.16
15	1	336.35	254.97	81.38	32,125.10
19	6	336.35	212.75	123.60	26,749.50
24	6	336.35	137.96	198.39	17,228.60
29	0	336.35	32.65	303.70	3,820.78

the amount for reduction of the principal increases. At the end of fifteen years and one month, for example, the monthly payment of $336.35 is divided into $254.97 for interest and $81.38 for principal payment, and the balance of the loan is $32,125.10.

Ratio of Loan to Appraised Value and Maturity of Real Estate Loans

Two important factors that must be considered in residential real estate lending relate to the maturity of the loan and the amount to be advanced to the borrower. An increase in either the maturity or the loan-to-value ratio increases the cost of the loan to the borrower and may increase the risk of nonpayment to the lender. Moreover, an increase in maturity and a decrease in the down payment reduce the liquidity of the loan. The increased cost to the borrower as the loan-to-value ratio and maturity increase is illustrated in Table 14–4, which shows the monthly and total cost of a mortgage on a house valued at $50,000. Note that as maturity increases the monthly cost declines, but the total cost increases. The monthly and total costs also increase as the loan-to-value ratio rises from 50 to 90 percent. Long maturities and low down payments may reduce the monthly payment, but they reduce the growth in the borrower's equity and increase his total cost. In general, lenders prefer short maturities and high down payments since the risk of default and loss as well as the interest-rate risk are reduced. In an effort to increase home ownership, however, Congress has provided insurance and guaranty programs designed to encourage private lenders to increase the maturity of residential real estate loans and lower the down payment.

National banks are permitted to make conventional residential real estate loans in an amount equal to 90 percent of the appraised value of the property if amortized over the 30-year period. Most state banks permit a similar amount. On FHA insured and VA guaranteed loans, banks can loan the amount covered by insurance and the guarantee. Although these amounts have varied over the years, they have always exceeded the amount that could be made on conventional real estate loans.

Table 14–4
Cost of Residential Mortgage on a House Valued at $50,000,
Assuming 9.5 Percent Interest and Various Loan-to-Value Ratios and Maturities

Assumed Loan-to-Value Ratio	Amount of Mortgage	10 Years		20 Years		30 Years	
		Monthly Payment	Total Cost	Monthly Payment	Total Cost	Monthly Payment	Total Cost
90	$45,000	$582.29	$24,874.80	$419.46	$55,670.40	$378.39	$91,220.40
80	40,000	517.60	22,112.00	372.86	49,486.40	336.35	81,086.00
50	25,000	323.50	13,820.00	233.04	30,929.60	210.22	50,679.20

In recent years real estate loan insurance has been developed by private insurance companies for conventional loans. The reasons for the development of this insurance were the lower down payments and the desire to increase the marketability of real estate loans. Many financial institutions, including banks, frequently sell loans to other investors such as insurance companies. Loans with a loan-to-value ratio of 70 percent are obviously more marketable than those with a 90 percent ratio since the risk of nonpayment is less. The amount of insurance required increases as the loan-to-value ratio rises. For example, a loan-to-value ratio of 80 to 85 percent requires an amount of insurance equal to 12 percent of the mortgage. The requirement is 17 percent on a mortgage with an 85 to 90 percent ratio and 22 percent on a 90 to 95 percent ratio. This reduces the possibility of loss from nonpayment and increases the loan's marketability. Private insurance is usually carried on a real estate loan for about 10 years. By that time the possibility of loss from default has been reduced to a level that the lender is willing to assume. The effective cost of private insurance is slightly less than the FHA insurance which currently has been placed at 0.50 percent of the mortgage. The rate on private insurance is 0.25 after a slightly higher rate for the first year of the loan contract.

The average maturity of residential real estate loans held by banks is shorter than that of other institutional lenders. The loan-to-value ratio is also lower in commercial banks. In early 1978, for example, the loan-to-value ratio of all lenders on new homes was 76.2 percent, compared to a ratio of 69.8 percent for commercial banks.

Interest Rates on Mortgages

The cost of mortgage credit consists of a contract rate and various fees and charges. In addition to the interest charge, lenders typically levy a commitment on *originating fee,* which covers the cost of placing the loan on the books. This is paid only once, when the loan is made, and varies from 1 to 1.5 percent of the total loan. In early 1978 the contract interest rate on conventional first mortgage loans for all real estate lenders on new homes was around 9.01 percent and the initial fees and charges approximated 1.43 percent. The contract rate for banks on the same type of loan was approximately the same, but the initial fees and charges were less. Mortgage rates tend to fluctuate with other capital-market rates, but their movements tend to be less volatile. When interest rates in general move upward, mortgage rates tend to lag behind the trend and fall more slowly when rates move down.

Just as there is no unique interest rate, we cannot talk about "the" mortgage rate. It has been pointed out that rates differ on FHA, VA, and conventional mortgages. Moreover, substantial differences exist among interest rates in different regions of the country. Generally, rates are higher in the South and West and lower in the North and East. This reflects the influence of supply and demand forces. Regional differences in rates indicate some lack of mobility of certain types of funds to capital-short areas of the country.

With sharp rises in housing costs and interest rates in recent years, some concern has been expressed about the ability of many purchasers, especially young adults, to afford adequate housing. An important key to affordability of home ownership is the size of the monthly payments necessary to retire a home loan. This amount is a function of the size and maturity of the mortgage and the interest rate of course. The rise in interest rates on mortgage loans in recent years has been due in large part to an increase in the capital value risk encountered by mortgage lenders rather than to any increase in the risk of default. Once a lender commits funds for a definite period, his financial position can be severely affected by a general rise in prices that reduces the value of the dollars that are repaid by the borrower in subsequent years. Persistent inflation drives up interest rates, which depreciates the value of mortgages, makes them less marketable, and reduces the net flow of funds in real terms to mortgage lenders. Consequently, the supply of funds for mortgages is reduced. Under such conditions, lenders raise interest rates on mortgages and/or increase down payment requirements, both of which tend to discourage home mortgage financing.

Because of the rising costs of housing, more flexible repayment plans have been developed. All of these plans differ from the traditional fixed-term, fixed-rate, level-payment mortgages that have been discussed and illustrated in Tables 14–3 and 14–4. One type of an arrangement is a mortgage written with a *balloon payment* at the time of maturity. This type of home loan, for example, might be written for 10 or 15 years rather than for 25 or 30. With a balloon payment provision, the monthly payment is lower than for a traditional loan since it includes a smaller payment on the principal. At the end of the contract period the large balloon payment is due. It is assumed that at that time most home owners will be in a financial position that will justify a new loan for all or a portion of the balloon payment. This kind of loan arrangement is helpful to home purchasers who need greater relief in the earlier part of the mortgage when incomes are probably lower than in later years when incomes are normally higher. Another arrangement referred to as a *step-rate mortgage* calls for regular predetermined rate increases spread over the life of the loan. The payments could be increased every five or six years. An arrangement designed especially for younger home buying families is a *graduated payment mortgage*. This kind of contract carries a fixed predetermined rate of interest and maturity. Monthly payments start lower than necessary to amortize the loan fully but rise gradually over time to cover the interest and to retire the principal of the loan. Very similar to the graduated payment mortgage is the *flexible payment mortgage,* where payments in the early years cover only the interest. Usually this period of low payments is limited to the first five years of the mortgage. After that, the payments are increased to amortize the principal over the remaining life of the loan.

Another variation is the *rollover plan,* which provides for periodic rate reviews. At these times the interest rate is adjusted to current market conditions. These reviews could be established, for example, every two, three, or five years. This plan has been used successfully in England and in Canada and is sometimes referred to as the Canadian rollover plan.

The most common flexible loan arrangement at the present time and one that is similar to the rollover plan is the *variable-rate mortgage.* A variable-rate mortgage calls for the rate of interest to change over the life of the contract in response to variations in some key interest rate or some index that reflects current credit conditions. Of course, with a variable-rate mortgage, the borrower would face the possibility of a rise in rates as well as a decline. A change in the borrower's effective rate could be effected in two ways. The monthly payment of the borrower could be increased or decreased, or the maturity of the note could be lengthened or shortened, with the monthly payment remaining constant.

The rationale behind variable-interest rates stems from problems associated with financial institutions that borrow short-term (savings deposits) and lend long-term funds. In periods of rapidly rising interest rates, savings institutions often find that savings deposits are withdrawn and placed in more attractive investments; consequently, the availability of mortgage funds is reduced. Supporters of variable-rate mortgages hold that such rates would alleviate this problem of the mismatch of the cost of funds versus the price charged for loans. They also contend that the construction industry would enjoy more stable operations and not suffer as much from the diseconomies of the boom-bust cycles, which adversely affect the building industry and ultimately consumers. Moreover, the plan would appeal to the homeowner who is locked into a high-rate loan by prepayment fees and other refinancing costs. At present, national banks are permitted to make variable-rate mortgages in those states that permit the inclusion of an interest rate escalation clause in the mortgage contract, but few states include such provisions. In fact, the variable rate of interest has not been employed extensively by mortgage lenders.

Several obstacles obstruct widespread adoption of the variable rate of interest. It is difficult to find a basic rate acceptable to lenders and borrowers to which the mortgage rate can be tied. Ideally, the basic rate should reflect local mortgage-market conditions accurately. In reality, no "basic" rate performs this function since market conditions vary from one locality to another. Those rates that have been employed or suggested have shortcomings. The bank prime rate is much more volatile than the average conventional mortgage-loan rate, and the corporate-bond rate, which is long-term and comparable in maturity to real estate loans, tends to rise more rapidly than do mortgage rates. Some mortgage lenders have recommended that an average rate or index be computed based on the rates of various classes of U.S. government securities. However, there have been periods in which yields on these securities have remained relatively stable as a result of political action while other market rates have fluctuated widely. Finally, and probably most importantly, borrowers generally favor rate reductions but seldom appreciate an increase in the interest rate on their mortgage. Thus, it seems that the mortgage rate is distinct from other rates because it is characterized by forces that do not exist in other credit markets. This is true of all interest rates, of course. If it were not, we would have a single rate of interest.

A plan designed for older homeowners is a *reverse annuity mortgage.* Many older homeowners live on fixed incomes and, because of rising property taxes and increased living costs that include outlays for various public utility services, sometimes have difficulty in making ends meet. A reverse mortgage permits such homeowners to receive a regular income by borrowing against the equity of their house. The homeowner simply receives a monthly payment during the life of the contract. At the maturity of the loan, it can be refinanced or paid in full. In the event of the death of the homeowner, the loan is paid when the estate is settled.

All of these innovations in mortgage financing are not available in some areas of the country because of usury laws or other state and federal regulations applicable to real-estate lending institutions. The most widely accepted plan is the variable-rate mortgage, and its authorization is very recent. Although state chartered savings and loan associations in some states have had the right to make such mortgages, it was not until 1979 that this authorization was extended to federally chartered institutions. Commercial banks generally do not make any of these types of mortgages. Consumers have not expressed a strong desire for any of these real estate lending ideas; in fact, some labor and consumer groups have not looked upon them favorably. Even though a very small amount of the residential real estate loans outstanding is of the new variety, we are likely to see greater interest expressed in this type of financing in the future and participation by commercial banks.

Truth in Lending

Real estate loan transactions are included in the Truth-in-Lending Act, which is discussed in greater detail in the following chapter. In fact, a major portion of the act is concerned with the borrower's right of rescission, which is applicable mainly to home mortgages and home-improvement loans. The right of rescission allows a borrower to cancel a credit arrangement within three business days if his residence is used as collateral for the credit. This provision allows the borrower time to contemplate the purchase, shop for better credit terms, or cancel a home-improvement project that may have been foisted on him or her by a high-pressure salesperson. However, a first mortgage to finance the purchase of a borrower's residence carries no right of rescission, although a first mortgage for any other purpose and a second mortgage on the same residence may be cancelled. The borrower may cancel the credit transaction and the transaction that predicated the credit application by signing and dating a notice of such a decision. All credit transactions where the right of rescission is applicable are required by the act to include in the borrower's papers two copies of a cancellation form. Before furnishing copies of the notice to the customer, the lender is to complete the copies with the name of the lender, the address of the lender's place of business, the date of consummation of the transaction, and the date, not earlier than the third business day following the transaction, by which the customer may give notice of cancellation. In a case where a homeowner has an emergency, s/he may waive the right to rescind a transaction provided s/he has determined that a three-day delay in performance of the lender's obligation would jeopardize the welfare, health, or safety of persons or endanger property s/he owns or for which s/he is responsible. All other conditions relative to the Truth-in-Lending Act, including the effective annual interest rate, disclosures, finance charges, penalties, and liabilities as discussed in previous chapters, apply to real estate transactions.

Mobile Homes

Recently, the use of mobile homes has risen spectacularly. For many years they were associated with travel trailers and not considered permanent living quarters like the single-family house, and statistics regarding mobile home financing were included with consumer debt rather than with residential financing (see Table 15–1). With growth in the use of mobile homes, this attitude is changing. In 1961 mobile home shipments accounted for 7 percent of total private housing starts; they now account for about 20 percent.

The increased demand for mobile homes is a result of several factors. They are less expensive than conventional housing and are usually sold with complete furniture packages. As larger units have become available, this type of housing has been more widely accepted. During periods of tight money it has often been easier to obtain financing for a mobile home than for a single-family residence, because during such periods more buyers are attracted by shorter maturities and higher interest rates on loans for mobile homes.

Mobile home financing has changed dramatically in twenty years. Originally, financing was secured through finance companies with limited participation by commercial banks. Then the Housing and Urban Development Act of 1968 provided for FHA and VA guarantees on mobile homes with maturities of 12 years or less. As a result, savings and loan associations, mutual savings banks, and commercial banks increased their activity in mobile home lending.

In many respects the sale and financing transactions involving mobile homes are similar to those involving automobiles. New mobile homes are normally sold by dealers who show them on display lots, and frequently the inventory is financed by banks. The financing of individual units is arranged at the time of sale by the dealer, and the note or paper is transferred to a bank. Since the bank is a third party to the sales transaction, the bank may require a *limited liability clause* or a reserve in the agreement with the dealer. Briefly, a limited liability clause requires the dealer to stand behind the borrower's loan in the case of default, whereas the purchase reserve involves the bank holding a percentage of the selling price until the mobile home is paid for. Additional protection for the bank is also required in a comprehensive mobile home insurance policy. This type of policy parallels the protection found in a traditional homeowner's policy. A second type of insurance, unique to mobile homes, is referred to as a *vendor's single-interest policy*. It can protect the lender and/or dealer from such losses as disappearance of the home, inability to repossess the unit, and collision. The basis for such coverage is an impairment of the lender's security interest. The establishment of such insurance plans protects the interest of the lender. Many commercial banks that make mobile home loans employ the services of companies that specialize in insuring and processing such loans. For a small fee, usually a percentage of the monthly payment, the insurance company provides a default insurance policy similar to private mortgage insurance for other homes. In the event of default, the insurance company pays the bank and proceeds to repossess the mobile home.

Land Development and Construction Loans

Commercial banks are relatively large lenders for land development and the construction of industrial, commercial, residential, and farm buildings. Such lending has proved to be profitable, and since such loans have a short maturity normally, they are quite liquid. Construction loans made by national banks are limited to a maturity of five years, and a majority of them are for 18 months or less. Such a limit is also applicable to many state banks.

Land development loans provide a line of credit to the developer for the construction of streets, sewers, and other public utilities to prepare building lots for house sites or resale. Banks lend no more than 75 percent of the appraised value of finished lots usually, and are quite selective in making land development loans. Land development loans require considerable supervision. The loan agreement includes a release mechanism that sets forth when, how, and at what price lots may be released. Moreover, the agreement specifies the amount of money from the sale of each lot that must be applied to the loan. Land development loans can be quite risky, since repayment often depends on the sale of the developed lots. The history of such financing indicates that some developments have been very popular while others have been a financial failure. An experienced, reliable, and financially sound developer is very important. Commercial banks are interested in a land developer who fully discloses the essential facts regarding the lots that are for sale. The reason is, of course, that this activity has attracted unscrupulous operators. Real estate history is replete with incidents of selling lots under water, miles from modern transportation and utilities, and on the side of mountains. Government regulations and more responsible people in the land development business have reduced such unethical practices. However, it is still possible to sell lots under water, but that fact must be revealed to the prospective purchaser.

One reason for providing land development loans is to get an inside track on financing the houses when the development is completed. Not only are residential loans desirable from the standpoint of collateral and income, but they frequently result in a deposit relationship for the lending bank.

Construction loans to contractors arise when the ultimate owner of a building may not be known at the time of construction, or when the owner is not able to provide enough financing or is concerned only with the finished product. For example, a builder specializing in single-family residences may have 50 or more houses under construction at one time. Obviously, a considerable amount of financing is required during the construction period. As another example, a business firm, individual investor, or a group of investors might agree to purchase an office building or a manufacturing plant, but first someone must finance and construct the building. It is during this construction period that bank credit is extended.

A construction loan assumes many characteristics of a commercial loan. In determining the amount to be loaned, the banker takes into account the estimated construction costs, the estimated market value of the completed building, and the managerial and financial ability of the contractor. Normally, construction loans are advanced in instalments as the building progresses. As is true of all lending, risk is ever-present in construction lending, which is the major reason for very close supervision. The lending officer of a bank must be knowledgeable in many areas—construction costs and materials, the value of a location, demand for buildings and the like. Unforeseen and adverse developments can occur. Weather may delay construction;

strikes and a shortage of skilled labor at unpropitious times can be expensive and frustrating. The delivery of materials can become slow and even unavailable at times. Construction costs can rise as the general level of prices spiral upward. Environmental legislation and interpretations by regulatory bodies can cause construction moratoriums. Demand for the finished product may also change, especially in speculative construction. These factors and others can adversely influence the ability of the contractor to complete the project.

The administration of a construction loan is quite involved. A performance or *completion bond* may be required of the contractor. Such a bond guarantees that the contractor will fulfill the existing contract: that is, complete the building. Should the contractor default, the insurance company or surety protects the policyholder against the loss involved up to the bond penalty. A completion bond insures the property owner that the project will be completed free of liens. However, completion bonds do not protect a bank in the event of default on repayment of the loan. Other documents that may be required are title insurance, a survey, fire and casualty insurance, a building permit, an environmental impact study, and so on. An important document is the *letter of commitment,* which is a contract or pledge by a long-term lender to make a follow-on loan on specified terms at a given time in the future. For example, if the building in question were an office building, a bank might not be in a position to finance the long-term loan because of its size, length of time to maturity, and the fact that this type of loan does not meet the established liquidity requirements. The permanent investor might be the company for whom the building was being built, an insurance firm, or possibly a pension trust.

Nonfarm, Nonresidential Properties

Commercial banks make a variety of nonfarm, nonresidential loans (see Table 10–1) which may be secured by properties such as stores, shopping centers, apartments, warehouses, and industrial buildings. These loans are called *income property loans,* and it is not uncommon for commercial banks to have a section devoted to this kind of lending within its real estate loan department. The income property term derives from the value of these properties which is established by their ability to produce an income stream. In arriving at the value of such properties, the lending officer estimates the future potential gross income from the property and calculates the expenses of operation required to arrive at the net income. The next and final step is to select a proper capitalization rate and a capitalization technique for estimating the value of the property.

Because of the liquidity needs of commercial banks, the maturity of income real-estate loans seldom exceeds 15 years, and the preference is for even shorter maturities. Income property loans are frequently made with a balloon payment at maturity. At maturity, this is paid in full or, in some cases, the amount may be refinanced at the rate of interest then prevailing. This arrangement reduces monthly, quarterly, or annual payments and permits the borrower to increase cash flow. The loan-to-value ratio of an income property loan is usually low. Bankers are sensitive to real estate loans that contain an inordinate amount of risk, and correctly so.

Another factor that enters into income property loan considerations is the deposit relationship. Frequently, large real estate loans do not result in deposit balances in proportionate dimensions; consequently, such loans are not looked upon with favor by commercial banks. Banks prefer to make real-estate mortgage loans to business firms that are depositors rather than to out-of-community firms that carry their deposit balances elsewhere. Banks also place greater emphasis on the credit worthiness of the borrower than do other income property lenders. For example, insurance companies that make such loans look to the income property as a source of repayment. Commercial banks place emphasis on this source too, but they consider other credit factors and sources of income as well.

Farm Real-Estate Loans

Although commercial bank loans secured by farmland amounted to nearly $8 billion at year-end 1977, (see Table 10–1), this amount was less than one-fourth of the total lending to the agricultural sector. It should not be assumed that the amount of credit secured by farmland was used exclusively for the purchase of land and buildings. To be sure, part of this credit was used to purchase fixed assets, but a large portion was used for current operations and the purchase of machinery. Although the proceeds of farm loans may be used for other purposes, a large portion of such loans is secured by real estate since it is the most common asset available. The irregularity of farm income and the feeling that land is a sound investment have contributed to the heavy reliance on real estate as security. Banks have not been attracted to farm real estate lending because of the maturity of the loans and the risks involved. The maturity of most loans is relatively long, since the purchase of a farm usually requires the working lifetime of a farmer. For this reason, the Federal Land banks that specialize in loans to farmers for the purchase of real estate are authorized to make loans for a 40-year period. Because of their liquidity needs commercial banks are not in a position to make loans of this maturity; therefore, individuals, life insurance companies, and Federal Land banks are the big farm real-estate lenders.

The high risk inherent in real estate lending to farmers stems from the nature of agriculture: namely, the unfavorable cost-price relationship that often exists for major agricultural products. This relationship is a product of the relatively inelastic demand for agricultural products (a slight increase in supply is accompanied by a sharp decrease in price) and a relatively elastic supply (a slight increase in price accompanied by a sharp increase in supply). This situation has resulted in a highly fluctuating farm income from which debts must be repaid.

The most important financial factor to be considered by a banker before granting a farm loan is the farmer's ability to generate a positive cash flow from the farm operation. A positive cash flow exists when the dollars received during a period exceed the dollars expended. Cash flow is not synonymous with profit, for it takes account of money received from all sources, including sale of capital assets and new borrowings, and expended for all purposes, including payments on capital equipment, debt reduction, and living expenses. Thus cash flow may be positive whereas the farm is being operated at a loss. Of course, cash flow cannot be positive for many years if the farm is never profitable. A positive cash flow during a period of negative profits means a decrease in assets, or an increase in liabilities, or both—with a corresponding decrease in net worth. After several unprofitable periods the farmer's ability to generate a positive cash flow will be destroyed because of inadequate inventories or equipment and too much debt. For any given period of operations, however, if a farmer can produce a sufficient cash flow to repay a loan after providing for essential farm expenditures and family needs, credit will be made available.

A farmer's net worth is of far less importance in the loan-granting decision. Even though a farmer owns the land and equipment unencumbered, if the farm does not produce an adequate cash flow, a bank loan should not be granted. True enough, the bank is relatively certain of repayment by forcing liquidation of some of the assets, but this is undesirable. The primary reason for taking security for a loan is to help assure repayment in cash, not through liquidation of the security.

Other Bank Real Estate Functions

As stated in Chapter 3, during the late 1960s and early 1970s many banks followed the lead of industrial corporations and began to diversify their operations. Mortgage companies and real estate investment trusts were formed and/or acquired by a number of banks and one-bank holding companies as a result of this expansion through diversification.

Mortgage Companies

A mortgage company can be a developer, packager, servicer of existing mortgages, or any combination of the three. Mortgage companies generally utilize borrowed funds to originate and close FHA, VA, and conventional mortgage loans which are then sold to various financial institutions and/or government agencies. In originating and packaging the loans, mortgage companies provide a beneficial service by attracting capital to a capital-deficient area to finance residential construction at slightly higher, but acceptable, rates. The mortgage company generally sells the loans outright in packages of $1 million or more, usually with the mortgage company servicing the loans: that is, collecting the monthly payments, escrow funds, etc., and making payment to the holders of the mortgage. A fee of 0.375 percent is normally charged for this service. At year-end 1978, mortgage companies were servicing mortgages in the amount of $160 billion. Some of the advantages to a commercial bank in having a mortgage company subsidiary can be easily understood when it is realized that mortgage companies are not limited to the geographical area of the bank, need not limit sales to the parent bank, and have a limited interest-rate risk exposure because of the short time between the originating and the selling of the mortgage.

Real Estate Investment Trusts

Real estate investment trusts (REITs) are relatively new financial intermediaries that specialize in the transfer of funds from financial markets to income-producing real estate. REITs provide professional management of a pool of real estate assets—equity, mortgages, or both—the income from which is not taxed at the corporate level. Enabling legislation was enacted in 1960 which makes the REITs exempt from corporate taxes provided that:

1 The REIT is a passive investor rather than an active participant in its properties

2 Seventy-five percent of the value of the REIT's total assets consist of real estate, mortgages, cash, cash items, and government securities

3 At least 100 persons own shares in the REIT and five or fewer persons may not own more than 50 percent of the outstanding shares during the last six months of any calendar year

4 At least 75 percent of the REIT's income is derived from rents, mortgage interest, and gains on the sale of real estate

Most of the organizers of REITs serve as their investment advisors since the trusts must be passive. Many of the advisors are commercial banks, one-bank holding companies, life insurance companies, or mortgage bankers. The advisor conducts the day-to-day operation of the trust and recommends investment opportunities to the trustees. For this service the advisor receives a fee. In organizational structure and objectives REITs are similar to mutual funds. Banks and one-bank holding companies organize REITs because the services that can be provided by this type of organization complement and expand those of commercial banks. Banks are prohibited from owning real estate except for their office buildings and in satisfaction of debts, and the maturity of some real estate loans is limited by law or by regulatory authorities. Since real estate trusts are more flexible financial institutions, a wide variety of real estate financing can be provided to bank customers. Not only is a one-bank holding company that serves as an advisor to a REIT in a position to increase its income by charging a fee, it is also able to expand its real estate financial services and thus offer complete financial packages. Moreover, it can use its special personnel more effectively and generate additional deposits.

REITs can be classified according to type and investment policy. There are equity, mortgage, and hybrid REITs. Obviously, equity trusts are those that focus on the ownership of real estate, while mortgage trusts invest in mortgages. Hybrid trusts hold mortgages as well as make direct investments in real estate. Ordinarily, equity trusts invest in real property which may or may not be encumbered by mortgages. The properties may be land, commercial, industrial, or residential. Equity REITs are normally classified as long-term investments and derive their income primarily from rents. Equity REITs own such property as shopping centers and office buildings. They may also own and lease land and develop properties.

Mortgage trusts derive their income primarily from interest earned on the mortgage portfolio and from commissions and discounts on mortgages. They would hold both short-term and long-term mortgages. The flexibility and specialization of REITs are evidenced in the type of investments made. Some specialize in making first mortgage construction loans, while others specialize in land development loans. Still others make standby commitments, gap loans, and wraparound mortgages. Equity REITs might own real estate outright or enter into a joint venture or as tenants in common.

To obtain funds for investment in mortgages and to buy income producing properties, REITs issue stocks, bonds, and commercial paper publicly and borrow from financial institutions. Since a real estate trust seeks to increase its yield on investments by the use of leverage, it, like other investors, encounters money rate and credit risks. This happened to several REITs in the mid-1970s. With rising interest rates, some were low on available funds and forced to borrow at relatively high rates which reduced their cash flow. Moreover, the return on some investments was reduced; and, in some instances, interest and principal payments on mortgages were suspended during the period of recession which also contributed to a squeeze on earnings. Some REITs were forced to write-down their assets, and the market value of their stock declined. With a rise in the real estate market in the late 1970s the financial position of many REITs improved, especially those with an equity position.

Questions

1. What factors have been responsible for the increase in bank loans secured by residential real estate?

2. Why must conventional loans conform more and more to the requirements established by the secondary market?

3. What is the relationship between the price and the yield on a mortgage loan? Explain "points".

4. What factors are important in evaluating the credit worthiness of an applicant for a residential real estate loan?

5. What are the steps in the appraisal process for residential and income properties? What are the different approaches to property appraisal?

6. Why is the appraisal of property important in making residential real estate loans? Why is such an appraisal often more difficult than that for a loan secured by an automobile or by stocks or bonds?

7. How do the long maturity characteristics of residential real estate mortgage loans subject lenders to increase (a) money rate risk and (b) credit risk. Explain.

8. What is a construction loan and what factors of risk are associated with such a loan?

9. How would you capitalize an income stream so as to show a proper value?

10. What is a real estate investment trust (REIT) and how does it complement the services offered by a bank?

SELECTED REFERENCES

American Institute of Real Estate Appraisers, *The Appraisal of Real Estate*, 6th ed. Chicago, American Institute of Real Estate Appraisers, 1973.

BROCKSCHMIDT, PEGGY, "The Secondary Market for Home Mortgages," *Monthly Review*, Federal Reserve Bank of Kansas City, September–October 1977.

CANDILIS, WRAY O., "Mortgage Rate Variability in the Housing Market," *Construction Review*, U.S. Department of Commerce, May 1973.

Committee for Economic Development, *Financing the Nation's Housing Needs*, New York, The Committee, April 1973.

National Association of Home Builders, *The New Mortgage Market*, Revised, Washington, D.C., National Association of Home Builders, April 1971.

WIEDEMER, JOHN P., *Real Estate Finance*, 2nd ed., Reston, Virginia, Reston Publishing Company, Inc., 1977.

15

Loans to Consumers

Consumer loans are made to finance consumption, as compared with loans made for productive purposes or for the purchase of assets that produce a flow of funds, such as stocks and bonds. Consumer loans make possible the consumption of goods and services in advance of the consumer's ability to pay; as a result, consumers can enjoy a higher standard of living. Such loans are made for a multitude of purposes, including the purchase of automobiles, household appliances, furniture, medical services, vacations and so on. Although the maturities of consumer loans vary, they are usually made for a period of two to three years. With the rise in consumer incomes and expenditures, consumer credit, including that provided by commercial banks, has been growing rapidly for many years.

Classification of Consumer Credit

Of the total amount of consumer credit extended by commercial banks, more than 80 percent is made on an instalment basis. The remainder is classified as single-payment loans. Both lenders and borrowers have discovered that repaying a certain amount of the debt each month or payday is more convenient than accumulating the funds and retiring the total debt at one time.

Instalment Consumer Credit

Commercial banks hold nearly 50 percent of the instalment credit of the nation. Of this amount, approximately 45 percent is classified as automobile paper, making commercial banks the largest single holders of this type of paper (See Table 15–1 below). The classification "mobile homes" includes the financing of mobile homes, trailers, campers, self-propelled motor homes, and similar vehicles. Although several reasons could be given for classifying mobile homes as real estate credit, the consumer credit statistics collected and published by the Federal Reserve System place these loans under the general heading of consumer credit. Several factors have been responsible for this practice, two of which are accretion and tradition. The financing of trailers came into being before mobile homes were financed by banks. Since trailer financing was similar in some respects to the financing of automobiles, such loans were placed in the same department. When banks entered the field of mobile home financing, these loans, too, were placed in the instalment loan department because of their similarity to trailer financing. Also, the legal documents used in the financing of mobile homes are more like those used in trailer and automobile financing than those in real estate financing. Moreover, the fact that mobile homes are more easily moved than are houses had something to do with their being considered as consumer loans. Finally, the maturity of mobile home loans normally is shorter than that for home loans. Although the maturity of mobile home loans varies, they usually range from 6 to 10 years compared to a maturity of 25 to 30 years for real estate loans.

Revolving credit includes bank card and check credit, and the category "all other" in Table 15–1 includes loans for the repair and modernization of owner-occupied dwellings and personal loans. Personal loans are made for a variety of purposes, such as the consolidation of debts and the payment of medical, education, or travel expenses, personal taxes, and insurance

Table 15–1
Type of Instalment Credit Held by Commercial Banks, October, 1978
(amounts in millions)

	Amount	Percent of Total
Automobile	$ 60,564	44.5
Indirect	33,850	
Direct	26,714	
Mobile Homes	9,553	7.0
Revolving Credit	24,434	17.9
All other	41,638	30.6
Total	136,189	100.0

Source: Board of Governors of the Federal Reserve System, *Federal Reserve Bulletin*, February, 1979. Figures may not add to totals because of rounding.

premiums. Such loans satisfy the need for relatively large amounts of borrowed funds for the purchase of durable commodities that can best be repaid on a monthly or instalment basis.

Noninstalment Consumer Credit

Commercial banks are by far the largest single holders of noninstalment consumer credit. Although this amount, which approximated $50 billion at the end of 1978, has increased considerably over the years, the percentage increase has been less than for instalment credit. Noninstalment loans are made for the same variety of purposes as are instalment loans and are not as large generally. The majority are not made in excess of 12 months.

Origin of Consumer Loans

Commercial banks may make consumer loans directly to borrowers who apply for credit at the bank. The banks also purchase the notes of consumers from retail dealers of commodities who have sold goods to consumers or from those who provide consumer services. Commercial banks purchase the paper of automobile dealers, furniture stores, and retailers in household appliances such as refrigerators, stoves, washing machines, dryers, televisions, and radios. The notes and supporting documents are usually referred to as *dealer paper.* These methods of lending have given rise to the terms *direct* and *indirect,* or *purchased,* loans. Sometimes, lending indirectly is referred to as *instalment sales financing.* Indirect financing by commercial banks has increased in recent years. Banks have also initiated programs involving the purchase of consumers' obligations for dental and medical services and financing insurance premiums.

Reasons for Indirect Lending

Commercial banks' practice of indirect consumer lending has developed for several reasons. Marketing methods and the ways that consumers shop for durable goods have encouraged its use. Most consumers shop first and then make their financial arrangements, a procedure encouraged by retailers who offer to sell on credit in order to increase sales. Since many retailers are financially unable to carry all their accounts receivable, they look to financial institutions as a source of credit. Most durable consumer goods are sold on terms that are readily acceptable to lending institutions. Indirect financing also provides an opportunity to obtain a volume of loans without a substantial increase in operating expenses. Direct lending involves loan interviews; this is an expensive process since it requires the time of trained personnel and various overhead expenses. Purchasing dealer paper is less expensive than lending directly. In addition indirect lending has certain advantages over direct lending that appeal to some banks. Loans purchased from some dealers may be more secure than direct loans since, in most cases, the dealer endorses the paper. If the dealer has substantial net worth, this arrangement adds financial strength to the notes purchased. The dealer may also be responsible for a certain amount of loan supervision, such as following up on delinquent accounts, repossession, and sale of repossessed merchandise, all of which saves a bank considerable time and expense.

Dealer Reserves

Most banks that engage in indirect financing provide for a dealer's reserve, which is held by the bank to protect both the dealer and the bank against losses that may arise on instalment paper. Such reserves are usually created from the difference between the amount charged the dealer by the bank for discounting the paper and what the dealer charges the purchasers for financing the contract. It may be likened to a finder's fee for originating the contract and completing the paper work associated with the loan. This reserve is important not only to the bank as a safety fund but also to the dealer, since it may represent a large part of his profit. On an automobile contract of $5,000 with a maturity of 36 months, for example, the reserve might approximate $300.

Most reserve agreements provide that the balance will accumulate until it reaches a certain percentage of the dealer's outstanding paper. When the reserve exceeds this stipulated percentage, the excess is paid to the dealer. The amount of the reserve required of dealers varies with the risk involved. For reliable dealers with years of satisfactory experience who generate a very desirable automobile paper from the standpoint of down payment, maturity, and credit investigation, a bank might require that the reserve be a percentage equal to 3 to 5 percent of the outstanding paper. For dealers in household appliances, the percentage might be established at double or triple this amount.

Significant Factors Involved in Indirect Lending

Since the purchase of dealer paper involves accepting the credit judgment of a dealer, many commercial banks have established standards to which dealer paper must conform. These standards may take the form of a gentleman's agreement, or of a more formal document known as a *dealer agreement* entered into by the bank and the dealer which sets forth the conditions that will govern the purchase of dealer paper. Banks do not knowingly purchase the paper of a dealer who is dishonest or who follows practices that are unethical. The dealer must also have an acceptable net worth and sound business and credit judgment.

Indirect financing has certain pitfalls, which explains why some commercial banks do not engage in this type of financing and others follow strict procedures. First, the bank may never see the customer and is not, therefore, in a position to make a personal appraisal. Secondly, the attitude of some people who purchase durable goods on instalment contracts is different from that of those who borrow directly from a commercial bank. Bank borrowers generally take the attitude that the obligation must be repaid. But some consumers who buy from a retailer feel the debt can be wiped out by returning the merchandise if it proves unsatisfactory or if they are unable later to meet the payments. Finally, when the lender does not interview the borrower the chances of fraud, forgery, and misrepresentation are greater. For these reasons commercial banks closely scrutinize the contracts submitted to them for purchase, especially if the dealer who endorses the paper is weak financially.

Commercial banks have initiated several plans for financing dealer paper, each with certain advantages and disadvantages for the bank. The most common plans have become known as *full recourse, nonrecourse,* and *repurchase.* Under a full-recourse plan, the dealer gives his unconditional guarantee on all notes or paper sold to the bank. If some of the paper becomes delinquent, the dealer is required to pay off the note, and various arrangements can be made as to when. This plan involves less risk to the bank than do the other plans, assuming the dealer is sufficiently strong financially to pay off the delinquent accounts. Since the dealer is required to stand behind all contracts, s/he has an interest in seeing that only sound sales are made. It is assumed also that adequate supervision will be exercised over the accounts, since not doing so may result in losses to the dealer. Moreover, in case of "skips" and delinquencies the dealer would take steps to see that the purchaser was located and the instalments paid. Many dealers favor this plan too, since the bank usually grants a lower interest rate than would be available under a plan requiring no endorsement.

A nonrecourse plan does not require the dealer's endorsement; consequently, the dealer has no liability once the paper is sold to the bank. Since the bank is assuming greater risk under this plan, it is usually more selective of the paper purchased, and the dealer receives no part of the carrying charge as a reserve or the bank will discount the paper at a higher rate than under a full recourse plan. Because of this, many dealers do not look with favor on this plan. Although some dealers from whom banks purchase contracts do operate under a nonrecourse plan, these dealers have an excellent record of generating satisfactory paper.

If a dealer is financially strong and responsible, a repurchase plan has some advantages. This is a form of nonrecourse or limited recourse agreement which provides for dealers to repurchase the net unpaid balance when the loan is past due and the goods are repossessed by the bank and delivered to the dealer within a prearranged period of time. For example, if the past-due period were established at 90 days and the bank failed to repossess the merchandise within that period, the dealer would have no liability. Since the dealer assumes less risk under a repurchase plan than full recourse, he is generally allowed a smaller participation in the finance income. Inasmuch as the dealer faces the problem of repurchasing the contracts, he would be encouraged to follow and maintain sound credit terms and to see that the customer made the payments as agreed. However, if the dealer were to go out of business, because of financial difficulties, the bank might encounter some trouble in liquidating all of the accounts.

Credit Factors Involved in Indirect Financing

The credit factors involved in indirect financing are no different than those in direct financing. But since an unknown party has much to do with the indirect-lending, banks are concerned about the evaluation for credit. Thus, they establish rules that they expect dealers from whom they purchase paper to follow. One of the most important is the determination of a purchaser's ability to pay for the merchandise. Banks insist that the dealer sell only to those who are employed, have a steady income, and have a record of repaying their obligations. Most banks require dealers to submit a credit application with each contract purchased and to secure a credit report from the local credit bureau.

Banks are also concerned with the down payment required on the merchandise and the maturity of the contract. Two golden rules of instalment sales financing are that the down payment should be sufficiently large to establish a buyer's equity in the merchandise and a feeling of ownership, and that the instalment payments be sufficient to increase the equity established by the down payment at a faster rate than the merchandise depreciates. If the down payment and monthly payments do not accomplish these objectives, the purchaser may develop a feeling of renting the goods rather than of owning them. Experience with instalment financing shows that most trouble is experienced with low down payment, long maturity contracts. Consequently, banks favor large down payments and short maturities.

Floor Planning

To merchandise such durable consumer goods as automobiles, washers, dryers, and televisions effectively, it is desirable to display them in a showroom or parking lot for customers to see and examine. This need has given rise to a form of financing known as *floor planning* or flooring. Although flooring is in reality a business loan rather than a consumer loan and could be discussed in the chapter on short-term lending, it is discussed here because it is closely related to indirect lending and is considered part of a dealer-financing plan. Flooring is seldom provided by banks as the only form of dealer financing. It is not regarded as the most desirable form of credit since it provides a lower rate of return and has a higher than normal risk. This type of dealer financing is provided primarily because it is an excellent means of obtaining dealers' contracts.

Flooring is a form of inventory financing reserved normally for the financing of goods that have several common characteristics. Such goods are easily identified and have a factory-inscribed serial number to facilitate identification. Only goods that have relatively high value and an established market in which value can be easily determined are floored. They are whole products, not parts that require assembly, and are goods on which valid liens can be given. Finally, they are goods with a sufficiently broad market so that no specialized demand will contribute to a high obsolescence rate.

Control of the inventory under a flooring arrangement may present a problem and, to a great extent, this creates the high risk. The major problem is to floor the correct amount of units. If the amount floored is too little, sales and profits will be down; therefore, the dealer becomes weaker financially than if there were a larger amount of sales and a high level of profitability. If too many units are provided, however, the inventory may become stale and eventually obsolete, especially if new models are introduced during this time. Providing the correct amount of inventory is difficult because of seasonal factors and economic conditions that constantly affect retailing.

Another problem encountered in flooring is the failure of a dealer to pay for all the items sold. This is referred to as *sold out of trust* and occurs frequently when a dealer runs into financial difficulties or forgets to pay off a unit that has been sold at retail. Should this occur, what is called *double financing* results. This can become serious, especially if the goods are financed at or near inventory cost. In such a case, the dealer has no equity in the goods, and the bank might have a frozen loan on its hands. To protect itself against such developments, a bank engaged in flooring frequently checks the inventory of goods floored to determine whether they have been sold, to see that an adequate supply is on hand, and that inventory is maintained in an acceptable manner.

Innovations in Retail Banking

Banks, it seems, are constantly introducing services designed to attract new customers and make banking more convenient. Two highly publicized innovations are check-credit plans and bank credit cards, both of which involve the extension of credit, available on demand to an individual, basically in the form of instalment credit.

Check-Credit Plans

Check-credit plans link the extention of a line of credit to a checking account. They take a variety of forms, but all combine some characteristics of cashier's checks, traveler's checks, check guarantee, and overdraft banking. There are two general types of check-credit plans. The most common type relies on an individual's regular checking account and provides a prearranged automatic line of credit that is activated the moment the individual checking account is overdrawn. Under such a system checks are honored up to the authorized line, which might range from $100 to $500 or possibly even more. These plans are commonly called *overdraft accounts* for obvious reasons. In most plans a loan is automatically created once a check exceeds the balance in the account. In some plans, however, the bank may credit the account with loan increments of $50 to $100; that is, should the account be overdrawn in the amount of $37.50, a credit to the account would be added in the amount of $50. Such loans are usually repaid on a revolving basis. They may be liquidated as ordinary deposits are made to the account or, more commonly, by separate loan payments. Several banks have a *check guarantee* card that is tied to an overdraft account. Such a card is used to identify the customer. This arrangement has great appeal since the checking account is enhanced by broadening the acceptance of the check. Check guarantee cards usually bear an identification number, an expiration date, and the customer's signature. However, some banks have issued guarantee cards that have no overdraft arrangements to preferred customers for identification purposes.

A second type of check credit employs a special checking account and special checks provided by the bank. These checks may have a notable design and are encoded in a manner that provides identification as they are processed at the issuing bank. Sometimes an identification card is required when cashing these checks.

Finally, some banks provide checks that are predenominated and in this respect are similar to traveler's checks. A depositor with this arrangement activates borrowing at the bank as soon as the check arrives at the bank for posting to the account. As the customer writes checks on this check credit balance, the check draws down on the credit line that has been established previously. When payments are made on this account, the credit line is replenished.

Check-credit plans have several desirable attributes, as well as shortcomings, when compared with other alternatives available to banks in providing credit to consumers. Check-credit plans are less expensive to introduce and maintain and are more easily controlled than are credit-card plans, and losses from operation and fraud have proved to be less. The start-up costs of credit-card plans are quite high. These costs include promotion, the signing-up of dealers, the cost of cards and imprinters, and the issuance of cards. For a credit-card plan to be profitable a substantial volume of credit must be outstanding, which calls for a large number of cards in the hands of consumers and a large number of dealers who are willing to accept the card. Accomplishing all of this is expensive. Check-credit plans are made available only by application and after the bank has made a credit investigation and approved the person requesting the credit. Consequently, the bank is in a position to evaluate closely the credit of the applicant. The fact that check-credit plans usually have higher maximum credit lines than do credit cards is evidence of this feature. Check-credit plans appeal to small and medium-size banks because they are less expensive to inaugurate. Check-credit plans are also more flexible than are credit cards in that a single bank could have two or more plans, which could be adopted for large or small depositors.

Check-credit plans are generally less expensive to the consumer than are credit-card plans in that finance charges are usually less. The most frequent charge of check-credit plans is 1 percent per month, whereas the finance charge for bank credit cards varies from 1.25 to 1.5 percent per month. Despite the advantages of check-credit plans, banks adopting them have not been able to reach as many people with their services as have banks with credit-card plans. Credit cards have one great advantage over check credit —convenience. The promotion of many kinds of credit cards seems to have made an impression on the American consumer, and they are well accepted as a means of payment. Although more banks have check-credit plans than have credit cards, the amount of credit outstanding is less and the market share of check-credit plans has been declining. Recent data show that three-fourths of the total credit outstanding for these two credit plans is represented by credit cards.

Credit Cards

The most significant development in consumer lending during the past two decades was the phenomenal growth in the use of bank credit cards. Commercial banks entered the credit-card field in the early 1950s. They were not the first to issue credit cards, since major oil companies had issued cards for years and department stores, travel, and entertainment cards were inaugurated prior to the banking industry's entry. By 1959 nearly 60 banks were issuing credit cards. Some encountered difficulties generating a sufficient volume of business to make the service profitable and withdrew from this type of instalment lending. Although many banks throughout the nation contributed to the success of credit cards, the persistence of Bank of America has been noteworthy. Not only has this bank been successful in its credit card operation in California, but it has been able to franchise its card with other banks in every state and in some foreign countries.

Several factors have motivated banks to enter the credit-card field. It permits banks to offer new services to existing customers and is an excellent vehicle to attract new customers—individuals as well as retail merchants. Credit-card plans increase opportunities for promoting other bank services also. Although not a deciding factor, many banks probably have entered into this area of consumer lending to keep abreast of developments that may ultimately lead to an electronic money-transfer system. In the final analysis, of course, banks have been motivated to adopt credit-card plans because of the possibility of increasing profits.

Bank credit cards differ from check credit in several important aspects. Credit-card plans are not linked to a checking account as are check-credit plans. Credit-card plans involve a three-party arrangement—the cardholder, the bank, and a merchant. The embossed plastic card issued to consumers serves as evidence to merchants that a bank has granted a line of credit to the holder of the card. The card also serves as an accurate means of imprinting sales drafts. Retail merchants agree with the bank to accept the card for payment of goods and services. Merchants who have an account with a card-issuing bank may deposit their sales slips with the bank or with one of its agents and receive immediate credit to their account, less a small discount. In a very real sense, the bank is financing the merchants' accounts receivable, and in so doing relieves them of the costs involved in operating a credit department. If a merchant does not have an account with the bank but has a credit-card clearing agreement with it, the bank is required to make payment to the merchant by check for the sales drafts. Regulation B of the Board of Governors of the Federal Reserve System, which will be discussed in greater detail later in the chapter, prohibits any requirement that merchants have a deposit account with a bank with which they have a bank-card clearing agreement.

Although most cards are issued at no cost to customers of the bank, an increasing number of banks charge an annual fee for the card ranging from $10 to $20. A customer of the bank is considered eligible for a card if he has a satisfactory deposit and loan relationship. Noncustomers are issued a card in anticipation of their becoming customers. Each card carries with it an assigned line of credit which may be changed, depending on how prudently the privilege is handled and whether the customer requests it. If payment is slow and some payments are in default, the card might be withdrawn or the established line of credit reduced to a level more in keeping with the cardholder's ability to pay. Cards are reissued periodically, which permits banks to reevaluate the cardholder's credit. It is not uncommon to raise the credit line of a cardholder on request and after satisfactory experience. The cardholder is billed monthly and has the option of paying the balance within a certain period—usually 25 days—without interest or on a revolving-credit basis with a minimum monthly payment of $10. Many bank card holders use the card merely as a convenience instrument, paying the bill immediately upon receipt. When this occurs, the bank's income is considerably less than if the charges were converted into a loan. It is for this reason that some banks levy a flat charge on the use of the card and others are considering doing so.

Most banks set a ceiling sometimes referred to as a *floor limit* on retail purchases: that is, they limit the size of a transaction that can be made without obtaining approval from the bank. Since most credit-card operations are computerized, and banks have developed a rapid retrieval system for its customers' indebtedness and repayment records, approval can be provided the retail merchant in a matter of seconds via telephone. The ceiling may vary, depending on the type of store and its location as well as the type of goods and services purchased. A common ceiling at retail stores might be $50 to $100, but for airline tickets the limit might be $500. In addition to the purchase of retail goods and services, bank credit cards may be used for cash advances, that is, for receiving cash at the teller's window. Some banks also provide the overdraft feature by paying checks that overdraw the cardholder's account and adding the amount of the advance to the credit-card bill.

In providing credit-card services to customers, a bank has two alternatives. It can offer its own card by entering into a licensing or franchise agreement under which it becomes a participating or associate member with a group of banks or acts as an agent. Or, secondly, it can offer another bank's card. If a bank decides to offer its own card, it must attract a sufficient number of merchants to make the program worthwhile for individuals to use the bank's card, and there must be a large enough group of card holders to make it worthwhile for merchants to become associated with the plan. A credit-card plan requires considerable volume if it is to generate a profit. If cardholders use the cards as a convenience and pay their bills within the allotted time before a service charge is applicable, the plan will be less profitable than if they pay on the instalment plan and thus make full use of the service.

Although the cost of operating a credit-card plan varies with the bank and the area to be covered, it is an expensive operation generally since considerable time, expertise, and promotion are required to make it successful. For this reason the number of bank credit cards has declined, and two national cards—VISA and Master Charge—command the bulk of the credit card business.

A popular arrangement in providing credit-card services is through a franchised program in which the bank issues a nationally known credit card such as VISA or Master Charge. The major advantages of this franchised arrangement are that the bank receives a great amount of assistance on credit-card marketing, processing, and promotion at a cost much less than if it attempted to set up its own credit-card program. Some drawbacks remain. The bank agrees to handle the sales slips of any bank that uses the card, which contributes to a wider acceptance of the card. In this approach, however, some loss of identification for the bank occurs in that the name of the bank is not as conspicuously displayed as is the name of the credit card. However, it should be remembered that the name of the card and the fact that is it acceptable in many areas make it valuable and appealing to customers and merchants. The bank, in reality, has nationwide scope in that its customers can use the card thousands of miles away from the bank and in foreign countries.

Sometimes several banks enter into what might be described as a cooperative agreement to provide a credit-card program. Under such an arrangement each bank issues its own credit card, provides for its own promotion, and signs up merchants; but the principal bank in the group provides the computer and accounting facilities. The "associate" members pay a fee for these services. The arrangement involves less expense than if each bank issued its own card. Small banks often enter into an agreement as a licensee with a larger card-issuing bank to accept the sales slips of retail customers and pass them on to the card-issuing bank. Small banks do this as a defensive measure: if they did not perform this service, the retail merchants would change their account to the card-issuing bank. Such agent banks are reimbursed for this service and, above all, they get to keep the account of the retailer, and their customers have the services of a credit-card operation.

More than 10,000 banks provide credit-card services presently, far more than the number with check-credit plans, and thousands of foreign banks in over 100 countries are associated with the two national systems. VISA and Master Charge report that approximately 1.3 million merchants and about 3.5 million outlets accept either one or both credit cards. The number of credit-card holders has increased significantly in recent years and now exceeds 75 million. Approximately 80 percent of the revolving credit held by commercial banks is derived from credit cards.

Credit cards are a unique method of settling financial obligations and are a firmly established banking service. They provide a convenient charge-account service with revolving credit privileges at retail outlets. They also serve as travel and entertainment cards and, as discussed earlier, can be used to borrow cash at the teller's window.

The most important problems associated with bank credit cards are lost and stolen cards. Card holders are sometimes careless with their cards, and thieves are constantly on the lookout for them. It is not uncommon for cards to be removed from mailboxes, and it has been reported that even postal employees have been guilty of taking cards. It should not be assumed that bank credit cards are the only valuables stolen, however. Checks are removed from mailboxes, cash and currency are frequently taken, and the purse snatcher is still with us. Although banks in cooperation with merchants have done an excellent job in catching illegal possessors of credit cards, stolen cards still concern banks that provide this service.

Merchants have found credit cards advantageous. Travel-oriented merchants especially find that honoring bank credit cards is a useful method of attracting tourists. Although the discount charged by banks on merchants' charge slips varies, depending on the type and the amount of business generated, the average national charge is approximately 3½ percent. This cost is considerably below the cost of operating a credit department, which has been estimated at an average of 5 to 6 percent of sales.

Credit cards are designed primarily for revolving credit at the retail level. Credit cards are not adapted to use with big-ticket items such as boats, automobiles, or expensive household appliances, which constitute a large portion of the consumer credit outstanding. Credit limits on most cards are normally below the cost of such items. Loans for the purchase of such expensive goods are usually well secured, and no arrangement has been designed as yet to provide security for such purchases when the consumer uses a credit card. For the time being it seems that such large consumer loans will continue to be made on a closed-end basis.

A limitation to the use of credit cards is that the credit standards established by banks may not be consistent with those of merchants who agree to honor the cards. Some might be willing to extend credit to customers that banks would not. Of course, some low-margin retailers have been discouraged from signing up with bank credit-card plans by the merchant discount. Food chains have not accepted credit cards because of reluctance to encourage credit purchases of food and the fact that the cost of the discounted sales draft would reduce what is considered a low net profit margin. Studies have shown that consumers are not overwhelmingly in favor of making credit cards acceptable at food stores, but this attitude could change. Although some food stores have accepted cards, the movement has not been widespread. Thus far, large department stores have been unwilling to join bank credit-card plans. They are fearful that customer loyalty might suffer and that they would lose a strong marketing tool. Moreover, with their own credit-card plans they are in a position to tailor their credit plan to serve their customers' needs. With increased competition in retailing and the introduction of the discount store, which generally accepts bank credit cards, this attitude may also change. With credit-card systems reducing their credit risk and with a discount charge of from 3 to 4 percent, which is considerably below the cost of operating a credit department, merchants are likely to reevaluate the cost of this service. Thus, we may see some large department stores accepting bank credit cards in the future.

As discussed earlier, many banks now provide an overdraft privilege associated with the bank credit card. For example, if a credit card holder were granted an overdraft privilege of $500, it would go into effect the moment a check was drawn that exceeded the balance in that account. The loan would become a bank-card loan and would be repaid in accordance with the established rules governing credit card charges. Some interesting descriptions have been applied to this kind of arrangement. One bank refers to it as ACT, meaning Automatic Cash Transfer, and another employs the descriptive term "Ready Reserve."

The introduction of bank credit cards has proved to be one of the most significant developments in banking and finance. Such cards facilitate the extension of consumer credit and serve as a medium of exchange. Moreover, they may serve as *debit cards,* that is, they may be employed to access certain customer accounts. For example, they may be used to secure cash 24 hours a day via cash dispensing machines. They may be used in such machines to deposit checks, to transfer funds from demand to time deposits, and to make payments on loans. They make banking far more convenient for customers. The potential use of bank credit cards is great. Although the concept of a checkless-cashless society may never materialize completely, it appears that the bank credit card will contribute to the movement in that direction. In some areas of the country, banks and retailers are experimenting with what are commonly referred to as POS or point of sale transactions. This involves the insertion of a bank credit or debit card into special electronic devices located at the retail counters of merchants for the purpose of transferring funds from the purchaser's account to that of the retailer. Such electronic devices could be connected with bank computers throughout the nation, an arrangement that could even be extended worldwide. Many benefits could derive from such a system, including the elimination of float, the use of tons of paper, the cost of handling such paper, and the writing of bad checks, which is of concern to retailers. Although there would be a reduction in some costs, there would be an increase in others, such as the cost of providing the devices, the means of transmission, computers, and so on. Even though such point-of-sale terminals are in place in a few areas of the nation, various factors have hindered large-scale development. The cost is of no little consequence not to mention the question of who should own and be permitted to use the facilities, government regulations, and the consumer's attachment to the use of cash and checks as a medium of exchange. Duplication of some elements of the system, such as transmission lines would be uneconomic; consequently, in an effort to maintain a competitive environment, these should be available to users at reasonable cost. Even though several parties would benefit from such an arrangement, it is not easy to allocate cost. Because such a system smacks of a "natural monopoly," some agency or agencies of government would undoubtedly supervise its ownership and use. Due to such unresolved issues, some participants are reluctant to move aggressively in this area. As these problems are resolved we are likely to see an increasing role played by bank cards in banking and finance.

Regulation of Consumer Credit

Consumer credit has been subject to more regulation than has any other type of credit provided by lending institutions. For many years the regulations centered around interest rates—the maximum amount that could be charged—but recently the emphasis has been on disclosure, discrimination, and billing.

Truth in Lending

The Truth-in-Lending Act covers three major areas. The first section is concerned with disclosure and requires creditors to provide customers with certain cost information, including the annual percentage rate of the finance charge on a consumer loan. Regulation of the advertising of consumer credit constitutes the second part of the act. The third part is concerned with rescission, which applies mainly to home mortgages and home-improvement loans (which was discussed in the preceding chapter on real estate lending).

The Truth-in-Lending Act is primarily a piece of disclosure legislation. The law requires that certain information be presented in a standardized manner by all lenders. The objective of the law is to provide borrowers with data on finance charges so that they will be able to compare the cost of credit. Finance charges can be confusing, since several different methods are used to compute the interest rate on a loan. If a loan is based on simple interest, the borrower's interest for each period is computed on the unpaid balance of the loan. For example, if the loan is repayable in monthly instalments and the stated annual rate is 12 percent, the interest cost each month is 1 percent of the unpaid balance at the beginning of the month. If the discount-off-the-face method is used, the finance charge is computed on the total amount of the loan, and the borrower receives the face amount of the loan, less the finance charge. Thus, if the loan were a single payment, one-year loan of $100 at a nominal interest rate of 10 percent, the borrower would receive $90, and the effective rate would be 11.1 percent. For many years a popular method of computing the finance charge on instalment loans was known as the *add-on method*. With this method, the finance charge is added to the principal amount of the loan and the total is divided by the number of payments to arrive at the amount of each payment. For example, if the principal amount of a loan were $100 and the nominal interest rate 10 percent, the total amount of the one-year loan would be $110. If the loan were repayable in twelve monthly instalments, the amount of each payment would be $9.17, and the effective interest rate would be approximately 18.2 percent. The reason the effective rate is higher than the nominal rate is that with an instalment loan the borrower does not have the use of the full amount of the loan for the entire year. Recently more and more banks are using the *simple-interest-method* of rate computation because it is easier for the borrower to understand.

The Truth-in-Lending Act applies to credit extended to all individuals for personal, family, household, or agricultural use, up to a limit of $25,000, unless the collateral is the borrower's residence. The most important requirement of this act is that the consumer be presented with a copy of the credit agreement, which contains the finance charge and the annual percentage rate along with other data. The finance charge includes all charges made in connection with the extension of the credit. Among the many charges that might be included are interest, loan fees, finder's fee, service charge, points, investigation fees, and premiums for life insurance, if insurance is required by the lender. Some costs associated with loan agreements are not included as part of the finance charge. These include taxes, license fees, certain legal fees, some real estate closing costs, and other costs that would be paid if cash were used instead of credit. The annual percentage rate (APR) is the finance charge expressed as an annual interest equivalent.

The advertising provision of the act requires as a general rule that terms be stated clearly, accurately, and conspicuously on all promotional material. All advertising must state the finance charge and the annual percentage rate, the amount of any required down payment, the dollar amount of the finance charge, and the number of instalments or the period of payment. Although banks come under the advertising requirement of the Truth-in-Lending Act, they are certainly not singled out from other lenders. In fact, the advertising requirements will have a minimal effect on bank advertising. The advertising requirements were directed primarily at some retailers and other lenders that have made use of such terms as "no down payment," "take 36 months to pay," or "only $5 per month."

Equal Credit Opportunity Act

The Equal Credit Opportunity Act, frequently referred to as ECOA, prohibits discrimination in any aspect of a credit transaction including advertising, application forms and procedures, standards of credit worthiness, record keeping, and collection procedures. The Act prohibits discrimination on the basis of sex, marital status, age, race, color, religion, national origin, or receipt of public assistance benefits. Although the Federal Reserve Board is responsible for promulgating regulations to implement the ECOA, enforcement has been placed in the hands of several federal agencies including the Federal Reserve Board, the Federal Deposit Insurance Corporation, the Comptroller of the Currency, and the Federal Trade Commission. Banks and financial institutions that regularly extend credit to individuals must comply with the provisions of this legislation.

Regulation B of the Board of Governors sets forth the requirements of ECOA. The regulations are far-reaching, even to the point of containing model application forms designed for use in a particular type of consumer credit transaction. Some significant provisions of this legislation are:

1 creditors may not ask for information about an applicant's spouse unless the applicant resides in a community property state, the spouse is to be liable for debt repayment, or the applicant chooses to rely on the spouse's income to repay the loan;

2 creditors may not request information about a credit applicant's marital status, nor can they demand information about childbearing capability or birth control practices;

3 a creditor cannot inquire whether any of the applicant's income, as stated in the application, is derived from alimony, child support, or support maintenance payments unless the creditor appropriately discloses to the applicant that such income need not be revealed if the applicant does not desire the creditor to consider such income in determining the applicant's credit worthiness.

Several significant rules must be adhered to in the extension of credit. Credit scoring systems that are statistically sound and comply with the regulations may be used as long as the age, sex, and marital status of an applicant are not adversely taken into consideration. The creditor cannot take into account a telephone listing of the applicant in evaluating credit worthiness. If an applicant requests unsecured credit and relies in part upon property to establish credit worthiness, the creditor may require the signature of the applicant's spouse or other person on an instrument necessary to make the property relied upon available to satisfy the debt in the event of default. Similar arrangements are in order if secured credit is requested. Creditors are required to notify an applicant of action taken on a credit request within 30 days. Notification can be given orally, but if the applicant requests written notification, it must be forthcoming.

A development that has influenced the extension of consumer credit, especially indirect lending, has been the constant erosion of the holder-in-due-course doctrine. This long standing principle relates to the legal treatment of negotiable instruments, such as promissory notes, executed between buyers and sellers. Under this doctrine a purchaser in good faith of a negotiable instrument acquires it free of any claims the maker of the instrument might have against the original holder. The purpose of the doctrine is to promote the free flow of trade. Without established standards of performance on the part of all parties concerned, commerce and trade would be precarious and fraught with uncertainty. As already discussed, the practice of indirect financing has developed over the years whereby a negotiable instrument is created at the point of sale and then sold to another party—the lender in the transaction. Abuses have crept into these transactions when sellers have sold faulty merchandise. The note or dealer paper that arises from such a transaction is then sold to another party, often a bank, who buys it in good faith, thereby becoming a holder-in-due-course and entitled under the law to collect from the maker of the note. Criticism of this practice has developed. In many instances the courts and state legislatures have denied the holder-in-due-course status to lenders, especially if they are knowledgeable about the transaction and have participated in the credit approval process. On the national level the Federal Trade Commission has gone even further and holds the protective clauses available under the holder-in-due-course doctrine as unfair trade practices and prohibits their use in consumer credit contracts.

When the holder-in-due-course principle is abrogated completely, banks and other lenders can protect themselves by purchasing dealer's retail paper only with full recourse and by requiring a reserve fund. Since commercial banks generally buy consumer notes only from responsible and financially sound dealers who stand behind their products, elimination of the holder-in-due-course doctrine from the retail area should have little impact on them. The demise of this doctrine is a result of the violation of an acceptable and desirable code of ethics by a few sellers. Without the holder-in-due-course doctrine a buyer can return faulty merchandise to the dealer in certain circumstances and refuse to pay the promissory note, even if it has been purchased by a lender in good faith. In some cases buyers of merchandise do this even though they themselves have caused the damage to the product. Since these developments do occur, lenders tend to raise their credit standards to guard against such losses and, in so doing, limit the availability of consumer credit. Credit standards can be raised by refusing to purchase contracts from dealers who are weak financially and by scrutinizing each individual contract more closely.

Fair Credit Billing Act

The Fair Credit Billing act is an amendment to the Truth-in-Lending Act and is purportedly designed to protect consumers from inaccurate and unfair billing. This amendment gives customers 60 days after billing to make a complaint in writing, and during this period no interest can be charged on the disputed amount. Complaints must be resolved within 90 days. Complaints arising from inaccurate and unfair billing before and after the introduction of this legislation have not been significant. Disputes usually arise when customers forget that they made certain purchases, but once they are presented with their signed sales drafts, the issue is cleared up quickly. Additional regulations applicable to credit cards have had the effect of increasing the liability of commercial banks that issue cards, and have resulted in increased costs. In many states a credit-card holder is allowed to withhold payment and assert claims against the card-issuer where shoddy goods and services have been delivered. This change also eliminates the holder-in-due-course protection that has for years been available to lenders. However, the amount of a claim under this provision may not exceed the amount of the sales draft, and the credit-card holder must make a "good faith attempt" to obtain restitution from the merchant. The customer must also live in the same state where the purchase was made and/or within 100 miles of where the transaction occurred. The Truth-in-Lending Act also prohibits the issuance of unsolicited credit cards and places a limit of $50 on the liability of a credit-card holder for unauthorized use of a credit card.

Regulation of consumer lending, as with all other types of lending, raises important questions regarding social justice and the availability of credit. It is desirable that an adequate amount of consumer credit be made available for the purchase of consumer goods if many individuals are to have a high and rising standard of living. If interest rates are kept too low by legal ceilings, or if the debtor-creditor relationship is not fair and equitable, funds will not be made available or the laws will be violated.

Much of the concern about consumer interest rates and debtor-creditor relations stems from lack of knowledge about personal finances on the part of consumers and their occasional unwillingness to repay loans once they become financially strained. Through poor planning, some consumers buy goods they cannot afford, thinking that the monthly payments will be easy. Once good intentions are shattered, it is easy to blame the seller, the lender, or society in general for one's plight. Fortunately the great majority of consumers handle their obligations properly. As in any kind of regulation, the zeal to arrive at a perfect state in consumer lending must be tempered by the fact that it is for the majority that regulations are imposed. The scales of social justice must balance if we are to have an adequate flow of credit for consumer purposes and the proper functioning of our financial system.

Questions

1. What are the social and economic implications of consumer credit? Evaluate them.

2. Although both single payment and instalment credit have increased, instalment credit has increased more rapidly. Why?

3. Of all the plans initiated to finance dealer paper, which would you recommend to a bank and why? Which plan would you recommend to a dealer and why? What factors led you to these conclusions?

4. Do you agree with the statement "the introduction of bank credit cards has proved to be one of the most significant developments in banking and finance"? Why or why not?

5. Why does indirect lending exist? Does it have something to do with our method of shopping? Explain.

6. What are the advantages of a dealer's "reserve"?

7. The amount of bank card credit is much larger than bank check credit. Why? Which would you, as an individual, prefer? Why?

8. Do you agree that the potential use of bank credit or debit cards is great? Give reasons for your position.

9. What problems may our society encounter in changing to a cashless-checkless society?

SELECTED REFERENCES

American Institute of Banking, *Instalment Credit, A Modular Course,* Washington, D.C., 1975.

LITTLE, ARTHUR D. INC., *The Outlook for the Nation's Check Payments System, 1970–1980,* Report prepared for the Monetary and Payment System Committee of the American Bankers Association, New York, 1970.

Board of Governors of the Federal Reserve System, *Bank Credit-Card and Check-Credit Plans,* Washington, D.C., July 1968.

Board of Governors of the Federal Reserve System, "Evaluation of the Payments Mechanism," *Federal Reserve Bulletin,* December 1972.

Federal Reserve Bank of Dallas, "The Payments Mechanism," *Business Review,* September 1976.

——, "Current Issues in Electronic Transfer of Funds," *Business Review,* February 1977.

——, "Electronic Funds Transfer and Monetary Policy," *Business Review,* August 1977.

MANDELL, LEWIS, "Credit Card Uses in the United States," Ann Arbor Institute of Social Research, University of Michigan, 1972.

National Committee on Consumer Finance, *Consumer Credit in the United States,* Washington, D.C., U.S. Government Printing Office, November 1972.

OSTERBERG, RONALD, "An Update of Automatic Teller Equipment," *Magazine of Bank Administration,* March 1973.

16

The Investment Account: Policies and Management

The investment account of a commercial bank consists of securities that do not qualify for inclusion in the secondary reserve. Investment account securities are acquired with primary emphasis on income, whereas secondary reserve securities are selected for their high degree of liquidity. These two classifications of assets cannot be distinguished by looking at a bank's balance sheet, however, since investments are listed according to issuer.

Characteristics of the Investment Account

In banking, the term investment is used to include those funds placed in the debt securities of enterprises, both public and private, for relatively long periods of time. Investments differ from loans in several respects. A loan carries the concept of the use of something for a relatively short period on the condition that it or its equivalent will be returned. An investment, on the other hand, implies the outlay of funds for the purpose of obtaining a flow of funds for a relatively long period before the outlay is returned. In bank lending, a borrower usually initiates the transaction, but in investing, the bank takes the initiative by entering the market to purchase assets. In most loan transactions, the bank is the major creditor and one of only a few creditors, while in investing, the bank is usually one of many creditors. Bank lending involves a personal relationship between the bank and the borrower, but investing is an impersonal activity.

A fine line separates the investment account from the secondary reserve: it is a matter of liquidity. A liquid asset can be sold rapidly: converted to cash on short notice. In this sense many securities in the investment account are as liquid as those in the secondary reserve. Liquidity has another dimension, however, in that a liquid asset undergoes little fluctuation in value. The more distant the maturity date of a credit instrument, the more its market value will change with a change in interest rates. Therefore, U.S. government bonds that mature in 20 years are less liquid than short-term bills due within 90 days, even though both are issued by the Treasury and the investor can sell the bonds as easily as the bills. The bonds are more burdened with money-rate risk.

The assets in the investment account are of longer maturity than are those comprising the secondary reserve. Management may consider those securities with maturities of twelve months and less as belonging to the secondary reserve and all others as falling into the investment account. Therefore, assets constantly move from the investment account to the secondary reserve. For example, a U.S. government note purchased today and maturing five years hence would be placed in the investment account today. But four years from now it would be considered a part of the secondary reserve, assuming that twelve months is the dividing line.

The investments of commercial banks are relatively important, from the standpoint both of size and of revenue produced. At year-end 1977 the investments of all U.S. commercial banks, including secondary reserves, amounted to $250 billion and comprised 24 percent of bank assets (see Table 16–1). One-fourth of these securities have maturities of one year and less and are normally classified as secondary reserves while the remainder are commonly categorized as investment securities. The investment portfolio of all banks produced approximately 17 percent of bank income.

Objectives of the Investment Account

The objectives of a commercial bank's investment account are to provide the bank with safety of funds, diversification, income, and liquidity. It is doubtful whether all the deposits of a commercial bank or the commercial banking system could be placed in desirable loans. It would also be unwise since such a practice would violate one of the fundamental principles of investment—diversification. In the event a bank followed such a practice, it would be relying heavily on the fortunes of the local economy. Prudent banking dictates that a bank acquire some of its assets elsewhere.

The income requirement of the investment account normally is higher than that of the secondary reserve. Pursuit of that higher income results in a sacrifice of liquidity, because in most economic periods the more liquid

Table 16–1

Investments of Insured Commercial Banks, December 31, 1977

(in thousands of dollars)

Investment securities—total	250,392,895
U.S. Treasury securities	95,961,373
Maturity—1 year and less	36,481,917
Maturity—Over 1 through 5 years	49,411,277
Maturity—Over 5 through 10 years	8,860,522
Maturity—Over 10 years	1,207,657
Obligations of other U.S. Government agencies and corps	35,812,115
Maturity—1 year and less	9,318,756
Maturity—Over 1 through 5 years	14,905,716
Maturity—Over 5 through 10 years	4,878,770
Maturity—Over 10 years	6,708,873
Obligations of States and political subdivisions	112,900,214
Maturity—1 year and less	18,429,872
Maturity—Over 1 through 5 years	31,617,986
Maturity—Over 5 through 10 years	33,222,146
Maturity—Over 10 years	29,630,210
Other bonds, notes, and debentures	5,719,193
Maturity—1 year and less	923,827
Maturity—Over 1 through 5 years	2,437,129
Maturity—Over 5 through 10 years	1,087,293
Maturity—Over 10 years	1,270,944
Corporate stock	1,611,533

Source: FDIC, *Annual Report*, 1977.

assets produce lower yields. This does not mean high-risk assets are deliberately placed in the investment account, because neither the regulatory bodies nor most bank managements would allow such an approach, but it does mean that the longer maturities used in the investment account do build in a higher level of risk than exists in the secondary reserve. The assets of the secondary reserve must be of "near-cash" quality and so highly marketable that they can be converted in a "push-button" fashion. This is not so true of the investment account. Its function is to replenish the secondary reserve through staggered maturities, and to meet demands in the event of financial stringency involving large unpredictable requests for funds because of withdrawals or loan demands in excess of the secondary reserve.

The investment account does not need the same liquidity as does the secondary reserve for several reasons. A portion of the primary reserve can be used if a sudden need for funds develops, and the secondary reserve could be reduced if need be. Some of the more liquid loans made on a demand basis could possibly be called, and those that are maturing might not be renewed. Borrowing funds from a Federal Reserve bank is certainly in order when liquidity needs are great. In the event some of the assets in the investment account had to be sold at a price below the purchase price, and if the bank had a reserve for bond losses, the seriousness of the situation would be lessened. Therefore, some "shock absorbers" or buffers stand between financial stringency and the investment account. It may seem that the investment account has incompatible goals—liquidity and income. To a great extent this is true, and a perfect balance of these objectives requires astute bank management.

If a mistake is made in this liquidity versus profitability tradeoff, it should be in the direction of liquidity, because the investment account should serve as a buttress to the secondary reserve. If the secondary reserve is drawn down to meet deposit withdrawals or increased demand for loans, it must be replenished in a short period of time to restore adequate liquidity to the bank. If generating funds by increasing liabilities—perhaps large certificates of deposit—does not replenish the secondary reserve, then the sale of investment account securities may be required. If such sales are required, it is usually during a period of tight money and high interest rates when the prices of debt securities are depressed. During such periods disintermediation becomes a problem for many banks.

The Risks Inherent in the Investment Account

The risks inherent in the investment account of a commercial bank can be classified as the *credit risk,* the *market risk,* and the *money-rate risk.* The credit risk of a security arises from the probability that the financial strength of the issuer will decline so that it will not be able to meet its financial obligations. Credit risk on obligations of a governmental unit is a product of the character of the debtor or *obligor,* the economy supporting the obligations, and the tax and borrowing power of the unit. When speaking of the character of the obligor, we are thinking in terms of the attitude of public officials and the people toward debt repayment. The attitude of the people is important, for it is from them that public officials derive their strength and mandate. Occasionally, political upheavals in other areas of the world have resulted in the repudiation of debts by governments.

The debt-paying abilities of governments change. This is true of nations as well as of local governments. The strength of an obligor's economy becomes very important when the obligation is a revenue bond, which is supported by special revenues such as those from an electric power plant or a sewer facility. The tax and borrowing powers of governments are essential for a high credit rating on general obligation or guaranteed bonds. Maximum tax rates limit a government in supporting its debt. Some governments are limited in their borrowing activities, which might become very important if sufficient funds were not available from taxes for the payment of principal and interest.

Securities of the federal government are considered free of credit risk because of its great tax and borrowing powers and the strength of the economy from which it derives its funds for the repayment of its obligations. State and local securities are not in the same enviable classification since there have been some defaults in past history, the economies of these governments are not as strong as the total economy, and their taxing and borrowing powers are not comparable. However, it is not our intention to imply that only the obligations of the federal government are acceptable assets to be placed in the investment account, since many bonds issued by states and local units of government are eligible.

Market risk refers to the possibility that unforeseen changes in the securities markets or the economy may reduce the investment appeal of certain securities so that their sale is possible only at large discounts from earlier values. For example, an economic recession might cause investors to avoid the bonds of small public bodies even though the debt servicing abilities of such issuers have not declined.

Although an asset may enjoy low credit and market risk, it is still subject to the money-rate risk; that is, the risk that market value will decline due to interest rate increases. This phenomenon is the result of the contractual rate of interest a bond carries when it is issued and the relative freedom of market rates to move up and down. A federal government bond, for example, which was issued in 1960 with a 3.5 percent coupon rate lost considerable value in later years because of the rise in interest rates during the 1960s and 1970s. Ordinarily, the more distant the maturity date of a credit instrument, the greater the money-rate risk.

Bond Prices, Yields, and Maturities

The rate of return on a fixed-income obligation may be stated in terms of the *coupon rate,* the *current yield,* or the *yield to maturity.* The coupon rate is simply the contractual percentage of par value the issuer must pay. A bond carrying a 5 percent coupon pays the holder $50 per year (assuming a par value of $1,000) regardless of the prevailing market rate of interest. The current yield is obtained by dividing the coupon return by the market price. This ratio is more applicable to measuring the rate of return received on preferred stock than on bonds, since it ignores maturity values and assumes payments will continue forever. The yield-to-maturity concept provides the best measure of returns on fixed-income investments. This measure considers the coupon rate, maturity value, purchase price, and time to maturity.

The yield to maturity can best be explained by a simple arithmetical computation. Assume that a bond was purchased bearing an interest rate of 6 percent and maturing in 20 years. If the bond were purchased at par (100 percent of face value) at a time when the current market rate of interest was 6 percent for comparable quality bonds, its market price would be $1,000 (assuming par value of $1,000). In this instance, the yield to maturity would be the same as the coupon rate. However, if the cost of this bond were 93.39 (bond prices are stated in percentages of face value) or $933.90, the yield would be greater than 6 percent. It is obvious that at maturity the bond would be redeemed for $1,000.00, and would have appreciated $66.10 at that time. In computing yield to maturity, however, this increase should be spread over the life of the bond. During the holding period it would produce an annual interest payment of $60.00, and appreciation would amount to approximately $3.31 per year ($66.10 ÷ 20 years), so the annual income would be $63.31.

To determine the yield the average investment must be ascertained. This figure can be found by taking the initial investment of $933.90, adding to it $1,000.00, the maturity value of the bond, and dividing by 2 to arrive at an average investment of $966.95. The annual return of $63.31 on the bond divided by the average investment gives a yield of 6.55 percent. In computing the yield on this bond, we have made the following steps:

Annual interest (6% of $1,000.00) of	$60.00
Plus annual appreciation ($1,000.00 − $933.90 = $66.10 ÷ 20 years) of	3.31
Equals total income of	$63.31
Total income ($63.31) divided by average investment ($933.90 + $1,000 = $1,933.90 ÷ 2 = $966.95) equals a yield of	6.55%

On the other hand, if the bond had cost $1,125.50 we would have to consider the premium of $125.50 in determining the yield. This amount would have to be written off over the 20-year period. We would not consider all the $60.00 interest as current earnings therefore, but would charge off $6.27 per year from the interest income, which would leave a net of $53.73. We would determine the average investment by adding $1,125.50, the price paid, and $1,000.00, the redemption amount. Dividing by 2 would give us $1,062.75. This amount divided into the net return would give a yield of 5.06 percent.

The steps we followed in this instance were:

Annual interest (6% of $1,000.00) of	$60.00

Less annual amortization ($1,125.50 – $1,000.00 =
$125.50 ÷ 20 years) of   6.27
Equals total income of $53.73
Net income ($53.73) divided by average investment
($1,125.50 + $1,000.00 = $2,125.50 ÷ 2 = $1,062.75)
equals a yield of   5.06%

The formula we have used to determine the approximate yield to maturity in this example is:

$$\text{Yield to maturity} = \frac{\begin{array}{c}\text{annual dollar return} \\ \text{from coupon}\end{array} \begin{array}{c}\text{+ annual accumulation} \\ \text{or} \\ \text{–annual amortization}\end{array}}{\dfrac{\text{current market price + par value}}{2}}$$

This formula produces approximations only. For bonds selling close to face value it gives reasonably accurate results, but for bonds selling at large discounts or large premiums this formula produces a significant error because it ignores the compounding effect that results as the receipt of coupon payments over time gradually amortizes the premium or accumulates the discount. More sophisticated methods can be employed in making yield-to-maturity calculations, of course, but such time-consuming steps have been eliminated by bankers and others actively involved in the bond markets. Several manufacturers produce desk-top or handheld calculators programmed to make calculations pertaining to financial instruments, including yield-to-maturity calculations and others specifically applicable to bonds.

Prior to the introduction of financial calculators, the *yield book* was relied on by virtually everyone who was involved in the bond market, and it is still by those who, for whatever reason, do not use a financial calculator. Understanding the yield book is vital to understanding the bond market. This book contains bond tables from which it is a simple matter to determine a bond's yield when price, coupon rate, and maturity are known.

The following page contains a section of a bond table for 6 percent bonds due in from 18 years, 6 months to 22 years. Since we assume in our examples that we were dealing with bonds maturing in 20 years, we may glance down the column headed 20 years until we find the price paid for the bond in the first example, 93.39. Keeping our eye on that figure and glancing to the extreme left column with the heading "yield," we see that the yield on the bond is 6.60 rather than 6.55 as we found it to be by arithmetical means. Checking on the same page for our second example, we discover that the yield is 5.00 rather than 5.06.

Bond prices and bond yields are inversely related. When bond prices are

Table 16–2
Bond Values: 6 Percent Bonds Due in 18 Years, 6 Months to 22 Years

6% Yield	Years and Months							
	18-6	19-0	19-6	20-0	20-6	21-0	21-6	22-0
4.00	125.97	126.44	126.90	127.36	127.80	128.23	128.66	129.08
4.20	122.99	123.40	123.80	124.19	124.58	124.95	125.32	125.68
4.40	120.11	120.46	120.80	121.14	121.46	121.78	122.10	122.41
4.60	117.31	117.61	117.90	118.18	118.45	118.72	118.99	119.24
4.80	114.60	114.85	115.09	115.32	115.55	115.77	115.98	116.19
5.00	111.98	112.17	112.37	112.55	112.73	112.91	113.08	113.25
5.20	109.43	109.58	109.73	109.87	110.01	110.15	110.28	110.41
5.40	106.96	107.07	107.18	107.28	107.38	107.48	107.58	107.67
5.60	104.57	104.64	104.71	104.78	104.84	104.90	104.96	105.02
5.80	102.25	102.28	102.32	102.35	102.38	102.41	102.44	102.47
6.00	100.00	100.00	100.00	100.00	100.00	100.00	100.00	100.00
6.10	98.90	98.88	98.87	98.85	98.84	98.82	98.81	98.80
6.20	97.82	97.79	97.75	97.73	97.70	97.67	97.64	97.62
6.30	96.75	96.70	96.66	96.62	96.57	96.53	96.49	96.45
6.40	95.70	95.64	95.58	95.52	95.47	95.41	95.36	95.31
6.50	94.66	94.59	94.52	94.45	94.38	94.32	94.25	94.19
6.60	93.64	93.56	93.47	93.39	93.31	93.23	93.16	93.09
6.70	92.64	92.54	92.44	92.35	92.26	92.17	92.09	92.00
6.80	91.65	91.54	91.43	91.32	91.22	91.12	91.03	90.94
6.90	90.67	90.55	90.43	90.32	90.20	90.09	89.99	89.89
7.00	89.71	89.58	89.45	89.32	89.20	89.08	88.97	88.86
7.10	88.77	88.62	88.48	88.35	88.21	88.09	87.96	87.85
7.20	87.84	87.68	87.53	87.38	87.24	87.11	86.98	86.85
7.30	86.92	86.75	86.59	86.44	86.29	86.14	86.00	85.87
7.40	86.01	85.84	85.67	85.50	85.35	85.19	85.05	84.91
7.50	85.12	84.94	84.76	84.59	84.42	84.26	84.11	83.96
7.60	84.24	84.05	83.86	83.68	83.51	83.34	83.18	83.03
7.70	83.38	83.18	82.98	82.79	82.61	82.44	82.27	82.11
7.80	82.53	82.32	82.11	81.92	81.73	81.55	81.38	81.21
7.90	81.69	81.47	81.26	81.06	80.86	80.68	80.50	80.32
8.00	80.86	80.63	80.42	80.21	80.01	79.81	79.63	79.45
8.10	80.04	79.81	79.59	79.37	79.17	78.97	78.78	78.59
8.20	79.24	79.00	78.77	78.55	78.34	78.13	77.94	77.75
8.30	78.44	78.20	77.96	77.74	77.52	77.31	77.11	76.92
8.40	77.66	77.41	77.17	76.94	76.72	76.50	76.30	76.10
8.50	76.89	76.64	76.39	76.15	75.93	75.71	75.50	75.30
8.60	76.13	75.87	75.62	75.38	75.15	74.93	74.71	74.51
8.70	75.39	75.12	74.86	74.62	74.38	74.16	73.94	73.73
8.80	74.65	74.38	74.12	73.87	73.63	73.40	73.18	72.97
8.90	73.92	73.65	73.38	73.13	72.88	72.65	72.43	72.21
9.00	73.21	72.93	72.66	72.40	72.15	71.91	71.69	71.47
9.10	72.50	72.21	71.94	71.68	71.43	71.19	70.96	70.74
9.20	71.80	71.51	71.24	70.97	70.72	70.48	70.25	70.03
9.30	71.12	70.82	70.54	70.28	70.02	69.78	69.54	69.32
9.40	70.44	70.14	69.86	69.59	69.33	69.09	68.85	68.62

Table 16-2 Continued

6% Yield	Years and Months							
	18–6	19–0	19–6	20–0	20–6	21–0	21–6	22–0
9.50	69.77	69.47	69.19	68.91	68.65	68.40	68.17	67.94
9.60	69.12	68.81	68.52	68.25	67.99	67.73	67.49	67.27
9.70	68.47	68.16	67.87	67.59	67.33	67.07	66.83	66.60
9.80	67.83	67.52	67.23	66.95	66.68	66.42	66.18	65.95
9.90	67.20	66.89	66.59	66.31	66.04	65.78	65.54	65.31
10.00	66.58	66.26	65.97	65.68	65.41	65.15	64.91	64.67
10.20	65.36	65.04	64.74	64.45	64.18	63.92	63.67	63.44
10.40	64.18	63.86	63.55	63.26	62.99	62.72	62.48	62.24
10.60	63.02	62.70	62.39	62.10	61.83	61.56	61.31	61.08
10.80	61.90	61.58	61.27	60.98	60.70	60.44	60.19	59.95
11.00	60.82	60.49	60.18	59.88	59.61	59.34	59.09	58.86
11.20	59.75	59.43	59.12	58.82	58.54	58.28	58.03	57.79
11.40	58.72	58.39	58.08	57.79	57.51	57.25	57.00	56.76
11.60	57.72	57.39	57.08	56.79	56.51	56.25	56.00	55.76
11.80	56.74	56.41	56.10	55.81	55.53	55.27	55.03	54.79
12.00	55.79	55.46	55.15	54.86	54.59	54.33	54.08	53.85

Source: *Expanded Bond Values Tables*, Boston: Financial Publishing Company, 1970.

low, bond yields are high; when bond prices are high, yields are low. Investors who purchase bonds when interest rates are low face the risk of a decline in value if rates increase. On the other hand, market appreciation will occur when interest rates fall.

This relationship between bond prices and yields means that the market value of commercial bank investment portfolios fluctuates with changes in interest rates. This principle may be illustrated by referring again to table 16–2. Assume that a bank purchases $10,000,000 worth of 6 percent, 20-year bonds at par. Shortly thereafter the market rate of interest rises to 7.10 percent, and the bank is forced to sell the bonds. The increase in the rate of interest results in a capital loss to the bank of $1,165,000, since the bonds would sell for only 88.35, or $8,835,000. Rising interest rates, therefore, have mixed blessings for commercial banks. New loan and investment commitments can be made at rates more advantageous to the bank, but the higher rates mean that depreciation has occurred in the investment account.

When this happens, it is commonly referred to as being *locked in*. The bank does not want to sell the bonds and take a huge capital loss. The alternative is to hold them until maturity or until interest rates decline, causing prices to increase. Even if the bonds recover in price, however, the bank has still suffered an opportunity loss because it could not invest or lend the funds locked in during the period of high interest rates.

Banks devote extensive attention to avoiding or minimizing such price declines in the investment account, for it must be a major source of liquidity during periods of credit stringency, when interest rates rise most. In many cases banks have little choice but to take losses in order to restore their primary and secondary reserves if deposits have declined or it is necessary to meet increased loan demands. Obviously, the money-rate risk is of great importance to bank portfolio managers.

The degree of money-rate risk associated with bonds normally varies with the length of their maturities. The shorter the maturity, the more stable the price; the longer the maturity, the less stable the price. Reference to the bond table further illustrates the relationship between yields and prices. For example, if the market rate of interest moves from 6 to 7 percent, the price of a 20-year, 6 percent bond would drop to 89.32; but a 5-year, 6 percent bond would drop to only 95.84. This is a sizeable difference, and it explains why short-term securities are frequently more attractive to some investors, especially commercial banks, than are long-term obligations. However, one point of qualification should be made; interest rate increases (or decreases) often vary for different maturities. As an example, the rate change on five-year maturities could be much greater than on 20-year maturities. In fact, it is usually true that interest rate changes are greater for the shorter maturities.

Investment Policy

Every commercial bank has an investment policy, whether it is recognized or not. Even though a written statement of investment policy is desirable, few banks have them. The main objectors to a written investment policy are those who feel that the economic environment of banking changes so rapidly that a formal, written statement would become dated within a short time. It is true that banking operates in a changing environment, but changes do not occur so rapidly that they cannot be incorporated into a written policy.

The basic factors that will determine the objectives of a bank's investment policy are its income and its liquidity needs, and management's willingness to trade liquidity for greater income opportunities and vice versa—which means accepting greater or lesser degrees of risk. But risk is not limited to the investment account, and the risk generated by an aggressive investment account may be offset by conservative policies elsewhere. For example, a bank with a relatively large secondary reserve is in a better position to take more risk in its investment account than is one with a small and less liquid account. Moreover, a bank that has a portfolio of high quality loans and relatively stable deposits can assume more risk than can a bank without these characteristics. From the standpoint of the community, it might be preferable for the bank to pursue an aggressive lending policy and a conservative investment policy. This would mean a willingness to make loans in its home area, which might be considered somewhat risky but which would, for the most part, benefit the community. The higher risk in the loan portfolio would be countered with a very liquid investment portfolio.

The three approaches to the problem of determining what proportions of a bank's total assets should consist of loans and investments and what the makeup of each of these classes of assets should be are the pool-of-funds, the asset allocation, and the management-science approaches. These have been discussed in Chapter 5. None of the three approaches should be followed automatically by any bank however. Formulation of an investment policy must give cognizance to the entire risk exposure that bank management is willing to assume as well as the risk carried by the securities that comprise the investment account.

One of the acceptable methods of reducing risk in the investment portfolio of a commercial bank is by diversification—a basic and important rule of any investment policy. Diversification means holding an assortment of securities rather than very few. The diversification policy should consider maturity, geography, type of security, and type of issuer. Risks may not be completely avoided by diversification, but they can be reduced.

A commercial bank is most concerned with quality and maturity. Quality is not the problem it once was because of the large amount of U.S. Treasury and agency securities that are now available to commercial banks. The objective of quality diversification is to minimize the risk that the obligors might not meet their obligations as agreed. Therefore, diversification is more important when investing in securities of a lower quality.

Commercial banks hold a sizeable amount of the municipal debt of the nation, and here diversification becomes important. States and their political subdivisions differ considerably from an economic standpoint. Some are industrial, some commercial, some agricultural, while others are fairly well diversified. Some are heavily in debt, others, only lightly. When investing in municipal bonds, a commercial bank should not duplicate its loan portfolio. Loans are of local origin generally, and, as a result, a great part of the bank's assets depends on the economic stability of the local community. Therefore, the investment account affords the only avenue of hedging against any economic instability that may strike the local trade territory. Another factor to be considered in investing in local municipal obligations is that during a recession a bank may make loans to the municipalities for current operating purposes. If securities of these municipalities are held in large amounts, the pyramiding of credit extension in this manner would be unsound. Although there have been few defaults of municipal securities in recent years, local units of government are not immune to financial problems. This fact was evidenced by the financial problems of New York City and a default by the City of Cleveland in the late 1970s.

Maturity diversification is also desirable. The goal here is to keep the money-rate risk of the investment portfolio consistent with the income and liquidity objectives of the bank. As we have seen, securities that may not have any credit risk fluctuate considerably in price as interest rates change so that gains and losses frequently result when sales are made. The risk of significant loss dictates that banks stagger maturities in their investment portfolios. As various issues mature, the funds can be reinvested in other securities that best fit the investment portfolio if they are not needed elsewhere.

The investment policy should set forth the manner in which maturities are to be structured. One approach used by many banks is to *ladder* maturities, a process that involves the investment of an equal amount of funds in securities that mature each year up to, say, ten years. Thus, one tenth of the portfolio would mature in one year, one tenth in two years, one tenth in three years, and so on. Funds released from maturing securities are reinvested in the longest maturity category. This approach offers the advantages of simplicity, ease of management and supervision, and a usually stable earnings performance; but it precludes shifts in maturity schedules that might produce profits because of changes in the structure of interest rates. Under a pure ladder-of-maturities approach no effort is made to forecast interest rate movements. Many banks modify this approach and do restructure maturities when their rate forecasts indicate that benefits—either production of profits or avoidance of losses—will result from such restructuring.

Forecasting interest rate movements is far from being an accurate process. If confidence is placed in a forecast of declining rates and the bank lengthens its maturities, a severe loss of liquidity and perhaps serious losses could result if interest rates subsequently rise. The process of forecasting interest rates begins with understanding the existing rate structure. This structure is usually depicted by a *yield curve.*

A yield curve is a graphic presentation of yields to maturity for a certain class of securities that differ only as to maturity dates. It is prepared by plotting each issue's yield on the vertical axis of a chart and its maturity date on the horizontal axis. A smooth curve best depicting the overall yield structure of the securities is then fitted to the plotted points. Some points will be above the curve and some below. Since the curve represents the market in a given class of securities at one point in time, its shape may change significantly within a short time span. Yield curves may be constructed for any class of marketable debt instruments, but usually the curve of U.S. government securities receives most attention because of the number of issues and the absence of credit risk. The U.S. Treasury, in the *Treasury Bulletin,* publishes monthly the yield curve for Treasury issues.

The shape of the yield curve at any point in time is determined by a number of influences, including Federal Reserve monetary policy and maturity preferences of borrowers, but it also indicates the expectations of investors. A declining, or inverted, yield curve exists when short-term interest rates are higher than long-term rates. If a preponderance of investors believed the inverted shape would be permanent, they would simply place all of their investments in the shortest maturities. However, the inverted shape can only exist because a sufficient number of investors expect rates at all maturities to decline, and they want to "lock in" the prevailing long-term yields.

An increasing yield curve indicates that investors believe interest rates are soon to rise. Thus, investors reason that it would be better to take a low return in the short run and to purchase long-term securities when the yield increases and the prices of the securities are lower. The investment officer should evaluate the expectations that give the curve its shape, compare them with his or her own expectations, and invest according to his or her best judgment as to the portfolio that will most suitably comply with the bank's investment policy.

An investment strategy that has been adopted by a number of banks and which relies heavily on yield curve analysis is the *barbell* maturity structure. This approach places a significant portion of the portfolio in long maturity bonds and retains the balance in short maturities with few, if any, bonds maturing in the intermediate range. The two "bulges" at the short and long ends of the maturity structure give this strategy its name.

Under a barbell strategy, the amount invested in long-term bonds and the timing of those investments depend on the level of long-term rates and the direction in which those rates are expected to move. If long-term rates are expected to decline, a heavy commitment to the long end of the barbell is made. If rates at the short end of the yield curve are expected to be stable or declining, the short end of the barbell might include maturities of as much as three or four years, but if short-term rates are expected to rise, the short end of the barbell may consist of maturities so short that they are considered part of the secondary reserve.

If the bank is accurate in its interest rate forecasting, the barbell structure should be more beneficial than the ladder-of-maturities structure. The continued popularity of the laddered approach suggests that many bankers do not place a high degree of confidence in interest rate forecasts.

Commercial banks should not interpret diversification to mean the purchase of some securities of every eligible quality and maturity. It does not mean that every bank should own a few foreign bonds or a few revenue bonds located thousands of miles away, nor does it mean that maturities

382 The Investment Account: Policies and Management

should be staggered meticulously by months or quarters instead of by years. Too much diversification can become burdensome to the point where the effectiveness of the portfolio may be lessened.

The quality of the securities that make up the investment portfolio is so important that it must be mentioned in the statement of policy. High quality implies marketability and safety of funds, whereas low quality implies the opposite, even though the return may be greater. Investment officers must have some standards to guide them in their selection of securities, just as loan officers must have some criteria regarding the quality of loans that should be sought by the bank. A bank may wish to state in its investment policy that a certain percent of its investments must consist of U.S. government securities, since they are virtually risk-free if they are of relatively short maturity. The quality of municipals may be stated in terms of an acceptable rating by private rating agencies or of a quality considered suitable by the board of directors.

A statement of investment policy should designate the person responsible for handling the investment program. This is fundamental to the efficient operation of an investment portfolio, in that "too many cooks may spoil the stew." This person should be capable, well trained, and above all, cognizant of the bank's responsibilities to the community. One fault of most department heads in any organization, including banks, is the feeling that their responsibilities and activities should take precedence over other departments in the organization. The investment department must realize that its activities are subordinate in nature. Loans to customers, along with the primary reserve, come first in priority. The sale of a bond at a loss may be a hard blow to the investment department, but if the same funds can be employed more profitably in loans, the sale decision may be wise. Commercial bank management is a team undertaking, and the investment officer should be given full authority for the operation of the department, consistent with the investment policy established by the board of directors. If the size of the investment portfolio warrants it, this person should devote his or her full time to this important function and have capable personnel, facilities, and materials available to help carry out the policies.

An important influence on the management of an investment portfolio is the pledging requirement imposed by governmental units. Most governments—federal, state, and local—require commercial banks to hold securities of certain amounts and classifications to secure their deposits in those banks. For example, a state may require that its deposits be secured by obligations of the U.S. government, federal agencies, or the state itself in amounts totalling no less than 110 percent of those deposits. A bank that anticipates holding a significant volume of the state's deposits should establish in its investment policy the manner in which the pledging requirement normally will be met. The policy should also recognize the immobility such a pledging requirement injects into the investment portfolio. The investment manager may be prevented from making advantageous portfolio switches because of the frozen nature of pledged securities. The portion of the investment portfolio immobilized by such a pledge can reach 50 percent or more at some banks during periods when they have become somewhat illiquid in their effort to satisfy loan demands.

Since the board of directors is responsible for the proper investment of the bank's funds, periodic reports regarding the investment portfolio should be prepared for the board's use in evaluating investment management and establishing investment policy. These reports should be informative, clear, and concise. The board of directors is basically interested in the quality, diversification, and maturity schedule of the investments, and an appraisal at periodic intervals.

The investment policy of a bank should be reviewed occasionally and modified as economic conditions change. It is impossible to state how frequently this should be in terms of months or years. It should be reviewed when developments occurring within or outside the bank dictate. For example, if interest rates increase or decrease after several months or years of stability, a review is in order. If loans, in strong demand for months, decrease, the policy should be reviewed.

Trading

Trading can refer to "making a market" in certain securities or to buying and selling securities actively in the hope of profiting from short-term movements in prices. Making a market is the practice of a bank investment department, or any other underwriter, who acts as a merchant standing ready to buy or sell a particular issue at established bid-and-ask quotations. Commercial banks are permitted to underwrite municipal issues and commonly make a market for them, which is an acceptable function of an underwriter. A few large banks also have dealer departments that make a market in U.S. government securities. Banks that conduct dealer activities in securities have committed a certain amount of capital in support of such operations, and the securities involved are segregated from the investment account and are designated *trading account securities.*

Active trading of investment account securities in the hope of realizing profits is a practice that calls for close and continuous awareness of the securities markets, skillful trading techniques, and probably some good luck in order to achieve success. Before contemplating the practice of trading, a commercial bank should consider the objectives of the investment portfolio. As we have seen, the principal objectives are to provide liquidity and income commensurate with the risks involved; a bank that engages in trading extensively, consciously or unconsciously, is placing greater emphasis on income than liquidity as its investment goal.

Determining the Organization of the Investment Department

The size of the investment or bond department of a commercial bank depends on the size of the investment portfolio; the functions performed by the department, such as underwriting, trading, and services performed for customers; and the type of securities purchased and held in the investment portfolio. The investment function requires an analysis of the credit and money-rate risk of the assets to be purchased, an evaluation of the bank's ability to assume the degree of risk found, and, once they are placed in the investment portfolio, continual assessment of the securities.

A lack of organization is sometimes found in some smaller banks, but most large banks have people skilled in various phases of the investment program with funds budgeted for research and analysis. Such specialists have a wealth of materials in the form of information from investment services and financial and economic data that have bearing on various securities. Small banks generally do not have ready access to most of these aids. The investment function may be performed by any of the officers, who may also make loans and, possibly, perform additional administrative duties. Because of lack of time for specialization, the personnel in a small bank usually do not acquire the acumen of those who handle the investment accounts in larger institutions.

In many small, and some medium-sized banks, the trust and investment functions are combined. There are arguments both for and against this kind of organization of course. The most important argument in support of this combination is that both departments are concerned with the analysis of various securities; therefore, it is economical from a personnel standpoint to combine both functions in the same department. The most potent argument against it is that greater opportunity exists for self-dealing than if the two functions were separate and distinct. In the event these functions are combined, safeguards should be established to avoid direct as well as indirect self-dealing as far as trust funds are concerned. Complete separation of these functions is the ideal situation.

Many large banks make their own analysis of the securities purchased; the investment department determines whether the issue in question meets the specific needs of the bank. Other banks may rely on outside sources for this analysis. However, outside sources are not as aware of the bank's investment requirements as are those associated with it who have probably participated with the board of directors in the formulation of the policy.

The small bank may employ several means of overcoming its lack of proficiency in investment portfolio management. It can abstain from purchasing issues that require elaborate analysis and concentrate on credit risk-free securities, which would mean heavy purchases of U.S. government obligations. This may be desirable from the standpoint of safety and liquidity, but the bank may forego considerable income if the practice is followed for a long period. Many small banks follow this practice, however, coupled with the purchase of local municipals.

Small banks also utilize various statistical services. Many are worthy of consideration, but the small bank should not rely on them exclusively. Rating agencies do not always agree on each security, and they are as subject to error as others. Some people hold that rating agencies follow the market rather than lead it. Relying exclusively on ratings means that some small but high-quality issues would never be purchased.

A final means that many small banks employ is to utilize the services of their correspondents. The large correspondent banks ordinarily have experienced personnel who are available to customer banks in effectuating their investment policy. One major advantage of relying on a city correspondent is the confidential manner in which information is handled. If smaller banks do rely on their correspondents, the officers of the city correspondents will require all the details of the investment policy in order to advise the country bank correctly. Moreover, the city correspondents are in close touch with the large bond dealers and can complete purchases or sales at opportune times.

Questions

1. If interest rates rise by some amount, say one percent, at all maturity levels, why is it that long-term bonds will decline more in price than short-term bonds?

2. If the country was entering an economic recession, would you expect the prices of U.S. Treasury bonds to be rising or falling? Why?

3. What has been the trend of interest rates in the U.S. over the last 30 years? How would this trend influence the management of bank investment accounts?

4. Loan demand at a bank is probably at its highest level when the economy is operating at its strongest. At such a time the Federal Reserve is likely to become restrictive in its monetary policy. What is happening to the bank investment account at such a time?

5. Locate the August 30, 1974 issue of the *Treasury Bulletin* and look at the yield curve. What economic conditions and other influences caused the curve to have its inverted shape?

6. In the back issues of the *Treasury Bulletin* examine the yield curves for Treasury securities over the last few years. What is the most common shape of the yield curve?

7. Locate a yield book. When interest rates change, is the impact greater on the price of a low-coupon bond (say, 3 percent) or a high-coupon bond (say, 10 percent)? Why?

8. Looking again at the yield book, if rates rise one percent at all maturity levels, is the difference in the price decline between a 5-year and a 10-year bond the same as the difference in the price decline between a 20-year and a 25-year bond? Why not?

Selected References

BAUGHN, WILLIAM H., and CHARLES E. WALKER, (eds.), *The Bankers' Handbook,* rev. ed. Homewood, Ill., Dow Jones-Irwin, 1978, Section IV.

BEAZER, WILLIAM F., *Optimization of Bank Portfolios.* Lexington, Mass., D.C. Heath & Co., 1975.

BRADLEY, STEPHEN P., and DWIGHT B. CRANE, *Management of Bank Portfolios.* New York, John Wiley & Sons, 1975.

HOMER, SIDNEY, and MARTIN L. LEIBOWITZ, *Inside the Yield Book.* Englewood Cliffs, N.J., Prentice-Hall, Inc., 1972.

MCCRACKEN, JOHN, "Interest Rate Forecasting . . . and Other Popular Delusions," *The Bankers Magazine,* Winter, 1976, pp. 71–77.

NADLER, PAUL S., *Commercial Banking in the Economy,* 2nd ed. New York, Random House, 1973, chs. 5 and 6.

PULLIAM, KENNETH P., "A Liquidity Portfolio Management Strategy Approach," *Journal of Bank Research,* Spring, 1977, pp. 50–58.

ROUSSAKIS, EMMANUEL N., *Managing Commercial Bank Funds.* New York, Praeger, 1976, chs. 2, 3, 5, and 6.

VINING, JAMES L., "Higher Yields From the Bond Portfolio," *The Bankers Magazine,* Summer, 1977, pp. 56–62.

17

Investment Securities

The investment activities of commercial banks are closely regulated for the same reasons as are lending activities: to assure safety of depositor's funds. There are many limitations as to which securities are acceptable in the eyes of state and federal regulatory authorities. We will discuss the most important of these that apply to national banks.

Investment Regulations Pertaining to National Banks

An investment security is "a marketable obligation in the form of a bond, note or debenture."[1] From this concise definition it is obvious that two criteria must exist before a security is eligible for bank investment: the security must be marketable and it must be a debt instrument—banks are prohibited from investing in equity securities. There are minor exceptions to this rule however. National banks must belong to the Federal Reserve System and are required to own stock in their respective regional Federal Reserve banks. Also, a bank can own stock in an amount up to 15 percent of its capital and surplus in the corporation that operates its safe-deposit business, and it can own stock in amounts equal to its capital in the corporation that owns the buildings in which the bank is located. With the permission of the Board of Governors of the Federal Reserve System banks may also

[1] R. S. 5176, par. Seventh; 12 U.S.C., 24

invest an amount equal to 10 percent of capital and surplus in a foreign banking corporation. A bank may own stock in the Government National Mortgage Association, the Student Loan Marketing Association, and in the Federal National Mortgage Association if that association buys FHA and VA mortgages from the bank. There is no limit set on the amounts of stock that can be held in these three agencies, and that is also true of the stock of corporations authorized under Title IX of the Housing and Urban Development Act of 1968. With various limits, a national bank may also own stock in small business investment companies, agricultural credit corporations, banking service corporations, state housing corporations, and Minbank capital corporations.[2]

For purposes of regulating the investment and underwriting activities of national banks, the Comptroller of the Currency has defined three classes of securities. A type I security is one that "a bank may deal in, underwrite, purchase and sell for its own account without limitation. These include obligations of the United States, general obligations of any State of the United States or any political subdivision thereof and other obligations listed in paragraph Seven of 12 U.S.C.24." The other obligations listed in the code are those issued by various government agencies and under various government acts.

Type II securities are those "which a bank may deal in, underwrite, purchase and sell for its own account, subject to a 10 percent limitation. These include obligations of the International Bank for Reconstruction and Development, the Inter-American Development Bank, the Asian Development Bank, and the Tennessee Valley Authority, and obligations issued by any State or political subdivision or any agency of a State or a political subdivision for housing, university or dormitory purposes."

Type III securities are those "which a bank may purchase and sell for its own account, subject to a 10 percent limitation, but may neither deal in nor underwrite." The most important securities in this classification are corporate debt instruments, including those convertible into common stock, foreign corporate or government bonds, and assessment and revenue bonds of states and political subdivisions issued for purposes other than housing or university dormitories.

These definitions contain, indeed consist of, the Comptroller's limitations. There are no prescribed percentages of each type that a bank may hold, except that the amount held of type II or type III securities issued by one obligor cannot exceed 10 percent of the bank's capital and surplus. Banks are expected to exercise prudence in the selection of their investment securities and to maintain credit files adequate to demonstrate prudence.

---

[2]A Minbank capital corporation is a corporation organized for the purpose of extending credit to members of minority population groups.

The Comptroller's regulations state that a bank may purchase a type II or III security when "it determines that there is adequate evidence that the obligor will be able to perform all that it undertakes to perform in connection with the security." Further, a bank may "purchase a security of type II or III for its own account although its judgment with respect to the obligor's ability to perform is based predominantly upon estimates which it believes to be reliable." The limit for such securites is 5 percent of capital and surplus for all obligors combined. If a bank is in doubt about a security, it may request a ruling from the Comptroller.

Banks will become owners from time to time of common stocks pledged as collateral on loans that become uncollectable. These stocks must be disposed of within a reasonable time. In the view of the Comptroller, that is generally regarded to be five years.

Banks may purchase debt instruments convertible into common stock or with stock purchase warrants attached, but they must reduce the cost of such securities by amounts equal to the value of the conversion features. This requirement discourages the purchase of such securities if they are selling far above their market values as pure debt instruments.

The National Bank examiners look closely at the investment account to determine the quality and hence the market value of the securities held. For this purpose, securities are placed in three categories: investment securities, doubtful securities, and loss. Investment securities, as the term implies, are those that meet the standards of quality laid down by law and the regulatory authorities. Doubtful securities mean that a credit problem exists and the possibility of the obligor meeting interest and/or principal payments is questionable. Should a bank have doubtful securities in its portfolio, a portion of their book value is deducted by the examiner in his computation of the bank's adjusted capital and reserves. Securities are placed in the loss classification if, in the evaluation of the bank examiner, a loss exists; consequently, these securites must be written off.

Determination of Quality

Regulatory authorities are concerned with the quality of the securities purchased by commercial banks. For example, the Comptroller's Office states that its definition of investment securities "does not include investments which are predominantly speculative in nature." Quality, however, is difficult to define, recognize, and regulate. Many circumstances are responsible for the quality of bonds commonly purchased by commercial banks, but it is not always easy to recognize these circumstances when purchases are made. The investment of funds is not an exact science. There is no sure way to invest funds for long periods since many uncertainties face the obligors that issue securities commonly purchased by commercial banks. Almost any security is speculative to a degree; however, some are more speculative than others. Quality is, to a great extent, relative.

Marketability has been emphasized as a criterion for quality by regulatory agencies. This attitude raises the question of a definition of marketability. There are certainly different degrees, depending on the size of the issue, the credit worthiness of the issuing body, and general economic conditions; but, as a general definition, a marketable instrument is one that is actively traded and thus easily sold. Active trading usually results when both the issuer and the issue are large. Issues of the U.S. government are traded in an active market; those of a small country school district are not. School district bonds might be sold only by making large price concessions. Probably the difference separating the bid and ask quotations for a bond is as good a test of marketability as can be found. Financial authorities say that a spread of one point or more between the bid and asked quotations indicates limited marketability.

Two recognized private agencies in the country rate corporate and government securities from the standpoint of quality. These agencies—Standard and Poor's and Moody's—do not rate all issues but confine their ratings to those that have a relatively broad market.[3] In general, investors have great respect for these ratings, and so does the Comptroller's office, which looks with favor on those securities rated in the upper four brackets. However, the Comptroller's Office recognizes that there are thousands of issues of small localities outstanding that are not as marketable as a U.S. government bond, but are of high quality and are eligible for a bank's portfolio.

To insure high quality of the securities placed in the investment account by a bank, the Comptroller's Office requires that all investment securities be supported by adequate credit files. Banks are prohibited from relying exclusively on the evaluation of others. The objective of this regulation is to encourage bank management to make desirable decisions regarding the investment portfolio. It is believed that this cannot be done intelligently unless adequate information abut the issue and the obligor is available. This is desirable since banks, especially smaller ones, tend to rely on a city correspondent, an investment counselor, or a bond dealer, some of whom might have a special interest in certain issues.

[3]Moody's rating of bonds is as follows:

Aaa	Best quality	Baa	Medium grade	Caa	Poor standing
Aa	High quality	Ba	Have speculative elements	Ca	Speculative in
A	Upper medium grade	B	Lack characteristics of		a high degree
			a desirable investment	C	The lowest rated

Classification of Eligible Securities According to Obligor

Eligible securities may be classified according to obligor: federal government, federal agencies, state and local units of government (municipals), and corporate securities. Although municipal issues make up the largest portion of commercial bank investment portfolios, as a single obligor, the federal government is by far the most important.

Federal Government Securities

To a large extent the debt of the federal government is the legacy of the Great Depression, World War II, and deficit financing. The growth of this debt reflects the budgetary position of the government and the methods employed to finance deficits.

Treasury securities are classified as public and nonpublic and marketable and nonmarketable issues. Since commercial banks may purchase only marketable public issues, our discussion will center on these types of securities. Marketable public issues include Treasury bills, notes, and bonds. The amounts outstanding of each type of security as of December 1978 were: bills, $161.7 billion; notes, $265.8 billion; bonds, $60.0 billion.

Treasury Bills. Bills are short-term securities with original maturities of three, six, nine, or twelve months. Because of their short maturities and high marketability, Treasury bills are the most liquid of all U.S. government securities and meet the liquid-asset needs of banks very well. Bills are discount instruments; that is, the investor does not receive separate interest payments, but instead earns interest income by paying a price below the face value of the bill and receiving face value at maturity. If the bill is sold before maturity, the seller receives less than face value, but will have earned interest income if the bill is sold for more than was paid for it. This should be the case unless interest rates have risen sharply since the purchase date.

From time to time the Treasury issues a special bill termed a Tax Anticipation Bill, or TAB. The TABs are issued with maturities of six or nine months, and are designed to provide a convenient investment vehicle for corporations to place funds temporarily in anticipation of quarterly income tax payments. The bills mature about a week after tax payment dates and may be used at par value to meet tax instalments or may be turned in for cash at maturity.

Because Treasury bills are issued in tremendous volumes, an active and efficient secondary market exists. Thus banks are not limited to purchasing newly issued bills and, in fact, buy most of their bills in the secondary market. A given bill may be bought and sold several times while it is outstanding. Because of their superior quality and tremendous volume, yields on Treasury bills are pivotal rates in the money market. Changes in bill rates will likely affect rates on other types of short-term obligations since investors continually compare the relative attractiveness of investment alternatives.

It is customary to speak of Treasury bill yields, although bills are quoted on a bank discount basis. The computation of Treasury bill price discount and equivalent bond yield is illustrated below.[4]

Let A = number of days to maturity
     E = discount basis expressed as percentage
     F = discount from par in dollars
     G = dollar price
     I = investment return

To find the price of a Treasury bill due in 40 days on a 6.25 percent discount basis, let

$$F = \frac{E}{360} \times A$$

$$= \frac{.0625}{360} \times 40$$

$$= .6944\%, \text{ or } \$0.6944 \text{ per } \$100.00 \text{ maturity value.}$$

The price of the bill will be quoted in the market as:

$$G = \$100 - F$$
$$= \$100 - \$0.6944$$
$$= \$99.3056$$

The investment return, or equivalent bond yield, will be higher than the discount-basis return because the discount is expressed as a percent of $100.00 and not as a percent of the $99.3056 actually invested, and because bond yields are computed on a 365-day year while bill discount rates and prices are based on a 360-day year. The result is:

[4] *The First Boston Corporation Handbook of Securities of the United States Government and Federal Agencies and Related Money Market Instruments,* 27th ed. (New York: First Boston Corp., 1976), pp. 56–59.

$$I = \frac{\$0.6944}{\$99.3056} \times \frac{365}{40} = 0.0638, \text{ or } 6.38\%$$

Treasury Notes and Bonds. Treasury notes are issued with maturities of from one to seven years. Bonds may have any maturity but are usually issued with maturities of five years or more. Notes and bonds are issued with specified coupon rates. A forthcoming new issue is announced in detail by the Teasury two or three weeks in advance, tenders are accepted at the Treasury or any Federal Reserve bank, and an allotment is made by a predetermined method if the issue is over-subscribed. Several issues of bonds are callable prior to maturity. For example, the 4.25 percent bonds of 1987–92 mature in 1992 but may be called in, or anytime after, 1987. The bond will be called, of course, only if market rates at the time of call are below the coupon rate.

The Dealer Market

The secondary market for U.S. government securities is maintained by relatively few business organizations which buy and sell securities for their own accounts. These organizations may be commercial banks, but most are nonbank securities dealers. Most of the nonbank dealers conduct a wide range of investment activities.

The market for government securities made by a particular dealer is depicted in the firm's quote sheet. The quote sheet lists all issues in which that dealer is willing to trade, the bid and asked price of each issue, net change of the bid price from the previous day's close, yield to maturity before and after taxes, a historical price range, amounts of each issue outstanding, and the dollar value to 1/32 of 1 percent.

The spread between a dealer's bid and asked price represents the gross profit of a trade. When dealers want to increase their trading volume or reduce their holdings of a particular issue, spreads between bid and asked prices are narrowed. The spread between highly demanded issues is quite small because of competition between dealers. Prices on U.S. government bonds are stated in terms of 1/32 of 1 percent. As maturities increase, spreads quoted by dealers increase usually and may reach as much as 1 percent on long-term bonds that are inactively traded.

Marketing Treasury Obligations

Commercial banks are involved in the marketing of U.S. Treasury obligations through their participation in the weekly auctions of Treasury bills, cash offerings, and refundings. Bills are issued through auctions conducted by the Federal Reserve banks. The auctions normally take place each week on Monday, with delivery and payment on the following Thursday. Competitive bids are entered by investors on a basis of 100, with the highest bid accepted first, then the next highest, and so on, until the desired amount has been sold. For example, a bid of 98.914 would be filled entirely before any bills were granted to a bid of 98.913. Investors who do not wish to enter competitive bids may enter noncompetitive tenders. In this case, investors are assured of having their orders filled, but must pay the average price as determined from the accepted competitive bids. Only relatively small amounts—usually no more than $500,000—may be purchased on a non-competitive basis.

When the Treasury wishes to raise new money by offering short-term securities, it may resort to the issuance of a *strip* of bills. Under this arrangement, increased amounts of outstanding bills are offered for bids, and investors and dealers must bid for a package of bills rather than for individual issues. For example, at any one time there are 13 issues of 91-day Treasury bills outstanding, which means that one issue matures each week. The Treasury may wish to raise $1.3 billion of new money by offering a strip of bills that will include an additional $100 million of each of the outstanding bill issues.

A Treasury offering of notes or bonds may be on an auction or a subscription basis. If the auction process is followed, it is similar to a bill auction except that bids are in terms of yield instead of price, with the lowest yield bid receiving the full amount of its order before the next highest bid receives any securities. Noncompetitive orders are usually accepted for relatively small amounts. If the subscription process is followed, all terms of the forthcoming issue are set in advance (amount to be sold, maturity and call dates, coupon rate, and price). The issue usually carries an attractive yield relative to existing market rates, so over-subscription is normal. Each of the subscribers then receives a small fixed amount, usually $200,000, and a percentage of the balance of their subscription as determined by the ratio of total subscriptions to the amount of the security to be issued.

Subscribers to Treasury bonds are usually required to pay cash for the bonds purchased. Occasionally commercial banks may pay for securities purchased by crediting the Treasury's tax and loan account. This privilege is frequently extended to banks in connection with the auction of tax anticipation bills or special strip offerings of bills.

Since banks participating in an offering with the tax and loan payment privilege experience an increase in deposits through no advancement of their own funds (required reserves increase, of course), it is to be expected that banks bid aggressively on such issues. The value of the tax and loan payment privilege to the individual banks depends partially on the length of time the Treasury deposit remains at the bank. As a service to their customers, U.S. government securities dealers estimate the value (expressed in basis points) of the tax and loan feature to banks.

Several issues of Treasury bonds have a provision whereby they are accepted by the Internal Revenue Service at face value in payment of federal estate taxes if the person owned them at time of death. Bonds with such a provision are commonly referred to as *flower bonds*. Thus estate planning results in a demand for these issues when they are selling at a discount. Since many of these have low coupon rates, they sell at sizeable discounts and, as a result of the estate-planning demand, low yields; consequently, they are relatively unattractive to banks. Congress eliminated the flower bond provision on all bonds issued after March 1971; the last of these bonds will mature in 1998.

Government Agency Issues

The obligations discussed above are direct obligations of the U.S. government. In additon to these securities, various government agencies issue obligations in the securities markets not guaranteed by the U.S. government. Among the most important of these agencies are the Federal Home Loan Banks, Government National Mortgage Association, Bank for Cooperatives, Federal Intermediate Credit Banks, Federal Land Banks, and the Tennessee Valley Authority. Several of these agencies borrow on both a short- and a long-term basis.

Yields on government agency bonds are above those on direct issues. The spread varies with money-market conditions, investor preference, and the features of the particular issue which affect its liquidity. At the end of June 1978, agency issues held by banks totaled approximately $39 billion and comprised 15 percent of bank investments.

Municipal Securities

Municipals. This is a broad term employed in financial circles to include securities issued by states and their political subdivisions and, sometimes, even the obligations of territories and possessions of the United States. The political subdivisions of states whose obligations are classified as municipals are cities, counties, towns, boroughs, and villages. State and local governments may also create various types of districts with the authority to issue obligations classified as municipals, such as school, road, water, library, and sanitary districts. Municipal securities are difficult to classify as to source of payment because of the many variations that exist. The usual classifications are general obligation, revenue, and assessment; but, not too infrequently, one finds an obligation with some features of two or all three of the classifications.

General Obligation Bonds. The most common type of municipal security and the largest single class is the general obligation or, as it is sometimes called, the *full faith and credit* obligation. The term full faith and credit means that the full taxing power of the obligor is pledged to assure payment of the obligation; technically, such securities have a tax lien on all taxable property within the obligor's domain up to 100 percent of the property. The term also means that the issuing body will exert every effort to collect taxes to pay the principal and interest on the obligations. From a credit standpoint, general obligations are the best type of municipal security and are the most sought after of all municipals by investors, including commercial banks. The credit worthiness of general obligations is also recognized by bank regulatory authorities.

Revenue Bonds. Revenue bonds are obligations issued by publicly owned business agencies or authorities. The principal and interest are payable solely from the earnings of the business. Examples of revenue bonds are the obligations issued by municipally owned water works, electric power departments, and sewer districts or toll bridge and toll road authorities created by states. The issuance of revenue bonds stems from the debt limitations that were imposed on municipalities when they had fewer proprietary functions than they now have. If municipalities have used up their ability to issue general obligation bonds, revenue bonds provide an alternative method of financing revenue-producing facilities. The quality of revenue bonds is not usually as high as that of general obligation bonds, and commercial banks purchase fewer of them for their investment accounts.

Assessment Bonds. Assessment bonds are obligations that have been issued to finance a particular improvement, such as the pavement of a street or the installation of a sewer. Such obligations are payable from the proceeds of a specific assessment based, for example, on frontage footage or on some other measure levied against each piece of property located in the area that receives the benefit. In some cases local governments may agree to make up any deficit that occurs, however, and if this should happen, assessment bonds would assume the characteristics of general obligation bonds. Many other assessment bonds, if the assessed property is very valuable in relation to the amount of the assessment, are desirable obligations. Experience with such securities over the years has not been as satisfactory as with general obligation and revenue bonds, and commercial banks do not, as a result, invest heavily in them.

Hybrid Bonds. In addition to general-obligation, revenue, and assessment bonds, there are municipal obligations that possess features of one or more of these securities. In a sense, these bonds are hybrids. The full faith and credit of the issuing government could be added to a revenue bond. In this instance, it would be relied on only in the event revenue from the public utility was insufficient to pay the principal and/or interest. This type of bond would certainly be of a higher quality than if only one source of funds were available to support it. It would therefore command a higher price or lower interest rate in the market. Water bonds could be supported, in addition to revenues from the operation of the water department, by specific taxes levied on the property in the water district. This feature would certainly improve the credit quality of the issue and result in a more attractive investment. Revenue bonds may also be issued by a district having the authority to levy supplementary taxes on all property in the district to meet any deficit that may arise.

Some states have issued general obligation bonds payable primarily from the revenue derived from particular taxes, and others have issued bonds with no pledge of the full faith and credit of the state but with only the pledge of the revenue from a particular tax. These bonds are sometimes referred to as tax revenue bonds.

Public bodies frequently issue short-term *anticipation notes* to provide temporary funds until receipt of the proceeds from a new bond issue, tax revenues, or other anticipated income. Another form of short-term, tax-exempt security which many banks purchase is the *project note*. These notes are issued to provide construction funds for urban renewal, neighborhood development, and low-cost housing projects. They are issued under agreement with the Department of Housing and Urban Development, are sold through auctions by that agency, and are guaranteed by the U.S. Government.

Corporate Issues

Commercial banks are permitted to purchase bonds and notes of private corporations if these meet the tests of investment securities. They are not very important in the investment portfolios of commercial banks however. Prior to the 1930s, such securities were relatively important because of the absence of municipal and federal securities and the emphasis placed on income. Now, because of the high income tax rates under which banks operate, taxable revenues from corporate issues are less attractive than the tax-free payments received from municipals.

Bank Underwriting of Municipal Securities

Unlike U.S. government securities which are issued without the services of an underwriter, municipal securities are issued through a competitive bidding process in which commercial banks and other underwriters compete for a given issue. The underwriter offering the bid with the lowest interest cost to the issuer is awarded the right to market the issue. Member banks are prohibited from underwriting assessment bonds or revenue bonds for other than housing, university, or dormitory purposes.

From a bank's standpoint, the most important part of the underwriting process is the preparation of the bid. The announcement of a new bond issue is made in the form of a published *invitation to bid.* The invitation describes the issue and informs prospective bidders of procedures to be followed in submitting bids. If the issue is small, a bank may bid on it without forming an underwriting syndicate. On large issues, syndicates consisting of a number of banks and other underwriters will be formed to spread the risk of underwriting and assist in marketing the issue. For large issues, for example from $100 million to $250 million, a syndicate may include as many as 100 banks and other underwriters, and several syndicates may bid on the issue. Prior to making its bid, an agreement is drawn under which the syndicate spells out the responsibilities and liabilities of syndicate members if a bid is successful.

The first step in determining the bid is *scaling,* that is, determining the reoffering scale, which is the list of yields investors will be offered by the underwriter on the various maturities of the issue. The reoffering scale is determined by conditions in the municipal securities market. The underwriter scales presently outstanding issues of municipal securities of the same quality rating as the one on which the bid is being prepared by listing the yields at which the various maturities of these issues are trading in the market. This process is, in fact, the development of a yield curve for a particular quality group of municipal securities. The underwriter will plan to offer the new issue to the public at yields equal to or slightly higher than those available in the open market.

The next step is the determination of the *coupon structure*—the coupon rates that will be assigned to the various maturities of the bond issue. The coupon structure is not the same as the reoffering scale because the underwriter usually will sell some of the bonds at a price above par and some below par. Setting the coupon rate above or below the scale will result in an offering price above or below par.

The coupon structure is determined in part by what the market will consider attractive, but it is also a factor in the bidding strategy. Putting the highest coupon rates on the shortest maturities results in a lower net interest cost to the issuer. The calculation of the net interest cost as an amount and as a rate is demonstrated in Table 17–1, which depicts a hypothetical bond issue and a bid by the underwriter of 100.50, or $1005 per $1000 bond. The bid price determines the net interest cost and, of course, that bid resulting in the lowest net interest cost will be the one accepted.

The formula used to calculate net interest cost is:

$$\begin{matrix} \text{net} \\ \text{interest} = \\ \text{cost} \end{matrix} \frac{\text{(total interest cost for the life of the issue) less (premium)}}{\text{total number of bond years}}$$

$$\begin{matrix} \text{net} \\ \text{interest} = \\ \text{cost} \end{matrix} \frac{\text{total interest of } \$871,800 \text{ less premium of } \$8,500}{17,900 \text{ bond years}}$$

$$\frac{\$863,300}{17,900} = \$48.229 \text{ net interest cost per } \$1000 \text{ bond per year}$$

$$\frac{\$48.229}{\$1000} = 4.8229 \text{ percent}$$

This formula gives the net interest cost per bond year. It should be noted that bond years are calculated by multiplying the number of years a maturity group will be outstanding by the number of bonds in the group.

The underwriting spread is the difference between the bid and the price at which the underwriter will offer the bonds to the public. The spread is the underwriter's gross profit. If the underwriter is confident of a rapid sale of the issue or if much of it has been presold to investors before the bid is determined, he will consider the risk of buying to be small and will be more aggressive by entering a bid with a small spread—perhaps $8 or $10 per bond. If the issue is not expected to be very attractive or if the underwriter

Table 17–1
Computation of Net Interest Cost to Issuer

Amount	Coupon Rate	Years to Maturity	Bond Years	Coupon in $	Total Interest
$ 50,000	.060	1	50	$60	$ 3,000
50,000	.060	2	100	60	6,000
50,000	.060	3	150	60	9,000
50,000	.060	4	200	60	12,000
100,000	.058	5	500	58	29,000
100,000	.058	6	600	58	34,800
100,000	.058	7	700	58	40,600
100,000	.058	8	800	58	46,400
100,000	.058	9	900	58	52,200
100,000	.058	10	1,000	58	58,000
100,000	.058	11	1,100	58	63,800
100,000	.058	12	1,200	58	69,600
100,000	.058	13	1,300	58	75,400
150,000	.040	14	2,100	40	84,000
150,000	.040	15	2,250	40	90,000
150,000	.040	16	2,400	40	96,000
150,000	.040	17	2,550	40	102,000
$1,700,000			17,900		$871,800

has been unsuccessful in prebid selling efforts, the bid will be made with a much larger spread, perhaps $16 to $18 per bond, to compensate for the greater selling effort that will be required in case the bid is successful.

Besides the underwriting spread from which the bank will derive its profit if the issue is sold as planned when the bid is made, a bank may derive benefit also from public deposits resulting from its underwriting efforts. If it is a participant in an underwriting, a bank may have a deposit stemming directly from the sale of the issue. In addition, if the bank is known for its willingness to make bids on issues of governmental units in its region, the goodwill generated may result in sizeable public deposits.

Trends in Bank Investments

Bank investments have changed significantly over the years, both in relative amount and composition (see Figure 17–1). Investments as a percent of total assets have declined substantially since reaching a high point during World War II. This high level was the result of U.S. government borrowing to finance the war and the dearth of loan demand during the war years. Banks participated heavily in financing the war by increasing holdings of

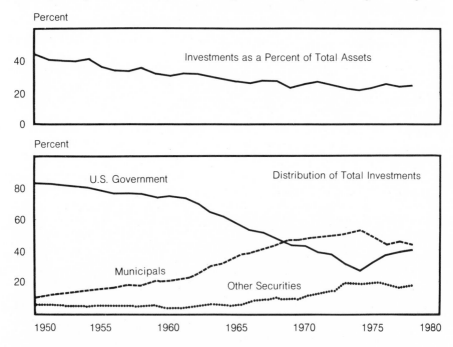

Fig. 17-1 Investments of Commercial Banks. (Source: Federal Deposit Insurance Corporation, Annual Reports.)

U.S. government securities from $22 billion at the end of 1941 to $91 billion at the end of 1945. The entire investment account totaled less than $100 billion in 1945, but this equaled 62 percent of bank assets.

Bank portfolios totaled $254 billion by June 30, 1978, but this was only 21 percent of bank assets. This relative decline resulted from a generally high loan demand since World War II, the expansion of some classes of loans (for example, consumer loans), and the higher rate of earnings that loans normally produce. While the size of the investment account has had a relative decline, the proportion composed of municipal securities has expanded dramatically. In 1945, municipals accounted for only 4.2 percent of the investment account—on June 30, 1978 they made up 45.5 percent.

The most important reason banks have invested so heavily in municipal issues is because of the relatively high returns provided. The interest payments on these issues are not taxed by the federal government or the state governments in many cases. This tax-exempt feature has the approximate effect of doubling the rate of return to banks paying the full corporate tax rate over that of a security with the same taxable interest payment. Of course, because they are tax exempt, market yields on municipals are below those of similar quality taxable issues, but not enough to offset more than part of the tax exemption benefit.

Municipal securities carry more credit risk than do U.S. government issues, and they are less marketable. By increasing the emphasis on municipals, banks have become somewhat less liquid; that is, the investment account embodies more risk as a result of the pursuit of higher earnings. Also, since loans are less liquid than are investments, the diminishing relative size of the investment account points to an even greater decline in the liquidity of bank assets. The significance of this decline was discussed in Chapter 8.

Questions

1. The Comptroller's regulations refer to a process called "overtrading" as an improper investment practice. Overtrading results when a bank engages in a "swap" of one security for another, receiving a price well above market for the security it is eliminating while paying a commensurately higher price for the security it acquires. Why would such a practice have appeal to portfolio managers, and why would the Comptroller consider it inappropriate?

2. How much emphasis should be placed on the ratings of the private rating agencies in selecting municipal bonds for a bank's investment portfolio?

3. Should national banks be allowed to invest in corporate common stocks such as those listed on the New York Stock Exchange?

4. How do Treasury bills differ from Treasury notes?

5. When a bank sells bonds at a loss, it can deduct those losses without limit from

other income in determining federal income taxes. How does this differ from the way individuals and non-financial corporations must treat such losses?

6. Look at the Government bond quotes in the *Wall Street Journal.* What does a quote of, say, 98.14 convert to as the dollar price of a $1,000 bond or note?

7. Notice in the Government bond quotes that the yields to maturity for certain long-term bonds, such as the 3's of February, 1995, are much lower than other issues; for example, the 8–5/8's of August, 1993. Why is this?

8. Notice that the spread—the difference between bid and ask quotations—varies from one Treasury bond to another. Why?

9. Except for a few specified types, banks cannot underwrite revenue bonds, yet they are allowed to acquire such issues for their portfolios. Why do you suppose this restriction on underwriting exists?

10. What is the difference between marketability and quality as these terms apply to debt securities? Can a security be high in one and low in the other? If so, give examples.

Selected References

DARST, DAVID M., *The Complete Bond Book.* New York, McGraw-Hill Book Company, 1975.

FRANCIS, JACK CLARK, *Investments: Analysis and Management,* 2nd edition. New York, McGraw-Hill Book Company, 1976, chs. 7 and 8.

HOFFLAND, DAVID L., "New York and the Municipal Bond Market," *Financial Analysts Journal,* March/April 1977, pp. 36–39.

LEVINE, SUMNER N., (Editor), *Financial Analyst's Handbook I: Portfolio Management.* Homewood, Ill., Dow Jones-Irwin, Inc., 1975, chs. 6, 9, 11, 12, 13, 15, 29, 30 and 33.

MENDELSON, MORRIS, and SIDNEY ROBBINS, *Investment Analysis and Securities Markets,* New York: Basic Books, Inc., 1976, chs. 18–21.

NAGAN, PETER S., "Focus on Investments," *Banking,* monthly.

RABINOWITZ, ALAN, *Municipal Bond Finance and Administration,* New York, Wiley-Interscience, 1969.

ROSS, IRWIN, "Higher Stakes in the Bond-Rating Game," *Fortune,* April, 1976, pp. 132–42.

Salomon Brothers, *An Analytical Record of Yields and Yield Spreads.* New York, Salomon Brothers, 1974.

SHERWOOD, HUGH C., *How Corporate and Municipal Debt is Rated.* New York, John Wiley & Sons, 1976.

Twentieth Century Fund, *The Rating Game,* New York, Twentieth Century Fund, 1974.

18

Trust Services of Commercial Banks

A person's accumulation of wealth, the need for expert management of this wealth, and the desire to pass it on to various beneficiaries have given rise to a multitude of trust services. Trust services are closely related to banking in that such skills as the maintenance of records, safekeeping, the deposit function, financial analysis, and decision making are all attributes of commercial bankers. With the growth of financial assets throughout the nation the market for trust services has grown tremendously.

Trust services result in a *fiduciary* relationship: that is, one party acting for the benefit of another in matters coming within the scope of their relationship and, in most instances, involving the holding of property commonly administered by the trustee for the benefit of a third party or parties. In general, the functions of a trust department may be classified into three broad services: the settlement of estates, the administration of trust and guardianships, and the performance of agencies. Trust services are detailed, highly technical, and "legalistic" in nature, so our approach will be cursory and very general.

Advantages of a Corporate Trustee

Trust services may be performed by individuals or corporations, including the trust departments of commercial banks. Because of the advantages of a corporate trustee over an individual acting in this capacity, most trust services are performed by bank trust departments. These advantages are experience, permanence, financial responsibility, responsiveness to obligations, specialization, group judgment, impartiality, and adaptability. The terms of a trust agreement may be in effect for many years or may in some cases continue in perpetuity; therefore, a trustee must have permanence if the terms of the trust are to be carried out effectively and efficiently. Trusts are limited by common and statutory law. Common law limits a trust to the lives-in-being plus 21 years. Several states by statute limit trusts to what is legally referred to as *measuring lives,* that is, to a term measured by the lives of not more than two persons who are named in the will and who are living at the time of the testator's (one who created the will) death. Trusts established under a will have an average life of from 20 to 25 years. Those established by a donor have a shorter life. Trusts seldom last longer than 40 years. Charitable trusts, can be created for perpetuity however. It is obvious that an individual, who is mortal, cannot serve as a trustee as well as can a corporate entity with continuous existence. Continuous capacity is similar to continuous existence and implies the abilty to perform the terms of a trust agreement. Since a corporation in general has perpetual existence, capable and efficient personnel can be employed to carry out the provisions of the trust and other trust services to which the corporation is obligated. Individuals may become incapacitated or for other reasons—personal or business—find it impossible to perform the services of a trustee without great sacrifice.

Many trusts and trust services involve large sums of money and/or property. People who create trusts or have other trust services to be performed are interested in the financial capacity of the trustee to carry them out. Few individuals have sufficient funds to assure the creator of a trust that they are financially able to meet this test. Trust services and trust agreements must be carried out punctually and with dispatch; consequently, bank trust departments are more responsive to their obligations than would be an individual who has many other obligations.

The volume of trust activity has grown very rapidly in recent years. Probably the main reason for this growth is the high degree of specialization that exists in trust departments. A very important advantage that corporate trustees have over an individual trustee is group judgment, since several technicians—specialists in the fields of law, investments, and taxation—are normally in a better position to render sound judgment and advice than is a single individual. Corporate trustees are also better qualified to act impartially than are individuals. Finally, a corporate trustee with its many specialists is more adaptable than an individual who cannot be expert in all required skills.

Development and Regulation of Trust Services in Commercial Banks

Trust functions were first performed by individuals and insurance companies in this country, and it was not until the demand for fiduciary services became great that trust companies were organized. Although state banks have performed trust services for many years, national banks are relative latecomers to the field. Not until 1913, with the passage of the Federal Reserve Act, were national banks granted the right to perform fiduciary services. At the present time, approximately 4200 banks provide trust services, many of which use the word "trust" in the name of the bank. All banks do not offer trust services since the demand is not great in every area of the country and the cost of operating a trust department is quite high. Trust services are concentrated in banks located in areas where there is centralization of both wealth and population. For example, of the total trust assets of $503 billion held by insured commercial banks at the end of 1977, almost $131 billion were held by nine New York banks.

Since handling trusts and performing trust services involve a great deal of social responsibility, society has seen fit to regulate the performance of these services very closely. Only a few states permit banks, by virtue of their having a charter to carry on commercial banking activities, to render trust services also. Most states require that a state bank must first obtain a special permit or license from the proper state authority to operate a trust department. State banks that are members of the Federal Reserve System must also receive permission from the Board of Governors to perform trust services. In addition to a special permit or license, most states require state banks to make a special deposit of securities with the state treasurer or some other designated state official to guarantee the faithful performance of their duties as a trustee. Trust activities of national banks are under the supervision of the Office of the Comptroller of the Currency. Although this office does not require the pledging of securities or other assets, if national banks operate in states that require the pledging of specific assets, they are obliged to comply with state law.

Trust Services Performed for Individuals

Space does not permit the discussion of all the trustee services rendered to individuals by commercial banks. Only the major functions will be mentioned, which include the settlement of estates, the administration of trusts, serving as guardian and conservator of estates, and performance of agency for individuals.

Settlement of Estates

The property of deceased persons must be distributed in accordance with law. Some persons die *testate,* that is, leaving a will that declares their wishes regarding matters to be attended to after death and normally relates to the disposition of property. Others may die *intestate,* leaving no will. Unless negligible in amount, estates must be settled by an executor or administrator under the direction of a court of law. A person dying testate appoints in his will an executor to carry out his wishes—often the trust department of a commercial bank. The person who settles an estate in which no will existed is called an administrator and is appointed by the court; this responsibility too may fall to the trust department of a commercial bank. In addition to serving as executors and administrators of estates, trust departments may serve in two other capacities: as administrators with the will annexed or as administrators to complete the settlement of an estate. An administrator with the will annexed exists when a will names no executor or when the one named is unwilling or unable, by law or otherwise, to serve, or has died. In these instances, the court will appoint one. An administrator to complete the settlement of an estate exists when an executor or administrator of an estate dies, resigns, or is removed before the estate is fully settled.

The Uniform Probate Code, which was first adopted in Idaho in 1971 and has since been adopted in various forms by several other states, uses the term "personal representative" in place of executor and all the various administrator designations. The Uniform Probate Code was an attempt to simplify and bring uniformity to the complex estate settlement process and its state-by-state variations. At this time the success of the Uniform Probate Code is yet to be determined.

The basic duties of an administrator or an executor are to obtain court authority to act, assemble and safeguard the assets of the estate, pay administrative expenses and debts of the estate, pay taxes due, distribute the net estate, and render personal services to members of the family. Since property must be distributed in accordance with law, a will must be probated: that is, proved to be the last will and testament of the deceased. The executor will receive from the court *letters testamentary,* an official document that authorizes him to proceed with the settlement of the estate. If no will was made,the court must appoint an administrator whose responsibilities are basically the same. Assembling the assets of an estate may be a meticulous and time-consuming process. Bank accounts must be located, brokerage accounts closed, safe deposit boxes opened and the contents surveyed and removed, and life insurance policies collected and presented for payment if payable to the estate. If real estate, growing crops, or livestock are a substantial part of the estate, they must be inventoried and cared for. Business interests might have to be supervised and continued in operation, and household furniture and heirlooms inventoried and protected.

Safeguarding the assets of an estate may become an enormous task. An appraisal must be made by persons skilled in this type of work; if there are perishable goods they must be cared for and disposed of with a minimum of loss. If a business has to be sold, timing of the sale is important in order to secure a satisfactory price; the same is true of the sale of securities. Real property might have to be insured, rented, and cared for so that it would not become nonproductive, lost to the estate, or decline in value. The administrator or executor must arrange for payment of all debts, taxes, and administrative costs of the estate. Funeral expenses, appraiser's and attorney's fees, and court costs must be met. The objective of safeguarding the assets is obviously to preserve the value of the estate.

The next step in settling an estate is to distribute the assets. If a person dies intestate, distribution must be carried out in accordance with the law: that is, so much of the assets will pass to the living spouse, children, grandchildren, and so forth. If there is a will, its provisions must be followed, assuming that they are not in conflict with the laws governing the distribution of property. In addition to these steps, the executor or administrator may have to offer a variety of personal services to the family of the deceased person. Funeral arrangements might become a responsibility. In many instances, the immediate cash needs of the family prove to be a major problem. Obviously, serving as administrator or executor requires special skills and tact.

Administration of Personal Trusts

One of the most important functions performed by trust departments of commercial banks is the administration of personal trusts. A trust arises out of an agreement between the creator of the trust and a trustee and involves the transfer of property from the creator, or trustor, to the trustee who holds title to and administers the property for the benefit of the trustor, a beneficiary, or beneficiaries. Several methods may be employed in the creation of a personal trust, one of which is making a will. This is done by instructing the trustee to hold and administer property and distribute its income to designated beneficiaries and is commonly referred to as a *testamentary trust.* A person may create a *living trust* during his lifetime. In this method, the creator enters into an agreement with the trust department of a commercial bank and delivers to it certain properties—the trust—and the department holds, invests, and disposes of its income and principal in accordance with the agreement. In certain instances the creator may retain some control over the trust, and it is usually revocable and subject to amendment. In some cases the trust is irrevocable, however, and the creator has no control over it. When an irrevocable trust is created, the creator has, in fact, made a gift of the property and it cannot be reclaimed. Gift tax laws apply in such situations.

Many reasons exist for the creation of a personal trust, whether through one's will or with a trust agreement while one is living. A trust allows the owner of property to control its disposition and the distribution of income earned from the property long after death. A trust can relieve the beneficiary, perhaps an aged spouse, of the burden and responsibility of caring for the property and yet allow him or her to enjoy the benefits of the property. The beneficiaries may be children who are unable to care for the assets; possibly the beneficiary is a "spendthrift," and the creator feels that if the property were to be given in one lump sum it would soon be consumed irresponsibly and the beneficiary would then live in poverty. In other cases, the beneficiary might be incompetent or otherwise incapacitated.

Other factors may influence the creation of a trust. Assets placed in a living trust ordinarily do not go through probate on the death of the creator. If the trust does not continue after death, then the trust assets are distributed by the terms of the trust. Thus the period of probate, which at times might extend four or five years after death, is avoided. The probate fee is also avoided. As the living trust is a private agreement between the creator and the trustee, so the nature and extent of trust assets are never made public. Probating an estate is a matter of public record, however, and all assets going through probate are disclosed. Thus the privacy afforded by a trust may be valuable to many families.

Prior to the Tax Reform Act of 1976, there were clear-cut tax advantages for persons of means in creating trusts whereby on the death of the creator the trust assets were managed for the benefit of, perhaps, the surviving spouse. On the death of the spouse, the assets then might distribute to the children. Ownership never vested in the surviving spouse, so no estate tax resulted on the second death as would have been the case if the survivor had inherited ownership of the assets on the first death. The Tax Reform Act of 1976 did not eliminate all tax advantages of generation-skipping trusts, but it did complicate the estate planning process whereby the decision is made whether or not to use a trust. One important function of the trust officer is to assist individuals in estate planning.

Serving as Guardian and Conservator of Estates

In most states a minor is considered legally incapable of managing and holding property. When minors inherit property a guardian is appointed to hold it for their benefit; frequently, this responsibility falls to the trust department of a commercial bank. There are two kinds of guardians, a guardian of property and one of the person. Where this is the case, trust departments serve in most states only in the capacity as guardian of the property. As the term implies, a conservator of an estate has the objective of preventing the wasting of an estate. This arrangement usually arises when a property owner becomes physically incapacitated and is unable to care for and manage property. Guardianships and conservatorships are created by a court of law, and the fiduciary must perform them in accordance with statutory law and under the jurisdiction of the court. Trust departments of commercial banks perform these functions, but they do not constitute an appreciable part of their business.

Performance of Agencies

Trust departments perform agency services for individuals, the most important of which are custodian, managing agent, and attorney-in-fact. An agency differs considerably from a trust. In a trust, property is transferred to the trustee; in an agency arrangement the title to the property does not pass to the agent normally but remains with the owner. An agency exists when a person, referred to as the *principal* in legal terms, authorizes another, called the *agent,* to act on his behalf. An agency is a contractual arrangement, and before acting in this capacity a trust department of a commercial bank requires an agency agreement between the two parties or a letter of instructions from the principal. Agencies are generally less structured than are trusts and can be terminated with less formality.

One form of agency is a custodianship. In a custodianship the trust department accepts and cares for certain properties. For example, securities are accepted, and the trust department collects the income and notifies the customer of all collections. In addition, arrangements can be made for the trust department to collect the principal on matured bonds, notes, or mortgages; exchange securities; and even buy, sell, receive, and deliver securities.

A managing agency is an enlargement on the custodianship. Not only does the trust department have the authority to hold securities and collect the income but it also has the authority to manage the principal's investments or business affairs. The trust department can be given the authority to pay various bills for the principal, make recommendations on the purchase and sale of securities, pay taxes, renew insurance policies, receive income from all sources, and exercise stock rights. It would be difficult to mention all the services that can be performed by a managing agency since they are "tailor-made" arrangements and can be all-inclusive, if such is desirable. It is possible, under a managing agency, for a person to enter into an agreement where his total investment portfolio is handled by a trust department while he sojourns for a year on the Riviera.

An attorney-in-fact is one who has been given authority by a principal to do certain legal functions on behalf of the principal. Attorneys-in-fact are agents and frequently exist under a custodianship and managing agency arrangement. An attorney-in-fact is created by the principal giving to the trust department the *power of attorney.* Trust departments usually receive and prefer special powers rather than general powers. Such special powers would include the right to draw checks; endorse notes, checks, and other documents requiring endorsement; borrow funds; assign stocks and bonds; and execute deeds and leases. Sometimes a trust department acting in the capacity of custodian or managing agent is also appointed as an attorney-in-fact.

Trust Services Performed for Businesses

Just as they perform trust services for individuals, trust departments of commercial banks do so for businesses. These major functions are administration of trusts, performance of agencies, and liquidation of business enterprises. Business firms make use of commercial banks' trust services for several reasons. One major reason is the skills possessed by trust departments. Some large corporations have capable people who could possibly perform these functions, but this would be an uneconomic use of personnel; therefore, they look to the trust department of their bank. The services of a trust department are also used in some situations because a corporate trustee is required by law.

Most trusts established by corporations are for pension, profit sharing, and stock-bonus purposes; for bond issues; for redemption and sinking funds; and for the issuance of collateral trust bonds or certificates. Many businesses have established pension and profit-sharing plans and stock-bonus trusts to provide security for their employees' old age and retirement, stimulate higher productivity on the part of the work force, reduce labor turnover, care for employees who become incapacitated, and to enable employees to participate in the ownership of the firm. It is also a way of increasing payments to employees since they do not pay taxes on the employer's contributions to most plans until the funds are paid out; at that time, the employee will probably be in a lower income bracket. This feature has done much to encourage corporations to establish pension and profit-sharing trusts, and they are of great value to employees and also to the employer in retaining competent help.

The various plans designed for the benefit of employees may take several forms, but usually when the trust department of a commercial bank accepts a trust of this type and it is a self-funded plan, the trust department invests the funds, keeps records on how much each employee is to receive, and makes payments to employees in accordance with the trust agreement. If the plan is operated on an insured basis, the trust department purchases individual annuity contracts for each employee covered by the plan out of the contributions made by the employer. Employee benefit plans are not limited to private corporations, of course, and the administration of public plans—those for city, county, state, fire and police department, and other public employees—constitutes an important part of trust business.

Employee benefit plans of all types comprise an important part of trust business. Of the $503 billion of trust assets at the end of 1977, almost $232 billion was in employee benefit accounts. The competition to be trustee and investment manager—often the functions are separated—of large corporate or public employee benefit plans is intense. In such a competition a trust department may find the potential customer is being courted by several other trust departments or bank-holding company investment subsidiaries from various parts of the United States, by investment counselors and by insurance companies. In such competitions many factors are important, but investment philosophies and performance records usually receive primary attention. If the bank's trust department is not named investment manager, it may still be named trustee and perform all functions except investment management. In some cases a trust department may act as trustee for a large corporate retirement fund which has several investment managers.

A common trust function performed by commercial banks is that of trustee in connection with a bond issue or what is usually referred to as *trustee under indenture.* When corporations borrow money for long periods, bonds, notes, or debentures are generally issued. If these securities are secured, and they are normally, the question arises as to who will hold the security. This is a logical function of a trust department under an agreement designed to protect both the bondholder and the corporation that issues the bonds. The trustee under the trust indenture usually has legal title to the assets on which the lien is imposed, acts on behalf of the bondholders, and has the power to foreclose on the pledged property should the obligor default on the payment of principal or interest. Many activities are performed with this type of trust including the transferring of ownership of securities; making payments of interest and principal; releasing mortgaged property; handling sinking funds that have been created for the redemption of bonds; and maintaining records and making reports to bondholders, the issuing corporation, regulatory bodies, and stock exchanges. If the securities issued are collateral trust bonds, the trust department holds title to the stocks and bonds pledged as security. In some instances the trustee may issue equipment trust certificates, which are credit instruments secured by equipment such as railway cars and engines. Title to the equipment is transferred to the trust department, and the railroad pays a rental for the use of such equipment to the trustee, who in turn makes payment to the holders of the certificates. The Trust Indenture Act of 1939 gave to the Securities and Exchange Commission the power to approve or disapprove trust agreements providing for the issuance of debt instruments that are offered publicly in an amount in excess of $1 million for corporations other than railroads and charities. This legislation has done much to increase the amount of trust business for commercial banks' trust departments.

Trust departments perform several agencies for business firms. They serve as transfer agents, concerned with transferring the ownership of a corporation's stock. Serving as an exchange agent is very similar to being a transfer agent. When performing this service, the trustee receives one kind of securities and delivers another type in accordance with a prearranged plan. The exchange might involve a stock split, a stock conversion, combination of two or more business firms, or the distribution of securities arising out of a reorganization. In the capacity of a registrar, trust departments are responsible for seeing that stock is not issued in excess of the amount authorized. Since a trustee cannot act in the capacity of both a transfer agent and registrar for stock listed on the New York Stock Exchange, there is an independent check on the shares of stock issued by a corporation. Corporations with many stockholders are not particularly interested in handling payment of dividends on their stock because of the great volume of intermittent work; therefore, they turn to the trust department of a commercial bank to serve as a dividend-disbursing agent. The trust department receives payment from the corporation when dividends are due and in turn prepares the checks and mails each stockholder his dividend payment. Trust departments perform several other types of agencies for corporations such as acting as an agent for the redemption of preferred stock and subscription warrants.

Trust Services Performed for Charitable Institutions and Others

Trust departments of commercial banks provide trust services for parties other than individuals and businesses. They may serve as trustee of community trusts which derive their funds in the form of gifts and bequests from citizens of the community. These trusts are created for purposes such as promoting research; assisting schools and charitable and benevolent institutions; care of the sick, aged, and needy; aiding in the rehabilitation of victims of alcohol and narcotics; care of wayward or delinquent persons; public recreation; and improving working conditions. Trusts are established by civic clubs to award scholarships to students. Many of our educational institutions receive a portion of their income from trusts that have been created for such purpose by wealthy people. The same is true of many of our hospitals, art centers, orphanages, and homes for the aged.

Trust departments also perform agencies for parties other than individuals and businesses. They act as an agent for endowments and in so doing become a managing agency. Trust departments sometimes act as agent for municipal and state governments, serving as paying agents for the bonds issued and sometimes countersigning the bonds, which authenticates them. As paying agents, they are also in a position to see that the correct amount is issued. Since relatively large deposits sometimes accompany the performance of paying agent for municipalities, this type of trustee service is sought by trust departments of commercial banks.

Responsibilities of Trust Departments

A considerable amount of responsibility is involved in performing trust services. The basic duties and responsibilities of a trust department to the parties they serve have been laid down by statutory law, government regulations, and court decisions over the years; because of the extent of this subject matter, space does not permit a thorough analysis. One outstanding work on trust services has stated that "the basic responsibilities of a trustee are (1) to be faithful, (2) to conform to instructions, (3) to be competent and (4) to be diligent."[1] Faithfulness, in the performance of trust services, implies many things. The trustee should be loyal to the creator and beneficiary and never be motivated in any of its dealings by self-interest. Reasonable charges for the performance of services offered are acceptable, but the use of trust funds for personal gain is absolutely prohibited. A trusteeship is an agreement involving confidence and trust; and the trustee is legally bound to adhere to the agreement, must have high standards of honesty and business conduct, and is expected to defend the agreement if necessary.

A trust department must follow the instructions and terms of the trust agreement, will, court order, or agency agreement under which it performs. It cannot accept a responsibility and then decide that other actions would be better. This does not mean, however, that in the case of some unusual events changes could not be made in its performance. If such changes are desirable, the trustee is required to go to court and seek permission to make them. It is impossible to foresee all contingencies that may occur when the agreement is drawn, but care should be exercised so that they can be met, as far as humanly possible.

Individuals and businesses who use trust services and the courts expect and are entitled to a high degree of competence. Trust departments cannot plead ignorance or forgetfulness. Trustees are required and expected to

---

[1]American Institute of Banking, *Trust Department Services* (New York: American Bankers Association, 1954), p. 172.

exercise constant diligence to accomplish the objectives of a trust or agency agreement.

These responsibilities are great, but it must not be assumed that trustees are guarantors. They cannot perform miracles, nor are they expected to do so. They are, however, guarantors if losses arise because of their own negligence. A trustee who leaves securities out of the vault that should obviously have been kept there or fails to collect interest on a bond as instructed would be held liable. In general, a trustee is charged to use a degree of diligence, prudence, care, and management that men of discretion and intelligence would have used in the performance of a similar task. In evaluating this highly debatable matter, the courts, if called on to render a judgment, would look at all the facts surrounding the occurrence of a disputed act. It would not "second guess" the trustee. If a trust department invested a reasonable portion of a particular trust in a security today that was considered a highly acceptable investment by prudent men and it suddenly declined in value several years hence, the trustee would not be held liable. If, however, the trustee had the right of discretionary management and knew, as did others, that a particular investment was not good, yet did not attempt to rid the trust of this investment and purchase something more desirable, it would be at fault.

Trust Investment Objectives and Policies

Obviously one of the great responsibilities of a trustee in handling trusts is to invest funds properly. Each individual trust account has its own unique features and requirements, so each account should have its own specific investment objective. A high level of safe, secure income may be most suitable for a $100,000 trust managed for the benefit of a 90-year-old widow, while the pursuit of growth through a portfolio consisting mostly of a diversified group of common stocks may be most suitable for a 40-year-old businessman with a large income from his profession. Whatever the nature of the trust account, the trust department should seek the highest return it can attain while recognizing the constraints limiting the selection of investment assets. Many constraints may be imposed on the investment of trust funds by law, by the trust contract itself, by the type of trust, and by the underlying investment philosophy of the trust department. Trust agreements may specifically state what investments shall be made and held. Others may state that the investment function shall be carried out in accordance with state law, and finally, some agreements make no provision regarding this matter whatsoever. In some accounts, the investment responsibility is shared with another party who could be the creator of the trust, a cotrustee, or beneficiary. In a few accounts, the trust department has no investment authority.

For years trustees operated under *legal lists:* that is, lists of investments spelled out in the laws of the various states as being eligible for investment by trustees. However, with the passage of time it became evident that governments had no monopoly on investment knowledge and judgment and that to attain the objectives of many trust agreements greater freedom should be given to trustees. Because of this feeling, practically all states have liberalized such laws and have introduced what is commonly called the *prudent-man rule.* The prudent-man rule is an outgrowth of various court decisions and has been adopted either by court decision or by statute. It was well defined in the famous court decision of *Harvard College and Massachusetts General Hospital v. Francis Amory* in 1830 when the Supreme Judicial Court of Massachusetts said:

> All that can be required of a trustee to invest is that he shall conduct himself faithfully and exercise a sound discretion. He is to observe how men of prudence, discretion and intelligence manage their own affairs, not in regard to speculation but in regard to the permanent disposition of their funds, considering the probable income, as well as the probable safety of the capital to be invested.

In justification of this reasoning the court stated that:

> Trustees are justly and uniformly considered favorably, and it is of great importance to bereaved families and orphans that they should not be held to make good losses in the depreciation of stocks or the failure of the capital itself, which they held in trust, provided they conduct themselves honestly and discreetly and carefully, according to the existing circumstances in the discharge of their trusts. If this were held otherwise, no prudent man would run the hazard of losses which might happen without any neglect or breach of good faith.[2]

While prudent man statutes are at the state level, the federal government made an entrance into the area of trustee investment standards with the passage of the Employee Retirement Income Security Act of 1974 (ERISA). While ERISA pertains only to the administration of private retirement plans, and thus does not directly affect other trust business, it sets forth a prudent-man standard that all trust departments must observe in the investment of private retirement fund assets. Many have called it a "prudent expert" standard, since it calls for evaluation of trustees against trustees. Section 404 of the act states that the trustee shall exercise ". . . the care, skill, prudence, and diligence under the circumstances then prevailing that a

---

[2]26 *Massachusetts Reports* 447.

prudent man acting in like capacity and familiar with such matters would use in the conduct of an enterprise of a like character and with like aims."

Trust departments are charged with using good judgment and diligence in making investments of trust funds, with due regard to both the safety of principal and the production of income. Although this concept may appear somewhat vague, it becomes more concrete when one considers the problems of actual investment. Trustees should not err on the side of safety by investing exclusively in short-term U.S. government securities, nor should they emphasize income and possible gains to the extent of placing all the funds in securities with great credit risk. Trustees must "hew a fine line"— they must employ diversification and prudence in investing and perform consistently with the objectives of their numerous trust agreements and managing agencies.

Liabilities of Fiduciaries

Trust departments assume great liability in the administration of trusts. When losses occur, the court may impose a surcharge: that is, require the fiduciary to pay to the beneficiary either the asset or assets that were lost, plus the income that would have been earned or an amount equal to the damage suffered. In other words, a surcharge restores the benficiary's interest to what it would have been if the fiduciary had not failed in the performance of duty. The major reasons for surcharging are as follows:

Breaches of trust for which fiduciaries are always held liable are:

1 Fraud, such as misappropriation of the corpus or income for the benefit of others than the heirs or beneficiaries. This type of breach is not only surchargeable against the fiduciary, but makes him liable also to criminal prosecution.
2 Failure to pay taxes due.
3 Failure to reinvest trust funds for an unreasonable length of time, thereby causing loss of income to the trust.

Acts of negligence or omissions of duty include:

1 Making an unauthorized investment that gives rise to loss (*State v. Washburn*, Conn. 187, 34 Atl. 1034 [1896]).
2 Failure to diversify investments as authorized by the instrument or law, when this failure results in undue losses to the trust. (*West v. Bialson*, 365 Mo. 1103, 293, S.W. 2d 369 [1956]).
3 Carelessness in permitting an agent or co-trustee to breach the trust instrument, which causes losses to the trust fund. (*Cred v. McAleer*, 275 Mass. 353, N.E. 761 [1931]).
4 Failure to collect rents or other income when due, thereby depriving the trust of income.

5 Retaining securities or other assets for an unreasonable time after they fall below the standards for trust investment, or holding too long securities that when received in the trust, were ineligible for investment of trust funds. (*Babbit v. Fidelity Trust Co.*, 72 N.J. Eq. 745, 66 Atl. 1076 [1907].[3]

Size of Trust Activities

The amount of trust business conducted by banks is quite large. The amount of all trust assets held by insured commercial banks in 1977, as well as the distribution of assets by type of trust account is presented in Table 18–1. The $503 billion in trust assets were approximately 33 percent greater than the amount held in 1973. The largest type of trust account in 1977 was trusts established for employee benefits such as pension, profit sharing, and stock bonus plans. Employee benefit plans have shown rapid growth in recent years. A large portion of the assets listed in Table 18–1 was in the form of financial securities. Approximately 50 percent of trust assets were in the form of common stocks.

Common Trust Funds

A unique innovation in handling small trusts is the common trust fund, a single trust made up of funds drawn from a number of smaller trusts, each of which acquires a share of the principal and income of the common trust fund in proportion to the amount invested. Participation in the common trust fund is represented by units. Additional units are issued to participating trusts at their net asset value, which is determined by dividing the existing number of units into the market value of the fund, and shares may be redeemed at net asset value at various predetermined evaluation dates. Since a trust department performs no selling function, no charge is imposed when a trust becomes part of a common trust fund. The income of a common trust fund is exempt from taxation; only the income to each participating trust is taxed.

The major problems associated with handling small trusts are diversification of investments and costs of administration. All trusts need diversification, which is difficult to achieve with small trusts. Small trusts, too, may require just as much of a trust department's time as do large ones; hence, the costs of administration become important. The common trust fund is an answer to both these problems. It was the need for efficiency in the handling of small trusts that brought about broad usage of common trust

[3] *Financial Handbook,* fourth edition, revised printing, edited by Jules I. Bogen. Copyright © 1968 The Ronald Press Company, New York.

Table 18–1

Trust Assets of Insured Commercial Banks and Asset Distribution
by Type of Trust Account, 1977 (in thousands of dollars)

		Trusts and Estates			Agencies		
		Employee Benefit	Personal Trusts	Estates	Subtotal	Employee Benefit	All Others	Total
U.S. Government and Agency Obligations	1	23,237,140	15,230,009	1,791,369	40,258,519	5,457,538	12,088,675	57,804,733
State, County, Municipal Obligations	2	120,481	21,300,909	807,287	22,228,677	65,538	9,549,389	31,843,604
Other Obligations	3	48,770,207	20,440,469	1,177,255	70,387,933	15,056,547	14,994,153	100,438,628
Common Stocks	4	104,330,071	95,256,795	5,027,195	204,614,062	12,807,751	35,204,111	252,625,923
Preferred Stocks	5	952,221	2,101,840	132,282	3,186,341	190,721	907,332	4,284,398
Real Estate Mortgages	6	2,125,873	2,618,695	350,437	5,095,008	2,075,947	548,848	7,719,803
Real Estate	7	2,064,382	9,548,358	2,334,683	13,947,423	139,581	2,082,703	16,169,707
Savings and Loan Association Accounts	8	858,687	743,859	258,581	1,861,128	84,413	277,628	2,223,168
Time Deposits Own Bank*	9	1,963,120	2,621,279	945,376	5,529,772	213,330	2,812,324	8,555,430
Time Deposits Other Banks	10	3,805,827	1,254,108	279,197	5,339,132	305,762	1,070,065	6,714,959
Demand Deposits Own Bank	11	495,404	1,199,955	248,571	1,943,927	31,086	402,021	2,377,033
Demand Deposits Other Banks	12	19,917	107,420	7,389	134,727	1,519	12,553	148,799
Miscellaneous	13	6,418,864	3,192,646	600,443	10,211,957	226,456	1,370,267	11,808,682
Total Assets	14	195,162,201	175,616,340	13,960,057	384,738,608	36,656,192	81,320,082	502,714,881
Total Number of Accounts	15	331,892	885,314	105,684	1,322,890	14,683	143,509	1,481,082
Bank Record Count								4,156
R/C Total Assets								934,566,096

*Includes 1,183,606 held in time deposit open accounts for reserve purposes only.

Source: Board of Governors of the Federal Reserve System, Federal Deposit Insurance Corporation, and Office of the Comptroller of the Currency, *Trust Assets of Insured Commercial Banks—1977*, Washington, D.C., 1978.

funds in the 1930s and 1940s. However, when Regulation 9 of the Comptroller of the Currency was originated in 1962, replacing Regulation F of the Board of Governors of the Federal Reserve System as the main regulatory instrument for national bank trust departments, it removed the size limit on the amount of participation a trust could have in a common trust fund. The only size limitation imposed by Regulation 9 is that no trust can hold more than 10 percent of the units of a common trust fund.

The earliest common trust funds were almost all balanced funds. These portfolios consisted of stocks and bonds in some relatively constant ratio, say 40 percent stocks and 60 percent bonds, and most trust departments had only one fund. All trusts that participated in the fund had no choice as to asset mix. Over the years, trust departments developed separate funds for various categories of assets. Now a trust department may have two or more stock funds, each different in its emphasis on seeking growth or income; a taxable bond fund (or a bond and mortgage fund); a municipal bond fund producing income exempt from federal income taxes; a money market fund composed of short-term, highly liquid assets for temporary placement of money; and any number of even more specialized funds. With a variety of common trust funds, a given trust can have its investments tailored to its own needs by placing whatever amount seems appropriate in each of two or more funds.

Trust Department Organization

Many different organization plans have been created for trust department operations, depending, obviously, on the amount and kind of trust business performed. Reference has already been made to the requirement that trust work be kept separate from the commercial banking activities. In large banks that have a substantial amount of trust business, this requirement has resulted in an entirely separate department located in quarters apart from the other banking activities. However, in small banks with a small amount of trust business this is not feasible or physically possible. In many small banks that have trust powers, one officer may perform all the trust work along with his other duties.

In very large banks where the amount of trust work is counted in the millions of dollars, the trust organization becomes quite detailed and specialized. For illustration, a hypothetical organization chart for a large trust department that might be found in a large bank is presented (see Figure 18–1). The executive trust officer is responsible for the successful and efficient operation of the department and concerned primarily with the formulation and implementation of trust policy, along with other administrative officers of the bank and the trust department. The trust committee, which

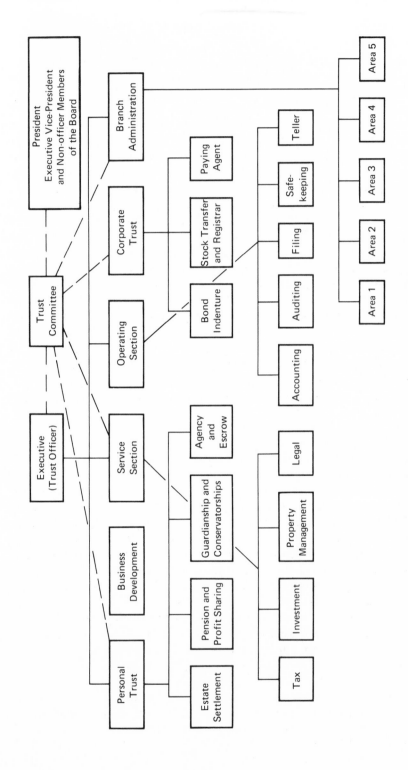

Fig. 18-1 Hypothetical organization of a trust department of a large commercial bank.

must review and approve many of the activities of the trust department, is composed of the trust officer, possibly the executive vice-president, some of the officers of the department such as an attorney skilled in investments, and an officer from the personal and corporate trust divisions.

In our hypothetical example the work of the trust department has been divided into six broad divisions or areas of operation. The personal trust division is concerned with estate settlement, the administration of personal and pension and profit-sharing trusts, guardianships and conservatorships, and personal agencies such as custody and agency management. The corporate division handles bond indentures, stock transfer and registration, and acts as a paying agent. The service section serves all divisions that need legal advice, tax and investment information, and real estate management. The operating section is responsible for accounting, auditing, filing, safekeeping of the properties held by the trust department, and providing teller services. The business development section handles advertising, personal representation and contacts, and estate planning, a very important part of the trust department if it is to expand and operate profitably.

Fees of Trust Departments

Trust departments of commercial banks are compensated for their trustee services by fees which are in many instances, especially in settling estates, established by statute or by probate courts. Most agency fees, however, are negotiated, and correctly so, since the work involved varies considerably, making the problem of established rates by law difficult, if not impossible. Trustee fees may consist of annual charges on the income of a trust, annual commissions on principal, and, in some instances, a commission collected on the principal when the trust is terminated. Fees are far from uniform throughout the country and the variability makes generalization hazardous. However, rates normally charged for handling personal trusts range from .5 to .75 percent of the principal annually. For a managing agency consisting of stocks and bonds similar to those held by personal trusts, the cost would be about the same. If the agency consisted of mortgages, notes, and contracts involving some additional supervision and expense, the cost would be slightly higher; if the trust department's function were to manage real estate properties and a business involving even greater activity, the fee would be still higher. For the performance as executor or administrator, the charges permitted by most states are graduated. In Oregon, for example, the fees permitted are 7 percent on the first $1,000 of property for which the executor or administrator is responsible, 4 percent of the next $9,000, 3 percent on the next $40,000, and 2 percent on all above $50,000. Thus, for serving as executor or administrator of an estate of $50,000, the charge would be $1,630; for one of $400,000, the charge would be $8,630.

It is an accepted fact among commercial banks that a substantial volume of trust business is necessary before a trust department is a profitable undertaking. This is because of the relatively large amount of fixed expense or overhead that trust departments must have in the form of capable personnel, which may be termed *high-priced talent.* Even though a trust department may have only a small amount of trust business, its ability to perform must be assured. The liability involved in providing trust services is too great to settle for inefficient personnel. Trust services are highly personal, and as a result the cost of operating a trust department closely parallels the cost of personnel. Some banks have capable personnel but unused capacity; they have decided to operate on this basis in anticipation of a volume of trust business that will warrant such an expenditure. Banks feel they must prove their ability to perform trust services before trust business will be forthcoming. In general, corporate accounts are more profitable than are personal accounts since a more constant application of detailed knowledge in the fields of investment, taxes, law, etc., must be applied. Some banks probably operate trust departments at a loss but feel their services will not be complete without trust services, and some probably operate at a loss but do not realize it because of the absence of an adequate system of cost accounting. As trust business expands, and there are several indications that it will, more banks will find their services a desirable and profitable phase of commercial banking.

Conflict of Interest Questions

Because of the great variety of trust accounts, the large number of customer relationships and account objectives, and the extensive amount of information to which trust departments become privileged, conflict-of-interest questions arise frequently. Such questions may also arise because the trust department, like the rest of the bank, wants to operate its activities at a profit.

Many trust departments that operate at a profit do so only because of a credit received from the commercial side of the bank for demand deposit balances of trust accounts. These balances earn nothing for the individual trust accounts but are usable funds to the commercial side of the bank. It has been asked whether such balances are at times larger than needed to operate the trust accounts efficiently.

The Hunt Commission made several recommendations directed at possible conflicts of interest.[4] It recommended that rules be adopted that would

[4] *The Report of the President's Commission on Financial Structure and Regulation* (Washington, D.C., Government Printing Office, December 1971), pp. 101–2.

prevent trust department investment managers from having access to commercial department credit information in banks with total assets over $200 million. This recommendation is based on the belief that access to such information can give trust investors unfair advantage over other investors. In small banks, the access to credit information is not likely to produce advantages because small banks seldom lend to large, publicly held corporations. This is an interesting recommendation because, in a very real sense, it would reduce the free flow of information that could be vital for effective performance. However, in October, 1977, the Comptroller of the Currency proposed "Chinese Wall" legislation to prevent national bank trust departments from using inside information material in its investment decisions.

One important recommendation of the Hunt Commission was that appropriate regulation be implemented to assure that brokerage commissions generated by the trust department not be used to attract or hold deposit balances or loans of brokerage firms with the commercial division of the bank. In the past, banks have allocated trust department securities transactions to brokerage firms in accordance with the broker's volume of deposits and other business done with the commercial division of the banks.

Recently some concern has been expressed about the concentration of trust assets. Charges have been made that bank trust departments are in a position to control effectively many large corporations if they wish by voting shares which they hold in trust accounts. The accuracy of such charges is open to dispute—two basic questions must be answered before such a conclusion can be reached. First, what amount of stock is necessary to exercise control; second, if control is possible, does it exist? The amount of stock necessary for control has concerned researchers for years. An early study on the subject of economic power in corporate finance admitted that the percentage of stock needed for control of a company varied widely, but it arbitrarily selected 20 percent as a criterion.[5] This figure was lowered to 10 percent by another researcher[6] and in a staff report of the Committee on Banking and Currency of the U.S. House of Representatives a figure of 5 percent was used.[7] Obviously, by lowering the percentage, such charges take on more credence. The use of 5 percent as a criterion of control by the staff of the Committee on Banking and Currency was not scientifically explained or supported by empirical data. The subcommittee arrived at the percentage when authorizing the study before the research was conducted. On this basis, the House committee found that trust departments of one or

[5]A. A. Berle and Gardner C. Means, *The Modern Corporation and Private Property* (New York, Macmillan Co., 1932), p. 93.

[6]R. J. Larner. "Ownership and Control in the 200 Largest Non-financial Corporations," *American Economic Review*, September 1966, p. 779.

[7]U.S. Congress, House, Subcommittee on Domestic Finance, Committee on Banking and Currency, *Commercial Banks and Their Trust Activities: Emerging Influence on the American Economy*, vol. I and II, 90th Congress 2d sess., 1968.

more banks held a minimum of 5 percent of the stock of 29 percent of the 500 largest corporations of the nation. Although this may be true, it does not prove control since it does not take into consideration whether bank trust departments had the right to vote the stock in question. Although trust departments hold stock, it does not follow that they exercise sole voting rights of the stock held. In the first place, they may not have the right to vote the stock. Secondly, they might be permitted to vote the stock only with the consent of a cotrustee or after consulting with the beneficial owner. Finally, they might hold stock that has no voting rights. Accurate data on the amount of stock over which banks have exclusive voting rights are not available, but some estimates made by trust officers range from 37 to 50 percent of the stock held.[8] Should these estimates be correct, the amount of control implied by the staff study would certainly be reduced. Despite the absence of data regarding control, the Hunt Commission recommended that corporate trustees be required to file annual reports of trust holdings with appropriate regulatory authorities. It was apparently felt that a requirement to report trust holdings would reveal the potential influence of trust departments and thus discourage abuse.

Other conflict of interest questions may arise regarding possible preferential investment treatment for some trust accounts, the purchase of assets such as mortgages from the commercial side of the bank to be placed in trust accounts, and relationships with securities brokers.[9]

Questions

1. Why is probate normally required for a will?
2. What are some reasons why a person might name a bank trust department as executor of his estate rather than, say, his cousin Bob or aunt Lucy?
3. What are some reasons for the concentration of trust assets in banks in the eastern United States?
4. How does a trust differ from an agency?
5. How can the investments of a trust be tailored to the specific needs of that trust and still consist entirely of common trust fund units?
6. What are some possible conflicts of interest resulting from the trust department being part of the bank?
7. What may be some of the major reasons for the low profitability of many trust departments?

[8]James S. Byrne, "Concentration Begets Investigation Into Institutions, Bank Trust Departments," *American Banker*, July 28, 1970.

[9]Edward S Herman, "Conflicts of Interest: Commercial Bank Trust Departments," (New York, The Twentieth Century Fund, 1975).

8.　If trust business is not very profitable for many banks, why would those banks continue to have trust departments?

9.　From what sources, besides other bank trust departments, would the most competition for the various types of trust business be likely to come?

SELECTED REFERENCES

American Institute of Banking, *Trust Functions and Services.* New York, American Bankers Association, 1971.

GREEN, DONALD S., and MARY SCHUELKE, *The Trust Activities of the Banking Industry.* Chicago, Association of Reserve City Bankers, 1975.

KENNEDY, JOSEPH C., and ROBERT I. LANDAU, *Corporate Trust Administration and Management,* 2d ed. New York, New York, University Press, 1975.

KENNEDY, WALTER, and PHILIP F. SEARLE, *The Management of a Trust Department.* Boston, Bankers Publishing Co., 1976.

MACE, MYLES L. and CHARLES T. STEWART, "Standards of Care for Trustees," *Harvard Business Review,* January-February 1976, pp. 14–16+.

STEPHENSON, GILBERT THOMAS *Estates and Trusts,* 2d ed. New York, Appleton-Century-Crofts, Inc., 1965.

Trust and Estates. Monthly, all issues.

United States Comptroller of the Currency, *Regulation 9. Fiduciary Powers of National Banks, Collective Investment Funds, and Disclosure of Trust Department Assets,* as amended April 25, 1975. Washington, D.C., U.S. Government Printing Office.

19

International Banking

In addition to the usual domestic activities of commercial banks with which we have thus far been concerned, many banks provide international banking services. Although not as important in dollar amounts as the domestic side of banking, international activities of commercial banks have grown phenomenally in recent years. The types of international services offered by banks have expanded, the volume of services has increased, and the number of banks providing these services has multiplied. In general, international banking includes all those services demanded by customers engaged in international trade, investment, and travel, and in reality is an extension of the services provided in domestic banking.

In providing international banking services to customers, several avenues are open to banks. They may have an *international department* which specializes exclusively in international banking services. A bank with an international department would have several strategically located correspondent banks in foreign countries through which the various services would be provided. Banks may have branches and/or subsidiaries located abroad through which the international services are offered. With this type of arrangement, a much broader array of services can be provided. Although a bank with an international department is able to engage in international banking, a bank with branches abroad has greater flexibility and is in a position to provide more personalized services. A branch and/or subsidiary arrangement, for example, would be better able to accept and service deposits (a large part of which would be denominated in the money of the host country) of foreign nationals and Americans abroad. Moreover, the bank with branches abroad would, in general, be in a better position to lend to (or invest in) business firms, governments, and individuals in foreign countries.

A final arrangement is termed a *representative office,* where a representative is maintained abroad to give financial advice and assist customers in their borrowing and depositing activities with the domestic bank. A representative office does not accept deposits or make loans abroad. It may be maintained because the country in which it is located has not granted a franchise for the establishment of a branch, or the domestic bank has not yet decided to establish a branch, possibly because of insufficient banking business to maintain a full-fledged branch. In other words, it may be an interim arrangement.

Development of International Banking

International banking is a recent development in the United States. For many years the financing of international trade was dominated by European institutions. From the twelfth to the mid-sixteenth century, banks in Italy were supreme in the area of international finance. Banks in Belgium and Holland then became important, and soon after the establishment of the Bank of England, Great Britain became the center of international finance —a role that was maintained until World War II. Banks in the United States were slow in entering into the financing of international trade primarily because of the lack of capital and the great need for domestic financing. Also, the momentum of an early start on the part of European banking houses was of no little consequence. Finally, the early prohibitions against national banks establishing foreign branches and the acceptance of bills of exchange precluded a large part of the banking system from financing international commercial transactions. Although state-chartered banks were free to engage in international banking, as were private unincorporated banks, the aggregate amount conducted by these institutions was not great prior to World War I.

With the passage of the Federal Reserve Act in 1913, the door was open to American banks to engage in financing international transactions. Member banks were permitted to accept bills of exchange arising from international transactions. Moreover, banks with capital and surplus of $1 million or more were permitted to establish branches abroad. Although these provisions were significant, the development of international banking was slow. The volume of acceptances did not increase to significant proportions, and during the three years following the enactment of the Federal Reserve Act only one national bank established branches abroad. To stimulate further expansion in the area of international finance, the Federal Reserve Act was amended in 1916 to permit national banks to invest in corporations engaged principally in foreign banking. These corporations had to enter into an agreement with the Federal Reserve Board regarding the type and manner of activities, and from this arrangement they became known as *agreement corporations.* The Federal Reserve Act, however, did not provide for the federal chartering of agreement corporations, and this was not conducive to an increase in this type of international banking institution.

The Edge Act

An additional inducement to the development of international banking was the enactment by Congress in 1919 of the Edge Act, authorizing the Board of Governors of the Federal Reserve System to charter corporations for the purpose of engaging in international and foreign operations abroad. Two types of corporations were permitted to be established under this act— banking and financing. Banking corporations were authorized to hold demand and time deposits of foreigners and to acquire equity investment in foreign corporations engaged in banking. Financing corporations were permitted to invest in foreign corporations other than banks but were not permitted to accept deposits. Both types of corporations could buy and sell foreign exchange; receive checks, drafts, bills, acceptances, notes, bonds, coupons, and other securities for collection abroad; and buy and sell securities for the accounts of customers abroad.

This approach to international banking was confusing, and the logic of such an arrangement was debatable. Finally in 1963, financial and banking corporations were permitted to merge all functions into one corporation. Regulations covering these corporations, organized under Section 25(a) of the Federal Reserve Act as amended, are spelled out in Regulation K of the Board of Governors of the Federal Reserve System. When such a corporation has aggregate demand deposits and acceptance liabilities exceeding its capital and surplus, it is considered to be "engaged in banking" and subject to the rule limiting loans and investments to one person or organization to 10 percent of its capital and surplus. Otherwise a corporation is considered an investment corporation and may lend or invest up to 50 percent of its capital and surplus to one person or organization.

Since 1963 the number of Edge Act corporations has increased substantially. In the 1960s several banks from outside the state of New York formed Edge Act affiliates and located them in New York City. In the 1970s the trend was toward the formation of Edge Act offices located in other areas of the country. By mid-1977, 113 Edge Act corporations were in operation, with out-of-state banks having established offices in New York, Los Angeles, Miami, Houston, Chicago, San Francisco, New Orleans, Wilmington, and

Norfolk.[1] These offices were formed in these particular cities because of the increase in the demand for various financial services arising out of the financing of foreign trade. While they are limited to financing foreign commerce and investments, these offices are a means of bypassing the prohibitions in the United States on interstate banking. An Edge Act corporation may act like a branch office in many ways and provides a presence for an out-of-state bank in direct competition with banks domiciled in the cities named above, competing for the international banking business that is available in those cities.

Expansion Abroad

At the present time, American banks have a great network of international banking facilities throughout the free world. Approximately 150 banks in the United States have an international banking department. The number of correspondent banks abroad that are associated with U.S. banks in providing these international banking services varies but is in the thousands. Branch offices of U.S. banks are widely distributed throughout the world. About 45 percent of all overseas branches are located in Latin America and the Caribbean. In terms of volume of assets, branches in the United Kingdom account for more than one-third of all assets of foreign branches, and those in the Bahamas and Cayman Islands offshore banking centers account for about one-fourth. The customers of foreign branches are more widespread in their geographical distribution than are the branches themselves (see Table 19–1), but nearly one-half of all assets of foreign branches are amounts due from customers in Europe, about one-fifth from customers in Latin America and the Caribbean, and the balance from other areas.

Table 19–1
Assets of Overseas Branches of Member Banks, 1977

	Number	Assets (in billions)
United Kingdom and Ireland	61	$ 82.7
Continental Europe	110	32.5
Bahamas and Cayman Islands	132	64.5
Latin America	199	8.7
Far East	138	29.1
Near East and Africa	42	6.8
U.S. overseas areas & trust territories	48	3.5
Total	730	227.9

Source: Federal Reserve Bank of Chicago, *International Letter*, July 7, 1978.

[1]Donald E. Baer, "Expansion of Miami Edge Act Corporations," Federal Reserve Bank of Atlanta *Economic Review*, September/October 1977, pp. 112–117.

In addition to branches abroad, other methods are employed in extending foreign banking services. Some U.S. banks have a minority interest in foreign banks, that is, own stock in foreign banks, and a few banks provide foreign banking services in consortia with other banks. Bank of America, for example, has joined with Banque Nationale de Paris, the largest bank in France; Banca Nazionale del Lavoro, the largest bank in Italy; Barclays Bank, the largest bank in Great Britain; the Dresdner Bank (Germany); the Banque de Bruxelles (Belgium); and Algemene Bank Nederland (the Netherlands) to form a new banking organization which is known as Société Financière Européenne. Another example of this type of organization is the International Commercial Bank owned by Irving Trust of New York; First National Bank of Chicago; Commerzbank, A. G., Duesseldorf; National Westminister Bank Ltd., London; and the Hong Kong and Shanghai Banking Corporation of Hong Kong.

In recent years, most of the expansion of U.S. banks has been by acquiring subsidiaries, in consortia, and joint effort rather than by branching. Several factors have been responsible for this development. In the first place, foreign countries are generally more inclined to accept the entry of American banks if the undertaking is in conjunction with nationals of the country. Part of this attitude stems from nationalistic pride; also, domestic bankers are less likely to be critical of this type of arrangement than of a branch of a U.S. bank. Many foreign countries do not admit branches of American banks freely. They normally do so only if such a business venture is advantageous to the economic development of their country. A host country does not look with favor on a branch entry if the state in which the head office is located does not have a reciprocal arrangement for branches of the host country's banks, and some American states are not noted for their willingness to accept foreign branches. In 1961, New York relaxed some of its restrictions on foreign branches when the authorities of such countries as Brazil, Venezuela, the Philippines, and Japan threatened to impose restrictions on American banks. California also liberalized its banking laws in 1964 as they applied to foreign banks, although it still does not permit the operation of foreign branches. In many instances, expansion by branching or by establishing a new subsidiary abroad is an expensive and time-consuming process. Opening a new office would require an outlay for building and equipment and the training of personnel. Moreover, it might take considerable time to develop a clientele. Expansion by acquisition of a subsidiary and the other methods would normally require less initial outlay, and the operation would start with some already established customer relationships. Therefore, a profitable undertaking would probably be realized in a relatively short time which, of course, might not always be the case with a new branch abroad. In addition, the ownership of a subsidiary corporation limits the liability of the parent bank. The establishment of a branch office may expose the entire assets of the parent to liabilities arising from the operation of the branch. The reluctance of many banks to assume this additional risk has thus favored other forms of organization for offices in foreign countries.

The establishment of branches abroad depends in large part on the attitude of foreign countries in regard to competition from foreign banks. Those countries that need capital and the expertise of lending and investing in general welcome U.S. banks with open arms and permit a wide array of banking services. Some countries, however, permit entry somewhat reluctantly and limit the banking activities of foreign banks, and others even prohibit the entry of foreign banks. In recent years, a rising tide of nationalism in many countries has slowed down the expansion of American banks abroad. Canada, for example, has objected to the ownership of a bank by the First National City Bank of New York, and after much discussion an agreement was reached whereby the U.S. bank would reduce its ownership to 25 percent by 1980. This is an interesting development since several U.S. states permit Canadian banks to operate freely. In banking, as in many other areas, reciprocity is more illusory than real. The rise of nationalism that has slowed down U.S. expansion has encouraged some banks to purchase an interest in foreign banks. Some countries, however, limit the percentage of foreign ownership. In 1973, two countries liberalized their attitude toward the entry of U.S. banks. Japan, which had permitted only two banks to operate branches for a number of years, approved the entry of eight additional U.S. banks; and the U.S.S.R. permitted two banks to establish representative offices. This change in attitude resulted from increased trade with Japan in recent years and the opening of trade relations with U.S.S.R.

Reasons for the Growth of International Banking

Several factors have been responsible for the growth of international operations by U.S. commercial banks in recent years. The growth of the United States economically and financially in the postwar period certainly cannot be overlooked. The general worldwide reduction of tariffs and the dismantling of other restrictions imposed on international trade and payments contributed to the growth of world trade, which in turn stimulated international banking. The growth of exports and imports of the United States has been phenomenal in the post World War II period. Since that time the value of our exports has increased from $10 billion to $144 billion, and our imports rose from approximately $9 billion to nearly $172 billion. At the same time world trade was increasing from approximately $50 billion to $1.3 trillion in 1978. Our investments abroad have shown a more startling increase than has the growth of exports and imports, especially since 1958 when several leading European countries agreed to establish external convertibility of their currencies. At the end of 1976 U.S. assets abroad had increased to $347 billion, from $86 billion in 1960. Our net international investment position exceeded $82 billion, compared to about $45 billion in 1960. U.S. investments abroad require numerous financial transactions, which are handled almost exclusively by American banks. Since American business firms prefer to deal with banks with which they are acquainted and which understand their operations, banks were encouraged to follow business firms abroad. Likewise the recent rise in investments by foreigners in the United States has been followed by an increase in the activity of foreign banks in the U.S., especially from Japan, Korea, Europe and to a lesser extent the Middle East and Latin America.

The relatively liquid position of banks at the beginning of the 1960s also contributed to their expansion into foreign markets. A liberalization of our restriction on the entry of foreign banks into certain states contributed to the expansion of branches abroad in the early 1960s. A final factor has been the technological advances in transportation and communication. With improvements in air travel, wire transfer, etc., the task of maintaining constant surveillance of foreign markets and overseas operations has become less burdensome and much more efficient.

International Services of U.S. Banks

Although many international banking services are similar to those provided by banks on the domestic level, some differences make them unique and therefore require elaboration. The uniqueness of international finance has been responsible for many of the activities performed in the international department of a bank. For example, the international department usually has separate divisions such as bookkeeping, credit information, and business development. Because of the many activities and services offered by the international department, it is frequently referred to as a bank within a bank. The implication of such a statement, of course, is that a customer can find all the services required for the successful implementation of his international activities within this single bank department. The variety of activities performed and the services offered arise primarily from the differences that exist in monetary standards, business practices, and languages among the various countries that engage in foreign trade.

One of the interesting but not unusual activities of an international department, for example, is that it maintains its own bookkeeping department. This is because deposits are received from foreigners—banks, business firms, and some individuals. The foreign department of a bank also will carry accounts in banks in foreign countries. Foreign accounts in American banks are almost always denominated in American dollars, and the deposits of American banks in foreign banks generally are denominated in foreign currency. Foreign deposits in American banks are usually in the form of demand deposits, but frequently time deposits are carried as well. Time deposits of foreigners are subject to Regulation Q (interest rate ceilings) with the exception of those held by foreign governments and by international financial institutions of which the United States is a member. Many services are provided by banks that engage in international banking. We will discuss the most important.

Transfer of Funds

Several methods might be employed in transferring funds between various parties living or traveling in different countries. Most of the funds, especially those from business transactions, are transferred by air remittance, cable remittance, and foreign drafts. Transferring funds via air mail is a relatively simple procedure. The customer of an American bank, for example, who wanted a certain amount of funds transferred to a party in England would pay the bank the amount in cash or by a check drawn on his account. The bank in turn would send an air mail letter instructing the bank in England to pay the exact amount to the party designated in the letter. The letter would specify the details of the payment: amount, name and address of beneficiary, name of the sender, and authorized signatures. Immediately on receipt of these instructions, the foreign bank would proceed to verify the signatures of the officials who had been authorized to sign for the bank and contact the beneficiary to make payment. The funds (denominated in pounds) would be deducted from the American bank's account in the foreign bank. A fee would be charged by the American bank to cover the expenses incurred by both the American and the foreign bank in this transfer of funds.

Sometimes it is necessary to transfer funds more quickly than by letter. Under such conditions the transfer would be made by cable or by telephone. Since it is impossible to verify signatures by this method, authenticity of the message would be verified by code or test-key arrangement. Obviously, this method of verification would be prearranged although the code or key would change from day to day to insure secrecy.

A draft is a very common method employed in transferring funds to another party in a foreign country. A foreign draft is a negotiable instrument drawn by a bank on a foreign correspondent bank. Drafts are normally employed when the customer of a bank wants to have an actual negotiable instrument to mail to the beneficiary abroad. When a draft is issued, the

American bank sends the foreign bank a special letter of advice which includes all the salient details of the draft. Since the draft is not paid until the letter of advice is received, it serves as a protection against fraud.

Commercial banks aid in the transfer of funds by selling traveler's checks. Although only a few banks issue traveler's checks, most banks sell them for domestic and foreign use. For years the traveler's checks of U.S. banks have been acceptable in most foreign countries. Because of this almost universal acceptance abroad, tourists rely heavily on this instrument that results in the transfer of funds from this country to another.

Financing International Trade

One of the most important functions performed by U.S. banks engaged in international banking is to finance exports and imports of the United States and trade between foreign countries. Just as domestic trade requires various financing methods, there are several ways of financing international trade. They are: cash in advance, open account, documentary collection, and letters of credit. Of all of these methods, the most important is the letter of credit. In 1955, it was estimated that about 70 percent of the foreign trade was financed by letters of credit. This ratio declined to 60 percent in 1960, and at the beginning of the 1970s an estimate placed it at 50 percent.

Although terms of cash in advance involve little risk and are highly advantageous to exporters, they are not very popular as a means of financing foreign trade because of the many disadvantages presented to the foreign buyer. The buyer is forced to have a considerable amount of his working capital tied up for long periods of time, and he is also at the mercy of the exporter because of the possibility of the shipment of inferior merchandise, delayed shipments, and even bankruptcy of the exporter. Nonpayment of foreign accounts arises many times out of unstable economic and political conditions, which are frequently encountered, and the difficulty in obtaining adequate credit information about foreign customers. Thus the cash-in-advance method of settlement is used primarily when the risk of not receiving payment is quite high.

Sales on open account reverse the risk exposure entailed in terms of cash in advance. Just as cash in advance presents some disadvantages to the foreign purchaser, the open account presents similar disadvantages to the exporter. If the foreign purchaser is slow in paying his bills, the exporter will experience a drain on his working capital which ultimately will adversely affect his turnover. The chief objection to this method of financing is that the exporter does not have any negotiable instrument evidencing the obligation, which would become very important in the event of a dispute over delivery, loss, or quality of product. Open-account financing has one great advantage, however—it is very simple. Moreover, it is a way of avoiding financing and service charges incurred with other credit arrangements. Sales on an open-account basis are used when exporters are dealing with buyers they know very well who are located in well-established markets. This method is also used when sales are made to foreign branches or subsidiaries of domestic concerns. In times of peace and stability in the foreign exchange market, sales on open account tend to increase, but when economic and political clouds gather, less reliance is placed on this method.

Bills of Exchange

While widely accepted in domestic trade, terms of cash in advance and on open account are less widely employed in foreign trade because of their many disadvantages. Consequently, heavy reliance is placed on bills of exchange and letters of credit as methods of payment, both of which involve the services of commercial banks. A bill of exchange is an unconditional order in writing addressed by one person to another, signed by the person giving it, and requiring the addressee to pay a certain sum of money to order or to bearer on demand, or at a fixed or determinable time. To illustrate this type of financing, let us assume that Dixie Textile Company, an American importer, has agreed to purchase some woolen goods from John Bull, Ltd., an exporter in England. The English exporter prepares the goods for shipment and delivers them to the shipping company for delivery to Dixie Textile Company in the United States. The exporter then executes a draft, or a bill of exchange, that directs the American importer to pay, we shall say, $100,000 for the goods.

The exporter must take this instrument along with the other documents necessary for the transaction to the bank, which we will assume is a branch of Barclays Bank in London, and request the bank to send these documents to its correspondent bank in the United States. On receipt of these documents, the American bank makes a presentation to the buyer for payment. Once the buyer has paid the bank, all the documents are turned over to the importer who, in turn, goes to the dock to claim the goods. The U.S. bank in this situation is acting only as an agent and performs a collection function. For this service the bank is paid a fee by the English bank which normally varies from .1 to .25 percent of the amount of the bill of exchange or a stated dollar charge. Obviously, this example may have many variations. If, for example, the goods have to be examined and approved for entry into the United States by the Department of Agriculture or another government agency, Barclays Bank might instruct the bank in America to deliver the documents against trust receipts which stipulate that payment for the goods would be made after they have cleared inspection.

Letters of Credit

A letter of credit is a financial instrument issued by a bank on behalf of one of its customers, which authorizes an individual or a business firm to which it is addressed to draw drafts on the bank for its account under certain conditions as set forth in the document. In a letter of credit, the financial strength or credit of the bank is substituted for that of the bank's customer simply because the credit of the bank may be more substantial and more widely known. Another reason for heavy reliance on the letter of credit is that it is a desirable way of establishing certain quality standards or classifications that the goods must meet. Finally, it permits the seller to receive almost immediate payment for his goods, as soon as they are shipped; as a result, the cost to the importer is less than if the seller had to wait for payment for an extended period. Irrevocable letters of credit are used in international finance and, as the name implies, cannot be changed without the consent of all parties concerned.

Risks are numerous in international trade; accidents at sea, strikes, riots, and civil commotions in port cities; all of which can cause damage to ships and their cargo. Typically, many documents are necessary to complete an international transaction, and these must be specified in an application for a letter of credit. Several copies of a commercial invoice are needed for office use, and customs' invoices are required before some goods can be brought into this country. Probably the most important document stipulated in an application for a letter of credit is the negotiable *on-board ocean bill of lading*. This document is a receipt that the cargo was received and was loaded on board ship. Whoever holds the on-board ocean bill of lading has title to the goods. Therefore, the bank must have this document before payment is made.

After an importer has completed arrangements for the issuance of a letter of credit by his bank, it is usually forwarded by the issuing bank to the beneficiary's bank abroad. The receiving bank is instructed to deliver the letter of credit to the beneficiary. After receipt of the letter of credit, the foreign exporter arranges for the shipment of the goods to the American importer in accordance with the terms of the letter of credit. When the exporter has prepared all documents required and delivered the goods to the ship, the documents are then attached to a draft and submitted to the exporter's bank along with the letter of credit. If the documents are in order, the bank then negotiates the draft and forwards the documents to the bank in the United States. The handling of the draft at this point depends on whether it is a sight or a time draft. If it is a sight draft, which means that it must be paid on sight, the bank pays the draft immediately. Several procedures could be employed in transferring the funds to the exporter's bank. The U.S. bank could merely credit funds to the exporting bank's account if the foreign bank carried a correspondent account with the bank in the United States. If it did not carry an account and the U.S. bank carried an account with the foreign bank, a transfer from the importing bank to the exporting bank could be effected. The U.S. bank could also order the transfer of funds from its account in another bank in the exporting bank's country to the bank that originated the draft. Whatever method is employed, the funds would be paid to the exporting bank within a very short time, and this bank would then transfer the funds to the exporter of the goods.

Banks that issue letters of credit may be paid in cash—a simple transfer from the customer's account to the bank. If, however, the importer does not have all or a part of the funds, he must negotiate a loan from the bank. This loan could be unsecured, assuming the borrower has sufficient credit worthiness, or it could be a loan secured by the goods just imported. If these goods are ready for sale, they could be released to the importer on a trust receipt. As they are sold, the loan is repaid, or they might be placed in a warehouse, with the warehouse receipts serving as collateral for the loan. Whatever the arrangement, the importer receives the order bill of lading which gives him title to the goods. If the goods were to be used in further manufacture, a different kind of loan might be made and with a longer maturity.

Bankers' Acceptances

Drafts authorized by a letter of credit may have various maturities. A sight draft, as we have said, must be paid when recieved. If the draft is drawn for 180 days, let's say, we would have an additional step in our financial transaction, that is, the creation of a bankers' acceptance, which is a draft that has been accepted by the drawee bank. The draft is changed into an acceptance by the stamping of the word "accepted" across the face of the draft, the signature of a bank officer who has been authorized to sign such documents, and a brief description of the transaction that gave rise to it. The bankers' acceptance can be returned to the drawer, who could hold the instrument until it is due to be paid and then present it to the accepting bank for payment. Bankers' acceptances are seldom disposed of in this manner, however, since the drawer of the original draft is not in the financing business and would, therefore, prefer to have his money immediately for the operation of his business.

An exporting bank could authorize a U.S. bank to sell the acceptance in the market. Since the acceptance market is old and well established, such a request would ordinarily present no problem. The U.S. bank could buy its own acceptance, which is not uncommon, especially when loan demand is relatively low. Acceptances are sold at a discount, and the difference between their price and the face value is the return received by the buyer.

Acceptance financing is a well-established form of financing, and bankers' acceptances in the money market are considered a prime asset. This high regard stems from the maturity and security of the acceptance. The maturity of bankers' acceptances usually will be for a maximum of 180 days,[2] which definitely places them in the category of a highly liquid asset. They are of high quality credit, since they are the promise to pay of a well-regarded bank. Finally, they are eligible for discount at a Federal Reserve bank if they conform to the standards established by law. The high value placed on bankers' acceptances as an asset in the money market is reflected in their yield. Although the yield on acceptances fluctuates, the yield on prime acceptances generally is only slightly above that on 90-day U.S. Treasury bills and noticeably below the rate on commercial paper. The fact that bankers' acceptances can be discounted at a Federal Reserve bank is quite important and is one reason for banks holding them in their investment portfolios and considering them part of their secondary reserves.

The creation of bankers' acceptances by commercial banks is closely regulated by the Federal Reserve System; moreover, their use is limited. The total value of bankers' acceptances that a bank can create must not exceed 50 percent of the bank's capital and surplus unless prior approval from the Federal Reserve System has been obtained, and under no circumstances can the amount exceed 100 percent of these two capital items. They are also subject to the 10 percent lending rule previously discussed in the chapters on lending; that is, the amount of acceptances drawn by a single drawer is limited to 10 percent of the bank's capital surplus. The Federal Reserve Act limits the use of bankers' acceptances to the exportation and importation of goods as just discussed, the domestic shipment of goods, and the storage of readily marketable commodities, provided a bank obtains a warehouse receipt or other comparable document as evidence of the transaction. These restrictions on bankers' acceptances stem from the fact that their creation is similar to the creation of demand deposits via the lending function, and such monetary creation is closely regulated by the central bank.

Although bankers' acceptances can be used in financing the domestic shipment of goods, they are somewhat cumbersome because of the documentation required and are therefore not widely used for this purpose. Their usage has grown, however, especially in tight money periods when loanable funds are less plentiful than in normal times. They are used extensively in financing the storage of readily marketable goods in foreign countries. In addition to these three basic uses of bankers' acceptances, they are

---

[2]Bankers' acceptances may have maturities exceeding 180 days, but longer maturities are not eligible for rediscount with Federal Reserve Banks.

also used to alleviate seasonal shortages of dollar exchange in those countries that rely heavily on a single crop or a few specialized exports. Several one-crop countries need dollar exchange for the purchase of machinery and material before a crop is harvested, processed, and sold in international trade. Under such conditions, banks in those countries can draw drafts on American banks and thus obtain dollar exchange which will be repaid after the crop is exported. This type of financing is closely regulated by the Federal Reserve System. Any member bank may accept drafts for this purpose if the country is on the list that has been approved by the Board of Governors of the Federal Reserve System. The maturity of these acceptances is limited to three months. Member banks may accept drafts only in an amount equal to 10 percent of the drawee bank's unimpaired capital and surplus, and total drafts accepted may not exceed 50 percent of the bank's capital and surplus. Most of the dollar exchange is created for Latin American countries, particularly for the coffee crop.

Export Financing

In our discussion of the use of letters of credit an example was given involving the importation of goods into the United States. Letters of credit also are employed in the exportation of goods from the United States. Foreign purchasers may ask their bank for a letter of credit for the same reasons that our importers requested its use when importing from a foreign seller. Although foreign importers may not want to use letters of credit when purchasing goods from a financially responsible U.S. exporter, the American exporter may nevertheless insist on their use for several reasons. The foreign purchaser may not meet the credit standards of the American exporter; therefore, the exporter may demand a bank obligation to eliminate the credit risk, although additional cost is involved. If the exchange situation in the buyer's country indicates that a delay might occur in the transfer of payment to the United States despite the financial responsibility of the buyer, the exporter may insist on a letter of credit. In fact, if the exporter considers the risk of nontransfer of funds to be quite high, he may ask his bank to add its confirmation to that of the foreign bank before he agrees to the transaction. In an arrangement of this kind, the U.S. bank adds its confirmation to that of the foreign bank to honor drafts and documents that are presented in accordance with the terms of the credit. However, confirmed letters of credit are not common, especially in times of international political and financial stability. Since the U.S. bank is providing a service that reduces the risk against which the U.S. exporter wants to be protected, obviously this service must be charged for.

Foreign Exchange Market

International payments necessitate converting one currency into another. The French exporter of rare wines to a buyer in the United States is not interested in dollars but in French francs, and the United States exporter of machinery to a purchaser in Argentina wants dollars rather than pesos. Whether the foreign transaction involves the purchase or sale of goods, tourism, or capital movements for investment purposes or interest arbitrage, there is a need for the exchange of currencies of the various countries. This demand is met by the foreign exchange market, which is dominated by commercial banks. Although the foreign exchange market is one where money is exchanged, there is no central marketplace such as the one for stocks and bonds on the New York Stock Exchange or for grains on the Chicago Board of Trade.[3] The foreign exchange market is a mechanism rather than a place. The market is very informal, has no fixed hours, is comprised of approximately 25 regular participants about half of which do the bulk of the business, and probably most interesting of all, has no written rules of trading. Its conduct is based on the principles and code of ethics that have evolved over time. The major framework is a system of direct communications among the participants, which include primarily domestic and foreign banks and a few brokers.

Making a Market

Many banks throughout the nation provide facilities for handling foreign exchange but only a few make and maintain a market—take a position or maintain an inventory in foreign currencies. These banks are really the hub or foundation of the foreign exchange market. Only a few are in this category, most located in New York City. The West Coast market is growing, however, with the establishment of Edge Act affiliates of New York banks and offices of several foreign banks. Although many other banks provide their customers with foreign exchange services, they arrange for this service through these very few banks. A bank located in Harrisburg, Illinois, for example, which needs 6,320 West German deutschemarks for a customer who must pay a German exporter for a new printing machine would probably arrange for these funds from a bank in St. Louis or Chicago. Most banks have access to daily quotations of the various foreign currencies. Although the price of currencies may change frequently, a current quotation can be obtained by making a telephone call to a dealer in foreign exchange.

[3]A futures market for a limited number of foreign currencies has been established on the Chicago Board of Trade. These contracts, if open at maturity, would have to be fulfilled by purchasing spot exchange.

To provide customers with foreign exchange services, some American banks must hold foreign exchange inventories in the form of deposits with foreign banks. These deposits or inventories are maintained by the purchase and sale of balances owned by both foreign and domestic banks, individuals, and business firms. Inventories may also be augmented by the purchase and sale of bills of exchange, traveler's checks, bond coupons, dividend warrants, and other assets denominated in foreign currencies. How much of an inventory and the variety of currencies held depend on the amount of activity a bank has in a given currency. Obviously, the largest percentage of its inventory will be in those currencies that are in greatest demand. High on the list would be the pound sterling, the Canadian dollar, the Japanese yen, and the West German mark. In other words, the inventory would contain the currencies of those countries with which we trade, in which we invest, and in which Americans tour.

Exchange Risks

Providing a market in foreign exchange is not without risk, and it is for the assumption of risks that a charge is imposed in the form of a spread between the bid and ask prices of currencies. The risks involved in foreign exchange trading stem from the fact that the exchange rates of the various currencies are subject to change as a result of a country's economic health and political stability. A country with a favorable balance of payments, for example, would have a stronger currency in the exchange markets than one suffering from a deficit. In recent years, England and France have suffered some devaluations, while West Germany has enjoyed a relatively strong currency. The United States dollar on occasions has been questioned in international markets because of its chronic unfavorable balance of payments for most years since 1950, and was devalued in relation to other currencies in late 1971 and again in early 1973. Since 1973, the major currencies of the world have been *floating;* that is, the exchange rate has been subject to day-to-day fluctuations according to the current demand for and supply of a given currency. Maintaining an inventory in a currency that is liable to drop in price is risky. To have been sitting with an inventory of $100 million in French francs in November 1968, when the franc was devalued by approximately 10 percent, was embarrassing and highly unprofitable. A bank that deals in foreign exchange must have business in sufficient regularity and volume so that losses can be offset against gains, rather than each transaction being offset against another. Moreover, managers of foreign exchange departments must be alert not only to changes in exchange rates but also to the cause of these changes so that steps can be taken to reduce risk. Large foreign exchange losses were the reported cause of the 1974 failure of a German bank and large losses incurred by other banks in England and

Switzerland, and at least one American bank was reported to be in serious financial straits for the same reason.

Spot and Forward Rates

In general, two classes of foreign exchange are traded in the foreign exchange market—*spot* and *forward.* Spot exchange is for immediate delivery, and forward exchange is for delivery sometime in the future. The rate of exchange at which spot purchases and sales are made is called the spot rate, and the term for delivery in the future is the forward rate. If the forward rate is above the spot rate, the difference between the two is called a *premium;* if the relationship is reversed, the difference is called a *discount.*

The rationale for quoting forward rates lies in the exchange-rate risk inherent in all international commercial and financial transactions. As long as spot rates fluctuate, even within narrow limits, risk is involved for those who expect to convert one currency into another. An American exporter who sells goods to a purchaser in England for sterling payable in three months is concerned about the rate at which he can convert his sterling claims into dollars. Let us assume, for example, that the goods were sold for £100,000 on February 13, 1975, when the spot rate for the pound was $2.3910 (see Table 19–2). If the pound is at the same quotation on May 13, 1975, the American exporter would receive pounds from the purchase which could be converted into 239,100 U.S. dollars (100,000 times 2.3910). Let us further assume that if this price were received, the exporter would realize a profit of $24,900 on this transaction. However, if for some reason or reasons a pound is worth only $2.2650 on May 13, the American exporter would only receive 226,500 (100,000 times 2.2650) U.S. dollars after the conversion was made. This unforeseen development would be upsetting to the exporter, since the profit would be reduced to a mere $12,300. Thus,

Table 19–2
Foreign Exchange Quotations

	Feb. 13, 1975	Mar. 1, 1978
Canada (dollar)	.9980	.8945
Britain (pound)	2.3910	1.9415
30-day futures	2.3788	1.9407
90-day futures	2.3552	1.9396
Denmark (krone)	.1804	.1808
France (franc)	.2325	.2115
Portugal (escudo)	.0410	.0251
Sweden (krona)	.2510	.2182
Switzerland (franc)	.4045	.5495
West Germany (mark)	.4304	.4960

Source: U.S. National Bank of Oregon.

because of a drop of less than $0.13 in the price of the pound, his profit is cut by nearly 51 percent. Of course, it could be reasoned that if the pound had increased in value to, let's say, $2.5020, he would have experienced an increase in his profit of $11,100. This is indeed correct, but the issue that is now raised is whether assuming this risk is really a logical or legitimate function of the businessman who exported the goods. It probably is not, and this businessman should stick with his trade and let someone else assume the risk that arises because of changes in exchange rates.

The American exporter could protect himself in this particular transaction by entering the forward exchange market. He could do this by entering into a contract with a commercial bank in which he promises to deliver, at a stated future date, pounds in exchange for dollars at the market price existing for forward pounds at the time the contract was initiated. On February 13, the forward rate (90-day future) was $2.3552. Once the sale transaction is completed he is assured of receiving $235,520 for his goods, which is only $3,580 less than on the day the sale was made. Now if the pound were to drop to $2.2650, the deal looks good. Thus, for giving up $3,580 he has protected himself against a possible loss of $12,600 or more. The student here might raise a question concerning the wisdom of entering into a contract with the exporter whereby the English importer has three months to pay for his goods. This is because the importer does not have the funds; if the American exporter insisted that payment be made at the time of sale, the English importer might purchase the goods from another exporter who would be willing to extend credit. Competition is indeed a great motivator.

It is not uncommon for an importer to enter into or buy a forward contract in some currency. This type of transaction can be illustrated by assuming that an American importer purchased some furniture from a manufacturer in Denmark for 553,097 kroner on March 1, 1978, payable within three months. On March 1 the Danish krone was quoted at .1808 which is another way of saying that the American importer had paid $100,000 (553,097 times .1808) for the furniture since he would have to pay that amount as of that date for the 553,097 kroner. If, however, on June 1 the price of the Danish krone had increased to .1906 it would cost the importer not $100,000 to purchase this number of kroner in the market, but $105,420 (553,097 times .1906), or $5,420 more than on March 1 because of the krone's increase in the foreign exchange market relative to the American dollar. This development would be considered by the importer in the same vein as by the exporter in our other example—a bad deal. To protect himself from this risk the American importer could, however, enter into a purchase contract whereby he would agree to purchase kroner at a certain price to be delivered on June 1. If the forward exchange rate were .1824 on March 1, the importer knows that the furniture is really costing him $100,884 (553,097 times 0.1824) or only $884 more than it would have cost him on the date the contract was made. This difference is not substantial if consideration is given to the possibility of the krone moving up to .1906, which would require an additional outlay of $5,420 over the purchase price as of March 1. Thus, it is fairly clear that the process of covering exchange risks through the financial exchange markets is essentially a way of eliminating the uncertainties of the forward exchange element from an international financial or commercial transaction.

International Lending

As in domestic operations, the greatest amount of income in international banking is derived from lending. Banks that engage in international lending do so through any one or a combination of an international department, branches, or other types of organization involving locations abroad. The bulk of foreign lending is done by those U.S. banks with locations in foreign countries, however. Banks with an international department only concentrate their efforts on financing international trade by extending credit to domestic customers for the production of goods that will be exported abroad, or lending to domestic firms for the purchase of goods from abroad that will be sold domestically or used in the further production of goods and services in this country. In reality this is domestic rather than international lending, however. The total amount of international lending by U.S. banks is not known, since published data are not available on the loans made by affiliates of U.S. banks, those banks that are owned jointly with other foreign banks, and banks abroad in which U.S. banks have a minority interest. Information is available on the amount of foreign loans of American banks within this country, however (see Table 19-3). By September 1978 claims on foreigners, including loans, collections, and acceptances by banks in the U.S. exceeded $100 billion, and claims on foreigners by foreign branches of U.S. banks approached $300 billion.

Risks of International Lending

In many respects, lending abroad is similar to lending domestically. The credit principles discussed in previous chapters are certainly not ignored. In addition to these basic factors, two others play a very important role in the granting of credit to foreign borrowers: *currency risk* and *political risk*. The currency risk is concerned with convertibility and the stability of the monetary unit of the borrower's country. A bank is interested in the monetary unit being convertible and the loan being repaid in a medium of exchange of the same value as when the loan was made. This might not be realized, however, in the event of inconvertibility or the devaluation of the monetary unit in

Table 19-3
Claims on Foreigners Reported by Banks in the United States (in millions of dollars)
Selected Years, 1950–1978

End of Year	Grand Total	Short Term Total	Payable in Dollars Total	Loans	Collections Outstanding	Acceptances	Other*	Payable in Foreign Currencies	Long Term Total	Long Term Loans	Long Term Other
1950	1,288	898	657	328	203	na	126	241	390	na	na
1960	5,312	3,614	3,135	1,297	605	na	1,233	480	1,698	na	na
1970	13,877	10,802	10,192	3,051	2,389	3,985	766	610	3,075	2,698	377
1971	16,939	13,272	12,377	3,969	2,475	4,254	1,679	895	3,667	3,345	322
1972	20,739	15,676	14,830	5,671	3,276	3,226	2,657	846	5,063	4,588	475
1973	26,688	20,726	20,064	7,689	4,307	4,156	3,912	662	5,962	5,412	580
1974	46,235	39,056	37,859	11,287	5,637	11,237	9,698	1,196	7,179	6,490	689
1975	59,767	50,231	48,888	13,200	5,467	11,147	19,075	1,342	9,536	8,316	1,219
1976	81,135	69,237	67,552	18,215	5,756	12,358	31,222	1,685	11,898	10,093	1,804
1977	92,562	79,913	77,811	19,955	6,176	14,212	37,469	2,101	12,649	10,676	1,972
1978 (Apr.)	98,197	85,166	83,088	21,284	6,910	13,783	41,110	2,078	13,031	11,051	1,980

*Includes claims of U.S. Banks on their foreign branches and claims of U.S. agencies and branches of foreign banks on their head offices and foreign branches of their head offices.

Source: Board of Governors of the Federal Reserve System, *Supplement to Banking and Monetary Statistics*, Section 15, International Finance, 1962; and *Federal Reserve Bulletins*.

which the loan is repaid. In other words, a risk exists because of changes that might occur in the convertibility of a currency or in its exchange rate. As long as a country has its international payments and receipts in approximate balance or has sufficient international reserves to cover a deficit in its balance of payments, the currency risk is minimal. If, however, the country does not have an equilibrium in its balance of payments and does not have sufficient reserves, its currency may decline in value; thus, the amount repaid would purchase fewer dollars in world markets. Moreover, if a country's international payments persistently exceed its receipts, it may establish exchange controls. Should this come about, the borrower who may be financially sound otherwise might have difficulty in securing funds to repay the bank.

Closely associated with the currency risk that must be considered in international lending is the *political risk.* Political risk refers to all matters political ranging from minor but unforeseen regulations that might be imposed on the bank or the borrower to the expropriation of property and expulsion from the country. Consideration would have to be given to such items as the country's internal and external debt; for if external debt were exceptionally large and economic developments were such that tax revenues were insufficient in amount to meet the principal and interest payments, steps such as additional taxation might be taken that would reduce the ability of the borrower to repay his loan to the bank. A risk that must be considered is the imposition of restrictions, which might prevent the delivery and acceptance of merchandise. Some foreign importers are required to secure an import license from their government to import goods, and this privilege might be cancelled after goods are purchased and shipped. Rebellion, civil commotion, and war are hazards that may be encountered in international lending. In this general area, a most significant risk is concerned with the expropriation of property. U.S. banks have been forced out of several countries including Spain, Chile, and Cuba. Some South American countries have taken United States properties, and in recent years the political climate in a few countries is certainly not of a tone that would encourage lending by U.S. banks.

Types of Loans

Foreign borrowers include individuals and business firms just as in this country. Commercial banks also, either individually or jointly, may extend credit for short periods to central banks, a practice that is not followed in the United States. These funds may be used by a central bank to make credit available to other commercial banks or may be employed in the central bank's foreign exchange operations. Banks abroad may have deposits from central banks and extend credit to central governments, neither of which is done in this country. If the U.S. Treasury needs funds, it borrows in the money and/or capital markets via the issuance of securities. This, of course, is done abroad; but in some countries, particularly where the money and capital markets are not as well developed as here, government borrowing from commercial banks is not uncommon. Loans to governments might be made directly or indirectly through central banks or foreign banks. In some countries, especially in developing areas, the government may be the strongest and most financially responsible borrower. In many cases, the borrowing government will in turn make the funds from U.S. banks available to local borrowers through various government agencies or development banks.

The purpose and type of loans made to foreign business firms do not differ greatly from business loans made in the United States. U.S. banks generally do not, however, make as many term loans abroad as they do domestically; it is not uncommon, especially in making loans with a relatively long maturity, for an American bank and a bank abroad to participate with a bank located within a third country in making the loan. In this way the risk is reduced, and at the same time the U.S. bank has acquired some expert judgment on the part of the local banker. Because of our huge investments in foreign countries in manufacturing, mining, and other forms of business enterprise, there are many American firms abroad who look to U.S. banks and branches for credit. Since American bankers have great knowledge of American firms, it is in this area of lending that they excel. Although U.S. banks abroad make personal loans, they do not engage in personal lending to the extent that they do in this country.

Just as in this country, foreign loans may be unsecured or secured, and the type of collateral taken as security varies. Since most of the loans in dollar amount are made to large business concerns, governments, and banks, a larger percentage of foreign loans is made on an unsecured basis than is the case domestically. This is especially true of those banks that do not have branches abroad. Unsecured loans might take the form of authorizing foreign banks or trading companies to draw drafts on U.S. banks up to a prearranged amount or merely signing a note supported by a loan agreement. Banks are interested in reducing the risks of lending, and this is done to some extent by diversifying their lending among several countries rather than concentrating it in one single country. It is not uncommon for several banks to form a syndicate to participate in a large loan to a borrower in a single country. The bank that negotiates the loan, the *lead* bank, is responsible for the investigation of the risks involved, the actual drawing-up of the loan agreement, collecting the interest and principal on the loan and disbursing the proceeds among the participating banks, and other supervisory activities that might be involved during the course of the loan. Some banks have sustained losses by relying on information provided by the lead bank or syndicate manager. While the syndicate manager has certain responsibilities[4] to the participating banks, each bank should evaluate the risks independently and not rely solely on the lead bank.

Insurance and Guarantees

Banks are able to reduce their foreign lending risks by loaning to exporters who insure their trade credits with the Foreign Credit Insurance Association (FCIA). This is a voluntary organization of more than 60 stock and mutual insurance companies throughout the United States which provides insurance coverage up to a certain percentage of the trade credit against nonpayment arising from credit losses and losses from political hazards. Political risks are reinsured through the Export-Import Bank, which is described below. The FCIA makes a thorough credit investigation of the foreign purchaser as well as the political risks in his country. In general, the insurance covers up to 90 percent of the credit risk and up to 95 percent of the risks from the political hazards. Insurance premiums paid by the exporters vary with a rating established for each country and foreign borrowers but average approximately .5 percent of the sale price. FCIA provides coverage for both short-term credits, which are defined as those up to 180 days maturity, and intermediate-term credits from 180 days up to 5 years.

A government institution that will sometimes guarantee foreign loans made by commercial banks, in addition to other activities in the area of international lending, is the Export-Import Bank (Exim Bank). The Exim Bank deals primarily with risks beyond the scope of private capital or that private lenders are unwilling to assume because of the high risks involved. The bank extends credit to foreign buyers to purchase material and equipment produced or manufactured in the United States. The bank's role in international finance may take the form of direct loans, participation in loans with other lenders, or guaranteeing loans. The Exim Bank's guarantee program is very similar to the insurance provisions of the FCIA. This international financial institution tends to operate in the area of capital loans and in relatively large amounts rather than in working-capital loans. Moreover, it is more interested in financing capital equipment, such as commercial airplanes or generators for a hydroelectric installation, than consumer goods.

Eurodollar Lending

Eurodollar lending derives its name from the source of funds rather than from differences in lending techniques. Branches of U.S. banks abroad originate deposits in their locales and normally lend these funds in the same

---

[4]A. D. Calhoun, Jr., "Eurodollar Loan Agreements: An Introduction and Discussion of Some Special Problems," *Journal of Commercial Bank Lending*, September 1977, pp. 27–31.

areas. In recent years there has developed what is referred to as *Eurodollar deposits*. These dollars are purchased by banks and loaned to business firms and governments; hence, the term Eurodollar lending. Eurodollars originate from dollar deposits with U.S. banks that are acquired by foreigners and redeposited in banks outside the U.S. For example, a French bank with a surplus of francs might exchange them with the French central bank for dollars that have accumulated because of a surplus in the French balance of payments. The French bank could then deposit these funds in a London bank and receive a stipulated rate of interest. These same funds could, in turn, be reloaned to another bank in Switzerland which could make the funds available to a producer of steel in Spain. Since the origin of this kind of deposit was in Europe and most of these deposits are found there, the market has been termed the Eurodollar market. Other currencies have also become part of the Eurodollar market such as the pound sterling, yen, deutschemark, French and Swiss franc, and the guilder. Dollars account for about 80 percent of the market, however. There are similar developments in Asia and other parts of the world; hence, the term *Asian dollar*. Hong Kong and Singapore are the centers of this market. The trading center for Eurodollars is London. The rate paid for Eurodollars is referred to as the London interbank offered rate, usually shortened to LIBOR.

Several factors have been responsible for the rise in Eurodollars—American aid abroad after World War II, a rise in our imports, and during the last few years, our substantial deficits. Moreover, the high esteem placed upon the value of the American dollar in international transactions contributes to an increasing number of countries tying their currencies to the American dollar and expressing their reserves in dollars. Eurodollar lending has also been encouraged by the reserve requirements placed on bank deposits in the U.S., the insurance on deposits, and the taxation of corporate income. U.S. banks must maintain a certain amount of their deposits as reserves at Federal Reserve banks and pay a fee to the FDIC for the insurance of deposits. This is not required of all foreign banks; consequently, the lending of funds in American banks must be done at a slightly higher cost than if the funds were held abroad and not returned to the U.S. The fact that income is taxed when returned to the United States also encourages both lenders and borrowers to maintain funds outside the continental limits of the United States where such income is not taxed, or if taxed, the rate is considerably lower. Although in the last few years there have been changes in the taxation of corporate income earned abroad, for many years this was an important factor contributing to the establishment of foreign branches and to the rise in the Eurodollar market as well.

Eurodollar lending is in relatively large amounts—ranging from a minimum of $1 million to as much as $1.5 billion. Usually a larger international bank puts together a Eurodollar loan and then proceeds to find other banks that would like to participate in that type of credit. Once the banks agree to the terms, rate, repayment schedule, and so on, the loan is consummated. The rate that is agreed upon is a certain amount above the LIBOR rate on the date the funds are advanced. If the rate offered on the loan is not of sufficient amount above the LIBOR rate, the loan would not be granted. Sometimes this type of lending is referred to as *spread banking* indicating that the crucial factor in engaging in this kind of lending is the spread between the cost of funds on the one hand and rates paid on the other. In addition to an interest payment, participants in Eurodollar loans sometimes receive a fee such as one-eighth to one-half of one percent of the amount of the loan. Occasionally there is a flat fee. The managing bank is not responsible for the soundness of the Eurodollar credit. Each participant must make its own decision on the credit worthiness of the borrower. Because of the volatility of rates, the interest rate on loans is adjusted every six months. The maturity of most Eurodollar loans varies from five to ten years. Eurodollar loans are made to a wide variety of businesses throughout the world. Such loans have been made to the government of Malaysia, a subway system in Brazil, the central bank of Mexico, an oil monopoly in Venezuela, Mobil Oil of Indonesia, and so on. Eurodollar lending has shown rapid growth. The pool of funds from which loans are made is quite substantial. At mid-year 1978, for example, it was estimated that Eurodollar deposits approximated $515 billion.

Collections

An important bank service that contributes to the flow of international trade is making collections. This is the process of presenting an item to the maker or drawee for payment. In the area of domestic banking, this is sometimes referred to as *clearing checks,* that is, routing the checks that have been deposited in bank A to the maker of the check who has an account in bank B, several miles from bank A. Domestic checks are cleared or collected through the facilities of the Federal Reserve System, the correspondent banking system, and local clearing houses. In the area of international banking, only one of these arrangements exists for clearing items—the correspondent banking system.

The international items collected by banks may be clean, that is, without documents attached or documentary, which means accompanied by documents. Such items as checks, traveler's checks, and money orders drawn on banks or agencies are usually clean items and are normally exchanged at a bank for local currency. An American traveler, for example, may cash a personal check or a traveler's check for $100 in a Paris bank. The funds are paid to the American tourist in French francs, and the check is then airmailed to the French bank's correspondent, let's say in New York, which credits the French bank's "due to account" either for immediate credit subject to final payment or as a collection, which means that the procedure will be credited to the "due to account" when payment is carried out.

Clean collections are relatively simple and do not present many problems. Documentary collections are a bit more complicated and are at present more important as far as international trade is concerned. These collections cover both exports and imports and may be in the form of either sight or time drafts. We have already had an example of an international financial transaction that required a collection effort, namely, the importation of goods under a letter of credit that required an American bank to collect funds from the importer and return the funds to the bank abroad. We have also had an example of the collection under a bill of exchange. In this example the bill of exchange was due at sight and the documents were sent to the U.S. bank, which was asked to release the documents only after payment had been made. Frequently exporters will ask their banks to provide them with blank drafts and collection instructions which they will use in their international dealings. The amount of collections outstanding is relatively large when compared to acceptances (see Table 19–3)

Questions

1. What different organizational arrangements are used by American banks to meet the needs of their customers for international banking services?

2. Discuss the factors that caused U.S. banks to be relatively uninvolved in international banking activities prior to World War II.

3. How can an American bank effectively engage in interstate banking in connection with its international banking activities?

4. What is the meaning of reciprocity as it applies to international banking offices?

5. How would tourists traveling abroad assure themselves of sufficient funds for expenses and purchases without the risks of carrying large amounts of the currency of each of the nations they expect to visit?

6. Define each of the following terms: (a) letter of credit, (b) bill of exchange, (c) bankers' acceptance, (d) bank draft, (e) spot exchange, (f) forward exchange, (g) on-board ocean bill of lading, (h) floating exchange rates.

7. Where is the foreign exchange market located? How does it operate?

8. How do the risks of international lending differ from those of domestic lending?

SELECTED REFERENCES

CALHOUN, A. D., "Eurodollar Loan Agreements: An Introduction and Discussion of Some Special Problems," *Journal of Commercial Banking*, September 1977, pp. 23–43.

VAN VLIERDEN, C. M., and W. HURST, "International Relationships of U.S. Banks," *The Bankers Handbook*, Revised Edition (Homewood, Ill., Dow Jones-Irwin, 1978) Edited by W. H. Baughn and C. E. Walker.

BAER, D. E., "Expansion of Miami Edge Act Corporations," Federal Reserve Bank of Atlanta *Economic Review*, September/October 1977, pp. 112–117.

CORSE, C. T., "International Term Loan Agreements and Loan Syndications," *Journal of Commercial Bank Lending*, March 1978, pp. 12–22.

SUMMERS, B. J. "Foreign Banking in the United States,"Federal Reserve Bank of Richmond *Economic Review*, January/February 1976, pp. 3–7.

Federal Reserve Bank of San Francisco, "International Banking," *Economic Review*, Spring 1976.

Federal Reserve Bank of San Francisco, "Banking in the World Economy," *Economic Review*, Fall 1977.

HOLMES, ALAN R., and FRANCIS H. SCHOTT, *The New York Foreign Exchange Market*, Federal Reserve Bank of New York, 1965.

Index